LIGHT FROM THE ANCIENT PAST

VOLUME II

The publishers have retained the original
page, chapter, and illustration numbers of
the one-volume hardbound edition, and have
included in each of the two paperbound
volumes the complete indexes, including the
index of scriptural references.

LIGHT FROM
THE ANCIENT PAST

The Archeological Background
of
Judaism and Christianity

By JACK FINEGAN

PRINCETON UNIVERSITY PRESS

VOLUME II

TO THE MEMORY OF

JESSE COBB CALDWELL

AND

HANS LIETZMANN

Preface

THE purpose of this book is to give a connected account of the archeological background of Judaism and Christianity. Within the last century and a half and largely within the past few decades, oriental archeology has pioneered a new past, in which are revealed more extensive vistas and higher cultures than hitherto were imagined. The account which can now be given of the rise of civilization in the Middle East, of the development of art, and of the formulation of ethical, philosophical, and religious ideas is of fascinating interest in itself. It is also of great significance for an understanding of Judaism and Christianity, both of which in their origin and earlier history were integral parts of that ancient world. To see that world come vividly and startlingly alive is to find biblical and early Christian history invested with a fresh sense of reality and interest. There are, moreover, many points at which biblical records and archeological discoveries are in direct contact, and increasingly in the later centuries there are many archeological remains which are primary historical monuments of Judaism and Christianity. A knowledge of these facts is now indispensable to all serious study of the Bible, and the proper utilization of the abundant new archeological materials may even be said to constitute one of the most important tasks in that study.

The presentation of this archeological background in the present book is in the form of a continuous account extending, in round numbers, from 5000 B.C. to A.D. 500. After an introduction dealing with the nature of archeological work in general, the narrative begins with the rise of civilization in the valley of the Tigris and Euphrates rivers where the origins of the people of Israel traditionally are located and where antecedents of their mythology and law are found. Then the development of culture in the valley of the

Nile is sketched, and the Exodus of the Israelites and their use of Egyptian materials in the Psalms and Proverbs are considered. Moving to Palestine, the "bridge" between these two ancient homes of empire, archeological findings are summarized, illuminating both Canaanite and Israelite times. Then the later Assyrian, Neo-Babylonian, and Persian empires are described, upon whose imperial policies the fate and future of the kingdoms of Israel and Judah depended. With the world at last under Roman domination, the cities of Palestine are pictured as they were in the time of Jesus, and afterward a glimpse is obtained of the chief places in which the work of the apostle Paul was done. In view of the great importance of the writings collected in the New Testament, a study is made of ancient writing materials and practices and of the transmission of the text to the present time. Then the Roman catacombs are investigated, together with their art and inscriptions, and a brief account is given of characteristic early Christian sarcophagi. Finally, the development of distinctive places of Christian assembly is indicated and the basilicas of Constantinian times are described—basilicas whose successors were the Byzantine churches of the East and the Romanesque and Gothic cathedrals of the West. With the clear emergence of the Christian community, centered in the place where the gospel of Jesus Christ is proclaimed, our story comes to an end.

In the earlier part of the narrative it is the broader background of the general history and civilization which is most illuminated by archeology and to which the major part of the portrayal is devoted. In the later part not only is the general history relatively simpler and more generally known, but there are also many more monuments of Judaism and Christianity themselves. Therefore in the course of the book a steadily diminishing amount of space is apportioned to the general history and a steadily increasing amount given to the specifically biblical and early Christian materials.

In order to give a more vivid sense of direct contact with the living past, frequent quotations are made from the ancient sources, and numerous photographs are presented of actual places and objects. Many of the sites are ones which I have visited and many of the objects are ones which I have studied in the museums of Chicago, Philadelphia, New York, London, Paris, Berlin, Rome, Cairo, and Jerusalem. An extensive literature has been consulted and all references cited, both ancient and modern, have been taken from personally used sources. The full title and date of each book are given upon its first appearance, with the exception of those works for which abbreviations are employed and which appear on pages xxxv-xxxvii. The maps and plans were prepared in detail by myself, and executed and lettered by Mr. William Lane Jones.

In the writing I thought often of Dean Jesse Cobb Caldwell of the College of the Bible, Drake University, who taught me the importance of history, and of Professor Dr. Hans Lietzmann of Friedrich-Wilhelms-Universität, Berlin, who instructed me in early Christian archeology, and I have dedicated the book to their memory. In the publication I was also very grateful to Mr. Datus C. Smith, Jr., former Director of Princeton University Press, for his deep understanding, constant interest, and many courtesies.

In the present second edition the structure of the book remains the same but the results of many new excavations and further studies are incorporated. Among other things there is reference to fresh work or publication relative to Jarmo, Matarrah, Samarra, Baghouz, Tepe Gawra, Eridu, Lagash, Nippur, Saqqara, Amarna, Kawa, Abu Usba, Yarmuk, Jericho, Abu Ghosh, Abu Matar, Khirbet el-Bitar, Hebron, Dotha, Nebo, Gilgal, Ai, Gibeon, Hazor, Megiddo, Ugarit, Shiloh, Tell en-Nasbeh, Shechem, Tirzah, Dibon, Nimrod, Herculaneum, and Rome; to new studies on the Habiru; to newly discovered documents including extensive Sumerian literature, the law codes of Ur-Nammu, Eshnunna, and Lipit-Ishtar, Egyptian execration texts, Babylonian chronicles, the Dead Sea scrolls, and the Nessana and other papyri; to new translations of ancient sources; and to recent researches in Egyptian, Assyrian, Babylonian, and biblical chronology. The literature dealt with extends up to January 1, 1959. Mention may also be made of my own articles on Christian Archaeology in *The Encyclopedia Americana*; on Baalbek, Babylon, Behistun Rock, Cuneiform, Jerusalem, Layard, Sir Austen Henry, Near Eastern Architecture, Nineveh, Persepolis, Petra, Ras Shamra, Tyre, and Ur in *Collier's Encyclopedia*; on Christian Archaeology in the *Twentieth Century Encyclopedia of Religious Knowledge, An Extension of the New Schaff-Herzog Encyclopedia of Religious Knowledge*; and on Achaia, Adramyttium, Adria, Agora, Amphipolis, Appian Way, Areopàgus, Athens, Berea, Beroea, Cenchreae, Corinth, Dalmatia, Elymais, Ephesus, Fair Havens, Forum of Appius, Illyricum, Italy, Lasea, Macedonia, Melita, Neapolis, Nicopolis, Philippi, Puteoli, Rhegium, Spain, Syracuse, Thessalonica, and Three Taverns in the forthcoming *The Interpreter's Dictionary of the Bible*; and Research Abstracts in Archeology in *The Journal of Bible and Religion* in October 1947 and following years. For their kindness and efficiency in everything concerned with the publishing of the present revised edition it is a pleasure to thank Mr. Herbert S. Bailey, Jr., Director and Editor, and Miss Harriet Anderson of Princeton University Press.

Pacific School of Religion
Berkeley, California

Jack Finegan

Acknowledgments

IN addition to the acknowledgments made in the List of Illustrations, thanks are also due to the following for kind permission to make reproductions: to the American Academy of Arts and Sciences, Boston, for Figures 152 and 153; to the American Schools of Oriental Research, New Haven, for Figure 195; to the Biblioteca Apostolica Vaticana, Rome, for Figure 145; to the Trustees of the British Museum, London, for Figures 24, 46, 72, 74, 78, 90, 146, 147, and 149; to the University of Chicago Press for Figures 30, 40, and 43; to the Clarendon Press, Oxford, for Figures 64 and 148; to Les Éditions d'Art et d'Histoire, Paris, for Figure 82; to Éditions Albert Morancé, Paris, for Figures 42 and 49; to the Egypt Exploration Society, London, for Figures 39 and 141; to the Field Press (1930) Ltd., London, for Figures 68 and 69; to the President and Fellows of Harvard College, Cambridge, for Figure 114; to Arthur Upham Pope, Director of the Iranian Institute, New York, for Figure 87; to the Director of the Istanbul Arkeoloji Müzeleri Müdürlügü, Istanbul, for Figure 118; to Kirsopp Lake for Figure 148; to Kirsopp and Silva Lake for Figures 152 and 153; to Librairie Orientaliste Paul Geuthner, Paris, for Figure 21; to Librairie Hachette, Paris, for Figure 97; to Macmillan and Co. Ltd., London, for Figures 4, 5, and 6; to the New York Public Library for Figure 113; to Sir Humphrey Milford, Oxford University Press, Oxford, for Figures 60, 61, 62, 70, 141, 186, 190, and 193; to the Government of Palestine for Figures 190 and 193; to the Palestine Exploration Fund, London, for Figures 59 and 66; to Presses Universitaires de France, Paris, for Figure 150; to George Routledge and Sons Ltd., London, for Figure 35; to C. F. A. Schaeffer for Figures 60, 61, and 62; to the Service des Antiquités de l'Égypte, Cairo, for Figures 38 and 44; to George Steindorff for Figure 47; to Emery Walker Ltd., London, for Figure 143; and to the Trustees of the late Sir Henry Wellcome, owners of the copyright, for Figure 70. The following pictures are from books whose copyright is vested in the Alien Property Custodian, 1945, pursuant to law, and their reproduction is by permission of the Alien Property Custodian in the public interest under License No. JA-964: Figure 154, Copyright 1919 by Gesellschaft zur Förderung der Wissenschaft des Judentums, Berlin; Figure 151,

Copyright 1929 by Peter Hanstein, Bonn; Figure 76, Copyright 1938 by J. C. Hinrichs, Leipzig; Figures 84, 85, Copyright 1925 by J. C. Hinrichs, Leipzig; Figure 168, Copyright 1927 by Josef Kösel & Friedrich Pustet K.-G., Munich; Figures 41, 138, Copyright 1936 by Phaidon Verlag, Vienna; Figures 75, 134, Copyright 1925 by Propyläen-Verlag G.m.b.H., Berlin; Figures 156, 157, 158, 160, 161, 163, 164, Copyright 1933 by Verlag für Kunstwissenschaft G.m.b.H., Berlin-Friedenau; Figure 127, Copyright 1923 by Ernst Wasmuth A.G., Berlin. Because of the war and other circumstances, it was impossible to communicate with certain publishers and individuals, and for pictures used under such conditions appreciation is recorded here.

Thanks are likewise expressed to The Westminster Press, Philadelphia, for permission to derive various details of Plan 1 from G. Ernest Wright and Floyd V. Filson, eds., *The Westminster Historical Atlas to the Bible*, 1945, Pl. xvii; and to Princeton University Press for permission to quote from *Ancient Near Eastern Texts Relating to the Old Testament*, ed. James B. Pritchard, 2d ed. 1955.

Except where otherwise indicated, the scripture quotations are from the *Revised Standard Version of the Bible*, copyrighted 1946 and 1952 by the Division of Christian Education of the National Council of Churches, and used by permission. For permission to quote from *The Bible, An American Translation*, by J. M. Powis Smith and Edgar J. Goodspeed, acknowledgment is made to the University of Chicago Press.

Contents

List of Illustrations

(Figures numbered 1 through 98 appear in Volume I.)

xxiii

xxv

Following
Page

xxxii

LIST OF MAPS AND PLANS
(Maps 1-4 appear in Volume I.)

MAPS

PLANS

List of Abbreviations

AASOR   *Annual of the American Schools of Oriental Research.*

AB   *The Art Bulletin.*

ADAJ   *Annual of the Department of Antiquities of Jordan.*

AJA   *American Journal of Archaeology.*

AJP   *The American Journal of Philology.*

AJSL   *The American Journal of Semitic Languages and Literatures.*

AJT   *The American Journal of Theology.*

ANEA   James B. Pritchard, *The Ancient Near East: An Anthology of Texts and Pictures.* 1958.

ANEP   James B. Pritchard, *The Ancient Near East in Pictures Relating to the Old Testament.* 1954.

ANET   James B. Pritchard, ed., *Ancient Near Eastern Texts Relating to the Old Testament.* 2d ed. 1955.

ANF   Alexander Roberts and James Donaldson, eds., rev. by A. Cleveland Coxe, *The Ante-Nicene Fathers, Translations of the Writings of the Fathers down to A.D. 325.* 10 vols. 1885-87.

AO   *Archiv für Orientforschung.*

AP   *Archiv für Papyrusforschung.*

ARAB   Daniel David Luckenbill, *Ancient Records of Assyria and Babylonia.* 2 vols. 1926-27.

ARE   James Henry Breasted, *Ancient Records of Egypt.* 5 vols. 1906-07.

AS   *Assyriological Studies.* Oriental Institute.

ASBACH   Joseph C. Ayer, *A Source Book for Ancient Church History.* 1913.

ASV   *American Standard Version.*

ATR   *Anglican Theological Review.*

AZKK   *Die Antike, Zeitschrift für Kunst und Kultur des klassischen Altertums.*

BA   *The Biblical Archaeologist.*

BASOR   *Bulletin of the American Schools of Oriental Research.*

BDSM   William H. Brownlee, *The Dead Sea Manual of Discipline,* BASOR Supplementary Studies 10-12. 1951.

BDSS   Millar Burrows, *The Dead Sea Scrolls.* 1955.

BJRL   *Bulletin of the John Rylands Library, Manchester.*

BML   Millar Burrows, *More Light on the Dead Sea Scrolls.* 1958.

CAH   J. B. Bury, S. A. Cook, F. E. Adcock, M. P. Charlesworth and N. H. Baynes, eds., *The Cambridge Ancient History.* 12 vols. and 5 vols. of plates, 1923-39.

CALQ   Frank M. Cross, Jr., *The Ancient Library of Qumran and Modern Biblical Studies.* 1958.

CAP   R. H. Charles, ed., *The Apocrypha and Pseudepigrapha of the Old Testament in English with Introductions and Critical and Explanatory Notes to the Several Books.* 2 vols. 1913.

CBQ   *The Catholic Biblical Quarterly.*

CIG   *Corpus Inscriptionum Graecarum.* 1828-77.

DACL   *Dictionnaire d'archéologie chrétienne et de liturgie.* 1924ff.

DJD   *Discoveries in the Judaean Desert.* I, *Qumran Cave I,* by D. Barthélemy and J. T. Milik. 1955.

DLO   Adolf Deissmann, *Licht vom Osten, Das Neue Testament und die neuentdeckten Texte der hellenistisch-römischen Welt.* 4th ed. 1923.

DM   *The Mishnah Translated from the Hebrew with Introduction and Brief Explanatory Notes,* by Herbert Danby. 1933.

EB   *The Encyclopaedia Britannica.* 14th ed. 24 vols. 1929.

GBT   Lazarus Goldschmidt, *Der babylonische Talmud.* 9 vols. 1899-1935.

GCS   *Die griechischen christlichen*

Schriftsteller der ersten Jahrhunderte.

GDSS Theodor H. Gaster, *The Dead Sea Scriptures in English Translation.* 1956.

HDB James Hastings, ed., *A Dictionary of the Bible.* 4 vols. 1898-1902.

HERE James Hastings, ed., *Encyclopaedia of Religion and Ethics.* 12 vols. 1910-22.

HFDMM W. H. P. Hatch, *Facsimiles and Descriptions of Minuscule Manuscripts of the New Testament.* 1951.

HJ *The Hibbert Journal.*

HPUM W. H. P. Hatch, *The Principal Uncial Manuscripts of the New Testament.* 1939.

HTR *The Harvard Theological Review.*

HUCA *Hebrew Union College Annual.*

ICC *The International Critical Commentary.*

IEJ *Israel Exploration Journal.*

JANT M. R. James, *The Apocryphal New Testament.* 1942.

JAOS *Journal of the American Oriental Society.*

JBL *Journal of Biblical Literature.*

JBR *The Journal of Bible and Religion.*

JCS *Journal of Cuneiform Studies.*

JE Isidore Singer, ed., *The Jewish Encyclopedia.* 12 vols. 1901-05.

JEA *The Journal of Egyptian Archaeology.*

JHS *The Journal of Hellenic Studies.*

JJS *Journal of Jewish Studies.*

JNES *Journal of Near Eastern Studies.*

JPOS *The Journal of the Palestine Oriental Society.*

JQR *The Jewish Quarterly Review.*

JR *The Journal of Religion.*

JRAS *The Journal of the Royal Asiatic Society.*

JSS *Journal of Semitic Studies.*

JTS *The Journal of Theological Studies.*

KAT J. A. Knudtzon, *Die El-Amarna Tafeln.* 2 vols. 1908-15.

KFTS Samuel N. Kramer, *From the Tablets of Sumer.* 1956.

KJV *King James Version.*

KPGÄ Friedrich K. Kienitz, *Die politische Geschichte Ägyptens vom 7. bis zum 4. Jahrhundert vor die Zeitwende.* 1953.

KRAC Theodor Klauser, ed., *Reallexikon für Antike und Christentum, Sachwörterbuch zur Auseinandersetzung des Christentums mit der antiken Welt.* 1950ff.

LCL *The Loeb Classical Library.*

LLP Louise Ropes Loomis, *The Book of the Popes (Liber Pontificalis), I, To the Pontificate of Gregory I.* 1916.

LXX The Septuagint. Henry Barclay Swete, ed., *The Old Testament in Greek according to the Septuagint.* I, 4th ed. 1909; II, 3d ed. 1907; III, 3d ed. 1905. Alfred Rahlfs, ed., *Septuaginta, id est Vetus Testamentum Graece iuxta LXX interpretes.* 2 vols. 1935. *Septuaginta, Vetus Testamentum Graecum auctoritate Societatis Litterarum Gottingensis editum.* 1931ff.

MMVGT James H. Moulton and George Milligan, *The Vocabulary of the Greek Testament Illustrated from the Papyri and Other Non-Literary Sources.* 1949.

MPG Jacques Paul Migne, *Patrologiae cursus completus. Series graeca.*

MPL Jacques Paul Migne, *Patrologiae cursus completus. Series latina.*

MTAT Samuel A. B. Mercer, *The Tell El-Amarna Tablets.* 2 vols. 1939.

NGM *The National Geographic Magazine.*

NPNF Philip Schaff, ed., *A Select Library of the Nicene and Post-Nicene Fathers,* First Series. 14 vols. 1886-89.

NPNFss Philip Schaff and Henry Wace, eds., *A Select Library of Nicene and Post-Nicene Fathers of the Christian*

Church, Second Series. 14 vols. 1890-1900.

NSH   Samuel M. Jackson, ed., *The New Schaff-Herzog Encyclopedia of Religious Knowledge.* 12 vols. 1908-12.

NTS   *New Testament Studies.*

OIC   *Oriental Institute Communications.*

OIP   *Oriental Institute Publications.*

OL   *Orientalistische Literaturzeitung.*

OP   *The Oxyrhynchus Papyri.*

PATD   Samuel B. Platner and Thomas Ashby, *A Topographical Dictionary of Ancient Rome.* 1929.

PBA   *Proceedings of the British Academy.*

PCAE   Richard A. Parker, *The Calendars of Ancient Egypt.* SAOC 26, 1950.

PCAM   Ann Louise Perkins, *The Comparative Archeology of Early Mesopotamia.* SAOC 25, 1949.

PDBC   Richard A. Parker and Waldo H. Dubberstein, *Babylonian Chronology 626 B.C.- A.D. 75.* 3d ed. 1956.

PEFA   *Palestine Exploration Fund Annual.*

PEFQS   *Palestine Exploration Fund Quarterly Statement.*

PEQ   *Palestine Exploration Quarterly.*

PWRE   Pauly-Wissowa, *Real-Encyclopädie der classischen Altertumswissenschaft.*

QDAP   *The Quarterly of the Department of Antiquities in Palestine.*

RAAO   *Revue d'assyriologie et d'archeologie orientale.*

RAC   *Rivista di archeologia cristiana.*

RB   *Revue Biblique.*

RBT   Michael L. Rodkinson, *New Edition of the Babylonian Talmud.* 10 (xx), vols. 1903, 1916.

RHR   *Revue de l'histoire des religions.*

RSV   *Revised Standard Version.*

SAOC   *Studies in Ancient Oriental Civilization.* Oriental Institute.

SBT   I. Epstein, ed., *The Babylonian Talmud* (Soncino Press). 1935ff.

SHJP   Emil Schürer, *A History of the Jewish People in the Time of Jesus Christ.* 5 vols. 1896.

SRK   Paul Styger, *Die römischen Katakomben, archäologische Forschungen über den Ursprung und die Bedeutung der altchristlichen Grabstätten.* 1933.

TL   *Theologische Literaturzeitung.*

TMN   Edwin R. Thiele, *The Mysterious Numbers of the Hebrew Kings.* 1951.

TU   *Texte und Untersuchungen zur Geschichte der altchristlichen Literatur.*

TZ   *Theologische Zeitschrift.*

UMB   *The University Museum Bulletin.*

VT   *Vetus Testamentum.*

WCCK   D. J. Wiseman, *Chronicles of Chaldaean Kings (626-556 B.C.) in the British Museum.* 1956.

ZA   *Zeitschrift für Assyriologie.*

ZÄS   *Zeitschrift für ägyptische Sprache und Altertumskunde.*

ZAW   *Zeitschrift für die alttestamentliche Wissenschaft.*

ZDPV   *Zeitschrift des Deutschen Palästina-Vereins.*

ZNW   *Zeitschrift für die neutestamentliche Wissenschaft und die Kunde der älteren Kirche.*

ZTK   *Zeitschrift für Theologie und Kirche.*

LIGHT FROM THE ANCIENT PAST

V

The Holy Land in the Time of Jesus

1. THE RISE OF ROME AND THE ROMAN EMPIRE,
c.753 B.C.-A.D. 476

IN EARLY Christian times the Mediterranean world was ruled by Rome. Stone Age remains in the neighborhood of Rome attest the great antiquity of human settlement in that vicinity. The actual founding of the city was supposed, according to Roman traditions, to have occurred in 753 B.C., and that date was taken as the initial point in the usual chronological system which reckoned *ab urbe condita*, from the founded city.[1]

The early kings gave way in 509 B.C., according to the traditional chronology, to a republican form of government which endured until 27 B.C. Rome was the natural center of the Mediterranean, and her supremacy in the West was established indisputably by the defeat of Hannibal of Carthage in the battle of Zama in 202 B.C. In the East, Greece and western Asia Minor were conquered by the middle and end respectively of the second century B.C., but it remained for the

[1] In the A.U.C. era the year was originally reckoned as beginning with a festival which fell on April 21, but writers usually refer to the year as beginning when the consuls took office and, from A.U.C. 601 on, this was generally January 1. In the Julian calendar, of course, the year began on January 1. For the Roman and Christian calendars see Walter F. Wislicenus, *Der Kalender in gemeinverständlicher Darstellung*. 1905; Hans Lietzmann, *Zeitrechnung der römischen Kaiserzeit, des Mittelalters und der Neuzeit für die Jahre 1-2000 nach Christus*. 1934. For a table of parallel years of the Greek, Seleucid, Roman, and Christian eras see SHJP I, ii, pp.393-398.

Roman general Pompey (106-48 B.C.), whose bust is shown in Fig. 98, to close the circle of empire around the eastern end of the Mediterranean.

The opposition to Rome in the East was headed by King Mithradates VI Eupator of Pontus, member of a dynasty which belonged to the highest Persian nobility, who warred with the Romans in Asia Minor for twenty-five years, and by his son-in-law King Tigranes of Armenia, member of a dynasty founded by Artaxias, a general of Antiochus III. Tigranes was for a time the most powerful ruler in western Asia, and used Antioch in Syria as one of his residential cities. The defeat of Mithradates and Tigranes by Pompey led to the consolidation of Roman power in the eastern Mediterranean, to the establishment of Syria as a Roman province, and to the inclusion of Palestine in the empire (cf. p. 246).

While Pompey was winning the East, Gaius Julius Caesar (c.102-44 B.C.) was rising to political importance in Rome. For a time the two men shared power, then faced each other in civil war. Pompey was defeated at Pharsalus in 48 B.C. and afterward was murdered in Egypt, whither he fled for refuge, while the last of his forces were crushed at Munda in Spain in 45 B.C. Thereafter Caesar was undisputed master of the Roman world, a glory which he enjoyed for only a brief six months before being assassinated on March 15, 44 B.C.

Two relatives of Julius Caesar were then the chief claimants to his empire. The first was Marcus Antonius, commonly called Mark Antony, who was related on his mother's side to Julius Caesar, and who was consul with Caesar in 44 B.C. The second was Gaius Octavius, whose grandmother was Caesar's sister, and who was adopted and made heir by Caesar, thereby acquiring the designation of Gaius Julius Caesar Octavianus. Associating himself with Cleopatra, the heiress of the Ptolemies in Egypt, Mark Antony was dominant in the East, while Octavian appropriated Italy and the West. The final trial of strength between the two rivals came in the naval battle of Actium (September 2, 31 B.C.), where Antony was decisively defeated. In the following year Alexandria was taken and Antony and Cleopatra committed suicide.

From 31 B.C. on, Octavian was the real master of the empire, and two years later the restoration of peace was marked by the closing of the doors of the temple of Janus for the first time in two hundred years. In recognition of Octavian's distinguished services to the state, the Roman Senate in 27 B.C. conferred upon him the title Augustus,

meaning august or majestic. This appellation of dignity was borne by him as the first Roman emperor, and was adopted by all the later Caesars or emperors of Rome.

Under the rule of Augustus (d. A.D. 14) and his successors, for two centuries the Mediterranean world as a whole enjoyed an internal peace, the *Pax Romana,* which it never before had had and which for so long a period it has never since possessed. The author of this outstanding achievement is portrayed in the statue shown in Fig. 99. This work of a master sculptor[2] was found near Prima Porta north of Rome in the ruins of the villa of Livia, the wife of Augustus; the statue is now in the Vatican. The emperor is represented in the prime of manhood and at the height of his power, and his features are delicate and refined. On his breastplate is carved in relief an allegory of empire. Beneath Caelus, the Sky, drives Sol, the Sun, in his four-horse chariot—symbol of the new order in all its splendor.

In the New Testament the birth of Jesus is dated in the reign of Augustus (Luke 2:1)[3] and the beginning of the public ministry of Jesus is placed in the reign of Tiberius (Luke 3:1).[4] The latter was

[2] Gerhart Rodenwaldt in AZKK 13 (1937), pp.160-163.

[3] In A.D. 533 the Roman monk Dionysius Exiguus suggested counting years no longer from the founding of Rome (cf. above p.247 n.1) but rather from the birth of Christ. Clement of Alexandria (A.D. c.200) stated (*Stromata.* I, xxi, 147; ANF II, p.333): "And our Lord was born in the twenty-eighth year, when first the census was ordered to be taken in the reign of Augustus." Octavian became emperor and received the title Augustus on January 16, A.U.C. 727. Counting A.U.C. 727 as his first year, his twenty-eighth year was A.U.C. 754, and this was taken as the year A.D. 1. Augustus died August 19, A.D. 14 (A.U.C. 767), having reigned forty-one years. Clement of Alexandria, however, in a paragraph preceding the quotation given above, attributed to him a reign of forty-six years, four months, and one day. Counting back exactly that far from August 19, A.D. 14 would bring one to a starting point of April 18, 33 B.C. Reckoned from that initial point, the twenty-eighth year of Augustus began on April 18, 6 B.C. At all events it is clear that Dionysius Exiguus was not entirely correct in the year selected for the beginning of the Christian era.

[4] Luke gives the date as "in the fifteenth year of the reign of Tiberius Caesar." The more usual method of dating in this period was by indicating the honors accorded to the emperor and specifying the number of times he was invested with the tribunician power, designated consul, and acclaimed imperator (Carl H. Kraeling in ATR 24 [1942], p.344). When tribunician years were not stated, it was usually the custom in the first century A.D. to count the years of an emperor's reign from the death of his predecessor or the day on which he himself began to rule (W. M. Ramsay, *Was Christ Born at Bethlehem?* 1898, pp.133, 202). Augustus died August 19, A.D. 14; Tiberius was formally proclaimed emperor within less than one month on September 17 (H. Dessau, ed., *Prosopographia Imperii Romani.* II [1897], No. 150, pp.182f.; M. Cary, et al., eds., *The Oxford Classical Dictionary.* 1949, pp.906f.). The first year of Tiberius began, accordingly, on August 19 or September 17, A.D. 14, and his fifteenth year began at the same time in A.D. 28. The appearing of John the Baptist and the inauguration of the public work of Jesus may be dated, therefore, with considerable

the successor of Augustus, and reigned from A.D. 14 to 37. The marble head of Tiberius shown in Fig. 100 is in the Boston Museum of Fine Arts, and portrays him as yet a lad with fresh and pleasing features.[5]

---

probability in the fall of A.D. 28. For other ways of reckoning see Werner Foerster, *Neutestamentliche Zeitgeschichte*, II, *Das römische Weltreich zur Zeit des Neuen Testaments*. 1956, p.268, n.37.

[5] The successors of Augustus and Tiberius in the Julio-Claudian line were Gaius (A.D. 37-41), generally known as Caligula, Claudius (41-54), and Nero (54-68). In 68 Galba, Otho, and Vitellius all claimed the throne, but the final winner in the struggle was Vespasian (69-79). The Flavian Dynasty which he founded included also Titus (79-81) and Domitian (81-96). The rulers who followed belonged to the house of Nerva and included Nerva (96-98), Trajan (98-117), and Hadrian (117-138). Then the Antonines came to the throne, including Antoninus Pius (138-161), Marcus Aurelius (161-180), and Commodus (180-192). The Severan house embraced Septimus Severus (193-211), Caracalla (211-217), Elagabalus (218-222), and Severus Alexander (222-235). The succeeding military emperors were Maximinus Thrax (235-238), Gordian III (238-244), Philip the Arab (244-249), Decius (249-251), Gallus (251-253), Valerian (253-260), and Gallienus (260-268). After Gallienus was murdered, Claudius II reigned briefly (268-270), but it remained for Aurelian (270-275) to restore unity. He was followed by Tacitus (275), Probus (276-282), Carus (282), Carinus and Numerian (283), and Diocletian (284-305). Diocletian reorganized the empire in 286 by entrusting the West to his friend Maximian while he retained the East for himself. This arrangement was modified further in 292 when the two Augusti each recognized a Caesar as a subordinate colleague. Thus Galerius Caesar was associated with Diocletian Augustus in the East and Constantius Chlorus Caesar with Maximian Augustus in the West. Diocletian and Maximian abdicated in 305, leaving Galerius and Constantius Chlorus as Augusti in control of the empire. Galerius was able to secure the promotion to the rank of Caesar of his faithful servant Flavius Valerius Severus and of his nephew Daia Maximinus, hoping thus on the death of Constantius Chlorus to become the sole master of the empire. Constantius Chlorus died in 306, but his soldiers continued to be loyal to Constantine, son of Constantius Chlorus and Helena. Maximian now reassumed the dignity which he had relinquished in 305, and with his son Maxentius brought the number of Roman rulers to six. In the struggle that followed, Maximian was killed in 310, and Maxentius was defeated by Constantine at the decisive battle of the Milvian bridge outside Rome in 312. Meanwhile in the East Licinius had become co-regent with Galerius and, upon the latter's death in 311, succeeded him on the throne. Constantine and Licinius now (313-323) exercised authority jointly as colleagues in the West and the East respectively, and Licinius married the sister of Constantine. The two rulers warred however in 314 and again in 323. In the second conflict Licinius was defeated, and in 324 was executed at Constantine's command. Thus Constantine the Great emerged as sole ruler of the Roman Empire (323-337). After Constantine, his three sons divided the empire, but Constantine II (337-340) died in civil war against his brother Constans (337-350) and the latter was slain by the usurper Magnentius. The remaining son Constantius (337-361) had received the East, and now upon defeating Magnentius again united the whole empire under one authority. He was followed by Julian the Apostate (361-363), and Jovian (363-364). In 364 the empire was divided again, Valentinian I (364-375) taking the West and Valens (364-378) the East. The later emperors in the West were Gratian (367-383) and Valentinian II (375-392), Theodosius I (394-395), Honorius (395-423), Joannes (424), Valentinian III (425-455), Maximus (455), Avitus (455-456), Majorian (457-461), Libius Severus (461-465), Anthemius (467-472), Olybrius (472), Glycerius (473), Julius Nepos (473-475), and Romulus Augustulus (475-476). The last named king was deposed by the Teutonic invaders in 476 and replaced by Odoacer as the first barbarian ruler of Italy. Thus the Roman Empire in the West came to an end. In the East the emperors who

In connection with the birth and the public appearance of Jesus, Luke not only refers to the Roman emperors Augustus and Tiberius, but also gives more detailed mention of a number of lesser governors and officials. The passages (Luke 2:1f.; 3:1f.) are as follows:

"In those days a decree went out from Caesar Augustus that all the world should be enrolled. This was the first enrollment, when Quirinius was governor of Syria.

"In the fifteenth year of the reign of Tiberius Caesar, Pontius Pilate being governor of Judea, and Herod being tetrarch of Galilee, and his brother Philip tetrarch of the region of Ituraea and Trachoritis, and Lysanias tetrarch of Abilene, in the high-priesthood of Annas and Caiaphas, the word of God came to John the son of Zechariah."

Elsewhere Luke dates the promise of the birth of John the Baptist "in the days of Herod, king of Judea" (1:5), and Matthew places the birth of Jesus "in the days of Herod the king" (2:1), this Herod being identified (2:22) as the father of Archelaus.[6] In order to explain these references to Syrian and Palestinian authorities and to give an understanding of the inner political situation in Palestine in the time

---

followed Valens included Theodosius I the Great (379-395), who also ruled the West for a time, Arcadius (395-408), Theodosius II (408-450), Marcian (450-457), Leo I (457-474), Leo II (474), Zeno (474-491), Anastasius I (491-518), Justin I (518-527), Justinian I the Great (527-565), and a long line of further rulers who occupied the throne until Constantinople fell to the Crusaders in 1204 and became the seat of a Latin Empire. On the Roman emperors and Christianity see Ethelbert Stauffer, *Christ and the Caesars, Historical Sketches*. 1955.

[6] Since Herod died in 4 B.C. the birth of Jesus must have been at least that early, and Matthew 2:16 suggests that it may have been as much as two years before that. The date of Herod's reign is fixed by the following facts. Josephus (*Ant.* XVII, viii, 1; *War.* I, xxxiii, 8) tells of the death of Herod and says that at that time he had reigned thirty-seven years. He died shortly before a Passover (*Ant.* XVII, ix, 3; *War.* II, i, 3), and not long before his death there was an eclipse of the moon (*Ant.* XVII, vi, 4). This is the only eclipse of moon or sun mentioned by Josephus in any of his writings (William Whiston, *The Works of Flavius Josephus*, p.514 n.), and must be the lunar eclipse which was seen in Palestine on the night of March 12/13, 4 B.C., no such phenomenon having taken place there in 3 or 2 B.C. It is also known that Archelaus was deposed in A.U.C. 759 in the tenth year of his reign, which leads back to A.U.C. 750 or 4 B.C. for his accession and the death of his father (SHJP I, i, p.465 n.165). Thus Herod died in the spring of 4 B.C. and his thirty-seven year reign was 40-4 B.C. In 7 B.C. there was a triple conjunction of Jupiter and Saturn, a phenomenon which occurs once in 805 years and was observed by Johannes Kepler in A.D. 1603. The planets passed each other on May 29, September 29, and December 4, 7 B.C., and in 6 B.C. Mars moved past them too, in February of that year forming with them a triangle in the evening sky, a configuration known as a massing of the planets. These unusual astronomical happenings took place in Pisces, the sign of the zodiac which ancient astrologers called the House of the Hebrews, and it has been thought that this was the "star" which the wise men saw. See the pamphlets, *The Star of Bethlehem*, published by the Adler Planetarium, Chicago; and *The Christmas Star*, published by the Morrison Planetarium, California Academy of Sciences, San Francisco.

of Jesus, it is necessary now to tell briefly a complex and fascinating story which has its beginnings in the days of the Maccabean War.

2. THE TIME OF THE MACCABEES, c.168-63 B.C.

IT WAS an old priest Mattathias and his five sons who led the revolt against Antiochus IV Epiphanes (p. 246).[1] Of these sons, Judas, called Maccabeus, or the Hammer (165-161 B.C.), became the great general and gave his name to the struggle, while his brother Simon eventually ruled (142-135) as prince and high priest over a small independent kingdom. The dynasty thus founded was known as the Hasmonean, from Asamoneus the father of Mattathias.[2] In the succession of rulers Simon was followed by his son John Hyrcanus (135-104), and his grandson Aristobulus I (104-103), who assumed the title of king. Under the latter's brother, Alexander Janneus (103-76), the Jewish kingdom attained its greatest extent, reaching to limits practically the same as those of the kingdom of David. The title of king was stamped proudly in Hebrew and Greek upon the coins of Alexander Janneus.

But the sons of Janneus, Hyrcanus II and Aristobulus II, quarreled for the throne and both appealed to the Romans for help. Pompey had already (64 B.C.) made Syria a Roman province and was near at hand in Damascus. When Aristobulus lost the confidence of the Romans and his adherents entrenched themselves in the temple, Pompey besieged Jerusalem. The city fell after three months (63 B.C.) and Pompey outraged the Jews by entering the Holy of Holies. Aristobulus II was taken prisoner to Rome, and the elder brother, Hyrcanus II (63-40 B.C.), was established as high priest and ethnarch. From that time on the Jews were subject to the Romans.[3]

3. PALESTINE UNDER HERODIAN AND ROMAN RULE, 63 B.C.-A.D. 70

WHEN Pompey was defeated and Julius Caesar was established as master in Rome, Hyrcanus II and his friend Antipater, the Idumean,

---

[1] The history of the Maccabean struggle is narrated in a generally trustworthy way in I Maccabees. For the history from here on through the wars with Rome see Robert H. Pfeiffer, *History of New Testament Times with an Introduction to the Apocrypha.* 1949.

[2] Josephus, *War.* I, i, 3.

[3] *ibid.,* I, vii, 4; *Ant.* XIV, iv. For Palestine in the Roman period see G. M. Fitz-Gerald in PEQ 1956, pp.38-48.

attached themselves to Caesar's party and rendered him such services as to secure for Judea freedom both from taxes and from the obligation of military service. Antipater, who already, it seems, had attained the position of procurator of Judea,[1] was confirmed in this office by Caesar. He soon appointed his two sons, Phasael and Herod, governors of Jerusalem and Galilee respectively.

Phasael ended his life by suicide when Antigonus (40-37 B.C.), son of Aristobulus II and last of the Hasmonean rulers, captured Jerusalem with Parthian help. For Herod there was a greater future. In Rome he gained the favor of Mark Antony and Octavian, who at that time divided the Roman world between themselves, and was given by the Senate the rank of king of Judea (40 B.C.). By 37 B.C. Herod was able to besiege and take Jerusalem. Antigonus was beheaded by the Romans, and Herod assumed the Jewish crown, meanwhile having strengthened his claim by marrying the Hasmonean princess, Mariamne. When Mark Antony was defeated and Octavian emerged as the sole emperor of the Roman Empire, Herod knew how to continue in his favor and even to gain by imperial favor the doubling of his own territory.

HEROD THE GREAT

Herod "the Great"[2] ruled for thirty-seven years (40-4 B.C.) with much energy and success, but was always hated by the Jews as a half-foreigner[3] and a friend of the Romans. Moreover, he had little real interest in Judaism and was instrumental in spreading Greek culture throughout the land. The love of Herod for pagan civilization was reflected in most of his numerous building activities.[4] Temples dedicated to pagan gods and emperor worship, halls and theaters in the Greek style, palaces, castles, and baths were constructed throughout the land. On the site of ancient Samaria he built a new city, named Sebaste, in honor of the Emperor Augustus.[5] On the coast, on the site of the ancient Straton's Tower, he built a new city and port which he named Caesarea and which later was to be the capital of the country.

---

[1] *Ant.* xiv, viii, 1.

[2] This title is applied once to Herod by Josephus, *Ant.* xviii, v, 4. See now Stewart Perowne, *The Life and Times of Herod the Great.* 1956.

[3] As an Idumean he was called a "half-Jew" by Josephus, *Ant.* xiv, xv, 2. The Idumeans, or Edomites, living in southern Palestine had been conquered and compelled to accept Judaism by John Hyrcanus (*Ant.* xiii, ix, 1).

[4] *War.* i, xxi.

[5] The Latin title Augustus was rendered in Greek by Σεβαστός. cf. Dio Cassius (A.D. c.150-c.235), *Roman History.* liii, xvi, 8. tr. E. Cary, lcl (1914-27), vi, p.235.

But the most magnificent single piece of building done by Herod was carried out in strict conformity with Jewish principles. This was the restoration of the temple in Jerusalem,[6] which was begun in 20/19 B.C. Only priests were allowed to build the temple proper, and Herod himself refrained from entering the inner temple, whose precincts should be trodden by none but priests. The temple proper was built in one year and six months, but other building work was long continued, and was finished only in the time of the procurator Albinus (A.D. 62-64), a few years before the temple's final destruction.

THE SONS OF HEROD

A few days before his death in 4 B.C., the aged Herod rewrote his will providing for the division of his kingdom among his sons. Of the various sons of Herod's ten legal marriages several had perished in intrigues or had been put to death by their father's orders, including Alexander and Aristobulus, the sons of Mariamne (who also was slain), and Antipater, who was executed five days before Herod died. Three younger sons were to inherit the kingdom. Philip, the son of Cleopatra of Jerusalem, became tetrarch of Gaulanitis, Trachonitis, Batanea, and Panias (Paneas), regions north and east of the Sea of Galilee and mostly inhabited by pagans.[7] Over this territory Philip reigned well for nearly forty years (4 B.C.-A.D. 34). At the sources of the Jordan he rebuilt the city of Panias and gave it the name Caesarea in honor of the emperor.[8] To distinguish it from Caesarea on the coast[9] it was called Caesarea Philippi (Matthew 16:13; Mark 8:27). Also he raised the village of Bethsaida, which was situated at the lake of Gennesareth, to the dignity of a city, both by the number of inhabitants it contained and by its size, and named it Julias after the daughter of the emperor.[10]

Herod Antipas, the younger son of Malthace, became tetrarch of Galilee and Perea (4 B.C.-A.D. 39). He built a splendid capital for himself at a beautiful site in the western shore of the Sea of Galilee, and named it Tiberias in honor of Tiberius who was then on the Roman throne. Antipas brought trouble upon himself through put-

[6] *War.* I, xxi, 1; *Ant.* xv, xi.

[7] *War.* I, xxxiii, 8; *Ant.* xvii, viii, 1.

[8] *War.* II, ix, 1; *Ant.* xviii, ii, 1.

[9] For coastal Caesarea, founded by Herod the Great in 22 B.C., see A. Reifenberg in IEJ 1 (1950-51), pp.20-32.

[10] *Ant.* xviii, ii, 1; cf. *War.* II, ix, 1. Julias was the daughter of Augustus, but was banished in 2 B.C. Since Philip hardly would have named a city for her after that event, Julias must have been built before 2 B.C.

ting away his first wife, the daughter of King Aretas of Nabatea, to marry Herodias, whom he alienated from his half-brother, Herod.[11] Thereafter Antipas was defeated in war by Aretas, and when he sought the king's title from Caligula was banished instead to Lyons in Gaul, whither Herodias followed him.

Archelaus, the older son of Malthace, received the principal part of Herod's territory—Judea, Samaria, and Idumea—and was intended by Herod to have the title of king but actually was given only that of ethnarch (4 B.C.-A.D. 6). Insurrection was spreading throughout the land, however, and the rule of Archelaus was violent and incompetent. When he was deposed and banished to Vienne in Gaul in A.D. 6, his territory was put directly under Roman rule.[12]

THE PROCURATORS AND LEGATES

Authority over the former dominions of Archelaus was placed in the hands of a governor of the equestrian order, whose title was that of procurator, and who could receive help in case of need from the legate who governed the province of Syria.[13] The residence of the

[11] Herodias was a granddaughter of Herod the Great, her father being Aristobulus, the son of Mariamne, who was executed in 7 B.C. Mark 6:17; Matthew 14:3 (contrast Luke 3:19) call Herodias the wife of Philip, meaning doubtless the tetrarch of Trachonitis. Josephus (*Ant.* XVIII, v, 4) states that Herodias was married to Herod, the son of Herod the Great and the second Mariamne, the high priest's daughter. Also Josephus says that Herodias' daughter, Salome, was married to Philip, the tetrarch of Trachonitis. The relationships may have been confused in the Gospels, or it is barely possible that this Herod bore the surname Philip.

[12] *War.* II, viii, 1; *Ant.* XVII, xiii; XVIII, i, 1.

[13] In 27 B.C. Augustus divided the provinces of the Roman Empire into imperial and senatorial. (1) The imperial provinces, which the emperor continued to hold, were those which were most difficult to manage and which required the presence of a strong military force. They in turn were divided, with the exception of some which were administered by simple knights, into two classes: those administered by men who had been consuls, and those administered by men who had been praetors. The governors were nominated by the emperor, were directly responsible to him, and held office for a term the length of which depended on the emperor's pleasure. The governors of both consular and praetorian provinces were called *legati Augusti* (or *Caesaris*) *pro praetore*. (2) The provinces which were given over to the senate were those which did not require the presence of an army but only of a small garrison sufficient for the purpose of maintaining order. They were also divided into those administered by men who had been consuls and those administered by men who had been praetors. The governors of the senatorial provinces were appointed for a year at a time, were responsible to the senate, and were called proconsuls. (3) Certain other possessions were regarded as domains of the emperor and were placed under governors of the equestrian order responsible to the emperor. Their title was that of praefect or procurator, and the title procurator soon became the prevailing one. Judea thus belonged to the third and more exceptional class of provinces. Dio, *Roman History.* LIII, xii-xv; Strabo, *Geography.* XVII, iii, 25.

procurator was at Caesarea, but on occasions when special oversight was necessary he would live for a time in Jerusalem.

The first procurator of Judea was Coponius (probably A.D. 6-9), and his immediate successors were Marcus Ambivius (probably A.D. 9-12), Annius Rufus (probably A.D. 12-15), Valerius Gratus (A.D. 15-26), Pontius Pilate (A.D. 26-36), Marcellus (A.D. 36-37), and Marullus (A.D. 37-41).[14]

Of them all the most famous and perhaps the most ruthless was Pontius Pilate. Pilate was appointed to office through Sejanus, the anti-Semitic prime minister of Tiberius, and he gave offense to the Jews in many ways. His soldiers carried into the Holy City standards bearing the likeness of the emperor, which violated Jewish principles and provoked a determined and successful protest. Again, he took money from the temple treasury to build an aqueduct to Jerusalem, and mercilessly beat down the crowds which gathered to make petition against this act. Later he put inscribed shields in Herod's palace, which were taken down only when the Jews appealed to Tiberius. Yet another and otherwise unknown act of violence is referred to in Luke 13:1, where Pilate is said to have mingled the blood of certain Galileans with that of their animal sacrifices. Finally he slaughtered and imprisoned a multitude of Samaritans who had gathered at Mount Gerizim to search for some sacred vessels which were believed to have been buried there since the time of Moses. The Samaritans complained to Vitellius, the legate in Syria, and Pilate was replaced by Marcellus. Agrippa I charged against Pilate, according to a letter quoted by Philo, "corruptibility, violence, robberies, ill-treatment of the people, grievances, continuous executions without even the form of a trial, endless and intolerable cruelties," yet it must be admitted that the position of a Roman governor in Judea was very difficult, and no doubt it was to Pilate's credit that he retained office for as long as ten years.[15]

Of the Lysanias who is mentioned by Luke (3:1) as tetrarch of Abilene, little is known. The capital of the tetrarchy was at Abila, not far from Damascus, and an inscription of the time of Tiberius has been found there naming Lysanias as tetrarch.[16]

[14] For a tabulation of dated coins struck by the procurators from Coponius to Antonius Felix, including examples from the second to the sixth years of Pontius Pilate, A.D. 27/28 to 31/32, see A. Kindler in IEJ 6 (1956), pp.54-57; cf. Florence A. Banks, *Coins of Bible Days.* 1955.

[15] Josephus, *Ant.* XVIII, iii, 1f.; iv, 1f.; *War.* II, ix, 2-4; Philo (c.20 B.C.-A.D. c.54), *Legatio ad Gaium.* 38. ed. L. Cohn and P. Wendland VI (1915), p.210.

[16] CIG III, No.4521. This younger Lysanias to whom Luke refers and who undoubt-

The legates who ruled Syria at the end of the old era and the beginning of the new are usually listed as follows: M. Titius, 10-9 B.C.; C. Sentius Saturninus, 9-6 B.C.; P. Quinctilius Varus, 6-4 B.C.; P. Sulpicius Quirinius, 3-2 B.C. (?); C. Caesar, 1 B.C.-A.D. 4 (?); L. Volusius Saturninus, A.D. 4-5; P. Sulpicius Quirinius, A.D. 6-7. It must be admitted, however, that there are considerable gaps in the evidence upon which this list is based.[17]

Luke's reference (2:2) to the census that was taken at the time of the birth of Jesus, which was the first enrollment made when Quirinius was governor of Syria, constitutes a difficult problem. Josephus writes concerning Quirinius: "Now Cyrenius, a Roman senator, and one who had gone through other magistracies, and had passed through them till he had been consul, and one who, on other accounts, was of great dignity, came at this time into Syria, with a few others, being sent by Caesar to be a judge of that nation, and to take an account of their substance. Coponius also, a man of the equestrian order, was sent together with him, to have the supreme power over the Jews."[18] Tacitus (A.D. c.55-c.117) describes the public funeral Tiberius requested for Quirinius, and tells briefly of his life.[19] He says that Quirinius was born at Lanuvium, and that he won a consulate under Augustus. A little later he earned the insignia of triumph by capturing the strongholds of the Homanadensians beyond the Cilician frontier. Again he was appointed as adviser to Caius Caesar during the latter's command in Armenia.

Known dates of events mentioned in the foregoing passages are the consulship of Quirinius in 12 B.C., his going with C. Caesar to Armenia in A.D. 3, and his death and public funeral in A.D. 21. His governorship of Syria can also be fixed as beginning in about A.D. 6 by the fact that he took that office, as Josephus says, at the same time that Coponius went to Judea as procurator. Josephus also informs us that the taxings conducted by Quirinius while governor of Syria were made in the thirty-seventh year of Caesar's victory over Antony at Actium.[20] Since that battle took place on September 2, A.U.C. 723 or 31 B.C., the year indicated is that beginning Septem-

---

edly existed, is not to be confused with an older Lysanias who ruled at nearby Chalcis, 40-36 B.C.

[17] SHJP I, i, pp.350-357; E. Honigmann in PWRE, Zweite Reihe, IV, ii (1932), col. 1629; Erich Klostermann, *Das Lukasevangelium* (Handbuch zum Neuen Testament. 5 [2d ed. 1929]), p.33.

[18] *Ant.* XVIII, i, 1.

[19] *Annals.* III, 48. tr. J. Jackson, LCL (1931-37), II, pp.597-599.

[20] *Ant.* XVIII, ii, 1.

ber 2, A.D. 6. A census held in A.D. 6/7 is, of course, too late to be brought into connection with the birth of Jesus.

The fact, however, that Luke speaks of the census at the time of the birth of Jesus as the "first" which was made when Quirinius was governor, may suggest that the census attested above was a second one by that governor. The circumstance that Quirinius conducted the war against the Homanadensians, as stated by Tacitus, suggests that he was already at that earlier time in an official position, perhaps even governor, in Syria, inasmuch as that war was probably conducted from the province of Syria. That one man might hold the same governorship twice is proved by an inscription found in A.D 1764 near Tibur (Tivoli) and placed in the Lateran Museum, which mentions a person who governed Syria twice as legate of Augustus.[21] Some have wished to refer this to Quirinius himself, but since the name is missing in the inscription it cannot be demonstrated. The exact date of the Homanadensian war is also uncertain. Finding an apparent gap in the list of Syrian legates in 3-2 B.C., Schürer concluded that Quirinius was governor there at that time and in that position conducted the war.[22] It may be, however, that the war with the Homanadensians was as much earlier as 10-7 B.C. (cf. below p. 344 n.37), for it is argued that their opposition must certainly have been broken by 6 B.C. when the net of Roman roads was laid out in the province of Galatia.[23] If a gap could be found in the list of Syrian legates at that time it might be supposed that Quirinius was governor then,[24] even as Schürer by the same logic assigned him to a hypothetical place in 3-2 B.C. Or we may think, as W. M. Ramsay suggested,[25] that Quirinius was at that time a special officer sent out by Augustus to conduct the war against the Homanadensians and to see after other foreign relations of the province of Syria. In this position he might also have been responsible for the census in Palestine, which he probably could not have started until the war was over in 7 B.C. Conditions in Palestine, a land normally difficult for the Romans to deal with, might have delayed the census even beyond that, say to 6 B.C. That two Roman officials could exercise administrative authority in the same province at the same time is shown by a statement of Josephus in which he speaks of "Saturninus and Volumnius,

[21] SHJP I, i, p.354 n.25.   [22] SHJP I, i, pp.351f.

[23] Groag in PWRE, Zweite Reihe, IV, i (1931), col. 831.

[24] Egbert C. Hudson in JNES 15 (1956), pp.106f.

[25] Ramsay, *Was Christ Born at Bethlehem?* p.238.

the presidents of Syria."[26] Perhaps Quirinius was associated with Saturninus for a time in a similar way. If that were the case we would understand why Tertullian said that the census at the time of the birth of Jesus was "taken in Judea by Sentius Saturninus."[27]

One other inscription may be mentioned which deals with the career of a Roman officer, Q. Aemilius Secundus, who served under Quirinius when the latter was governor of Syria. Here Quirinius is called legate of Syria, and it is stated that by his orders Aemilius Secundus carried out a census of Apameia, where 117,000 citizens were enumerated.[28] While this may well have to do with the Syrian census of A.D. 6/7 rather than the hypothetical earlier census of Quirinius, it is still of interest in connection with the complex question which we have discussed.

As to the taking of such an enrollment in general, it is known from discoveries among the Egyptian papyri that a Roman census was taken in Egypt, and therefore perhaps also throughout the empire, regularly every fourteen years. Many actual census returns have been found, and they use the very same word (ἀπογραφή) which Luke 2:2 uses for the "enrollment." The earliest definitely dated example is from A.D. 34,[29] then there is one from A.D. 48,[30] another from A.D. 62,[31] and from then on there are numerous examples extending to A.D. 202 and attesting the fourteen year period.[32] Another such return, although now without a date, is believed to have been written in A.D. 20,[33] and yet another is thought to belong to A.D. 34, or 20, or possibly even 6.[34]

That A.D. 6 was a census year we have also seen already from the reference considered above from Josephus. Fourteen years before this would be the year 9 B.C. While actual returns have not been found for this date, there are poll tax lists for even earlier dates and they were presumably connected with some kind of census. It is a reasonable supposition, therefore, that the periodic enrollment was instituted by Augustus in 9 B.C.[35] There is reason to think the actual taking of a census came in the year following that in which the order

[26] *Ant.* XVI, x, 8.   [27] *Against Marcion.* IV, 19; ANF III, p.378.

[28] Ramsay, *Was Christ Born at Bethlehem?* pp.151, 274. The inscription was at one time considered a forgery but is now accepted as genuine (John E. Sandys, ed., *A Companion to Latin Studies.* 3d ed. 1921, p.763).

[29] MMVGT pp.59f. s.v. ἀπογραφή.   [30] OP II, No.255.

[31] OP II, p.207.   [32] *ibid.*   [33] OP II, No.254.

[34] OP II, No.256.

[35] Bernard P. Grenfell and Arthur S. Hunt in OP II, pp.209-211.

for it was given,[36] in which case 8 B.C. would be indicated here, and other reasons have already been given why if this census were taken in Palestine by Quirinius it might have been delayed to 7 or 6 B.C. when it would still fulfill the condition of Tertullian's statement in coming under Saturninus.

The papyri also attest the practice of going to one's own home place for enrollment. An edict of A.D. 104 says: "Since the enrollment by household[37] is approaching, it is necessary to command all who for any reason are out of their own districts to return to their own home, in order to perform the usual business of the taxation. . . ."[38] Also in a late third century letter a writer asks his sister to endeavor to enroll for him but to let him know in case that is impossible so he may come and do it himself:

"To my sister, lady Dionysia, from Pathermouthis, greeting. As you sent me word on account of the enrollment (τῆς ἀπογραφῆς) about enrolling yourselves, since I cannot come, see whether you can enroll us. Do not then neglect to enroll us, me and Patas; but if you learn that you cannot enroll us, reply to me and I will come. Find out also about the collection of the poll tax, and if they are hurrying on with the collection of the poll tax, pay it and I will send you the money; and if you pay the poll tax, get the receipt. Do not neglect this, my sister, and write to me about the enrollment, whether you have done it or not, and reply to me and I will come and enroll myself. I pray for your lasting health."[39]

Thus the situation presupposed in Luke 2:3 seems entirely plausible.[40]

When Philip died in A.D. 34 his tetrarchy was for a few years included in the province of Syria, then in A.D. 37 was given by Caligula, together with the title of king, to the brother of Herodias, Herod Agrippa I. In A.D. 39 the tetrarchy of Herod Antipas was added, and in A.D. 41 Claudius gave him also what had been the ethnarchy of Archelaus, so that from then until he died in A.D. 44 Herod Agrippa I ruled almost as extensive a kingdom as his grandfather Herod the Great.[41] In his time the emperor Caligula ordered a statue of himself erected in the Temple at Jerusalem. The order reached the legate of Syria, Publius Petronius, in the winter of 39/40,

[36] W. M. Ramsay, *The Bearing of Recent Discovery on the Trustworthiness of the New Testament.* 1915, p.255.

[37] τῆς κατ᾽ οἰ[κίαν ἀπογραφῆς].   [38] DLO p.231.   [39] OP VIII, No.1157.

[40] For further discussion of this problem see Lily R. Taylor in AJP 54 (1933), pp.120-133.

[41] Acts 12:20-23; *Ant.* XIX, viii, 2; Eusebius, *Church History.* II, x. tr. Arthur Cushman McGiffert, NPNFSS 1, pp.111f.

but he delayed the matter as much as he could and Agrippa I begged Caligula not to perform the outrage. Caligula agreed not to desecrate the Temple but still wanted emperor worship altars erected outside Jerusalem, and only his death on January 24, A.D. 41, ended the threat.

Upon the death of Herod Agrippa I his kingdom was reorganized by Claudius into a Roman province (A.D. 44-66), although some portions of the country, including the former tetrarchy of Philip and parts of Galilee and Perea, were after a time given to his son, Agrippa II (A.D. 50-100).[42] The procurators who now governed the land were Cuspius Fadus (A.D. 44-c.46), Tiberius Alexander (c.46-48), Ventidius Cumanus (48-52), Antonius Felix (52-60), Porcius Festus (60-62), Albinus (62-64), and Gessius Florus (64-66), and their cumulative cruelties drove the Jews to the great war (A.D. 66-73) which was climaxed with the destruction of Jerusalem in A.D. 70.

THE HIGH PRIESTS

Our brief outline of the history suggested by Luke's references may be completed by noting that from the time of Herod the Great to the destruction of Jerusalem, twenty-eight high priests exercised spiritual authority in Palestine.[43] The two to whom Luke (3:2) refers are

[42] In A.D. 50 Agrippa II received the kingdom of Chalcis in the Lebanon which had been ruled by his uncle, a grandson of Herod the Great, Herod of Chalcis (A.D. 41-48), and with it the right which Herod of Chalcis had obtained from Claudius of nominating the high priest and overseeing the Temple and its treasury. Also after the death of her husband, Bernice, second wife of Herod of Chalcis and sister of Agrippa II, lived with Agrippa II (cf. Acts 25:13, etc.). In A.D. 53 Agrippa II gave up the kingdom of Chalcis and in its place received from Claudius the former tetrarchy of Philip, while under Nero parts of Galilee and Perea were also given to him. Josephus (*War.* II, xiv, 4) dates the beginning of the great Jewish war in the seventeenth year of Agrippa and the twelfth year of Nero, A.D. 66 (SHJP I, ii, p.193 n.5; but see also S. Zeitlin in JQR 41 [1950-51], pp.243f.). In the war Agrippa II sided with the Romans and after it received additions to his kingdom over which he continued to reign until he died in A.D. 100. Then his territory was no doubt incorporated in the province of Syria.

[43] *Ant.* XX, x. The collation of Josephus' various notices of them gives the following list of twenty-eight names (SHJP II, i, pp.197-202): Appointed by Herod (37-4 B.C.): Ananel (37-36 B.C.), Aristobulus (35 B.C.), Jesus the son of Phabes, Simon (father-in-law of Herod the Great), Matthias (5-4 B.C.); Joseph, Joazar (4 B.C.); appointed by Archelaus (4 B.C.-A.D. 6): Eleazar, Jesus the son of Sie; appointed by Quirinius (A.D. 6): Annas or Ananos (A.D. 6-15), *Ant.* XVIII, ii, 1f.; Luke 3:2; John 18:13, 24; Acts 4:6; appointed by Valerius Gratus (A.D. 15-26): Ishmael (A.D. c.15-c.16), Eleazar the son of Annas (A.D. c.16-c.17), Simon the son of Kamithos (A.D. c.17-c.18), Joseph called Caiaphas, the son-in-law of Annas (A.D. c.18-36), *Ant.* XVIII, ii, 2; iv, 3; Matthew 26:3, 57; Luke 3:2; John 11:49; 18:13f., 24, 28; Acts 4:6; appointed by Vitellius (A.D. 35-39): Jonathan the son of Annas (A.D. 36-37), Theophilos the son of Annas (A.D. 37-40); appointed by Agrippa I (A.D. 41-44): Simon Kantheras, Matthias

Annas and Caiaphas. While Annas was actually high priest only in A.D. 6-15, he continued to be a dominant influence in the days when his sons Eleazar, Jonathan, Theophilus, Matthias, and Ananos, and his son-in-law Caiaphas (A.D. 18-36) held that position.

As appears in Mark 14:55 where "the chief priests and the whole council (συνέδριον) sought testimony against Jesus," the high priests were prominent in the Sanhedrin or supreme court of the Jews. In that body there were also leaders like the famous pair of teachers, Hillel (d. A.D. c.10) and Shammai, and the presidency of the Sanhedrin continued in the family of the former for generations.[44]

4. THE DEAD SEA SCROLLS AND THE QUMRAN COMMUNITY

REMARKABLE and widely heralded discoveries in recent years in the vicinity of the Dead Sea have brought to light the evidences of a community, together with the remains of some of its literature, which probably existed in the first and second centuries B.C. and only came to an end at the time of the great Jewish war in the first century A.D. These finds are therefore an important part of our material for a knowledge of what was happening in Palestine just before, during, and for a few decades after the lifetime of Jesus.

THE GEOLOGY OF THE DEAD SEA REGION

The region of the Dead Sea is of unusual interest geographically and geologically. The geography of Palestine has been outlined in Chapter III, and at this point a brief description of the geology, par-

---

the son of Annas (A.D. c.43), Elionaios; appointed by Herod of Chalcis (A.D. 44-48): Joseph, Ananias (A.D. c.47-c.59), *Ant.* xx, v, 2; vi, 2; ix, 2-4; *War.* II, xii, 6; xvii, 6, 9; Acts 23:2; 24:1; appointed by Agrippa II (A.D. 50-100): Ishmael (A.D. c.59-c.61), Joseph Kabi (A.D. 61-62), Ananos the son of Annas or Ananos (A.D. 62 for only three months), Jesus the son of Damnaios (A.D. c.62-c.63), Jesus the son of Gamaliel (A.D. c.63-c.65), Matthias the son of Theophilus; appointed by the people during the war (A.D. 67-68): Phannias.

[44] According to the Talmud (*Shabbath.* 15a; SBT p.63) the leadership of the father-and-son succession of Hillel, Simeon I, Gamaliel I, and Simeon II covered the one hundred years prior to the destruction of the Temple. Gamaliel I the Elder, as the grandson of Hillel is called, worked in the second third of the first century A.D. and is probably mentioned in Acts 5:34 and 22:3. Simeon II ben Gamaliel I was president of the Sanhedrin in the last two decades before the destruction of Jerusalem. Gamaliel II or Gamaliel of Jabneh (Jamnia), as he is called to distinguish him from his grandfather Gamaliel I, was head of the Jews in Palestine about A.D. 80-116, and may have been the first to whom was given the title of *nasi* or "prince," later replaced by "patriarch" (JE v, p.560).

ticularly with reference to the immediate region around the Dead Sea, may be given which will help to show the nature of the area the Qumran community was in.

The outer covering of this planet is made up of stratified rock formations perhaps fifty miles thick. The upper layers which contain distinctive fossils are classified within three time units known as eras: Paleozoic, meaning "pertaining to ancient life" (trilobites to reptiles), beginning an estimated 500,000,000 years ago; Mesozoic, "pertaining to middle life" (mammals to dinosaurs), beginning 200,000,-000 years ago; and Cenozoic, "pertaining to recent life" (horses to man), beginning 70,000,000 years ago. The rocks in the several eras are divided into systems and the name of the system also serves as the name of the time unit or period in which the system was formed. In the Paleozoic era the systems and periods run from the Cambrian up to the Permian; in the Mesozoic they are the Triassic, Jurassic, and Cretaceous; and in the Cenozoic era the system and period are both called Cenozoic. The systems in turn are divided into series of rocks each with its corresponding epoch of time. Thus the Cretaceous includes the Cenomanian and Senonian in Palestine, and the Cenozoic includes the Eocene, Miocene, Pliocene, and Pleistocene.[1]

In that part of the world with which we are concerned, at a very early time, long before the Cambrian period, a great block of granite was pushed up to the surface of the sea. This was essentially what we now know as Arabia. What we call Palestine was the coastland where this land mass met the adjacent sea. This ancient sea, which lay in the Mediterranean-Turkey-Iran area, has been named Tethys[2] by the geologists, and our Mediterranean Sea is what now remains of it.

The land mass just described was from time to time raised or lowered. In general this movement had two effects with which we are concerned. For one thing, as the land mass was lifted or lowered the sea was pushed back or allowed to encroach farther inland. Much of the time it reached to about where the Jordan Valley now is. It

[1] The Pleistocene epoch, when "most of the new" or present-day animals were in existence, corresponds approximately to the Ice Age in climate and to the Paleolithic Age in culture. It began perhaps 1,000,000 years ago and lasted until the Holocene when "all of the new" fauna were known. The Holocene, beginning 10,000 years ago, includes the Mesolithic, Neolithic, Chalcolithic, Bronze, and Iron Ages. For the divisions of geologic time see Chester R. Longwell and Richard F. Flint, *Introduction to Physical Geology.* 1955, pp.54f.
[2] Tethys was the wife of Oceanus.

was the deposits of the sea which formed the limestones and chalks of western Palestine, while the desert sandstones of Transjordan were formed where the land was dry.

Also, in the course of the lifting and lowering, the great crystalline block of granite, which was too rigid to bend, was itself at last actually broken and one part was pushed up and the other down. This made a deep rift which runs from north to south in Palestine along the line where the Jordan River now flows and on down through the Dead Sea, the Wadi Arabah, and the Gulf of Aqabah. In the extreme south the granite mass was pushed up so high that it can still be seen in the mountains around Aqabah.

Tracing now what happened in particular in succeeding periods, in the Paleozoic era and the Cambrian period a dark limestone was laid down upon the underlying granite platform. This limestone extends well to the east of the Jordan and may be seen in places where the valleys of Transjordan cut deeply into the earth.

As the Cambrian sea retreated there ensued in Transjordan a long period of desert conditions during which the colorful Nubian sandstone was formed which can be seen, for example, in the cliffs at the famous city of Petra.

In the Mesozoic era and the Cretaceous period the sea again extended over much of the land, and in this time most of the Palestinian rocks were formed. The Cenomanian series of rocks laid down in this period are limestones. These were deposited in greatest thickness in northern and central Palestine west of the Jordan where they are one thousand to two thousand feet thick. Since the limestone is usually quite hard it tends to stand up in mountains and hills and often forms deep gorges and steep cliffs. Being porous, the rock absorbs rain and pays it out in springs, and it also becomes dotted with caves. It is these limestones which form the central highlands of Palestine and also the cliffs on the west side of the Dead Sea.

Later in the Cretaceous period the Senonian rocks were deposited. In contrast with the relatively hard Cenomanian limestones, these rocks are often a soft chalk. Being easily eroded the chalk wears away into smooth and rounded hills and forms valleys which provide passes among the harder formations. It is the Senonian chalk which forms the Wilderness of Judea, which lies to the west of the Dead Sea and the lower Jordan Valley. This rock is extremely porous and with only two inches of rain in the year the result in this region is a most arid wasteland of desert hills and valleys.

In the Cenozoic era and period, the Eocene, Miocene, and Pliocene epochs were a time of mountain building. While the greatest ranges were pushed up in Iran and Anatolia, Palestine felt what has been called the "ground swell" from this activity. Not only was the underlying rock platform broken to make the great Rift Valley but also a whole series of faults was produced which run parallel to the valley and also off at angles from it. A main fault line is near Qumran and Jericho and accounts for the earthquakes which have left such marked evidences at both places.

On the whole, Palestine tended to be lifted up out of the sea at this time. By the end of the Eocene epoch Judea, Samaria, and eastern Galilee were probably dry land, and the waters which remained in the depression between western Palestine and Transjordan formed a large inland sea with its shore somewhat near Bethlehem. By the Pliocene epoch Mount Carmel was beginning to appear above the coastal sea, but the inland sea was being lowered as renewed faulting in that area pushed the valley floor down.

In the Pleistocene epoch there was much volcanic action on both sides of the Rift Valley in the north and also in the southern part of the plateau to the east; and at the same time there were also some sedimentary rocks laid down in the valley as well as on the Coast Plain. In this epoch the large inland sea was reduced to several separated basins. Calling them by the names of places now well known, they were from north to south the Huleh basin, the Tiberias-Beisan basin, the Jordan-Dead Sea basin, and the Aqabah basin. The Huleh basin and the Tiberias-Beisan basin were joined together at first, but in the middle of the epoch were separated by a dam of basalt which poured across the valley south of the present Lake Huleh.

The Pleistocene was the time of the Ice Age, and in Palestine this meant very heavy rains. The resultant floods produced a large salt lake which encompassed both the Tiberias-Beisan basin and the Jordan-Dead Sea basin and extended some distance south of the present Dead Sea. The deposits of this lake are to be seen in the gray marls of the Jordan Valley and the Dead Sea. At the same time the gravels were washed down which form the alluvium in the Jordan Valley and the mouths of the wadis which lead into the Rift.

In the last part of the Pleistocene epoch the rains diminished, the large salt-water lake shrank to become the fresh-water Sea of Galilee and the heavily mineralized Dead Sea, the Jordan River cut its immediate valley below the level of the marls the larger lake had left, and the tributary wadis carved their valleys deeper. Thus, during the past fifty thousand years, the great Rift Valley took on its present appearance.

So it was that in the time with which we are concerned the people of Qumran settled in a region where long before the Senonian chalk had produced a forbidding wilderness relatively isolated from the rest of Palestine, and where the wadis, cutting down through the Cenomanian limestone and through the marl, had made gorges and cliffs in whose steep walls were the caves which were to preserve the literature of a remarkable community.[3]

QUMRAN CAVE 1

Wadi Qumran is about seven miles south of Jericho and reaches the shore of the Dead Sea at a point some distance north of a spring known as Ain Feshkha. On a marl plateau beside the Wadi and between the Sea on the east and the limestone cliffs on the west is an ancient ruin, long known, called Khirbet Qumran. Farther south another valley, a continuation of the Kidron at Jerusalem, known here as Wadi en-Nar, descends to the Sea. Clinging to its steep walls is the Mar Saba Monastery, and some four miles to the northeast is another ancient ruin, Khirbet Mird. Yet farther south, a dozen miles below Qumran, is Wadi Murabba'at.[4] Throughout the area the hills are dotted with caves. It was in one of these, a cave in the limestone cliffs less than half a mile north of Khirbet Qumran, that the first find was made. This cave is hidden near the center of the cliffs in Fig. 101.

In 1945 a Bedouin of the Ta'amireh tribe by the name of Muhammad al-Di'b was seeking a lost goat in this region. Noticing a cave he threw stones into it and heard something breaking. Going down into the cave he found pottery jars which he broke open. In one of these was some rolled leather with writing on it. This material he took to his home and kept for two years, then took to a dealer in

---

[3] For the geology here summarized see Denis Baly, *The Geography of the Bible.* 1957, pp.14-26.

[4] For the enormous literature on the Dead Sea Scrolls and the Qumran community see Christoph Burchard, *Bibliographie zu den Handschriften vom toten Meer* (Beihefte zur ZAW 76). 1957. Other bibliographies are to be found in H. H. Rowley, *The Zadokite Fragments and the Dead Sea Scrolls.* 1952, pp.89-125; J. van der Ploeg in *Jaarbericht ex Oriente Lux.* 14 (1955-56), pp.85-116; BDSS pp.419-435; Charles T. Fritsch, *The Qumrân Community, Its History and Scrolls.* 1956, pp. 131-141; BML pp.411-424. And see now the *Revue de Qumran.* 1- (1958-).

antiquities at Bethlehem.[5] These were the now-famous scrolls from Qumran Cave 1, and finally in that year, 1947, they came in part into the possession of the Syrian Orthodox Monastery of St. Mark in Jerusalem, from which they were brought to the American School of Oriental Research in Jerusalem for study and were eventually purchased for the State of Israel; and in part into the possession of the Hebrew University in Jerusalem.

For convenient reference to these and the many other manuscripts and fragments that have been found, a system of abbreviations has been internationally adopted.[6] First, the material on which the writing is found is indicated, no sign meaning leather, p standing for papyrus, cu for copper, and o for ostracon. Second, the place of discovery is shown, 1Q, for example, meaning the cave mentioned above, Cave 1 at Qumran. Third, the contents of the document are shown. Biblical and apocryphal books are designated with customary abbreviations. Commentaries are indicated with the letter p standing for *pesher* or commentary. New works are marked with a letter corresponding to the first letter of their Hebrew title as known or as supposed. Thus the work commonly called the Manual of Discipline is designated 1QS, the S standing for the word קרס (*serek*) meaning the "Order" or "Rule" of the community; and The War of the Sons of Light with the Sons of Darkness is 1QM from מלחמה (*milhamah*) meaning "War."

The scrolls referred to above as coming to the American Schools of Oriental Research were the following: The Isaiah scroll (1QIs[a])[7] is a virtually complete copy of the book of Isaiah. It is written on a roll of parchment twenty-four feet in length and about ten inches high. Having been sealed in its container and left in a place where the climate is similar to that of the Fayum and Upper Egypt, the state of preservation is very good. The writing fills fifty-four columns with an average of thirty lines to the column. The text is substantially the same as the later standard Masoretic text.[8] This scroll is shown in Fig. 102. The bottom line in the not entirely visible right-hand column is the beginning of Isaiah chapter 40.

---

[5] For Muhammad al-Di'b's own story of the scroll discovery see William H. Brownlee in JNES 16 (1957), pp.236-239; and see also the somewhat different account in DJD I, p. 5.

[6] DJD I, pp.46-48.

[7] *The Dead Sea Scrolls of St. Mark's Monastery*, I, *The Isaiah Manuscript and the Habakkuk Commentary*, ed. Millar Burrows. 1950.

[8] The Masora is the early tradition as to the correct text of the Hebrew Scriptures, the Masoretes were the scribes who dealt with these studies. Caspar Levias in JE VIII, pp.365-371.

The Habakkuk Commentary (1QpHab)[9] contains the first two chapters of the book of Habakkuk with a commentary accompanying the text. This roll has suffered more disintegration than the preceding one and is broken off all along the bottom edge with the loss of several lines of text. As it now exists the roll is over four and one-half feet long and less than six inches high. The first fragment of this scroll, containing portions of columns 1 and 2, is shown in Fig. 103.

The Manual of Discipline or Rule of the Community (1QS)[10] is the name now commonly given to a book which contains liturgical and disciplinary instructions for the order of people who lived at Qumran. It is written on a parchment roll over six feet long and about nine inches high. Column 10 in this manuscript is reproduced in Fig. 104.

A fourth document the American Schools of Oriental Research found in too bad condition to be able to unroll. From a broken-off piece which contained the name of Lamech it was surmised, incorrectly, that this might be an otherwise lost apocryphal book of Lamech. Since the acquisition of these scrolls for Israel, this work too has been unrolled, and it is found that it is an Aramaic version of several chapters of the book of Genesis with additional stories and legends woven around the lives of the patriarchs. The roll is about nine feet long and twelve inches high, and the work is now known as a Genesis Apocryphon (1QApoc).[11]

The rolls which were acquired at the outset by Hebrew University included the following: A second copy of the book of Isaiah (1QIs[b])[12] is badly disintegrated but contains at least portions of a number of the chapters of the book and is most nearly complete from chapter 38 on to the end. The text is close to that of the Masoretic tradition.

A scroll which the editors call The War of the Sons of Light with the Sons of Darkness (1QM)[13] describes the conflict which is to

[9] *The Dead Sea Scrolls of St. Mark's Monastery*, I, *The Isaiah Manuscript and the Habakkuk Commentary*; tr. BDSS pp. 365-370; GDSS pp.249-256.

[10] *The Dead Sea Scrolls of St. Mark's Monastery*, II, Fascicle 2, *Plates and Transcription of the Manual of Discipline*, ed. Millar Burrows. 1951; tr. BDSM; BDSS pp.371-389; GDSS pp.39-60, 115-122; P. Wernberg-Møller, *The Manual of Discipline Translated and Annotated With an Introduction* (J. van der Ploeg, ed., Studies on the Texts of the Desert of Judah, I). 1957.

[11] Nahman Avigad and Yigael Yadin, *A Genesis Apocryphon, A Scroll from the Wilderness of Judaea, Description and Contents of the Scroll, Facsimiles, Transcription and Translation of Columns II, XIX-XXII*; cf. N. Avigad in BA 19 (1956), pp.22-24; detached fragments (1Q20) in DJD I, pp.86f.; tr. BML pp.387-393.

[12] *The Dead Sea Scrolls of the Hebrew University*, ed. E. L. Sukenik. 1955.

[13] *ibid.*; tr. GDSS pp.281-301; and selections in BDSS pp.390-399.

break out between the tribes of Israel and their enemies, the Kittim. The document details the equipment of the troops, outlines their battle formations and tactics, gives the prayers of the priests prior to battle, and closes with the hymn of thanksgiving which celebrates the victory. The roll, over nine feet long and six inches wide, was well preserved and even its original outer leather wrapping was still with it.

The scroll of Thanksgiving Psalms or Hodayot (1QH)[14] was received in three separate leaves of leather and about seventy detached fragments, but was once a connected roll about six feet long and thirteen inches high with about thirty-nine lines of writing in each of a dozen columns. This is a collection of hymns, composed in a style similar to the Psalms of the Bible, in which the writer gives thanks for the acts of kindness which God has done.

Since the three scrolls just described were acquired originally by Hebrew University, and since those handled by the American Schools of Oriental Research were later purchased for Israel, it is anticipated that they will be brought together in a projected Shrine of the Book at Hebrew University.[15]

Certain other fragments from Cave 1 have come into circulation through various channels. Portions of the book of Daniel are contained on three small pieces of leather (1Q71, 72), each two or three inches wide and four or five inches high. They include the point in Daniel 2:4 where the language changes from Hebrew to Aramaic, and also contain the names Shadrach, Meshach, and Abednego. The text is substantially the same as the Masoretic.[16] Two larger pieces contain two columns of writing which seem to belong to the Manual of Discipline. The text (1QSa)[17] begins, "This is the rule . . . ," and contains information about admission to the sessions of the community and to its common meal.

In 1949 Cave 1 was excavated by R. de Vaux, Director of the École Biblique in Jerusalem, and G. Lankester Harding, Director of the Department of Antiquities of Jordan. A great many fragments of pottery were recovered, enough to piece together into more than forty jars such as those in which the manuscripts were found, about two feet high and ten inches in diameter.[18] One of the jars from the

[14] ibid.; tr. GDSS pp.123-202; and selections in BDSS pp.400-415.
[15] Avigad in BA 19 (1956), pp.22f.; Yigael Yadin, The Message of the Scrolls. 1957, pp.39-52.
[16] BA 12 (1949), p.33; DJD I, pp.150-152.
[17] DJD I, pp.108-118; tr. GDSS pp.307-310.
[18] DJD I, pp.8-17.

cave is shown in Fig. 105.[19] Also many pieces of linen cloth were found, which had doubtless been used to wrap the scrolls since in at least one case cloth was still adhering to a piece of scroll.[20] In addition there were hundreds of fragments of manuscripts, many very tiny, most on leather, a few on papyrus, most in Hebrew, some in Aramaic. Represented are texts of Genesis, Exodus, Leviticus, Deuteronomy, Judges, Samuel, Ezekiel, and Psalms; commentaries on Psalms, Micah, and Zephaniah; apocryphal books including the book of Jubilees, and the Testament of Levi; books of discipline, of liturgy, and of hymns; and pieces as yet unidentified.[21]

THE DATE OF THE MANUSCRIPTS

Prior to the Qumran discovery the oldest known manuscript with an Old Testament text was the Nash Papyrus.[22] This papyrus, which is in the Cambridge University Library, contains the Ten Commandments and the Shema (Deuteronomy 6:4ff.). On the basis of comparison with Aramaic papyri and ostraca from Egypt on the one hand, and with Herodian inscriptions on the other, it has been dated in the Maccabean period, that is between 165 and 37 B.C.[23] When the first Isaiah scroll was first brought to the American School of Oriental Research in Jerusalem, John C. Trever compared it with a photograph of the Nash Papyrus and noted a striking similarity of script.[24] W. F. Albright supported this observation and dated the newly found scrolls in the second and first centuries B.C.,[25] while Solomon A. Birnbaum made an independent approach to the problem and arrived at similar results.[26] An intense discussion of the entire subject ensued and every possible dating of the scrolls was explored. Solomon Zeitlin thought they could not date before the Middle Ages and might even be a hoax.[27] The original paleographical

[19] cf. Carl H. Kraeling in BASOR 125 (Feb. 1952), pp.5-7.
[20] DJD I, pp.18-38. [21] DJD I, pp.49-155.
[22] Stanley A. Cook in *Proceedings of the Society of Biblical Archaeology.* 25 (1903), pp.34-56; Norbert Peters, *Die älteste Abschrift der zehn Gebote, der Papyrus Nash.* 1905.
[23] W. F. Albright in JBL 56 (1937), pp.145-176.
[24] Trever in BA 11 (1948), pp.46f.
[25] Albright in BASOR 115 (Oct. 1949), pp.10-19.
[26] Birnbaum in BASOR 115 (Oct. 1949), pp.20-22; and in BASOR Supplementary Studies 13-14. 1952.
[27] Concerning the Habakkuk Commentary, for example, he argued (in JQR 39 [1948-49], pp.236f.) that it was axiomatic that the Jews did not write commentaries on the prophetic books in the period prior to A.D. 70. See also his other articles in JQR, and *The Dead Sea Scrolls and Modern Scholarship* (JQR Monograph Series, 3). 1956.

conclusions have been supported, however, by other types of evidence soon to be mentioned, and there seems to be no doubt that these are genuine documents of remarkable antiquity. On primarily paleographic grounds the first Isaiah scroll may probably be put about 150 B.C., and the various manuscripts from Cave 1 and other similar caves of the Qumran area yet to be described may be assigned to three periods, Archaic, c.200-c.150 B.C., Hasmonean, c.150-c.30 B.C., and Herodian, c.30 B.C.-A.D. 70.[28] If the Isaiah scroll was written in the second century B.C., it is approximately one thousand years older than the oldest previously known Hebrew manuscripts of the Old Testament, such as Oriental Codex 4445 in the British Museum containing the Pentateuch and written probably about A.D. 820-850, and the St. Petersburg Codex of the Latter Prophets dated in A.D. 916.[29]

The pieces of linen cloth which were with the manuscripts in Cave 1 have also been studied.[30] The linen seems to have been a local Palestinian product. Some of the cloth had fringes and corded edges, and blue lines and rectangles showed that decorative designs were made. The cloth seems to have been used both for scroll wrappers and for jar covers. The employment of cloth wrappers for leather scrolls accords with references in the Mishnah where there is mention of scroll wrappers of linen[31] and with ornamentation.[32] In 1950 some of the linen cloth from Cave 1 was subjected to the Carbon 14 test and it was found that the flax of which it was made had ceased to grow 1,917 years before, that is in A.D. 33. There is a margin of error in the test of plus or minus 200 years, however, therefore the limits are actually between 167 B.C. and A.D. 233.[33] If the flax was cut and the linen made around the median date of A.D. 33, presumably the scrolls were wrapped and sealed in their jars sometime later in the first century. At all events the Carbon 14 date is at least in broad agreement with the paleographic conclusions.

[28] Frank M. Cross, Jr. in JBL 74 (1955), pp.148 n.3, 164. For the available examples of early Hebrew writing see S. A. Birnbaum, *The Hebrew Scripts*. 1954-. For a table of the letters of the Hebrew alphabet as written in the scrolls see Sukenik, ed., *The Dead Sea Scrolls of the Hebrew University*, p.40.

[29] Christian D. Ginsburg, *Introduction to the Massoretico-Critical Edition of the Hebrew Bible*. 1897, pp.469-476.

[30] Louisa Bellinger in BASOR 118 (Apr. 1950), pp.9-11; G. M. Crowfoot in PEQ 1951, pp.5-31; and in DJD I, pp.18-38.

[31] *Kil'ayim*. IX, 3; DM p.38.

[32] *Kelim*. XXVIII, 4; DM p.646; SBT p.134.

[33] ADAJ 1 (1951), p.6.

The pottery from Cave 1 also gave an indication of the date of the manuscripts which were with it. Two intact jars said to have come from the cave were sold by the Bedouins to Professor E. L. Sukenik at Hebrew University and, when the cave was excavated, the mass of potsherds recovered was found to represent the same type of pottery. This pottery was judged to belong to the end of the Hellenistic period in the first century B.C., while some additional pieces were recognized as Roman and thought to belong to the second or third century A.D.[34] When Khirbet Qumran was excavated both types of pottery were found, and the coins also discovered there showed that the Roman ware itself belonged to the first century A.D. and before the destruction of Jerusalem in A.D. 70.[35]

KHIRBET QUMRAN

The ruins known as Khirbet Qumran were explored by Charles Clermont-Ganneau in 1873-1874 and he called attention to the adjacent cemetery of a thousand or so tombs.[36] After the discovery of the manuscripts in the nearby cave, interest turned to the ruins again, and in 1951, 1953, 1954, 1955, and 1956 de Vaux and Harding excavated there.[37] A photograph of the site is shown in Fig. 106.

The main building was a large rectangular structure about 100 by 120 feet in size. At its northwest corner stood a massive two-story stone tower evidently intended for defense. In the southwest corner were a court and several large rooms. A low bench around the four sides of one room suggested a place of assembly. Fragments from an upper story room in this area fitted together to make a plaster table and bench, and when two Roman period inkwells were found, one of copper and one of terra cotta, it was seen that this must have been a scriptorium, doubtless the very place where many of the Dead Sea Scrolls were copied.

In the center of the building was a court and to the north and northeast of it were various rooms, one containing several fireplaces. In the southeast section were a lavatory, a workshop with iron implements, and two pools, one small and one large. The large pool was entered by fourteen steps with four guiding lanes on the upper

[34] The Dead Sea Scrolls of the Hebrew University, ed. Sukenik, p.20.

[35] James L. Kelso in JBL 74 (1955), pp.141f.

[36] Clermont-Ganneau, Archaeological Researches in Palestine during the Years 1873-1874. II (1896), pp.14-16.

[37] R. de Vaux in RB 60 (1953), pp.83-106; 61 (1954), pp.206-236; James L. Kelso in JBL 74 (1955), pp.141-146; Fritsch, The Qumrân Community, Its History and Scrolls, pp.1-25.

steps. There were also many other pools and reservoirs in and around the building, perhaps as many as forty in all.[38] The water for them was brought by a stone aqueduct from natural reservoirs at the base of the cliffs not far from Khirbet Qumran.

In an extension of the main building to the south was a large room, twenty-two feet long, which may have been used for a communal meal since a smaller room adjoining it was found to contain more than one thousand bowls stacked against the wall.

Near the ruins is a cemetery which, as Clermont-Ganneau observed, contains around one thousand tombs. Laid out in orderly arrangement, these are simple graves in which the bodies were protected with a layer of stones or bricks. The bodies lie supine, feet to the north. Lack of jewelry or pottery indicates the simplicity of the interment, but potsherds in the earth fill show that the cemetery is of the same age as the nearby ruins. According to what is known thus far, the main cemetery contains only adult male skeletons, but there are remains of women and children in smaller burial areas adjoining it.[39]

In the ruins of Khirbet Qumran some 750 coins were found and, together with the pottery and the evidences of architectural changes in the building, these provide clues for a reconstruction of the history of the site.

Even before the periods in which we are here interested there was an occupation, probably in the eighth and seventh centuries B.C., by the Israelites. It is also thought that Khirbet Qumran was the 'Ir-Hammelah or City of Salt of Joshua 15:62.[40]

The original building which we described above was probably erected in the reign of John Hyrcanus (135-104 B.C.), since many coins of this ruler were found. Likewise coins of Antigonus (40-37 B.C.), the last Hasmonean ruler, show that this period of occupation continued until the end of Hasmonean times. In the reign of Herod the Great, however, the place may have been abandoned, since but a single one of this king's coins was found. Such an abandonment could have been due at least in part to an earthquake. There are

---

[38] Since reservoirs with steps leading down into them are familiar in Palestine, many of these pools were no doubt simply intended for water storage, yet some may have been used for ablutions, while Ain Feshkha and the Jordan River also provided relatively nearby and abundant waters for washings and baptisms (CALQ pp.49f.).

[39] R. de Vaux in RB 63 (1956), pp.569-572.

[40] Martin Noth in ZDPV 71 (1955), pp.111-123.

evidences of such a disaster in discernible damage in the great tower and in a large diagonal crack running down through the steps into the large pool, and these may well be recognized as marks of the severe earthquake which Josephus says struck Judea in the seventh year of Herod, 31 B.C.[41]

The coins also suggest that the building was reoccupied under Herod's son Archelaus (4 B.C.-A.D. 6), when it was enlarged and the great tower strengthened, and that occupation continued until in the early part of the Jewish war. Arrowheads of iron and a layer of burnt ash attest the military conquest and the conflagration which then befell the place. Josephus states that in the spring of A.D. 68 Vespasian set out with his army from Caesarea to finish the conquest of Palestine and on the second day of the month Daisios reached and took Jericho whose inhabitants had already fled to the hill country.[42] It may readily be assumed therefore that it was at this very time, June, A.D. 68,[43] that the Roman army also took Qumran, and the presence of coins from Caesarea in the ruins confirms this conclusion.[43a]

Afterward Vespasian returned to Caesarea but left a garrison at Jericho,[44] and it was also by way of Jericho that Legion X came up to Jerusalem when Titus mustered his forces for the final attack upon the Judean capital in the spring of A.D. 70.[45] That the Tenth Legion had contact with Qumran is shown by one coin found there marked with an "X." From other coins and from modifications in the Qumran building evidently intended to make it into a barracks it seems that Roman troops were quartered there until about the end of the first century A.D.

Again during the second revolt (A.D. 132-135), Jewish forces occupied Qumran briefly. After that there were only temporary encampments attested by a few Byzantine and Arab coins.

[41] *Ant.* xv, v, 2; *War.* i, xix, 3. Since Josephus equates the date with the battle of Actium (31 B.C.) he must have reckoned 37 B.C. when Herod took Jerusalem as the first year of his reign. For other reasons why the community may have left Qumran under Herod the Great see Charles T. Fritsch in JBL 74 (1955), pp. 173-181.

[42] *War.* iv, viii, 1-2.

[43] For the months see PDBC p.24.

[43a] Perhaps the Qumran community was allied at this time with the Zealots who led the rebellion against Rome (H. H. Rowley in BJRL 40 [1957-58], p.144). For a theory which identifies the Qumran group with the Zealots see Cecil Roth in *Commentary.* 24 (1957), pp.317-324; and for the supposition that Simeon ben Kosiba was an Essene see L. E. Toombs in NTS 4 (1957), pp.65-71.

[44] *War.* iv, ix, 1.

[45] *War.* v, i, 6; ii, 3.

The periods just described may therefore be outlined as follows:[46]

Period I.	Construction under John Hyrcanus, 135-104 B.C.
	Earthquake
Abandonment	
Period II.	Restoration under Archelaus, 4 B.C.-A.D. 6
	Destruction, June, A.D. 68
Period III.	Military occupation, A.D. 68-c.100
Abandonment	
	Occupation during the Second Revolt, A.D. 132-135
Final Abandonment	

Thus it was from the time of John Hyrcanus near the end of the second century B.C. to the time of the great Jewish war and in particular the spring of A.D. 68, with an interruption in the time of Herod the Great, that Khirbet Qumran was occupied by the group with which we are concerned. Since the arrangements of the building we have described had to do with assemblage and ablution, with cooking, eating, and writing, rather than with residence, it seems probable that this was a community center and that the people must be thought of as having actually dwelt in the neighboring caves and perhaps also in tents and other less permanent structures. Soundings made at Ain Feshkha in 1956 by R. de Vaux also show remains at that site contemporary with Khirbet Qumran.[47] Therefore the entire occupation at this time must be pictured as extending over a very considerable area, with Khirbet Qumran doubtless representing the center of the whole settlement.

OTHER QUMRAN CAVES

In 1952 it became known that the Bedouins had found more manuscripts in another cave near the one where the original discovery had been made. Thereupon the École Biblique, the Palestine Archaeological Museum, and the American School of Oriental Research in Jerusalem joined in an expedition under Père de Vaux and William L. Reed to explore the Qumran area more thoroughly.[48] In a distance of about five miles from north to south thirty-nine

[46] De Vaux in RB 61 (1954), p.234.
[47] De Vaux in RB 63 (1956), pp.576f.
[48] R. de Vaux in RB 60 (1953), pp.540-561; William L. Reed in BASOR 135 (Oct. 1954), pp.8-13.

caves and crevices were found which contained pottery and other objects, the pottery being of the same sort already known from Cave 1 and Khirbet Qumran. Two caves had written material. One of these was that which the Bedouins had already found and which they had cleared so completely that only two small fragments of manuscripts remained in it. This cave, which was only about three hundred feet from the cave of the original discovery, is now known as 2Q. All together there came from it fragments of Exodus, Leviticus, Numbers, Deuteronomy, Ruth, Psalms, Jeremiah, and Jubilees, and also fragments of perhaps forty nonbiblical books including a liturgical document in Aramaic. The other cave (3Q) was over a mile north of Khirbet Qumran. In it were fragments of a dozen manuscripts including a few lines of Isaiah and, surprisingly enough, two copper rolls inscribed in Hebrew characters. Preliminary study had to be based on the letters which showed through on the back,[49] but the document was finally opened by cutting.[50] This was done in England in 1956 and then the rolls were returned to the Jordan Museum in Amman. Actually there were three strips of copper riveted together to form a document nearly eight feet long and one foot high. The script probably belongs to about the middle of the first century A.D. Listed are the hiding places, such as in cisterns, pools, and tombs, all over Palestine, of some sixty caches of treasure, mostly silver and gold, totaling over two hundred tons in weight. The language is colloquial, and it has been suggested that this is simply a compilation of traditional folklore concerning legendary ancient treasures. On the other hand it is notable that the text is inscribed in such a permanent way, and it may be that it is a genuine list of the treasures hidden away in their time of peril by the Essene communities, an order which had many goods even though its individual members were pledged to poverty.[51]

Later in 1952 the Bedouins found Caves 4, 5, and 6, all not far from Khirbet Qumran. Caves 5 (5Q) and 6 (6Q) had relatively few fragments of manuscripts, but Cave 4 (4Q) provided a discovery of scope exceeding that of the original Cave 1. This cave, which is in the same marl terrace on which Khirbet Qumran lies, is shown in Fig. 107. No less than tens of thousands of manuscript fragments were found here and acquired by the Palestine Archaeological Mu-

[49] K. G. Kuhn in RB 61 (1954), pp.193-205.

[50] J. T. Milik in BA 19 (1956), pp.60-64; H. Wright Baker in BJRL 39 (1956-57). pp.45-56.

[51] A. Dupont-Sommer in RHR 151 (1957), pp.22-36.

seum. A very great labor was involved in the ensuing endeavor to assemble such pieces as belonged together and to identify the books represented. By 1956 approximately 330 manuscripts had been identified, about ninety of them of biblical books.[52] Every book of the Hebrew Old Testament is represented excepted Esther. Most nearly complete is a copy of Samuel (4Q Sam[a]), the fragments of which represent forty-seven out of an original total of fifty-seven columns of text. This is written on leather to which later a backing of papyrus was added. The script appears to belong to the first century b.c. The text is not like the Masoretic as in the case of scrolls mentioned above, but rather is so much like the Septuagint that it must be in general the kind of Hebrew text upon which that translation was based.[53] There are also thirteen manuscripts of Deuteronomy, twelve of Isaiah, ten of Psalms, seven of part or all of the Book of the Twelve Prophets, and five of books of the Pentateuch. As in the case of the book of Samuel just mentioned, the text of the other historical books is like that of the Septuagint. In the Pentateuch some of the manuscripts resemble the Septuagint, some the Masoretic text, and some the Old Samaritan recension. An example of the last is a copy of Exodus (4QEx[a]), a scroll of about the same size as the first Isaiah scroll (1QIs[a]) containing sections from Exodus 6:25 to 37:15.[54] In the case of at least one of the Isaiah manuscripts from Cave 4 the text conforms closely to the Masoretic.[55] Of interest also are fragments of Ecclesiastes (4QQoh[a]) written in a beautiful Hebrew script of about 150 b.c., which show that at least by this date this book was accepted in the Qumran community.[56]

In the Cave 4 manuscripts there are also fragments of apocryphal books, of commentaries on Isaiah, Malachi, and Psalms, and of liturgical texts, and a page of *testimonia* (4Q Testimonia) or Old Testament texts expressing the Messianic hope (p.288 n.87). In addition, as study progresses on this extensive if fragmentary material, undoubtedly many more books will become known.

[52] Frank M. Cross, Jr., in basor 141 (Feb. 1956), pp.9-13.
[53] Frank M. Cross, Jr., in basor 132 (Dec. 1953), pp.15-26.
[54] Patrick W. Skehan in jbl 74 (1955), pp.182-187. The Samaritan Pentateuch has been edited by A. von Gall, *Der hebräische Pentateuch der Samaritaner.* 5 vols. 1914-18. It varies from the Masoretic text in about 6,000 cases, in 1,900 of which it agrees with the Septuagint. While many of the variants are evidently due to accidental or intentional changes, some of them, particularly those in agreement with the lxx, appear to represent good tradition. Pfeiffer, *Introduction to the Old Testament*, pp.101-104.
[55] James Muilenburg in basor 135 (Oct. 1954), pp.28-32; cf. Patrick W. Skehan in cbq 17 (1955), pp.158-163.
[56] James Muilenburg in basor 135 (Oct. 1954), pp.20-28.

Likewise other discoveries continue to be made in the Qumran region, and in 1956 unofficial reports told of the finding of important manuscripts, comparable to those of Cave 1, in Cave 11 (11Q) somewhat over half a mile north of Cave 1. These are now said to include copies of Leviticus and Psalms, an apocalyptic description of the New Jerusalem, and an Aramaic targum of the book of Job.[57] As the manuscripts and fragments come in they are brought together in the Palestine Archaeological Museum in Jerusalem and studied with painstaking care.

Outside of the immediate Qumran district but still in the general area west of the Dead Sea other finds have been made, notably in Wadi Murabba'at and at Khirbet Mird, but at both places most of the manuscripts are of later date than those of Qumran.

WADI MURABBA'AT

In Wadi Murabba'at four large caves were found by the Bedouins and were excavated by an expedition of the Jordan Department of Antiquities, the École Biblique in Jerusalem, and the Palestine Archaeological Museum in 1952.[58] As was shown by the pottery the caves had been occupied in the Chalcolithic, Bronze, and Iron Ages, and there were great quantities of potsherds from the Roman period, in particular the second century A.D. Caves I and II, the largest ones, each over 150 feet long and fifteen feet high and wide, contained manuscripts, with the majority of these in Cave II. Except for a Hebrew papyrus of the sixth century B.C. containing a list of names and numbers, most of the documents come from the second century A.D. There are fragments of Genesis, Exodus, Deuteronomy, and Isaiah, with a text identical with the Masoretic. There are cursive Aramaic, and Greek business documents, frequently with dates. And there are several Hebrew letters on papyrus, including two written by Simeon ben Kosiba. This is none other than the leader of the Second Revolt (A.D. 132-135), whose name was changed by Akiba to Bar Kokhba. Thus these caves must have been used as a hideaway of the revolutionists in their bitter struggle. In one of the ben Kosiba letters there is mention of certain Galileans who seem to be staying apart from the conflict, and it has been suggested that these could have been Christians.[59] Since in the Qumran manuscripts there was

[57] *Time*. April 15, 1957, p.60; CALQ pp.25f.
[58] G. Lankester Harding in PEQ 1952, pp.104-109; Frank M. Cross, Jr. in BA 17 (1954), pp.8-12; Fritsch, *The Qumrān Community, Its History and Scrolls*, pp.51-59.
[59] J. T. Milik in RB 60 (1953), pp.276-294.

yet much deviation from the Masoretic text, but the Wadi Murabba'at fragments are identical with it, it may be concluded with some probability that the standardization of this text took place between the First and Second Revolts, that is between A.D. 70 and 135.[60]

KHIRBET MIRD

In 1952 the Bedouins brought in manuscripts from the Wadi en-Nar region, and in 1953 an expedition of the University of Louvain found that the source was Khirbet Mird. This ruin is identified as the fortress Hyrcania which was used by the Hasmoneans and rebuilt by Herod the Great. The manuscripts include papyri from the early Islamic period; fragments of Greek codices, written in uncial letters, of the Wisdom of Solomon, Mark, John, and Acts, from the fifth to the eighth centuries; and Syriac fragments of Joshua, Matthew, Luke, Acts, and Colossians.[61]

THE ESSENES

Who were the people who, beginning in the second century B.C., had their center at Khirbet Qumran and who, shortly before disaster befell them in A.D. 68, deposited in the nearby caves their valuable manuscripts?

In a short passage in his *Jewish Antiquities*[62] and a longer section in the *Jewish War*[63] Josephus describes the Essenes as the third philosophical sect among the Jews after the Pharisees and the Sadducees, and in the *Life* he states that he himself had taken training with all three groups.[64] The Essenes, he says, live simply and have their property in common, with officers elected to look after the interests of the community. They settle in various towns. They clothe themselves in white, and do not discard their garments until they are entirely worn out. They pray before sunrise, labor till the fifth hour, then bathe in cold water. After this purification they assemble for a common meal, before and after which a priest says grace. Laboring after that until evening, they again sup in like manner. They display an extraordinary interest in the writings of the ancients. One desiring to join the order is proved for a year, then allowed to share in the waters of purification, but tested yet two years more

[60] Joachim Jeremias in ZAW 67 (1955), pp.289-290; Moshe Greenberg in JAOS 76 (1956), pp.157-167.

[61] J. T. Milik in RB 60 (1953), pp.526f.; Fritsch, *The Qumrân Community, Its History and Scrolls*, pp.50f.

[62] *Ant.* xviii, i, 5.   [63] *War.* ii, viii, 2-13.   [64] *Life.* 2.

before being admitted and allowed to take the common food. In doctrine the Essenes teach that souls are immortal, and when set free from the prison of the body will mount upward with joy. The Essenes disdain marriage but adopt children to raise in their own teachings; one order, however, allows marriage.

Philo[65] also tells about the Essenes at some length. They are, he says, more than four thousand in number. Their name is a variation of the word "holiness."[66] Some of them labor on the land and others pursue crafts of all peaceful sorts. They denounce slavery and abstain from oaths. They study particularly the ethical part of the laws of their fathers, and use allegory in their philosophy. They dwell together in communities and have a single treasury, common disbursements, and common meals. Characterized as they are by frugality, simple living, contentment, humility, love of men, and the spirit of fellowship, they are indeed "athletes of virtue."

Pliny[67] too writes briefly of the Essenes. He speaks of them as a "solitary tribe" who are located "on the west side of the Dead Sea, but out of range of the noxious exhalations of the coast," and who are remarkable for having no women, no money, and only palm trees for company. "Lying below the Essenes," Pliny continues, "was formerly the town of Engedi," and "next comes Masada." If "lying below" means "south of" then Pliny has listed the Essene center, Engedi, and Masada in order from north to south.

The Essenes, therefore, were a communal order with an important center on the west side of the Dead Sea. The location of this center north of Engedi, which is about half way down the west coast, can agree perfectly with the Qumran area in general and Khirbet Qumran in particular. Khirbet Qumran was a community center with special arrangements for ablutions, for communal eating, and for the copying of books. The Qumran manuscripts are copies of scriptural and other books including a rule of the order in which also ablutions and communal eating are prescribed. The correspondence of location and of attested practice at Qumran with the descriptions of Pliny, Philo, and Josephus make probable the identification of the community at Qumran as a group of Essenes,[68] or at least a

---

[65] *Every Good Man is Free.* 75-91. tr. F. H. Colson, LCL IX (1941), pp.53-63.

[66] Philo uses the word ὁσιότης. In Aramaic the word for "holy" is ḥese, and this may indeed be the source of the name. A. Dupont-Sommer, *The Dead Sea Scrolls*. tr. E. Margaret Rowley. 1950, pp.86f.

[67] *Natural History.* v, xv.

[68] A. Dupont-Sommer, *The Jewish Sect of Qumran and the Essenes.* tr. R. D. Barnett. 1954; H. H. Rowley, *The Zadokite Fragments and the Dead Sea Scrolls.*

group related to that movement. While the Essenes were also to be found in other places in Palestine, the relatively elaborate character of the main building at Qumran and the extent of the library even make it possible to suppose that at the time this was a headquarters for the entire movement.[69]

THE ZADOKITE DOCUMENT

There is also some connection between the discoveries at Qumran and two manuscripts which were found in 1896 in the *genizah* or storeroom of a medieval synagogue in Cairo.[70] Manuscript A, as the first of these is designated, consists of eight leaves copied probably in the tenth century A.D. Manuscript B is a single leaf, with a portion of the same work, probably copied in the eleventh or twelfth century. The entire work comprises two writings, the Admonition (pages I-VIII = chapters 1-9), and the Laws (pages IX-XVI = chapters 10-20), and is commonly known in its entirety as the Cairo Document of the Damascus Covenanters (CD), although a simpler name is the Zadokite Document. The reasons for the two names will be obvious in what follows. There is also a fragment of the same work (6QD) which was found in Cave 6 at Qumran.[71]

In this work we are told about a group of Jews who took thought of their trespasses and came to realize that they were "guilty men." After they had groped their way for some time, God raised up for them "a teacher of righteousness."[72] This group came forth "from Israel and Aaron," that is, from the laity and the priesthood (page 1, lines 5-11 = chapter 1, verses 5-7).[73] The priests, and possibly the en-

---

1952, pp.78f.; *The Dead Sea Scrolls and Their Significance.* 1955, p.20; and in TZ 13 (1957), pp.530-540.

[69] GDSS pp.2,328.

[70] S. Schechter, *Documents of Jewish Sectaries,* I, *Fragments of a Zadokite Work Edited from Hebrew Manuscripts in the Cairo Genizah Collection now in the Possession of the University Library, Cambridge, and Provided with an English Translation, Introduction and Notes.* 1910; CAP II, pp.785-834; Solomon Zeitlin, *The Zadokite Fragments, Facsimile of the Manuscripts in the Cairo Genizah Collection in the Possession of the University Library, Cambridge, England* (JQR Monograph Series, 1). 1952; Chaim Rabin, *The Zadokite Documents.* 1954; GDSS pp.61-85.

[71] Maurice Baillet in RB 63 (1956), pp.513-523.

[72] CALQ pp.95-119 identifies the teacher of righteousness with a Zadokite priest of Hasidic sympathies who probably began his ministry late in the reign of Jonathan (160-142 B.C.) and was persecuted by Simon (142-135 B.C.) who appears as "the wicked priest" in the Qumran literature. Rowley (in BJRL 40 [1957-58], pp.114-146) places the teacher of righteousness and the wicked priest in the time of Antiochus IV Epiphanes (175-164 B.C.) and the Maccabean uprising.

[73] tr. Rabin, *The Zadokite Documents,* p.2; cf. GDSS p.61.

98. Pompey

99. Caesar Augustus

100. The Young Tiberius

101. The Site of Cave 1 at Qumran

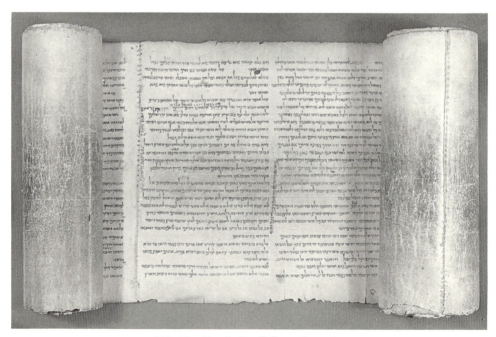

102. The Isaiah Scroll from Cave 1

104. Column Ten of the Manual of Discipline

103. The First Fragment of the Habakkuk Commentary

105. A Jar from Cave 1

106. Khirbet Qumran as Seen from Cave 4

107. Cave 4 at Qumran

108. A Palestinian Shepherd with his Sheep

109. The Jordan River

110. Plowing on the Hills above the Sea of Galilee

111. The Synagogue at Capernaum

112. The Synagogue Inscription of Theodotus

113. A Portion of the "Fourth Map of Asia" in Ptolemy's *Geography*

114. Herod's Towers at the West Gate of Samaria

115. The Garden of Gethsemane

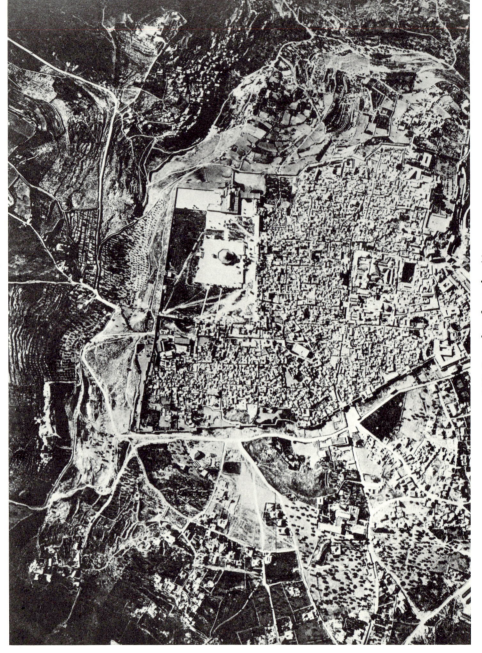

116. Jerusalem from the Air

118. Warning Inscription from Herod's Temple

117. The Wailing Wall

119. Titus, the Conqueror of the Jews

120. Relief on the Arch of Titus at Rome

tire group, are called "sons of Zadok" (IV, 3 = 6:1), the reference being to the leading priestly family of the time of David (II Samuel 8:17), who were designated as the only legitimate priests in the future Temple in the vision of Ezekiel (40:46, etc.).[74]

This group entered into a solemn agreement to keep away from evil men, not to rob the poor, to keep the Sabbath in every detail, to love each man his brother, and to keep away from all uncleanness, these and yet other items of the compact being "according to the findings of the members of the 'new covenant' in the land of Damascus" (VI, 15 - VII [XIX], 4 = 8:12-20).

The mention of Damascus at this and other points in the document has been taken to show that the group actually migrated to Damascus, but it may be that the geography is purely figurative, meaning that the residence of the group in the desert was a fulfillment of the prophecy of Amos (5:27) that the people would go "into exile beyond Damascus." Likewise a reference to 390 years (I, 5-6 = 1:5) is probably based on the 390 days of Ezekiel 4:5 and thus may have symbolic significance rather than being a clue for exact dating of the origin of the group.[75]

In its references to the "new covenant," the "sons of Zadok," and the "teacher of righteousness," and at a great many more points as well, this document (CD) agrees in language and ideas with the Qumran Manual of Discipline (1QS).[76] Because of these agreements, and also because an actual fragment of this work (6QD) was found at Qumran, the Zadokite Document may be taken as representing at least the same general movement as that of the community at Qumran. Since it speaks, however, of "the order (*serek*) of the meeting of the cities" (XII, 19 = 15:1) as well as of "the order of the meeting of the camps" (XII, 22-23 = 15:4), it seems to be concerned with groups established in urban places as well as more remote regions like Qumran, thus hardly represents the latter place alone. In the same connection the statement of Josephus that the Essenes settle in various towns may be recalled. Likewise there are variations in details of organization and life as reflected in the Zadokite Document and in the Manual of Discipline.[77]

[74] GDSS pp.4,333.

[75] Isaac Rabinowitz in JBL 73 (1954), pp.11-35; GDSS pp.4,24; Norman Walker in JBL 76 (1957), pp.57f.

[76] William H. Brownlee in BA 13 (1950), pp.50-54; P. Wernberg-Møller in JSS 1 1956), pp.110-128.

[77] Fritsch, *The Qumrān Community, Its History and Scrolls*, pp.79-86.

In the damaged line with which our text begins, the Manual of Discipline (1QS) is speaking, according to the probable reconstruction, about living in "the order (*serek*) of the community (יחד, *yaḥad*)" (I, 1).[78] The members of this community are described as in a "covenant (*berith*) of friendship" (I, 8), and the requirement is stated that they shall bring all their property into the community (I, 12). The priests, Levites, and people who belong are arranged in groups of thousands, hundreds, fifties, and tens (II, 19-21). No one may be admitted who is unwilling to enter the covenant and prefers to walk in his own "stubbornness of heart" (II, 25-26). A person of such iniquity cannot be sanctified by any washing:

> He cannot purify himself by atonement,
> Nor cleanse himself with water-for-impurity,
> Nor sanctify himself with seas or rivers,
> Nor cleanse himself with any water for washing! (III, 4-5).

The wicked may not, therefore, enter the water in which the holy men of the community purify themselves, for no one can be cleansed unless he has truly turned from his wickedness (v, 13). Those who have done so, however, are united together and form "a holy congregation (עדה, *'edah*)" (v, 20).

Even a group of the smallest allowable size, that is of ten men, may constitute a local unit of the order if one among them is a priest (VI, 3-4). Concerning their meals it is ordered that "they shall eat communally," and "when they arrange the table to eat, or the wine to drink, the priest shall first stretch out his hand to invoke a blessing" (VI, 2, 4-5). There must also never cease to be a man who expounds the Torah day and night, therefore the members must keep awake, no doubt in shifts, a third of all nights of the year for study and worship (VI, 6-8), this requirement presumably being intended to secure a literal fulfillment of Joshua 1:8 and Psalm 1:2.

When the community meets in public assembly, the "session of the many (רבים, *rabbim*)," as it is called, is presided over by a supervisor (מבקר, *mebaqqer*) or overseer (פקיד, *paqid*), these probably being two titles for the same officer (VI, 8, 12, 14).[79] One who wishes to join the community must be examined by the overseer and subsequently by "the many." During his first year the candidate must not touch "the purity" of the many, which presumably means that

[78] tr. BDSM p.6.
[79] BDSM p.25 n.24,27. See also Ralph Marcus in JBL 75 (1956), pp.298-302.

he must not participate in the purificatory rites of the group, and he is also not allowed to share in the common property. During his second year he still may not touch the drink of the many, presumably meaning that he may not join in the common meals. Only after successful completion of the entire two-year period, and after a final examination by the overseer, may he become a full member (vi, 13-23).

In connection with the admission of candidates, the enforcement of discipline, and the maintenance of high standards in the community, mention is also made of a council (עֵצָה, 'eṣah).[80] This body is made up of fifteen men, twelve laymen and three priests, "who are perfect in all that is revealed of the whole Torah" (viii, 1).

In the Zadokite Document (cd) the community has four classes, priests, Levites, and people, as mentioned in the Manual of Discipline, and also proselytes (xiv, 3-4 = 17:2-3). In agreement with the Manual, the arrangement is by thousands, hundreds, fifties, and tens, ten men sufficing to form a group providing there is a priest among them (xiii, 1-2 = 15:4-5). As in the Manual of Discipline so in the Zadokite Document the supervisor (mebaqqer) has to do with the admission of members to the community (xiii, 11-13 = 16:4-6; xv, 7-11 = 19:8-12), and he is also the spiritual guide of his congregation. The description of his duties employs scriptural allusions and draws particularly upon the idea of the shepherd in Ezekiel 34:12, 16. "He shall instruct the many in the works of God," it is ordered, "and make them consider his wonderful mighty deeds. And he shall recount before them the events of eternity. . . . And he shall take pity upon them like a father upon his sons, and shall bring back all them that have strayed of them . . . like a shepherd his flock" (xiii, 7-9 = 16:1-3). In addition to the supervisor of the individual "camp" there is also a "supervisor (mebaqqer) over all the camps," and it is required that he "shall be from thirty to fifty years old, one that has acquired mastery in every secret of men and in every language" (xiv, 8-10 = 17:6).

Fewer details are given by the Zadokite Document than by the Manual of Discipline concerning the requirements for entrance to the group, and it does not appear that such a lengthy probation is required. "With regard to everyone who turns from his corrupt way: on the day that he speaks to the supervisor (mebaqqer) of the many,

---

[80] Like the Greek βουλή by which it is often translated in the Septuagint (Deuteronomy 32:28, etc.), the Hebrew word means both "council" and "counsel."

they shall muster him with the oath of the covenant" (xv, 7-8 = 19:7-8). But the secret rulings of the order may not be divulged to the newly admitted one until he has passed the examination of the supervisor (xv, 10-11 = 19:10). It also does not seem that all property has to be turned over to the community, as in the Manual of Discipline, but rather that the member must give at least two days' wages each month to the supervisor and the judges who will use it for the poor and needy (xiv, 13-16 = 18:1-6). Marriage is also evidently allowed, since those who dwell in the "camps" are said to "take wives" and "beget children" (vii, 7 = 9:1).

The judges of the community, according to the Zadokite Document, are a group of ten men, four from the tribe of Levi and Aaron, that is priests, and six of Israel, that is laymen (x, 4-6 = 11:1-2), this court resembling the council of the Manual of Discipline but being somewhat different from it in makeup. The "assembly" (קהל, *qahal*) of the community is sometimes referred to (xii, 6 = 14:6; xiv, 18 = 18:6), the Hebrew word being the same as that commonly used in the Old Testament for the "assembly" (rsv) or "congregation" (kjv) of the whole people of Israel (Leviticus 4:14; Deuteronomy 31:30; etc.).

The communal meal is not mentioned in the Zadokite Document, due perhaps to the fact that the text is fragmentary, but purification with water is referred to and it is ordered: "Let no man bathe in water that is dirty or less than the quantity that covers up a man" (x, 11-12 = 12:1).

For the teaching of the community a long passage in the Manual of Discipline (iii, 13-iv, 26) is of special interest. "From the God of knowledge," it is affirmed at the outset, "exists all that is and will be." Then it is explained that God created man to have dominion over the world, "and assigned him two spirits by which to walk until the season of His visitation." These two are "the spirits of truth and perversion," or "the spirits of light and darkness." The prince of lights rules over the sons of righteousness and they walk in the ways of light; the angel of darkness rules over the sons of perversion and they walk in the ways of darkness. God made both spirits, but he delights forever in the spirit of light and has hated forever the spirit of darkness. Until now the two spirits "strive within man's heart," but in his wisdom God "has appointed an end to the existence of perversity," and "at the season of visitation, he will destroy it for ever." Such a doctrine of the conflict of light and darkness and the ultimate conquest of the latter is reminiscent of the teachings of Zoroastrianism, and the influence of Iranian dualism may be recognizable here.[81]

The War of the Sons of Light with the Sons of Darkness (1QM) is also concerned with this great conflict and describes the final battles in which the struggle will reach its climax. According to this writing, the climactic period of warfare will last for forty years (II, 6).[82] This may be the same period of about forty years which the Zadokite Document (CD) says will elapse from the time that the teacher of the community is gathered in or dies until the time when all the men of war are consumed who go with the man of falsehood (xx [MS. B], 14-15 = 9:39). This man of falsehood or man of lies is also referred to in the Habakkuk Commentary (1QpHab II, 1), and is evidently the "Antichrist" of the last days.[83]

At this time of "visitation" there will also come, according to the Zadokite Document, "the Messiah of Aaron and Israel" (VII [XIX], 21 = 9:10; XII, 23-XIII, 1 = 15:4). This Messiah who "shall arise from Aaron and from Israel" (xx [MS. B], 1 = 9:29) will bring to an end the old "epoch of wickedness" (XII, 23 = 15:4) and inaugurate the future age. In a small fragment recovered in the excavation of Cave 1 and sometimes known as The New Covenant (1Q34bis),[84] this new age is called the "epoch of favor" (II, 5). In a two-column fragment from the same source which has been called a Manual of Discipline for the Future Congregation of Israel (1QSa),[85] an "order" (serek) is set forth for the whole congregation ('edah) of Israel when, at the end of time, they live together in obedience to the ordinances of the sons of Zadok, the man who in the midst of inquity kept the covenant of God in order to make atonement (כפר, kaphar) for the land (I, 1-3). When this community of the future comes together for common deliberation, the priest as chief of the entire congregation comes first and then, in case he is present among them, the Messiah, that is presumably their anointed king,[86] takes his place, after that all the others in carefully determined grades. If they meet for a common meal, no one is to put his hand to bread or wine before

[81] Dupont-Sommer, The Jewish Sect of Qumran and the Essenes, pp.118-130; Karl G. Kuhn in ZTK 49 (1952), pp.296-316.

[82] GDSS pp.283, 315 n.10.

[83] GDSS p.103 n.41.

[84] DJD I, pp.152-155; tr. GDSS pp.311f.

[85] DJD I, pp.108-118; tr. GDSS pp.307-310; cf. H. Neil Richardson in JBL 76 (1957), pp.108-122.

[86] GDSS pp.278f.

the priest. It is the priest who must first pronounce the blessing over the bread and wine and stretch out his hand to the bread. Then the Messiah of Israel[87] puts his hand to the bread and after that the members of the congregation say the blessing. Such is the common meal of the community in the blessed future age (II, 11-22).

RELATIONSHIPS WITH EARLY CHRISTIANITY

It will have become evident that not a few points in the life and teachings of the community we have been describing suggest comparison with early Christianity. The extent and significance of the similarities have been judged variously by various investigators. One holds that the people of Qumran were Jewish Christians and the teacher of righteousness was Jesus himself,[88] but alone the chronology we have indicated above will not support this identification. Another thinks that the teacher of righteousness was crucified and held a place in the sect much the same as that of Jesus in Christianity,[89] but while a fragmentary Commentary on Nahum from Cave 4 (4QpNah) mentions a "Lion of Wrath" "who used to hang men up alive" (6-7) there is no proof that the teacher of righteousness was his victim.[90] Again it is held that so much in the Qumran community and its leader anticipated the work of Jesus that the latter was, at least in many regards, a veritable "reincarnation" of the teacher of

[87] The explicit designation of this leader as the "Messiah of Israel" suggests that the priest was the "Messiah of Aaron." Thus the future community would be presided over by two "anointed ones," one priestly and sacerdotal, the other lay and royal. This is in agreement with 1QS IX, 11 which speaks of "the Messiahs [plural] of Aaron and Israel." See Karl G. Kuhn in NTS 1 (1954-55), pp.168-179. A leaf from Cave 4 at Qumran (4QTestimonia) contains several Old Testament passages which were evidently used as *testimonia* or texts to express the Messianic expectations of the community. The citations are in succession Deuteronomy 18:18 (combined with 5:25-29), the announcement of the coming of the prophet like Moses; Numbers 24:15-17, the prophecy of Balaam about the star out of Jacob; and Deuteronomy 33:8-11, the blessing of Levi. It would appear that these were intended to refer respectively to the coming prophet (cf. Acts 3:22), the Davidic king (cf. Justin, *Dialogue with Trypho.* 106; and possibly Revelation 22:16), and the priestly Messiah (cf. *The Testament of Levi.* 18:2-14), so all of these personages figured in the expectations for the future. See DJD I, pp.121f.; F. F. Bruce in NTS 2 (1955-56), pp.179f.

[88] J. L. Teicher in JJS 5 (1954), pp.53f.

[89] J. M. Allegro in JBL 75 (1956), pp.89-95; and *The Dead Sea Scrolls and the Origins of Christianity.* No date, pp.99f.

[90] H. H. Rowley in JBL 75 (1956), pp.190f. GDSS pp.5, 333 even suggests that "teacher of righteousness" may have been the title not just of the founder of the community but of each of a series of its leaders, so that no single individual is necessarily indicated.

righteousness;[91] while on the other hand it is felt that the more the Qumran literature and the New Testament are compared the more skeptical one must become as to any direct contacts between the two.[92]

The judgment that will be expressed here, and briefly illustrated, is that the Qumran and related discoveries provide important information on a part of the background of early Christianity. The organization of the community of the covenant, as we have noted it above, manifests similarities with the organization of the early Christian church. The emphasis upon "community" (yaḥad) makes one think of the "fellowship" (κοινωνία) of the Jerusalem church (Acts 2:42), and both at Qumran and Jerusalem there was actual community of property. The word "congregation" ('edah) is that usually translated συναγωνή, "synagogue" in the Septuagint,[93] and this word is used for the Christian assembly in James 2:2. The "many" (rabbim) of the Qumran community are designated by a word (rab) to which in the Septuagint the term πλῆθος, "multitude," often corresponds,[94] and the latter word is used for the Christian group in Acts 6:2, 5; 15:12, 30.[95] The word "assembly" (qahal), used in the Zadokite Document, is usually translated by ἐκκλησία in the Septuagint,[96] and this is the word for "church" in the New Testament.

The "council" ('eṣah) of the community is designated by a word related to Greek συνέδριον;[97] in the New Testament this refers to local judicial councils of the Jews (Matthew 10:17) or to the supreme court, the Sanhedrin (Matthew 26:59); but Ignatius uses the Greek word for the assembly or council of the apostles to which he likens the elders of the church.[98] The make-up of this council in the Manual of Discipline, with its twelve laymen and three priests, at least makes one think of "the twelve" in the Jerusalem church (Acts 6:2), and of the three who were considered "pillars" (Galatians 2:9).

[91] Dupont-Sommer, The Jewish Sect of Qumran and the Essenes, pp.160f.; cf. Edmund Wilson, The Scrolls from the Dead Sea. 1955, pp.112f.

[92] Geoffrey Graystone, The Dead Sea Scrolls and the Originality of Christ. 1956.

[93] Exodus 12:3, etc. Edwin Hatch and Henry A. Redpath, A Concordance to the Septuagint and the Other Greek Versions of the Old Testament (Including the Apocryphal Books). 1892-1906, p.1309.

[94] Genesis 16:10, etc.

[95] Note the varying translations of the word in these passages in the Revised Standard Version: body, multitude, assembly, congregation.

[96] Deuteronomy 31:30, etc.   [97] GDSS p.332.

[98] To the Magnesians. VI, 1. ANF I, p.61; O. de Gebhardt, A. Harnack, and T. Zahn, Patrum Apostolicorum Opera. 1900, p.94.

Perhaps the most interesting of the possible antecedents to features of early church organization is the office of the supervisor (*mebaqqer*) or overseer (*paqid*). The two titles seem to have about the same meaning and the latter, *paqid*, is translated in the Septuagint by ἐπίσκοπος (Judges 9:28; Nehemiah 11:9, 14, 22). In the New Testament the same Greek word appears in the Revised Standard Version as "guardian" (Acts 20:28; I Peter 2:25) and "bishop" (Philippians 1:1; I Timothy 3:2; Titus 1:7).

The practices in the Qumran community of ablution and communal eating make one think of baptism and the breaking of bread in the early church (Acts 2:41f.). As the Greek word (βαπτίζω) signifies, the baptism of the church was an immersion, and we have noted the requirement of the Zadokite Document that ablution be in a quantity of water sufficient to cover a man. Likewise the insistence of the Manual of Discipline that the water is effective for cleansing only if the person has truly turned from his wickedness, is in agreement with the connection between baptism and repentance emphasized by both John the Baptist (Mark 1:4, etc.) and early Christianity (Acts 2:38, etc.). The baptism of John and of the church was an initial act performed once rather than a repeated washing like the ablutions of the community of the covenant, yet in this community also where, as we have seen, ablution was so closely connected with repentance and sanctification, it may well be that there was an initial bath at the time of admission. Again, as seen in the accounts of the Last Supper (Mark 14:22-25, etc.), the elements of the common meal of the disciples of Jesus were bread and wine, and the partaking was preceded by a blessing, just as in the covenant community. Likewise the common meal of the disciples of Jesus as also that of the community at Qumran expressed an eschatological anticipation of the Messianic banquet (Mark 14:25; I Corinthians 12:26). Yet the Christian records also connect the observance with the Passover (Mark 14:12, etc.), which was not the case at Qumran as far as we know.[99]

In its teachings it has been noted that the community of the covenant spoke of a conflict of light and darkness and looked forward to the final victory of the light. While this doctrine comes from a dualistic background, probably Iranian, it has been brought into harmony with Jewish monotheism by the explicit statement that God

[99] CALQ pp.177f. For further comparison between the Manual of Discipline and the Jerusalem church see Sherman E. Johnson in ZAW 66 (1954), pp.106-120.

made both the spirit of light and truth, and the spirit of darkness and perversion. Furthermore the teaching does not lead to extreme asceticism or libertinism, as Gnostic dualism often did, but is closely bound up with ethical ideals which belong to the Jewish tradition. The doctrine is accordingly much in line with the ethical dualism which is found in the New Testament, particularly in the Gospel according to John. For example, both the Manual of Discipline and the Gospel of John speak on the one hand of walking in the darkness (1QS III, 21; John 8:12; 12:35), and on the other hand of being "sons of light" (1QS I, 9; III, 24-25; John 12:36).[100]

Connections may be discerned also with the Letter of James. The otherwise enigmatical statement in James 4:5, "Do ye think that the scripture saith in vain, The spirit that dwelleth in us lusteth to envy?" (KJV) does not seem to refer to any passage in the canonical Old Testament but might be citing such a writing as the Manual of Discipline which says that "to the spirit of perversion belong greediness . . . wickedness and falsehood, pride and haughtiness of heart, lying and deceit, cruelty and gross impiety, quick temper and abundant folly and proud jealousy" (IV, 9-10). Likewise we have noted that it is James who uses the word "synagogue" ($\sigma\nu\nu\alpha\gamma\omega\gamma\acute{\eta}$) for the Christian "assembly" (James 2:2), this being equivalent to *'edah* or "congregation" as commonly used for the community of the covenant in the Dead Sea Scrolls.[101]

Likewise there is possible relationship between the Manual of Discipline and the thought of Paul. Near the end of our copy of the Manual of Discipline are these two remarkable passages:

> For as for me, my justification belongs to God;
> And in His hand is the perfection of my way. (XI, 2)

> In His compassion He has brought me near,
> And in His dependable mercy He will bring my justification.
> In His steadfast righteousness He has justified me
> And in His great goodness He will pardon [or, atone for] all
>   my iniquities;
> And in His righteousness He will cleanse me from man's impurity
> And from the sin of the children of men. (XI, 13-15)

[100] Karl G. Kuhn in ZTK 47 (1950), pp.209f.; Lucetta Mowry in BA 17 (1954), pp.78-97; W. F. Albright in W. D. Davies and D. Daube, eds., *The Background of the New Testament and Its Eschatology, Studies in Honour of Charles H. Dodd.* 1956, pp.167-171. The evidence now available suggests that John is no longer to be regarded as the most Hellenistic but rather, at least in some respects, the most Jewish of the Gospels (CALQ pp.161f.).

[101] GDSS pp.15-17.

When the writer speaks here of God's "righteousness" he uses the word צדק (*ṣedeq*), which is regularly translated by δικαιοσύνη in the Septuagint,[102] and is the Greek word so frequently used by Paul (Romans 1:17, etc.). For "justification" the writer of the Manual of Discipline uses משפט (*mishpaṭ*) (XI, 2), and when he says, "He has justified me," this is expressed with a verbal form of the same root, שפטני (*shepaṭni*) (XI, 14). In the Septuagint *mishpaṭ* is frequently translated by κρίσις generally meaning "justice,"[103] but in Leviticus 24:22 it is rendered δικαίωσις with the sense of "law," and in Isaiah 61:8 it is translated δικαιοσύνη in the sense of "justice." When Paul, on the other hand, speaks of "justification" he uses the noun δικαίωσις (Romans 4:25; 5:18), and when he speaks of being "justified" he uses the verb δικαιόω (Romans 2:13, etc.), thus employing terms which are of the same root with the word "righteousness" (δικαιοσύνη) itself. In the Manual of Discipline however, the words *ṣedeq* and *mishpaṭ* are practically of the same meaning, therefore the passages just quoted may still be considered rudimentary expressions of the doctrine of justification which was later developed so fully by Paul.[104]

Finally, the fact that the Qumran community was looking for the time when God would renew his covenant with them (1Q34bis II, 6) and when the Messiah would be in their midst (1QSa II, 20), links this congregation with the early church which was also a community of eschatological hope. But it was the faith of the church that the new covenant had now actually been established by Jesus (I Corinthians 11:25) whom it knew as the Christ (Mark 8:29). He was himself the expected prophet (Acts 3:22), priest (Hebrews 9:11f.), and king (John 1:49).[105]

That Jesus himself had direct contact with the Qumran community is not indicated, since at his baptism he "came from Nazareth of Galilee" (Mark 1:9).[105a] That John the Baptist could have had contact with this or another such group is suggested by the fact that, although he was born in "a city of Judah" (Luke 1:39), he was "in

---

[102] Leviticus 19:15, etc.　　　　　　　　[103] Genesis 18:19, etc.
[104] Sherman E. Johnson in HTR 48 (1955), pp.160-165.
[105] Bruce in NTS 2 (1955-56), p.180. For further discussion of the Messianic ideas at Qumran see William H. Brownlee in NTS 3 (1956), pp.12-30; and for possible identification of the Messiah with the Suffering Servant see William H. Brownlee in BASOR 132 (Dec. 1953), pp.8-15; 135 (Oct. 1954), pp.33-38. For theological conceptions in the Dead Sea Scrolls see Matthew Black in *Svensk Exegetisk Arsbok*. 18-19 (1953-54), pp.72-97.
[105a] See now Ethelbert Stauffer, *Jesus und die Wüstengemeinde am Toten Meer*. 1957.

the wilderness," that is presumably the general area west of the Dead Sea, "till the day of his manifestation to Israel" (Luke 1:80). That he even grew up in an Essene community is a possible surmise in view of the statement of Josephus that the non-marrying Essenes adopted other children to raise in their teachings.[106]

If John the Baptist had been in contact with the community of the covenant, the influence of that community could have been carried on into the early church through disciples of John who became followers of Jesus (John 1:35-37). Also, Acts 6:7 states that many priests accepted the Christian faith and, as we have seen, there were many priests in the community of the covenant, so it is at least possible that members of that community went directly into the group of followers of Jesus. Likely as it seems that some such contacts existed, even if they did not it is probable that "diffusion of ideas" from the various communities in Palestine which belonged to the movement now best known from Qumran could account for the influence attested by such evidence of relationship as has been cited.[107]

THE CALENDAR AT QUMRAN

A further topic of specialized interest with regard to the Dead Sea Scrolls is suggested by their emphasis upon times, seasons, and the calendar. The Manual of Discipline (1QS) describes the members of the covenant as desiring to walk before God "perfectly in all things that are revealed according to their appointed seasons" (I, 8-9; III, 10). They are also "not to advance their times, nor to lag behind any of their seasons" (I, 14-15). Likewise the duties of the council of fifteen include "the proper reckoning of the time" (VIII, 4),[108] while the wise man is admonished "to walk . . . according to the proper reckoning of every time," "to do God's will according to all that has been revealed for any time at that time, and to study all the wisdom found with reference to the times" (IX, 12-13).

Again in the latter part of our copy of the same Manual there is a long poem in which it is told how the devout worshiper blesses God at different times and seasons. The section with which we are concerned begins as follows (IX, 26-X, 1):

[106] William H. Brownlee in *Interpretation*. 9 (1955), p.73.
[107] J. Philip Hyatt in JBL 76 (1957), p.11. For further discussion of the relationships between the Qumran texts and early Christianity see Oscar Cullmann in JBL 74 (1955), pp.213-226; Sherman E. Johnson, *Jesus in His Homeland*. 1957, pp.23-67; Krister Stendahl, ed., *The Scrolls and the New Testament*. 1957.
[108] Another translation, however, is simply, "in conduct appropriate to every occasion" (GDSS p.55).

With an offering of the lips he shall bless Him
During the periods which Aleph ordained:
At the beginning of the dominion of light with its circuit;
And at its withdrawal to the habitation of its ordinance.

Aleph is the first letter of the Hebrew word for God (אלהים, *'Elo-him*) and is probably used here as a somewhat mysterious abbrevia-tion for God. The "beginning of the dominion of light" is evidently dawn, and it may be recalled that Josephus said the Essenes prayed before sunrise. The word "circuit" (תקופתו, *tequfato*) is the same that is used in Psalm 19:6[109] for the circuit of the sun. The "with-drawal" of the light is likewise the sunset, and the word (אסף, *'asaph*) is the same that is also used in the Old Testament for the setting of moon (Isaiah 60:20) and stars (Joel 2:10). Thus sunrise and sunset were taken account of by the community as times of worship.

After this the poem mentions the time "when luminaries shine from the abode of holiness" (x, 2-3). The word "luminaries" (מאורות, *me'orot*) is the same as that translated "lights" in Genesis 1:14, and the "abode of holiness" (זבול קודש, *zebul qodesh*) is the same as the "holy habitation" of God in Isaiah 63:15. According to Genesis 1:14 the "lights" serve "for signs and for seasons and for days and years," and the Qumran community undoubtedly looked to the heavenly bodies for the marking out of periods of time.

Using the same word "seasons" (מועדים, *mo'adim*) as is in Genesis 1:14, the poem next speaks of "the coming together of seasons to the days of a new moon" (x, 3). This probably means in effect, "when-ever the days and nights add up to a month,"[110] and indicates con-cern with this unit of time.

Following this the characters Mem and Nun are introduced into the poem (x, 4). As seemed probable in the case of the Aleph above (x, 1), there was doubtless also an esoteric meaning attaching to these letters. Mem, it may be noted, is the first letter of the word "luminaries" and also of the word "seasons." As it lends itself readily to doing, the letter Nun is written in the manuscript in a form which looks like a simple key, and the text reads, "the sign Nun is for the unlocking of His eternal mercies, at the beginnings of seasons in every period that will be" (x, 4-5). Together Aleph, Mem, and Nun form the word Amen, and it seems probable that this acrostic is in-tended. A possible allusion contained in it would be to Isaiah 65:16

---

[109] Verse 7 in the Hebrew text.　　　　[110] BDSM p.39 n.13.

where it is said that "he who blesses himself in the land shall bless himself by the God of Amen,"[111] while the probable relationship to the calendar will be explained below (p. 587).

Having spoken of days and months the poem refers also to times "at the beginnings of years and at the completion of their terms" (x, 6). In this connection there is mention of how the seasons are joined to each other, namely "the season of reaping to the season of summer-fruit, the season of sowing to the season of green herbage" (x, 7), this manner of speech being reminiscent of the Gezer calendar (p. 182). Then the poem speaks of the adding together of "seasons of years to their weeks, and the beginning of their weeks to a season of release" (x, 7-8). The week of years must refer to the provision found in Leviticus 25:1-7 according to which the children of Israel are to sow their fields for six years but in the seventh year to allow the land "a sabbath of solemn rest"; and the season of release must be the "year of jubilee" of Leviticus 25:8-55 when, after seven "weeks" of seven years, in the fiftieth year they are to proclaim liberty throughout the land and each return to his property and to his family.

The Zadokite Document (CD) reveals a similar interest in times and seasons and shows that the covenant community believed that it was faithful to the divine laws in these regards whereas all the rest of Israel had erred (III, 12-16 = 5:1-3): "But with them that held fast to the commandments of God who were left over of them, God established His covenant with Israel even until eternity, by revealing to them hidden things concerning which all Israel had gone astray. His holy sabbaths and His glorious appointed times, His righteous testimonies and His true ways and the requirements of His desire, which man shall do and live thereby, these He laid open before them; and they digged a well for much water, and he that despises it shall not live."

Over against the failure of Israel otherwise, it was the undertaking of those who entered the covenant "to keep the sabbath day according to its exact rules and the appointed days and the fast-day according to the finding of the members of the new covenant in the land of Damascus" (VI, 18-19 = 8:15). The "appointed days" must be those of the various religious festivals of the year. The "fast-day" (יום התענית, *yom ha-ta'anit*), although only designated with the

---

[111] See the margin of the ASV, and cf. II Corinthians 1:20; Revelation 3:14. BDSM p.38 n.2.

same general word for fasting which occurs in Ezra 9:5, is no doubt the most solemn fast of the year, the Day of Atonement (הכפרים יום, *yom ha-kippurim*), described in Leviticus 16 and 23:26-32, and in Acts 27:9 also called simply "the fast" (ἡ νηστεία).

Again, even as the Manual of Discipline referred to the "season of release" which must be the year of jubilee, so the Zadokite Fragment says that "the exact statement of the epochs of Israel's blindness" can be learned "in the Book of the Divisions of Times into Their Jubilees and Weeks" (xvi, 2-4 = 20:1). This seems plainly enough to be a reference to the writing commonly called the Book of Jubilees, the prologue of which begins: "This is the history of the division of the days of the law and of the testimony, of the events of the years, of their (year) weeks, of their Jubilees throughout all the years of the world."[112] Since two fragments of the book of Jubilees were found in Cave 1 at Qumran (1QJub = 1Q17 and 18), it is evident that the work was used by this community.[113]

In the Habakkuk Commentary (1QpHab) there is reference to the observance by the community of the day of atonement (*yom ha-kippurim*), and it is stated that "the wicked priest," an enemy for whom various identifications have been proposed, chose that very occasion to appear among them in order "to confound them and to make them stumble on the day of fasting, their Sabbath of rest" (xi, 6-8, commenting on Habakkuk 2:15).[114] That the wicked priest could break in upon the community on this solemn occasion would suggest that they were celebrating the fast on a day other than that which he himself recognized, and thus again it is indicated that the Qumran group was separated from other Jews by its calendar of festivals and fasts.[115]

The foregoing references suggest, then, that the Qumran community had its own religious calendar and that this was similar to the calendar of the book of Jubilees. This has now been confirmed by the discovery, announced in 1956 by J. T. Milik, in Cave 4 at Qumran of an actual liturgical calendar. The fragments on which this is contained appear to belong, paleographically, to the first part of the first century A.D. The calendar gives the dates of service in rotation of the priestly families and the dates of the religious festivals. These dates are always stated in terms of days of the week and sometimes

[112] CAP II, p.11.
[113] DJD I, pp.82-84.
[114] BDSS p.370; cf. GDSS pp.255, 268f.
[115] See S. Talmon in *Biblica.* 32 (1951), pp.549-563.

in days of the month. The liturgical days fall regularly on Wednesday, Friday, and Sunday. The passover is celebrated on Tuesday evening. The offering of the sheaf of first fruits (Leviticus 23:11) falls on the twenty-sixth day of the first month, a Sunday. The New Year begins on the first day of the seventh month, a Wednesday. The day of atonement, the tenth day of the seventh month (Leviticus 16:29), comes on Friday. The feast of tabernacles, the fifteenth day of the seventh month (Leviticus 23:34), is on Wednesday. Occasionally in the case of historical rather than liturgical dates, these are expressed in terms of Babylonian month names. This suggests that a calendar derived from Babylonia was in common use for everyday purposes, but that the other calendar which was presumably more ancient was adhered to for liturgical purposes.[116]

5. SACRED WAYS AND SITES

"HERE everything is historical," is the way Dr. Gustaf Dalman always answered the question as to whether this or that place in Palestine was historical.[1] As one seeks to follow the steps of Jesus in Palestine it is often the country itself rather than any specific object which speaks most clearly. Its hills, lakes, and rivers, its sky, sun, and springtime flowers, must be much the same as they were in Jesus' day. Also in many ways, at least until very recent times, the life of the people, their villages, activities, and customs, have remained little changed. One has seen the women at the village well, the sower going forth to sow, and the shepherd leading his sheep, exactly as it is said in John 10:4, "He goes before them, and the sheep follow him" (Fig. 108).[2] But it is also possible to make many positive identifications of places of New Testament significance and to discover many tangible remains from the Palestinian world in which Jesus walked.

BETHLEHEM

Bethlehem may be mentioned as early as in the Amarna letters.[3] The town is about six miles south and slightly west of Jerusalem, in the hill country of Judea. It is situated on the two summits and in-

---

[116] A. Jaubert in VT 7 (1957), pp.60f. See the Appendix of the present book for further discussion of the calendars.

[1] Dalman, *Sacred Sites and Ways*. 1935, p.13.

[2] See A. C. Bouquet, *Everyday Life in New Testament Times*. 1953; Eric F. F. Bishop, *Jesus of Palestine: The Local Background to the Gospel Documents*. 1955.

[3] ANET p.489 and n.21.

termediate saddle of a ridge some 2,500 feet in elevation. The terraced hillsides and fertile valleys justify the name which means "House of Bread." As of the year 1955 the Government of Jordan reported the population of the subdistrict of Bethlehem as 60,430. From the point of view of the Bible the greatness of Bethlehem lies in the fact that it was the city of David and the birthplace of Jesus Christ (I Samuel 16:4-13; Matthew 2:1; Luke 2:4).

Three and one-half miles southeast of Bethlehem are the remains of the Herodium. This was a stronghold of Herod the Great, which he erected on an unusual, conical, and artificially heightened hill. Two hundred steps of polished stones once led up to the circular towers of the fort on the summit, which contained richly furnished apartments for the king.[4] Here, at his desert watch-tower, Herod the Great at last was buried.[5] Today the hill is known as Frank Mountain and still has on its summit the ruins of Herod's towers.

Yet much farther southeast, on the western bank of the Dead Sea, was Masada, the "Mountain Stronghold." On a rock which rose high and steep on all sides, was a fortress which had existed from the time of Jonathan the high priest and had been fortified anew in the greatest strength by Herod the Great.[6] This was the very last stronghold of the Jews to fall to the Romans in the great war. Here the Sicarii[7] under Eleazar held out during a prolonged siege. When hope was gone, the besieged put one another to death rather than fall into the hands of their enemies. The fortress, blazing in flames, and containing only the multitude of the slain, was entered by the Romans in April, A.D. 73.[8]

NAZARETH

Nazareth lies high on a sharp slope in the Galilean hills. Its altitude is about 1,150 feet. From the summit above the village one looks south across the extensive plain of Esdraelon, west to Mount Carmel on the Mediterranean coast, east to nearby Mount Tabor,[9] and far north to snow-capped Mount Hermon (Psalm 89:12):

[4] *War.* i, xiii, 8; xxi, 10; *Ant.* xiv, xiii, 9; xv, ix, 4.

[5] *War.* i, xxxiii, 9; *Ant.* xvii, viii, 3.

[6] *War.* vii, viii, 3. A. Reifenberg, *Ancient Hebrew Arts.* 1950, pp.90f.; M. Avi-Yonah, N. Avigad, Y. Aharoni, I. Dunayevsky, S. Gutman, and L. Kadman in iej 7 (1957), pp.1-65.

[7] These fanatical patriots received their name from the short daggers (*sicae*) which they carried (*War.* ii, xiii, 3; *Ant.* xx, viii, 10).

[8] *War.* vii, ix.

[9] The Gospel according to the Hebrews made Mount Tabor the mountain of Temptation (jant p.2), while in the fourth century A.D. it was believed to be the mount of the Transfiguration and in the sixth century three churches were built on its summit in memory of the three tabernacles (Mark 9:5 = Matthew 17:4 = Luke 9:33).

The north and the south, thou hast created them:
Tabor and Hermon joyously praise thy name.

As of the year 1955 the Government of Israel reported the population of Nazareth as 22,000. Stores, blacksmith shops where the sickles characteristic of Nazareth are made, and carpenter shops open directly on the steep and narrow streets. Behind the present Greek Church of the Annunciation is a spring which is the only source of water in the village. A conduit carries this water farther down the hill to a place which since A.D. 1100 has been called Mary's Spring (Ain Maryam). Even as the mother of Jesus must once have visited the spring for water, so the women of Nazareth come to the same source today with their water pitchers balanced gracefully on their heads. The synagogue in which Jesus spoke (Luke 4:16), like other Jewish synagogues of the first century, was probably destroyed in the great Jewish war, and only replaced in the second or third century. The Church of the United Greeks has usually been held to mark the site of the ancient synagogue, but the place indicated by the Orthodox Greeks, where the Church of the Forty Martyrs was, has recently been held to be more likely.[10] There was also a basilica in Nazareth in Crusader and Byzantine times, and recent investigation in this area has disclosed traces of a pre-Byzantine church wall. There are several caves at the same place, one traditionally identified as the cave of the annunciation, and Iron II potsherds found in them prove that there was occupation at Nazareth as early as 600 B.C.[11]

An inscription said to have come from Nazareth was brought to Paris in 1878 and is in the Bibliothèque Nationale. Although the significance and even genuineness of the text are still under discussion, the date seems to be not later than the first half of the first century A.D., possibly in the reign of Tiberius. The inscription is headed "Ordinance of Caesar" and has to do with the inviolability of tombs. It expresses the imperial wish that one guilty of violation of sepulture be condemned to death. As far as is known such a provision was not a regular feature of contemporary Roman law. Accordingly it has even been suggested that this may represent a rescript of Tiberius which came in answer to a report from Pilate which included mention of the rumor (Matthew 28:13) that the disciples of Jesus stole his body from the tomb. At any rate the

[10] Clemens Kopp in JPOS 20 (1946), pp.29-42.
[11] CBQ 18 (1956), p.42.

fact that such a law could be stated makes more unlikely than ever the supposition that the disciples could have perpetrated such a theft.[11a]

Nazareth is now on the main highway which runs north and south through Palestine and stands also at the junction of that road with the branch which runs west to Haifa. Anciently the caravan road from Damascus to Egypt crossed the plain of Jezreel some six miles south of Nazareth, as does the Damascus-Haifa railroad of today, while a branch road to Akka passed at the same distance north of Nazareth. Also the main road from Sepphoris to Jerusalem ran south directly through Nazareth, while a branch from it ran through Japha to join the Damascus-Egypt road by way of Megiddo or Legio (el-Lejjun). Yet a third route south led from Nazareth through Endor and by way of Jericho to Jerusalem. Thus Nazareth was by no means a small out-of-the-way place hidden in a corner of the land, but was on or near important thoroughfares carrying extensive traffic.

Japha, only one and one-half miles southwest of Nazareth, was an important village at that time and Sepphoris, or Zippori, Galilee's largest city, was but three miles distant to the north. Neither Japha[12] nor Sepphoris is mentioned in the New Testament, but Josephus refers to both places frequently. Japha was one of the strongholds of the country. On one occasion it was occupied by Josephus that he might guard from there the roads of Galilee to the south,[13] and another time it stoutly resisted the armies of Trajan.[14] The remains of a synagogue of the Roman period have been found there.[15]

Sepphoris was "the largest city in Galilee."[16] In the time of Alexander Janneus it was so strong that his enemy, Ptolemy Lathyrus, was unable to conquer it.[17] A royal palace was established there in the days of Herod the Great, and in the insurrection which followed his death the revolutionary leader Judas made Sepphoris a main center of rebellion.[18] Then Varus came with the Syrian legions and, assisted by Aretas, took Sepphoris, made its inhabitants slaves and burned the city.[19] Herod Antipas walled the city and rebuilt it so

[11a] See J. Carcopino in *Revue Historique*. 167 (1931), pp.34f.; Jacques Zeiller in *Recherches de Science Religieuse*. 1931, pp.570-576; J. H. Oliver in *Classical Philology*. 49 (1954), pp.180-182; and for the hypothesis of a reply from Tiberius to Pilate, Ethelbert Stauffer, *Jesus, Gestalt und Geschichte*. 1957, p.111.

[12] It was the Japhia of Joshua 19:13.   [13] *Life of Josephus*. 52, cf. 45.

[14] *War*. III, vii, 31.

[15] L. H. Vincent in RB 30 (1921), pp.434-438.

[16] *Life*. 45.   [17] *Ant*. XIII, xii, 5.

[18] *Ant*. XVII, x, 5.   [19] *Ant*. XVII, x, 9.

splendidly that it became the ornament of all Galilee.[20] It probably was Galilee's capital until the founding of Tiberias. Having learned from its earlier experience the futility of revolution against Rome, Sepphoris did not join in the uprising of A.D. 66, and, by taking a stand for peace with the Romans, received a Roman garrison for its protection.[21] The remains of a fort and of a theater, both probably built by Herod Antipas, were unearthed at Sepphoris in 1931 by an expedition of the University of Michigan.[22]

Thus Jesus grew to manhood in a village which was close to some of the most stirring events of those times.[23]

THE JORDAN

The Jordan River, in the vicinity of which John the Baptist preached and in which Jesus was baptized, flows down through a flat, semi-desert valley, but the river itself is lined with rich foliage (Fig. 109). Locusts and wild honey (cf. Matthew 3:4) are still found and used on occasion by the Bedouins for food. The place where John baptized is called Bethany beyond the Jordan in John 1:28. A variant reading is the name Bethabara,[24] which was preferred by Origen (d. A.D. c.254) in his commentary on this passage.[25] Since Bethabara means "House of the Ford" it may have been a descriptive term for the same place. In that case, as the two designations suggest, Bethany beyond Jordan was probably on the far side of the river, but near a ford which would be a likely place for baptism. Since early centuries church tradition has located Bethabara near the ford called el-Hajleh where the main roads from Judea to southern Perea and from Jerusalem to Beth Haram cross the Jordan. John is also said to have baptized at Aenon near Salim (John 3:23). The name Aenon means "springs," and church tradition has pointed to a place of springs, six miles south of Scythopolis, as the site. The location is again near a main thoroughfare running up the Jordan Valley.[26]

[20] *Ant.* XVIII, ii, 1.

[21] *War.* II, xviii, 11; III, ii, 4; iv, 1; *Life.* 8,22,25,45,65,67,74.

[22] Leroy Waterman, *Preliminary Report of the University of Michigan Excavations at Sepphoris, Palestine, in 1931.* 1937, pp.28f.

[23] cf. S. J. Case, *Jesus, A New Biography.* 1927, pp.202-212.

[24] ASV margin.

[25] Origen, *Commentary on John.* VI, 24 (ANF IX, p.370); cf. Baedeker, *Palestine and Syria,* p.131.

[26] Carl H. Kraeling, *John the Baptist.* 1951, pp.8-10. See also Pierson Parker in JBL 74 (1955), pp.257-261. For the Jordan River in general see Nelson Glueck, *The River Jordan, Being an Illustrated Account of Earth's Most Storied River.* 1946.

THE SEA OF GALILEE

When Jesus left Nazareth and dwelt in Capernaum (Matthew 4:13) he left the highlands and took up his abode on the shores of a lake[27] lying some 696 feet below sea level. For the most part high plateaus surround the lake and slope steeply down to it. Viewed from the heights in the springtime, the Galilean lake seems the most beautiful place in Palestine, its blue surface set in the green frame of the hills. Flowers are then profuse and the radiant Syrian sunlight floods everything. One understands how Professor Adolf Deissmann could say in his *Licht vom Osten* that when a beam of the eastern sun falls into the darkness of a room "it begins to dawn, to glitter and to move; the one beam seems to double itself, to multiply itself ten-fold," and one appreciates his admonition, "Take then this single beam with you, as your own, beyond the Alps to your study: if you have ancient texts to decipher, the beam will make stone and potsherds speak . . . and, if the honor is vouchsafed you to study the holy Scriptures, the beam will awaken for you apostles and evangelists, will show you, yet more luminous than before, the sacred figure of the Savior from the East, to whose worship and discipleship the church is pledged."[28]

Narrow strips of land along the lake are very fertile, but back up on the stony hills cultivation is difficult and everything which has no deep roots withers beneath the blazing sun of summer. Fig. 110 which shows present-day plowing being done on these hills might almost serve as an illustration of the "rocky ground" in Jesus' parable of the soils (Mark 4:5 = Matthew 13:5 = Luke 8:6).

In visiting the chief sites on the Sea of Galilee, the pilgrim both in ancient and in modern times arrives at them most naturally in the order, Tiberias, Magdala, Capernaum, and Bethsaida.[29]

TIBERIAS

Josephus says that the capital city, Tiberias, which Herod Antipas built (p. 255), was on the lake of Gennesaret in the best part of Galilee.[30] Since Josephus mentions Tiberias just following his notice

---

[27] It was called "The Sea of Galilee" (Matthew 4:18; 15:29; Mark 1:16; 7:31; John 6:1); "The Sea of Tiberias" (John 6:1; 21:1); "The Lake of Gennesaret" (Luke 5:1); "The Water of Gennesaret" (I Maccabees 11:67); and "The Lake of Chennereth" (Eusebius, *Onomasticon* see under *Chennereth*, Χενερέθ, ed. Joannes Clericus. 1707, p.55).

[28] DLO p.v. tr. Jack Finegan.

[29] This was the route of the pilgrim Theodosius, A.D. c.530 (P. Geyer, *Itinera Hierosolymitana.* 1898, pp.137f.), cf. Petrus diaconus (Geyer, p.112) and Arculf (Geyer, p.273).

[30] *Ant.* XVIII, ii, 3.

of the coming of Pontius Pilate as procurator of Judea, it has been held that the city was built around A.D. 26. Evidence from coins and other data, however, suggests that the city was founded in A.D. 18, the year in which the Emperor Tiberius, for whom it was named, celebrated his sixtieth birthday and the twentieth anniversary of his holding of the *tribunica potestas*.[31] Josephus also relates that Herod Antipas had to remove many sepulchers in order to make room for his city. This kept strict Jews from settling there at first, and therefore the tetrarch had to secure inhabitants by bringing in foreigners and beggars. After the fall of Jerusalem, however, Tiberias became a chief seat of Jewish learning and in the second century the Sanhedrin, which had been moved from Jerusalem to Jamnia and then to Sepphoris, was established there. Despite its undoubted importance and magnificence at the time, Tiberias is mentioned only once in the New Testament (John 6:23).[32] Today the Arabs call the town Tabariya, and some ruins of the ancient city and its castle are still to be seen.

MAGDALA

Magdala was three miles north of Tiberias, at the southern end of the Plain of Ginnesar or Gennesaret, and is known today as Mejdel. This is doubtless the place from which Mary Magdalene (Matthew 27:56, etc.) came, and if Magadan (Matthew 15:39) and Dalmanutha (Mark 8:10) are to be traced to Magdal and Magdal Nuna or Nunaiya ("Magdal of fish") then they can be identified with the same place. If this is the city which Josephus called by its Greek name Tarichaeae, it had a population of 40,000 in his day.[33]

CAPERNAUM

The city on the lake which was of most importance in the ministry of Jesus was Capernaum. Insofar as Jesus had any fixed headquarters during his ministry in Galilee they were at Capernaum. The Gospels frequently mention his presence there[34] and Matthew calls it "his own city" (9:1; cf. Mark 2:1). Special reference is made to his teaching there on the sabbath day in the synagogue (Mark 1:21 = Luke 4:31), a building which was erected for the Jews by a sympathetic and generous Roman centurion (Luke 7:5). Finally Jesus pro-

[31] M. Avi-Yonah in IEJ 1 (1950-51), pp.160-169.
[32] John also (6:1; 21:1) calls the Sea of Galilee the Sea of Tiberias.
[33] *War*, II, xxi, 4.
[34] Matthew 8:5 = Luke 7:1; Matthew 4:13; 17:24; Mark 2:1; 9:33; Luke 4:23.

nounced a terrible woe against the city for its refusal to repent (Matthew 11:23 = Luke 10:15).

The site of Capernaum is doubtless that known today as Tell Hum,[35] where the most extensive ruins on the northwestern side of the lake are to be found. This location agrees with the geographical implications of an incident in which Josephus, suffering an accident near the Jordan and the city of Julias, was carried back to Capernaum for safety.[36] The other site whose identification with Capernaum has been considered seriously is Khan Minyeh, farther south along the shore beyond the springs known as Ain et-Tabgha and anciently called "Seven Springs."[37] But when the pilgrim Theodosius (A.D. c.530) came from Magdala to Capernaum he reached "Seven Springs" before arriving at Capernaum.[38] This he would have done if Capernaum were at Tell Hum but not if it were at Khan Minyeh.

The most important ruin at Capernaum is that of its famous synagogue.[39] This was explored by German archeologists and then excavated and restored (Fig. 111) by members of the Franciscan order on whose property the ruins stand. The synagogue was an imposing structure, built of white limestone, facing southward toward the lake and toward Jerusalem. In general, ancient synagogues in Palestine were built with this orientation toward Jerusalem, which in the case of those in northern Palestine was toward the south. This corresponded with the practice of offering prayer toward Jerusalem, which is reflected both in the Old Testament (I Kings 8:38, 44, 48; Daniel 6:10) and in rabbinical teaching, according to which Rabbi Hanna said to Rabbi Ashi, "Ye who are located on the north side of Palestine must recite your prayers towards the south (so that you shall face Jerusalem)."[40]

On the side toward the lake the Capernaum synagogue had three doors and a large window. The interior was more than seventy feet long and fifty feet wide, with a colonnade built around the three sides other than that at the entrance. Above was an upper floor, probably intended for women. There was also a colonnaded court

[35] The name may come from the fact that in later centuries the Jews made pilgrimages there to visit the grave of the prophet Nahum, or Rabbi Tanhum (Tanchuma).

[36] *Life.* 72.

[37] The present name is a corruption of the Greek Heptapegon (ἐπτάπηγον i.e. Χωρίον), "seven springs."

[38] Geyer, *Itinera Hierosolymitana*, p.138.

[39] H. Kohl and C. Watzinger, *Antike Synagogen in Galiläa.* 1916, pp.4-41; E. L. Sukenik, *Ancient Synagogues in Palestine and Greece.* 1934, pp.7-21.

[40] *Baba Bathra.* 25b (RBT 7 [v,xiii], p.77).

on the eastern side. Individual parts of the synagogue were gifts from various persons, and one fragment of a pillar still carries an inscription with the name of its donor, Zebida bar Jochanan, which is practically "Zebedee the son of John."

Ornamentation of the synagogue included figures of palm trees, vines, eagles, lions, centaurs, and boys carrying garlands. The attitude of the Jews toward such pictorial representations of living beings has varied greatly. Sometimes the letter of the law in Exodus 20:4 and Deuteronomy 5:8 was held to absolutely prohibit all such representations. The strenuous opposition of the Jews to the acts of Pilate in bringing standards with the likeness of the emperor into Jerusalem and in placing even inscribed shields in Herod's palace has already been noted (p. 257). Also in 4 B.C. the Jews at Jerusalem pulled down the golden eagle which Herod had put on the temple,[41] and in A.D. 66 Josephus was instructed to press for the destruction of the palace of Herod Antipas at Tiberias because it contained representations of animals.[42] In this connection Josephus expressly says that Jewish law forbade the making of such figures. But again the law was held to prohibit only the making of images for purposes of worship, and in this case animal and human motifs could be employed with perfect propriety. R. Eleazar b. R. Zadok, for example, who was well acquainted with Jerusalem before its destruction, said, "In Jerusalem there were faces of all creatures except men." Obviously the Capernaum synagogue represents in its decoration the more liberal policy.[43]

The synagogue at Tell Hum has been believed to belong to the time before A.D. 70,[44] but is more probably to be dated around A.D. 200 or later, since all the earlier Jewish synagogues appear to have been destroyed by Titus during the Jewish war and by Hadrian after the second century rebellion of Bar Kokhba.[45] Even so it is probable that the Capernaum synagogue stands on the site and follows the plan of an earlier synagogue or of earlier synagogues, and therefore may be safely regarded as a reconstruction of the one in which Jesus himself taught.

A number of other synagogues have been found in Galilee, but probably none of them is earlier than the third century A.D., while

---

[41] *War.* I, xxxiii, 2f.; *Ant.* XVII, vi, 2.   [42] *Life.* 12.

[43] Sukenik, *Ancient Synagogues*, pp.61-64.

[44] B. Meistermann, *Capharnaüm et Bethsaïde.* 1921, p.289; and *Guide to the Holy Land.* 1923, p.552; G. Orfali, *Capharnaüm et ses Ruines.* 1922, pp.74-86.

[45] Kohl and Watzinger, *Antike Synagogen in Galiläa*, p.218.

the famous synagogue of Beth Alpha, near Khirbet Beit Ilfa in the Valley of Jezreel, with its remarkable mosaic floor, belongs to the sixth century.[46]

An interesting inscription (Fig. 112) was discovered at Jerusalem, however, which undoubtedly is to be dated before A.D. 70.[47] It records the building of a synagogue by a certain Theodotus, whose family had had the honor of holding the office of ruler of the synagogue for three generations. Indeed the cornerstone had been laid already by the father and the grandfather of Theodotus, together with the elders (presbyters) of the synagogue and Simonides who doubtless had given some special gift toward the building. The enterprise, as Theodotus carried it to completion, included not only the erection of the synagogue proper but also the construction of a guest house and apartments for pilgrims from afar, together with arrangements for water for the ritual washings. The inscription reads: "Theodotus, son of Vettenos, priest and ruler of the synagogue,[48] son of a ruler of the synagogue, grandson of a ruler of the synagogue, built the synagogue for the reading of the law and for the teaching of the commandments;[49] furthermore, the hospice and the chambers, and the water installation for lodging of needy strangers. The foundation stone thereof had been laid by his fathers, and the elders, and Simonides."

CHORAZIN AND BETHSAIDA

Linked with Capernaum in the memorable woe which Jesus pronounced (Matthew 11:21-23 = Luke 10:13-15), and therefore presumably in the same general area, were two other cities, Chorazin and Bethsaida. Slightly less than two miles away in the hills above Tell Hum is a site called Kerazeh which doubtless is to be identified with ancient Chorazin. Again, the most impressive feature of the ruins is a synagogue, which was richly ornamented with sculptures showing animals, centaurs fighting with lions, and representations of grape-gathering and grape-pressing.[50]

The Bethsaida of the New Testament was probably the Bethsaida which Philip rebuilt and renamed Julias (p. 255). This city was just east of the Jordan near where the river flows into the Sea of Galilee,[51]

[46] E. L. Sukenik, The Ancient Synagogue of Beth Alpha. 1932.

[47] DLO pp.379f.; cf. Herbert G. May in BA 7 (1944), p.11.

[48] cf. Mark 5:35, etc.   [49] cf. Luke 4:16-21; Acts 13:15.

[50] Kohl and Watzinger, Antike Synagogen, pp.41-58; Sukenik, Ancient Synagogues, pp.21-24.

[51] Josephus describes Julias as being "in lower Gaulanitis" (War. II, ix, 1) and says that "below the town of Julias" the river Jordan "cuts across the Lake of Gennesar" (War. III, x, 7; cf. Life. 72).

and has usually been identified with et-Tell, a mound about one mile north of the lake. Some think that Bethsaida and Julias always remained distinct and that the village of Bethsaida itself may be represented by the site called Khirbet el-'Araj near the lakeshore.[52] These places are only a few miles distant from Capernaum across the lake, and Bethsaida might even be regarded loosely as belonging to Galilee. This would account for John's reference (12:21) to "Bethsaida in Galilee." Ptolemy also reckoned that Julias belonged to Galilee,[53] and in a similar way mention was sometimes made of "Judea beyond the Jordan."[54]

CAESAREA PHILIPPI

It was in the neighborhood of Philip's other city, Caesarea (p. 255), that Peter's confession was made (Mark 8:27 = Matthew 16: 13). Caesarea Philippi was some distance north of the Sea of Galilee on a plateau at the southern foothills of Mount Hermon. At this place a strong stream of water issues from a cave (Mugharet Ras en-Neba) in the hillside and is a main source of the river Jordan. Although the cave is filled now with fallen stone, it was described impressively by Josephus: "At this spot a mountain rears its summit to an immense height aloft; at the base of the cliff is an opening into an overgrown cavern; within this, plunging down to an immeasurable depth, is a yawning chasm, enclosing a volume of still water, the bottom of which no sounding-line has been found long enough to reach."[55] The cave was sacred to Pan and hence the place originally bore the name Panias (modern Banias). Herod the Great adorned the site with "a most beautiful temple of the whitest stone," dedicated to Caesar Augustus, and Philip transformed the place into a town of some size.

THE DECAPOLIS

The "Decapolis" which is mentioned on two or three occasions in the Gospels (Matthew 4:25; Mark 5:20; 7:31) was a kind of confederacy, at first consisting of ten towns, as the name suggests.

[52] Kraeling, *Rand McNally Bible Atlas*, pp.388f.
[53] *Geography.* v, 15. ed. Stevenson, p.128.
[54] Matthew 19:1. The fact that Luke 9:10 speaks of Jesus and the disciples going "apart to a city called Bethsaida" while in the Marcan parallel at the close of the section (6:45) the disciples are sent "to the other side, to Bethsaida" has led to the hypothesis that there was a second Bethsaida on the western side of the lake, but it is probable instead that there is confusion in the topographical references at this point. cf. C. C. McCown in JPOS 10 (1930), pp.32-58. The extreme skepticism of *Formgeschichte* concerning *Situationsangaben* (Rudolf Bultmann, *Die Geschichte der synoptischen Tradition.* 2d ed. 1931, pp.67-69, 257f.,355,365,379f.,389f.), however, would lead one to expect such confusions far oftener than they actually occur.
[55] *War.* I, xxi, 3; *Ant.* xv, x, 3.

These were Hellenistic towns which had been subjugated by Alexander Janneus and then set free from Jewish authority by Pompey. Thereafter they were subject to the legate of Syria but enjoyed a considerable degree of autonomy. According to Pliny (A.D. 23-79) the ten cities which comprised the league were Damascus, Philadelphia, Raphana, Scythopolis, Gadara, Hippo, Dion, Pella, Galasa, and Canatha.[56] Ptolemy, a portion of whose map of Palestine and Syria is reproduced in Fig. 113, lists eighteen "towns in Coelesyria and Decapolis": Heliopolis, Abila which is called Lysinia, Saana, Ina, Damascus, Samulis, Abida, Hippus, Capitolias, Gadara, Adra, Scythopolis, Gerasa, Pella, Dium, Gadora, Philadelphia, Canatha.[57]

Scythopolis was at the point where the plain of Esdraelon joins the valley of the Jordan. This was the site of Old Testament Beth-shean (p. 167), the name of which survives in the designation of the present-day village at that place as Beisan. A large stone amphitheater still remains there from the time of the Hellenistic city. Aside from Scythopolis, all of the towns of the Decapolis lay in the country east of the Jordan. Hippos (Kalat el-Husn),[58] Dion, Raphana, and Canatha (Kanawat) were east of the Sea of Galilee. Gadara is identified with the ruins of Umm Qeis, some five miles southeast of the Sea of Galilee, beyond the river Yarmuk. The ruins of the city's theater, cut out of the black rock, are still to be seen.

Gerasa lay yet farther south, some fifty miles from the Sea of Galilee, on one of the tributaries of the Jabbok. The site is known today as Jerash. Excavations conducted at Gerasa by Yale University and the British School of Archaeology in Jerusalem in 1928-1930 and by Yale University and the American Schools of Oriental Research in 1930-1931 and 1933-1934, have revealed that in the early centuries of the Christian era Gerasa was one of the most brilliant cities of Transjordan. The city was adorned with fine colonnaded streets, a circular forum, and beautiful temples and theaters. South of the city an impressive triumphal arch carried an inscription welcoming Hadrian on his visit to Gerasa in A.D. 130,[59] and most of the architectural remains are somewhat later than the New Testament period.

In Mark's narrative of the demoniac, and the swine which rushed into the sea, the scene is laid in "the country of the Gerasenes" (Mark

[56] *Natural History.* v, 16. tr. H. Rackham, LCL (1938-), II, p.277.

[57] *Geography.* v, 14. ed. Stevenson, p.127.

[58] Hippos was the Susitha of the rabbis, and the latter name survives in Susiyeh, a little distance to the southeast.

[59] C. H. Kraeling, ed., *Gerasa, City of the Decapolis.* 1938, p.401, Inscr. No.58.

5:1 = Luke 8:26). The reference, however, can hardly be to Gerasa, which was so far distant. Matthew (8:28) states that it was in "the country of the Gadarenes," and the reference to Gadara may be correct if that city's territory can be supposed to have extended to the shores of the lake. Otherwise, however, there is no evidence that Gadara's territory crossed the Yarmuk. According to some texts, Luke (8:26, 37, RSV margin) spoke of "the country of the Gerge-senes," and this makes it possible to suppose that somewhere on "the other side of the sea" (Mark 5:1 = Matthew 8:28; cf. Luke 8:26) there was a place called Gergesa, in whose vicinity the event took place. It has been suggested that this Gergesa is represented by the present Kersa, a small place on the eastern shore just below the Wadi es-Semak. In this neighborhood the hills do plunge steeply to the lake, as is presupposed in the Gospel narrative (Mark 5:13 = Matthew 8:32 = Luke 8:33).

Pella (Fahl) was midway between Gadara and Gerasa, across the Jordan somewhat south of Scythopolis. Pella was the city to which the Christians fled from Jerusalem in A.D. 68 and again in A.D. 135. Philadelphia lay south of Gerasa and was the southernmost of the cities of the Decapolis. Formerly it was known as Amman,[60] having been the chief city of the Ammonites. It was the Rabbah of the Old Testament (Deuteronomy 3:11; Joshua 13:25; II Samuel 11:1, etc.). The Hellenistic city at this site was built by Ptolemy II Philadelphus, and named for him. Both at Pella and at Philadelphia extensive ruins are still to be seen.

SAMARIA

The direct route from Galilee to Jerusalem ran through the land of Samaria, and Josephus says that it was the custom of the Galileans, when they came to the Holy City at the festivals, to journey through the country of the Samaritans.[61] By that route, which was the shortest and quickest, one could reach Jerusalem in three days' time.[62] Journeys by Jesus through the country of the Samaritans are noted in Luke 9:52 and John 4:4 (cf. Luke 17:11).

When the city of Samaria fell to the Assyrians, 27,290 of its people were carried off captive (p. 209). Doubtless these constituted the flower of the population, and those who remained behind were the poorest people. Then "the king of Assyria brought people from Babylon, Cuthah, Avva, Hamath, and Sephar-vaim, and placed them in

[60] Eusebius, *Onomasticon*, see under *Amman*, 'Αμμάν. ed. Clericus, p.15.
[61] *Ant.* xx, vi, 1.   [62] *Life.* 52.

the cities of Samaria" (II Kings 17:24) to take the place of those who had been deported. The descendants of the remnant of Israelites and the newly introduced foreigners constituted a mixed race which was looked upon with suspicion by the exiles who returned to Jerusalem. Any participation by the Samaritans in the rebuilding of the temple was spurned by the Jews (Ezra 4:3; Nehemiah 2:20), and Nehemiah expelled from Jerusalem the grandson of Eliashib, the high priest, because he was married to the daughter of Sanballat the Samaritan leader (Nehemiah 13:28). Eliashib's grandson was probably the Manasseh under whom the Samaritans set up their own rival priesthood and built their own temple on Mount Gerizim.[63]

The breach between the two groups was never healed. During the weak rule of the high priest Onias II (d. c.198 B.C.) the Samaritans carried off Jews into slavery,[64] and later John Hyrcanus made an expedition into Samaria and destroyed the Gerizim temple (c.128 B.C.).[65] In the time of unrest after the deposition of Archelaus (A.D. 6) the Samaritans defiled the Jerusalem temple by throwing in dead men's bodies at night.[66] Later a number of Galilean pilgrims were killed at Ginea (Jenin) as they started to cross Samaria on their way to Jerusalem. Thereupon a virtual civil war broke out which had to be appealed to Claudius Caesar (A.D. 51).[67]

The metropolis and chief center of the Samaritans was at Shechem,[68] between Mounts Gerizim and Ebal and on the most direct route from Galilee to Jerusalem. It was rebuilt as Flavia Neapolis in A.D. 72, and is today the village of Nablus, still inhabited by the remnant of the Samaritans. The village of Sychar which figures in John 4:5 has sometimes been identified with Shechem itself but is more probably to be found in the present-day village of Askar at the southeastern foot of Mount Ebal.[69]

"Jacob's Well" (John 4:6) is believed to be the well beside the main road, one and three-quarters miles southeast of Nablus and three-quarters of a mile southwest of Askar, but there are other wells in the neighborhood. This well, however, is near the crossing of the main north-south road with an important road running from the

[63] Josephus (*Ant.* XI, vii-viii) would make Manasseh the great-grandson of Eliashib, and place the schism in the time of Alexander the Great and Jaddua the high priest (332 B.C.), but that is probably one hundred years too late.
[64] *Ant.* XII, iv, 1.   [65] *Ant.* XIII, ix, 1; x, 2.   [66] *Ant.* XVIII, ii, 2.
[67] *Ant.* XX, vi; *War.* II, xii.   [68] *Ant.* XI, viii, 6.
[69] Walter Bauer, *Das Johannesevangelium* (*Handbuch zum neuen Testament.* 6 [3d ed. 1933]), p.66.

Jordan to the Mediterranean, and has been pointed to as Jacob's well by church tradition steadily since ancient times. From the well one looks directly up at the 3,000-foot summit of Mount Gerizim, concerning which the Samaritan woman said, "Our fathers worshipped on this mountain" (John 4:20).

The ancient city of Samaria itself was at this time a Hellenistic rather than a Samaritan city. Alexander the Great planted Macedonian colonists there (331 B.C.), and after many vicissitudes the city was bestowed upon Herod the Great by Augustus.[70] Herod rebuilt and greatly enlarged Samaria, honoring the Emperor Augustus both with the city's new name, Sebaste (p. 254), and with its temple dedicated to him.[71] This temple, which has been excavated, was approached by a massive stairway leading up to a large platform surrounded by pillars, behind which was the temple itself. At the foot of the stairway was an altar, near which the excavators found a fallen statue of Augustus.[72] Particularly impressive were the strong fortifications which Herod the Great erected at Samaria. An example of his work is to be seen in the great round towers flanking the west gate and shown in Fig. 114.[73]

In the early months of the Jewish revolt (A.D. 66) Sebaste was captured and burned by the rebels. Afterward, in the time about A.D. 180 to 230, Sebaste enjoyed a period of prosperity and was adorned with fine classical buildings, a columned street, and a Corinthian stadium.[74] In later times the Christian world was interested in Sebaste chiefly because it was supposed to be the place where John the Baptist was buried. Two shrines were dedicated to him here. One was at an old family burial place which dates probably from the second or third century and is in the eastern end of the city under the present mosque. It was identified as the tomb of John at least by the time of Julian the Apostate, for in an anti-Christian riot which took place at Sebaste during his reign the pagans demolished the tomb and scattered the ashes. The second memorial to the Baptist was at a high place south of the summit of the hill, where Herodias was supposed to have hidden John's head, and where eventually a Christian basilica was built.[75]

[70] *Ant.* xv, vii, 3; *War.* i, xx, 3.   [71] *Ant.* xv, viii, 5; *War.* i, xxi, 2.
[72] Reisner, Fisher, and Lyon, *Harvard Excavations at Samaria.* i, pp.48-50; Crowfoot, Kenyon, and Sukenik, *The Buildings at Samaria,* pp.123-127.
[73] Watzinger, *Denkmäler Palästinas.* ii (1935), p.52; Crowfoot, Kenyon, and Sukenik, *The Buildings at Samaria,* pp.39-41.
[74] Crowfoot, Kenyon, and Sukenik, *The Buildings at Samaria,* pp.35-37.
[75] *ibid.,* pp.37-39.

PEREA

If one did not wish to pass through Samaria, two other routes were possible from Galilee to Jerusalem. A western road ran down the coastal plain in the territory of the city of Caesarea, and then roads ascended to Jerusalem from east of Antipatris and from Lydda. Or one could take an eastern route by following down the valley of the Jordan River. From Capernaum such a route led through Tiberias and on south past Scythopolis, where there was a regularly used ford across the Jordan. Or it was possible to go around the eastern side of the lake and come south in the neighborhood of Hippos, Gadara, and Pella.

Beyond Pella one entered Perea proper. This land, Galilee, and Judea, were reckoned by the Jews as the three Jewish provinces, for Samaria was excluded from such dignity.[76] Josephus says that the length of Perea was from Pella to Machaerus,[77] that is from the Jabbok to the Arnon, and the breadth from Gerasa and Philadelphia to the Jordan,[78] although sometimes the name Perea was used loosely to include the region on north to the Yarmuk.[79] The actual name "Perea" is not used in the Gospels, where the usual designation for this country is "beyond the Jordan" (Mark 3:8 = Matthew 4:25, etc.).

Mark seems to indicate that the Perean route was taken by Jesus on his last journey to Jerusalem. He came "beyond the Jordan" (Mark 10:1 = Matthew 19:1), went "on the way, going up to Jerusalem" (Mark 10:32 = Matthew 20:17), and arrived at last at Jericho (Mark 10:46 = Luke 18:35; cf. Matthew 20:29). Opposite Jericho the Jordan was forded regularly either at Ghoraniyeh (Roraniyeh) or at el-Hajleh (p. 301).

JERICHO

Jericho itself, in New Testament times, had spread out beyond the hill on which the Old Testament city stood. The celebrated palm and balsam district of Jericho was given by Antony to Cleopatra,[80]

---

[76] *Baba Bathra.* III, 2 (RBT 7, p.100), "There are three lands concerning the law of *hazakah*: The land of Judea, the land on the other side of the Jordan, and of Galilee."

[77] Machaerus was a fortress on a mountain east of the Dead Sea. Alexander Janneus was the first to fortify the place, and Herod greatly enlarged and strengthened it, also building there a magnificent palace (*War.* VII, vi, 2). From Herod the Great it passed into the hands of Herod Antipas together with Perea in which it was situated. It was here, according to Josephus (*Ant.* XVIII, v, 5) that Herod Antipas imprisoned and beheaded John the Baptist (cf. Mark 6:17-29 = Matthew 14:3-12 = Luke 3:19f.).

[78] *War.* III, iii, 3.

[79] *War.* IV, vii, 3, calls Gadara, which was near the Yarmuk, the capital of Perea.

[80] *War.* I, xviii, 5.

but restored to Herod the Great by Augustus.[81] Here Herod built a citadel called Cyprus,[82] a theater,[83] an amphitheater,[84] and a hippodrome in which he planned to have the leading Jews murdered at the moment of his own death so that he would not lack for mourning.[85] The palace at Jericho in which Herod died afterward was burned down by Simon, a former slave of the king's, and then magnificently rebuilt by Archelaus.[86]

A portion of the Jericho of these times has been excavated by the American School of Oriental Research in Jerusalem and the Pittsburgh-Xenia Theological Seminary. This work was begun in 1950 under the direction of James L. Kelso.[87] The ruins investigated are at a site now known as Tulul Abu el-'Alayiq one mile west of modern Jericho at the place where the Wadi Qelt opens into the Jordan Valley. This is where the ancient Roman road entered the wadi to climb from the valley of the Jordan to the city of Jerusalem. There are ancient remains here on both sides of the wadi. The excavations on the south side uncovered an Arabic fortress of the eighth or ninth century; then a Roman structure of concrete masonry forming part of an elaborate civic center built probably by Herod Archelaus or possibly by Hadrian; below that, Herodian masonry; and below that, a Hellenistic tower constructed probably in the second century B.C. during the struggle between the Maccabees and the Seleucids. At the foot of the tell was a grand façade along the wadi. As in the case also of the Roman structure mentioned above, the masonry of the façade was lined with small, square-faced, pyramidal stones which give the impression of a net (*reticulum*), this type of work being known as *opus reticulatum*. The façade also was ornamented with semicircular benches and numerous niches. Flower pots found on the benches suggest that these provided a terraced garden, although they could also have been seats in an outdoor theater. The supposition that not a little of this work is to be attributed to Archelaus is strengthened by the finding of a number of coins of this ruler.

[81] *Ant.* xv, vii, 3; *War.* i, xx, 3.   [82] *Ant.* xvi, v, 2; *War.* i, xxi, 4, 9.
[83] *Ant.* xvii, vi, 3.   [84] *Ant.* xvii, viii, 2; *War.* i, xxxiii, 8.
[85] *Ant.* xvii, vi, 5; *War.* i, xxxiii, 6.   [86] *Ant.* xvii, x, 6; xiii, 1.

[87] James L. Kelso in BASOR 120 (Dec. 1950), pp.11-22; in BA 14 (1951), pp.34-43; and in NGM 100 (1951), pp.825-844; James B. Pritchard in BASOR 123 (Oct. 1951), pp.8-17; James L. Kelso and Dimitri C. Baramki, *Excavations at New Testament Jericho and Khirbet en-Nitla.* AASOR 29-30. 1955; James B. Pritchard, Sherman E. Johnson, and George C. Miles, *The Excavation at Herodian Jericho, 1951.* AASOR 32-33. 1958. For other Roman settlements in the *Regio Iericho* see Lucetta Mowry in BA 15 (1952), pp.26-42; and cf. M. Avi-Yonah, *Map of Roman Palestine.* 1940, pp.26f.

Soundings in the tell on the north side of the wadi have shown that a brick fortress and two stone buildings existed there. The architecture is so typical of what was already known at such places as Rome, Pompeii, and Tivoli, that the excavators say one might think a section of Rome itself had been miraculously transported on a magic carpet from the banks of the Tiber to the banks of the Wadi Qelt. Such was the winter capital of Judea in the time of the Herods, the New Testament city of Jericho.

FROM JERICHO TO JERUSALEM

From Jericho to Jerusalem (cf. Luke 10:30) is a distance of some seventeen miles. Approaching the Holy City, the Jericho road swings over the shoulder of the Mount of Olives. From the summit of the Mount of Olives one can look back across the entire eastern countryside of Judea. A tawny wilderness of hills drops away to the white Jordan Valley with its ribbon of green vegetation, and to the dull blue surface of the Dead Sea, some 1,290 feet below sea level, with the high wall of the mountains of Moab in the background. The arrival of Jesus and his disciples is introduced with the words: "And when they drew near to Jerusalem, to Bethphage and Bethany, at the Mount of Olives. . . ." (Mark 11:1 = Matthew 21:1 = Luke 19: 29). The exact location of Bethphage is unknown, but references to Beth Page in rabbinic literature point to its close connection with Jerusalem.[88] Bethany was doubtless on the east side of the Mount of Olives in the vicinity of the present village of el-Azariyeh, whose Arabic name preserves the tradition of the connection of Lazarus with Bethany (John 11:1).[89]

Gethsemane was apparently on the western slope of the Mount of Olives, just across the brook Kidron from the city of Jerusalem (Mark 14:26, 32 = Matthew 26:30, 36 = Luke 22:39; John 18:1). The precise location of the "enclosed piece of ground" (Mark 14:32 = Matthew 26:36, ASV margin) that was Gethsemane can hardly be determined now with certainty, since Josephus states that during the siege of Jerusalem Titus cut down all the trees and desolated the pleasant gardens for many miles round about Jerusalem.[90] The location of the beautiful little "Garden of Gethsemane" (Fig. 115) which

[88] Dalman, *Sacred Sites and Ways*, p.252.

[89] The "tomb of Lazarus" has been shown at this place at least from the time of the Bordeaux Pilgrim, A.D. 333 (*Itinerary from Bordeaux to Jerusalem*, tr. A. Stewart, Palestine Pilgrims' Text Society. 1887, p.25). Even if it is not genuine, its location doubtless corresponded with accurate knowledge of the position of Bethany.

[90] *War.* v, xii, 4; vi, i, 1.

belongs to the Franciscans corresponds very well to the general probabilities in the situation, however, and at least we can be certain that it was somewhere on the slope of this very hill that Jesus prayed.

JERUSALEM

From the western "descent" (Luke 19:37) of the Mount of Olives one looks directly across the Kidron Valley upon the Holy City. The city lies upon hills, 2,500 feet above sea level, yet in a sort of basin surrounded by somewhat higher ground. At the present time the city of Jerusalem is divided between the states of Jordan and Israel. As of the year 1955 the Government of Jordan reported a population of 92,658 in the sub-district of Jerusalem, and the Government of Israel reported for their side 146,000 inhabitants. The present city is built largely to the northwest of the ancient city, but it is possible nevertheless to recover a fairly accurate picture of the city of Jesus' time.

The site of Jerusalem (cf. pp.177f.) is a quadrilateral plateau, marked out on the east by the valley of the brook Kidron (II Samuel 15:23, etc.; John 18:1),[91] now known as the Wadi Sitti Maryam or "Valley of St. Mary," and on the west and south by the Valley of Hinnom (Wadi er-Rababi).[92] The steep walls of these valleys provided the city with naturally strong defenses on their respective sides but left the north and northwest sides vulnerable. The situation of Jerusalem is shown clearly in the aerial photograph reproduced in Fig. 116. In the immediate foreground are the slopes of the Mount of Olives and the Valley of the Kidron, at the left is the Valley of Hinnom, and at the right are the new northern suburbs. The prominent open area within the city walls is the Haram esh-Sherif where formerly the temple stood.

Within the city area there was a secondary valley, the Tyropeon,[93] which runs southward parallel to the Kidron Valley. Jerusalem has been destroyed and rebuilt so repeatedly that over much of the an-

[91] Eusebius, *Onomasticon*, see under *Cedron*, Κεδρών. ed. Clericus, p.52.

[92] The name Valley of Jehoshaphat (cf. Joel 3:2, 12) has been applied to both the Valley of the Kidron and the Valley of Hinnom. The Bordeaux Pilgrim, A.D. 333 (tr. Stewart, p.24), said, "Also as one goes from Jerusalem to the gate which is to the eastward, in order to ascend the Mount of Olives, is the valley called that of Josaphat," thus evidently referring to the Kidron Valley. Eusebius, however, states that this name was applied to the Valley of Hinnom (*Onomasticon*, see under Vallis Ennom, Φάραγξ 'Εννόμ. ed. Clericus, p.157).

[93] Josephus (*War*. v, iv, 1) called it "the Valley of the Cheesemakers" (Φάραγξ τῶν τυροποιῶν) and it is from this designation that the name Tyropeon is derived.

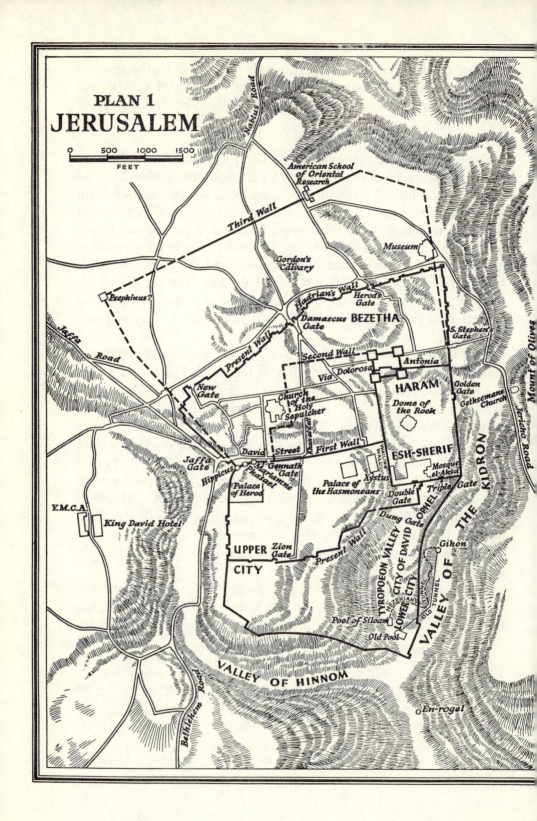

cient city forty to seventy feet of debris has accumulated, and the Tyropeon Valley today is largely filled up and remains only as a shallow depression called el-Wad. Formerly, however, it divided Jerusalem into two clearly defined parts. The broader and higher hill on the western side of the Tyropeon Valley was the site of the Upper City, which Josephus called the Upper Market. The lower eastern hill, which sloped down from the Temple area, was called Acra and was the site of the Lower City.[94] The Temple area itself was the "third hill" of Josephus, and northward of the Temple was the "fourth hill," where the growing city was spreading out. This last and newest part was called, according to Josephus, Bezetha (probably meaning "House of Olives") and also New Town.

In his description of Jerusalem, Josephus mentions three walls which were in existence in his time.[95] Of these, two had been restored by permission of Julius Caesar[96] and hence encompassed the city in the days of Jesus, while the third was begun by Herod Agrippa I. The latter desisted from finishing this wall, fearing that Claudius suspected him of intention to rebel, and the third wall was only completed by the Jews between A.D. 66 and 70. The first and most ancient wall ran from the side of the Temple area west to the three imposing towers named Hippicus, Phasael, and Mariamne. From there the wall ran south and then east along the edge of the Valley of Hinnom. Then it ran north and northeast, past the Pool of Siloam, and joined the Temple area at its southeast corner. From there the old wall was the same as the outer wall of the Temple. It ran north along the hill high above the Kidron Valley, and then, beyond the "Golden Gate," swung west to Antonia, the fortress which overlooked the Temple area at its northwest corner. From there it ran south along the western side of the Temple area to the point from which we described its beginning. The line of this wall from the Temple to Herod's citadel was probably just south of and parallel to the present David and Temple Streets, which are in the very heart of the modern city. The southern reaches of the wall as we have described it are now south of the present city wall and in less densely inhabited areas where

[94] *War.* v, iv, 1. According to Josephus' description, the Acra originally was higher than the Temple area and separated from it by a broad valley. The Hasmoneans cut down the height of Acra and filled in the intervening valley. Whether or not this tradition as to the earlier situation is correct, the hill doubtless was lower and the valley filled up in the time of Josephus, for he would have seen these facts with his own eyes. Josephus' error in locating the stronghold of David on the western instead of the eastern hill has already been noted (p.179 n.84).

[95] *War.* v, iv, 2.   [96] *Ant.* xiv, x, 5.

some excavation has been possible. Portions of the south and east walls and of the gates at the southwest and southeast corners of the ancient city have been uncovered.

"The second wall started," according to Josephus, "from the gate in the first wall which they called Gennath, and, enclosing only the northern district of the town, went up as far as Antonia." This wall apparently started north from the First Wall at a point some distance east of Herod's three great towers, for if the junction of the Second Wall had been at Hippicus, Phasael, and Mariamne these surely would have been mentioned instead of the otherwise never-mentioned Gate of Gennath, or Garden Gate. The latter gate was therefore presumably in the First Wall somewhere east of Hippicus, Phasael, and Mariamne.[97] In this case the Second Wall may have swung north just east of the present Church of the Holy Sepulcher, and then have turned eastward and run to Antonia. If this is a correct interpretation, the Second Wall was some distance inside the present northern wall of Jerusalem, which swings west far outside the Church of the Holy Sepulcher and runs east at a considerable distance north of the Temple area. As a matter of fact it is indicated now that the present north wall of Jerusalem corresponds to the north wall of the Roman colony of Aelia Capitolina founded by Hadrian in the second century (p.329).

If the foregoing interpretation is correct, the site of the present Church of the Holy Sepulcher (p.527) was in the time of Jesus outside the wall of Jerusalem, as the New Testament requires when it states that Jesus was crucified "outside the gate" (Hebrews 13: 12). The Church of the Holy Sepulcher is, of course, far inside the present northern city wall, and if that wall were to be identified with the Second Wall of Josephus then it would be necessary to seek the site of the crucifixion outside of it. It is far more probable,

[97] Dalman, *Sacred Sites and Ways*, p.375. A. T. Olmstead (*Jesus in the Light of History*, p.73 and Plan of Jerusalem) places the Gate of Gennath and the beginning of the Second Wall at the Tower of Hippicus. But immediately after stating that the second wall took its beginning at the Gate of Gennath, Josephus says that "The third [wall] began at the tower Hippicus" (*War*. v, iv, 2), which makes it improbable that the Gate of Gennath and the Tower of Hippicus were at the same point. Olmstead (pp.72,239) agrees, however, that the course of the Second Wall was such that the present site of the Church of the Holy Sepulcher lay in the time of Jesus outside the city wall. Against this view see N. P. Clarke in PEQ 1944, pp.201f. For some wall fragments which probably belong to the Second Wall and indicate a course for it such as I describe, and for the firm conclusion that the Second Wall did leave the site of the Church of the Holy Sepulcher outside the Jerusalem of Jesus' time see now André Parrot, *Golgotha and the Church of the Holy Sepulchre*. 1957, pp.21-23.

however, that the Second Wall ran inside the present location of the Church of the Holy Sepulcher and that the line of the present northern city wall only represents the wall built long after the time of Jesus by Hadrian. It is not necessary, therefore, to turn to a hill north of the present city wall known as "Gordon's Calvary" as the site of the crucifixion. The latter identification was suggested in 1842 by Otto Thenius, a German pastor from Dresden, to whom the hill in question seemed to have the appearance of a skull (cf. Mark 15:22 = Matthew 27:33 = Luke 23:33; John 19:17). Forty years later this view was adopted by General Charles G. Gordon and since has enjoyed a wide popular acceptance, the hill in question continuing to be known by Gordon's name.[98] A nearby rock-hewn tomb, known as the "Garden Tomb," may be as late as the third or fourth century A.D.

The Third Wall, which was built by Herod Agrippa I more than a decade after the death of Jesus, had its beginning, according to Josephus, at the familiar tower of Hippicus. Evidently it ran far north and then east, for it enclosed Bezetha, the newly-built part of the city north of the tower of Antonia and the Temple area, into which the city's increasing population had been overflowing, and which hitherto had been quite unprotected by a city wall. Finally it ran south or southeast and joined the Old or First Wall at the Valley of Kidron, that is at the northeast corner of the Temple area. The line of the present northern wall of Jerusalem would seem to fulfill these conditions, but discoveries have shown that Agrippa's "Third Wall" must have stood yet considerably farther north. Explorations carried out by Professors E. L. Sukenik and L. A. Mayer of the Hebrew University at Jerusalem traced considerable sections of a wall which ran north to a point near the present Swedish School, then east to the American School of Oriental Research, and finally southeast toward the Temple area.[99] A tower of this wall was found beneath the tennis court of the American School of Oriental Research in 1940,[100] and certain other portions of it were also found later.[101] Since these remains fit the description of Josephus, and since there was no "Fourth Wall" as far as we know, doubtless this was the Third Wall built by Agrippa.

[98] *Palästinajahrbuch des deutschen evangelischen Instituts für Altertumswissenschaft des heiligen Landes zu Jerusalem.* 9 (1913), pp.100f.; Bertha S. Vester, *Our Jerusalem, An American Family in the Holy City, 1881-1949.* 1950, p.97.

[99] Sukenik and Mayer, *The Third Wall of Jerusalem.* 1930.

[100] BASOR 83 (Oct. 1941), pp.5-7.   [101] BASOR 89 (Feb. 1943), pp.18-21.

Josephus described the towers Hippicus, Phasael, and Mariamne as "for magnitude, beauty and strength without their equal in the world."[102] In reality Hippicus was 80 cubits (120 feet),[103] Phasael 90 cubits (135 feet), and Mariamne 50 cubits (75 feet) in height. The bases were of solid masonry and above were rooms, battlements, and turrets. The three towers were named respectively for Herod's friend Hippicus, his brother Phasael (p.254), and his wife Mariamne whom he murdered (p.255). The towers doubtless stood in the neighborhood of the present Jaffa Gate, Hippicus and Phasael probably being represented by the northwest and northeast towers respectively of the present citadel (cf. p.179 n.84).

Herod's palace adjoined the three towers.[104] It was entirely walled about, to a height of 30 cubits (45 feet), the walls on the north and west being the same as the old city walls. Josephus professed his inability to describe it for its magnificence, but alluded to its "immense banqueting-halls and bedchambers for a hundred guests," and its grounds with canals and groves of various trees. In the days of the Roman procurators this building became their residence and seat of government when in Jerusalem,[105] which would suggest an identification of the Praetorium of Pilate (Mark 15:16) with Herod's former palace. Later tradition, however, located the Praetorium in the fortress Antonia. This fortress, which stood at the northwest corner of the Temple area, was rebuilt by Herod the Great and renamed Antonia in honor of Mark Antony, who at that time was still in power in the East.[106] It stood on a precipice nearly seventy-five feet high, and had four strong towers, themselves seventy-five or one hundred feet high, at its four corners. Within, it was fitted up with the magnificence of a palace, and Josephus says a Roman cohort was always stationed there.[107]

The central court of the Castle of Antonia has been excavated and underneath the so-called Ecce Homo arch which may belong to the time of Herod Agrippa I,[108] an earlier pavement has been brought to light consisting of huge slabs of stone three feet square and a foot or more thick. If Pilate was residing at the Castle of Antonia at the time

[102] *War.* v, iv, 3.
[103] The ordinary cubit was approximately 17½ inches, but there was also a royal or sacred cubit of about 20½ inches. For simplicity the figures above take the cubit as 1½ feet.
[104] *War.* v, iv, 4.   [105] *War.* ii, xiv, 8; xv, 5.
[106] *Ant.* xv, viii, 5; xi, 4; Tacitus (A.D. c.55-c.117), *Histories. v*, 11. tr. C. H. Moore, LCL (1925-31) ii, p.195.
[107] *War.* v, v, 8.   [108] Watzinger, *Denkmäler Palästinas.* ii, pp.57f.

when Jesus was brought before him, as he might well have been in order to be in close proximity to the Temple at the Passover season, then Antonia was the "Praetorium" and this courtyard pavement may have been the very Pavement that was called Gabbatha (John 19:13).[109] In that event the traditional Via Dolorosa[110] or "Way of Sorrows" which runs from here to the Church of the Holy Sepulcher may preserve the true general direction of the last journey of Jesus from the Judgment Hall to Golgotha.

At the eastern side of the Upper City and overlooking the Temple area across from its southwestern corner was a building that had been the palace of the Hasmoneans.[111] From it Herod Agrippa II enjoyed looking down into the Temple and observing what was done there. The priests obstructed his view by building a high wall which, when the affair was appealed to Nero, was allowed to stand.[112] On the lower slopes of the western hill, between Agrippa's palace and the Temple area, was the Xystus, apparently a sort of open-air gymnasium. From here a viaduct led across the Tyropeon and thus gave direct connection between the Upper City and the Temple area.[113] Remnants of the arches of two ancient bridges communicating between the Upper City and the Temple may still be recognized at the western wall of the Temple area. One, near the southwestern corner of the Temple area, is known as Robinson's Arch, and the other farther to the north, as Wilson's Arch.[114]

North of the Temple area, in the vicinity of the Church of Saint Anne, was the probable location of the Pool of Bethesda (John 5:2). Two cisterns found here gave the clue which led to further excavation, and the outlines of a large double pool have now been traced. The area occupied was over five thousand square yards in extent, and numerous fragments of columns and capitals show that fine balustrades and galleries surrounded the pools. Since these are in Roman style, and since a Hebrew graffito found there proves that the buildings were older than the time of Hadrian, it may be sup-

[109] Millar Burrows in BA 1 (1938), pp.17f.; Soeur Marie Aline de Sion, *La forteresse Antonia à Jérusalem et la question du Prétoire.* 1956.

[110] The first pilgrim to speak of treading "the way on which Christ walked carrying the Cross," and to describe its stations, was the preaching friar Ricoldus de Monte Crucis who visited Jerusalem in A.D. 1294. J. C. M. Laurent, *Peregrinatores Medii Aevi Quatuor.* 2d ed. 1873, p.112.

[111] Perhaps this is where Herod Antipas resided when in Jerusalem (Luke 23:7).

[112] *Ant.* xx, viii, 11.

[113] *War.* ii, xvi, 3; vi, vi, 2.

[114] Charles W. Wilson and R. E. Warren, *The Recovery of Jerusalem.* 1871, pp.58, 72-85.

posed that this impressive establishment was due to Herod the Great and was constructed in connection with his work on the Temple. The pools lay in a side-valley of the Kidron Valley, and were well situated to collect rain water. Perhaps some feature of the canals and conduits connected with the pools was responsible for the troubling of the water referred to in John 5:7. Since Jerusalem did not have too abundant water, it may be surmised that the Pool of Bethesda was utilized for many Christian baptisms, both in the first century and after. In the fifth century a Byzantine church was built at this place, some of the remains of which are still in evidence. Because of the perennial shortage of water at Jerusalem it may also be assumed as probable that conquerors of the city would not destroy its cisterns and pools, hence that the Pool of Bethesda was preserved and that the early Christian traditions about it were well founded.[115]

THE TEMPLE

The Temple itself was naturally the chief center of interest in Jerusalem. The Herodian temple[116] is described by Josephus[117] and also by the tractate Middoth ("Measurements"), which belongs to the second century A.D. and is to be found in the division Kodashim ("Holiness") of the Mishnah and the Babylonian Talmud.[118] These are the chief written sources which are available for the archeologist who endeavors to recover a picture of the Temple in the time of Jesus. In general they are good guides, but there is a tendency on the part of Josephus toward vagueness and exaggeration, and on the part of the author of Middoth toward ignoring things which were distinctively heathen.[119]

"In the fifteenth year of his reign," relates Josephus, Herod "restored the Temple and by erecting new foundation-walls enlarged

[115] Joachim Jeremias, *Die Wiederentdeckung von Bethesda.* 1949; cf. A. M. Schneider in *Beiträge zur biblischen Landes- und Altertumskunde.* 68 (1951), p.282. The feature of the troubling of the water has led some to identify the Pool of Bethesda with the Pool of Siloam, since the intermittent Gihon spring empties into the latter and could have produced the phenomenon. John 9:7, however, mentions the Pool of Siloam as a separate place, and therefore the hypothesis is unlikely.

[116] cf. above pp.179f. for the First Temple of Solomon, and p.195 for the Second Temple of Zerubbabel. For the entire history of the Temple see Parrot, *The Temple of Jerusalem.*

[117] *Ant.* xv, xi; *War.* v, v; cf. *Against Apion.* i, 22, where Josephus gives a quotation descriptive of the Temple from Hecataeus of Abdera (c.300 B.C.).

[118] DM pp.589-598; GBT IX, pp.675-689; SBT pp.1-38; cf. JE VIII, pp.545f.

[119] Hollis, *The Archaeology of Herod's Temple, with a Commentary on the Tractate 'Middoth,'* p.105.

the surrounding area to double its former extent."[120] This increase in the area available for the Temple and its courts must have been accomplished by building up the hill itself. Today there is to be seen underneath the southeastern corner of the Haram esh-Sherif an extensive system of vaults popularly known as "Solomon's Stables." In their present form these probably were constructed at a date later than that of Herod. They preserve, however, ancient materials and traces of old work which may indicate the kind of efforts Herod made to build up a larger court for the Temple. At its outermost "pinnacle" (cf. Matthew 4:5 = Luke 4:9), the Temple enclosure was lifted 170 feet above the gorge of the Kidron until, as Josephus said, "one who looked down grew dizzy."[121]

The limits of the Temple area as established by Herod the Great probably were the same as the present limits of the Haram esh-Sherif on the east, south, and west. On the north, however, the area now has been extended considerably farther than the limits of Herod's day. The Noble Sanctuary now includes part of the place where the Castle of Antonia then stood, and also extends over the fillings of what was then a ravine running diagonally into the Kidron Valley.[122] The northern limit in Herod's time was probably along a line joining the east wall at a point not far north of the present Golden Gate.

Whereas Solomon had built a wall on the east side of the sanctuary area but left the other sides exposed,[123] Herod the Great completed the enclosure of the Temple hill with lofty walls on all sides. Remains of the typical Herodian masonry, which employed very large stones carefully fitted together, still are to be seen in portions of the wall around the Haram esh-Sherif, notably including the "Wailing Wall" (Fig. 117). Above ground this wall probably has been reconstructed and the stones are not fitted together as carefully now as they were formerly, but otherwise it must appear much as it did in New Testament times. The nine lowest courses of stone consist of huge blocks, as was characteristic of Herodian masonry, the largest one being sixteen and one-half feet long and thirteen feet wide. Above are fifteen courses of smaller stones. The practice of the Jews, to lament the destruction of the Temple, is attested as long ago as

[120] *War.* i, xxi, 1.
[121] *Ant.* xv, xi, 5.
[122] Today the measurements of the area, outside the walls, are south side 929 feet, north side, 1,041 feet, east side 1,556 feet, west side 1,596 feet.
[123] *War.* v, v, 1.

the time of the Bordeaux Pilgrim (A.D. 333). He mentions two statues of Hadrian which had been erected at the place where the Temple stood and says that "not far from the statues there is a perforated stone, to which the Jews come every year and anoint it, bewail themselves with groans, rend their garments, and so depart."[124] What is meant by the "perforated stone" is uncertain but it may have been the sacred Rock (p.179) itself. Today it is the Herodian wall just described which is the wailing place of the Jews.

The outer court of the Temple area[125] was entered on the west by four gates, according to Josephus,[126] two of which were doubtless at the points indicated by Robinson's Arch and Wilson's Arch. Gates on the other sides are mentioned in the tractate Middoth. On the south were the two gates of "Chuldah,"[127] whose location is probably represented by the Double Gate and Triple Gate now walled up in the southern wall of the Temple area at a point some thirty-five feet below the present level of the Haram.[128] Ramps probably led from these gates up to the level of the court. On the east was the Shushan Gate, which probably was somewhat south of the present Golden Gate, a structure of the fourth or fifth century.[129] This is the gate which has been blocked up since A.D. 810 by the Arabs who fear that one day a conqueror will enter by it.[130] Finally, on the north was one gate, called Todi,[131] while in the northwest there were also steps to the Tower of Antonia. These last were the steps that the chief captain together with the soldiers and centurions "ran down" into the Temple on the occasion of the riot over Paul, and from which the apostle made his address to the people (Acts 21:32, 40).

[124] tr. Stewart, p.22.

[125] In the Gospels, "the temple" (τὸ ἱερόν) ordinarily means the entire area (Mark 11:11; 13:1, 3, etc.), although occasionally it refers to some particular part. "The sanctuary" (ὁ ναός) was the temple edifice itself, including the Holy Place and the Holy of Holies with the veil between them (Mark 15:38, etc.).

[126] *Ant.* xv, xi, 5; *Middoth.* i, 3 mentions only one, perhaps the principal one, on the west, named "Qiponos."

[127] Josephus says only (*Ant.* xv, xi, 5), "the fourth front of the temple, which was southward, had indeed itself gates in its middle."

[128] The "Single Gate" in the same wall is believed to be much later.

[129] This has been thought to be the Gate Beautiful of Acts 3:2, 10, ὡραία ("beautiful") having been taken over as *aurea* ("golden") in Latin, but more probably the Beautiful Gate was the one at the east entrance to the court of the women, which was distinguished by folding doors of Corinthian brass (*War.* v, v, 3).

[130] cf. Ezekiel 44:1f., which says that the east gate of the sanctuary should be shut because by it the Lord had entered in. For the traditions about this gate see Julian Morgenstern in HUCA 6 (1929), pp.1-37; 21 (1948), pp.459f.

[131] Josephus refers to it incidentally in *War.* vi, iv, 1.

Upon entering the outer court one found its walls lined with porticoes, or cloisters of double rows of marble columns, roofed with carved cedar. The east porticoes were said by Josephus to be the work of Solomon, and probably did at least survive from some earlier time, for they were in need of repair in the time of Herod Agrippa II.[132] This was probably the Solomon's Porch of the New Testament (John 10:23; Acts 3:11; 5:12). On the south, where the el-Aqsa mosque now is, were the royal porticoes, or Stoa Basilica, with 162 columns, each of such size that three men could just reach around it. These were arranged in four rows which formed three aisles.

Since even Gentiles were allowed access to this outer court, it is commonly designated the Court of the Gentiles. Within it was an inner court, set apart by a stone partition, beyond which none but Jews might pass. This was described by Josephus as follows: "Proceeding . . . toward the second court of the Temple, one found it surrounded by a stone balustrade, three cubits [about four and one-half feet] high and of exquisite workmanship; in this at regular intervals stood slabs giving warning, some in Greek, others in Latin characters, of the law of purification, to wit, that no foreigner was permitted to enter the holy place, for so the second enclosure of the Temple was called."[133] One of these stone slabs of warning was found at Jerusalem by M. Clermont-Ganneau in 1871 and is now in the Museum of the Ancient Orient at Istanbul, while part of another such inscription was discovered more recently.[134] The first-mentioned inscription is shown in Fig. 118. It is carved in a limestone block some twenty-three inches high, thirty-four inches long, and fifteen inches thick. The letters are over one and one-half inches in height. The inscription reads: "No foreigner[135] may enter within the balustrade and enclosure around the Sanctuary. Whoever is caught will render himself liable to the death penalty which will inevitably follow." In Acts 21:28f. Paul apparently was believed to have taken Trophimus beyond this barrier, and there may also be a side ref-

---

[132] *Ant.* xx, ix, 7.

[133] *War.* v, v, 2; cf. vi, ii, 4; *Ant.* xv, xi, 5. This is probably the same wall that is called the Soreg in *Middoth.* ii, 3, although the Soreg is described as only "ten handbreadths in height." Since in the Hebrew system one handbreadth equaled one-sixth of a cubit this would have been just about thirty inches in height. Perhaps there was at first only a low stone barrier on which the warning tablets were erected, and later the higher and exquisitely worked stone trellis was added which Josephus describes.

[134] QDAP 6 (1938), pp.1-3.

[135] The same word appears in Luke 17:18.

erence to it in Ephesians 2:14 where Paul speaks of "the dividing wall of hostility."

Within the wall beyond which Gentiles could not go were several courts together with their walls, gates, and terraces. The Women's Court represented the limit beyond which women might not go.[136] Farther on was the Court of Israel or Men's Court, and then the Court of the Priests.[137] In the Priests' Court and in front of the temple edifice itself was the altar upon which sacrifices and burnt-offerings were made.[138] It is not certain whether the altar stood upon the sacred Rock (es-Sakhra) or in front of it, but the former seems more probable (p.180).

The sanctuary or temple edifice itself stood within this inmost court and was approached by a flight of twelve steps.[139] It was built of white stones, to each of which Josephus assigns the enormous size of approximately thirty-five feet by twelve feet by eighteen feet.[140] In front its height and its breadth were equal, each being one hundred cubits (nearly 150 feet) according to Josephus, and it was covered all over with gold (cf. Matthew 23:16), so that it reflected the rising sun with fiery splendor.[141] Within, it was divided into two parts, the first of which was the Holy Place (cf. Exodus 26:33). In the Holy Place were the seven-armed lampstand, the table of showbread and the altar of incense. The second and most sacred part of the sanctuary was the Holy of Holies. "The innermost recess measured twenty cubits," says Josephus, "and was screened in like manner from the outer portion by a veil. In this stood nothing whatever: unapproachable, inviolable, invisible to all, it was called the Holy of Holy."[142] It was entered only once a year by the high priest on the Day of Atonement.[143]

The orientation of the Temple edifice was toward the east,[144] as was in accordance with general oriental practice, and the Holy of

---

[136] *War.* v, v, 2; *Ant.* xv, xi, 5; *Middoth.* ii, 5.

[137] *Middoth.* ii, 7.   [138] *Ant.* xv, xi, 5.

[139] *War.* v, v, 4.   [140] *Ant.* xv, xi, 3.   [141] *War.* v, v, 4f.

[142] *War.* v, v, 5; cf. Tacitus (*Hist.* v, 9) who says that after Pompey's conquest of Jerusalem and entry into the Temple (63 B.C.) "it was a matter of common knowledge that there were no representations of the gods within, but that the place was empty and the secret shrine contained nothing."

[143] Leviticus 16; *Tract Yomah.* RBT 3 (VI), pp.72f.

[144] cf. *The Letter of Aristeas.* 88. tr. H. St. J. Thackeray (1917), p.41: "The Temple looks towards the east, and its back is turned westwards." Precise measurements indicate that the east wall of the enclosure runs slightly toward the northwest, and is exactly at right angles to the line of direction between the sacred Rock and the summit of the Mount of Olives. But the eastern boundary of the "Platform of the Rock" runs due north and south and the inner courts and temple edifice probably had their eastern lines parallel with this.

Holies arose above or more probably, as we have seen (p.180), behind the ancient and sacred Rock.

The entire appearance of Herod's Temple must have been very impressive. Even Tacitus described it as "a temple of immense wealth,"[145] and the exclamation of one of the disciples of Jesus is recorded in the Gospels, "Look, Teacher, what wonderful stones and what wonderful buildings!" (Mark 13:1). Indeed the city as a whole must have presented the incoming visitor with a magnificent panorama. The Mount of Olives then as now would have provided the best point of view. From it one would have seen the Temple directly in the foreground, where the Dome now rises over the sacred Rock. Surrounded by sumptuous colonnades, its courts rose one within the other and each higher than the last to the inner sanctuary itself, whose marble and golden façade gleamed and glittered "like a snow-clad mountain."[146] At the northwestern corner of the Temple arose the powerful mass of the fortress Antonia, and beyond it, outside the wall, extended the villas of the northern suburb. To the south an uninterrupted sequence of houses and palaces fell away to the Pool of Siloam at the foot of the hill of Ophel. In the background on the western hill were ranged other populous quarters, crowned on the horizon by the imposing silhouette of Herod's Palace and Towers. "At no period of its history could the Sanctuary and City have presented a more inspiring aspect. The rhythm and harmony of Graeco-Roman art, so beautifully rendered against the oriental sky, restrained the louder tendencies of Herod himself, while infusing order and taste into the traditional chaos of the city."[147] The pride of the rabbis was not unjustified when they said, "He who has not seen Jerusalem in its beauty, has not seen a beautiful great city in his whole life; and who has not seen the building of the Second [i.e. Herod's] Temple, has not seen a handsome building in his life."[148]

6. THE LATER HISTORY OF JERUSALEM

BUT when the disciples were amazed at the splendor of the Temple, Jesus said, "Do you see these great buildings? There will not be left here one stone upon another, that will not be thrown down" (Mark 13:2 = Matthew 24:2 = Luke 21:6). His prophecy was fulfilled

---

[145] *Hist.* v, 8. [146] *War.* v, v, 6.

[147] J. Garstang in J. A. Hammerton, ed., *Wonders of the Past.* 1937, p.584.

[148] *Tract Succah.* v, 2. RBT 4 (VII), p.77; cf. *Baba Bathra.* I, 1. RBT 7, p.6, "It was said that he who had not seen the new Temple of Herod had not in all his life, seen a fine building."

swiftly. In A.D. 66, less than forty years after the death of Jesus,[1] the Jewish war broke out, an "utterly hopeless, and therefore unreasonable and disastrous struggle."[2] In A.D. 70, shortly before the Passover, Titus[3] (Fig. 119) and the Roman armies surrounded Jerusalem. A long and terrible siege ensued. Battering rams hammered against the walls, earthworks surrounded the city, and when the starving poor people slipped out to look for food the Romans caught and crucified them in sight of the city. Finally late in the summer Jerusalem fell, its beautiful temple was burned, and its people were slaughtered indiscriminately.[4] The city was razed to the ground and when Titus departed only Herod's towers—Hippicus, Phasael, and Mariamne—and a portion of the wall were left standing.

[1] According to John 19:14 the crucifixion was on the day of Preparation for the Passover, which doubtless means the fourteenth of Nisan, when the paschal lamb was slain. In agreement with this, Paul declares, "Christ, our paschal lamb, has been sacrificed" (I Corinthians 5:7); and a Baraitha or tradition of the Tannaitic period (A.D. 10-220) preserved in tractate Sanhedrin 43a in the Babylonian Talmud states, "On the eve of the Passover Yeshu was hanged" (SBT p.281; Morris Goldstein, *Jesus in the Jewish Tradition*. 1950, p.22). All four Gospels also place the crucifixion on a Friday, that day being followed by the sabbath and it by the first day of the week. The chronological problem, therefore, is to ascertain in what year, in the range of years which comes in question, the fourteenth day of Nisan fell on a Friday. By astronomical calculation this was the case in A.D. 30 and 33. In A.D. 30 Nisan 14 was Friday, April 7; in A.D. 33 it was Friday, April 3. If Jesus was baptized and began his public work in the autumn, A.D. 28 (see above p.250 n.4), crucifixion in A.D. 30 would mean a total ministry of about a year and a half, which is as much as the Synoptic record requires; crucifixion in A.D. 33 would mean a total of about four and a half years, which is enough to include the data of the Fourth Gospel. Perhaps John covers the entire ministry, the Synoptics only the latter and most critical part (Ethelbert Stauffer, *Jesus, Gestalt und Geschichte* [1957], pp.16f.). For the astronomical chronology see George Ogg, *The Chronology of the Public Ministry of Jesus*. 1940, pp.261-277; Johnston M. Cheney, "In What Year the Crucifixion?" paper read at annual meeting of the Society of Biblical Literature and Exegesis held at the Southern Baptist Theological Seminary, Louisville, Ky., Dec. 30-31, 1957. See also C. C. Torrey in JBL 50 (1931), pp.226-241; J. K. Fotheringham in JTS 35 (1934), pp.146-162; A. T. Olmstead in ATR 24 (1942), pp.1-26; and *Jesus in the Light of History*. 1942, pp.279-281; C. H. Kraeling in ATR 24 (1942), pp.336f.; T. J. Meek in JNES 2 (1943), pp.124f.; and articles in JQR 42 (1951-52), pp.37-44 (Percy Heawood), pp.45-50 (S. Zeitlin), pp.237-250 (Torrey), and pp.251-260 (Zeitlin). And see the Appendix in the present book.

[2] SHJP I, ii, p.209.

[3] The war against the Jews was begun by Vespasian but when he assumed the throne at Rome in A.D. 69 his son Titus took over the command of the Roman army in the Jewish war. Eventually Titus himself became emperor (A.D. 79-81).

[4] Rabbinic tradition (*Taanith*. IV. RBT 4 [VIII], pp.80,86f.) held that Herod's Temple was destroyed on the ninth day of Ab, even as the First Temple had been before it. II Kings 25:8f. and Jeremiah 52:12f. were interpreted by them as meaning that Nebuchadnezzar's men entered the Temple on the seventh day, ate and did damage in it also on the eighth and ninth and set it on fire toward the evening of the ninth, after which it continued to burn all day on the tenth. Josephus (*War*. VI, iv, 5) represents the same tradition that the Temple was burned by the Romans on the identical day that it was formerly burned by the king of Babylon, although he specifies the tenth instead of the ninth day of Lous or Ab. The month of Ab corresponded to our July-August.

In Rome the following year Titus celebrated his triumph, together with his father Vespasian. The triumphal procession was adorned by seven hundred of the most handsome Jewish prisoners and by abundant spoils of war. Speaking of the spoils, Josephus said, "Conspicuous above all stood out those captured in the temple at Jerusalem. These consisted of a golden table, many talents in weight, and a lampstand, likewise made of gold. . . . After these, and last of all the spoils, was carried a copy of the Jewish Law."[5] On the Arch of Titus, which was completed and dedicated *divo Tito*, "to the deified Titus,"[6] only after the death of the emperor (A.D. 81), was carved a representation of this event. It is in the form of a bas-relief (Fig. 120) on the passage of the arcade and shows a part of the triumphal procession. Roman soldiers, without weapons and crowned with laurels, are carrying the sacred furniture which was captured in the Temple. This included the seven-armed lampstand[7] and the table of showbread upon which the sacred trumpets are resting. Tablets fastened on staves are also to be seen, but the Law or Pentateuch mentioned by Josephus does not appear. In the relief on the other side of the passage Titus is shown, crowned by Victory, standing in a car drawn by four horses and conducted by a woman representing the city of Rome. In the relief under the vault the conqueror of the Jews appears once again, sitting on an eagle. The arch and the relief can be seen to this day in the city of Rome, a melancholy memorial to the Temple that is no more. The tradition still prevails there that no Jew ever passed beneath the arch.[8]

The Jewish national state and its central religious organization were now destroyed.[9] Judea was henceforth a Roman province separate from Syria and ruled directly by Roman governors residing at Caesarea. At Jerusalem, which had been razed to the ground, the Emperor Hadrian (A.D. 117-138) founded a new heathen city named Aelia Capitolina.[10] This provoked one more fanatical and useless

---

[5] *War.* VII, v, 5.   [6] M. da Firenze, *Itinerarium Urbis Romae*. 1931, p.141.

[7] Maximilian Kon (in PEQ 1950, pp.25-30) has shown that the seven-armed lampstand on the Titus Arch is a faithful representation of the Menorah in the Jerusalem Temple, even to the animal ornamentation on the base which shows the very kind of dragon which is explicitly allowed by the Talmud.

[8] JE XII, p.164.

[9] The Sanhedrin was superseded by the Bet Din, a court of much less political power (JE III, p.114), and the daily sacrifice was no more. Even the Jewish temple-tax was paid into the temple of Jupiter Capitolinus (p.371) in Rome (*War.* VII, vi, 6). But the Law still existed and the study of it was pursued more zealously than ever. The most notable center of rabbinical scholarship at this time was at Jamnia (p.303).

[10] *Colonia Aelia Capitolina*. It was called Aelia after Hadrian's family name, and Capitolina after the Capitoline Jupiter. cf. Ptolemy, *Geography*. v, 15. ed. Stevenson, p.128: "Hierosolyma which now is called Aelia Capitolia."

rebellion. It flamed out when Tineius Rufus was governor of Judea (A.D. 132). It was led by Bar Kokhba, "Son of a Star," in whom Rabbi Akiba saw the Messianic fulfillment of the prophecy in Numbers 24:17. The suppression of the rebellion was only completed by Julius Severus, who was sent to Judea from his governorship in Britain for that task. Bethar,[11] the last stronghold of Bar Kokhba and his followers, fell to Julius Severus in A.D. 135, and the final struggle of the Jews to regain independence was over.[12]

With the suppression of the rebellion, Hadrian, who was devoted to the erection of magnificent buildings and cities, was free to proceed energetically with the building of Aelia Capitolina. A Roman legion had continued to be garrisoned here since the time of Titus, and Greeks were now introduced in lieu of the Jews who were forbidden to enter the territory under pain of death. The city was divided into seven quarters, and many fine public edifices were built or rebuilt, including two baths, a theater, and the hippodrome. Two chief sanctuaries were established. On the site of the former Jewish temple of the Lord, a temple of Jupiter Capitolinus was erected.[13] In it Jupiter, Juno, and Minerva were represented and probably there was also a statue of Hadrian himself, while in the court in front of the temple there was a statue of the emperor on horseback. On the place where, according to Christian tradition, the sepulcher of Christ had been, a high terrace was constructed and a sanctuary of Venus (Aphrodite) erected.[14] On coins of the time it is represented as a round building with a dome. Within was a marble statue of the goddess.[15]

In A.D. 325 Jerusalem was made a Christian city by Constantine. The city was captured by the Neo-Persians under Khosroes II in A.D. 614, by the Arab Caliph Omar in A.D. 638, and by the Seljuk Turks in A.D. 1072. The crusader Godfrey de Bouillon took the city in A.D. 1099 and it was the seat of the Latin kingdom of Jerusalem until A.D. 1187, when it fell to Saladin. It was taken by the Ottoman Turks in A.D. 1517 and was entered by General Sir E. H. Allenby in December, 1917. In 1949 the Old City became a part of the Kingdom of Jordan, and the New City was made the capital of the State of Israel.

---

[11] Or Beth-ther. Probably the modern Bettir, some five miles southwest of Jerusalem. The rabbis said that like the Temple it too fell on the ninth of Ab (*Taanith.* IV; cf. p.328 n.4).

[12] Eusebius, *Ch. Hist.* IV, vi; Dio, *Roman History.* LXIX, 12-14.

[13] Dio, *Roman History.* LXIX, 12.

[14] Eusebius, *Life of Constantine.* III, 26 (NPNFSS I, p.527).

[15] Watzinger, *Denkmäler Palästinas.* II, pp.79f.

VI

Following Paul the Traveler

1. THE DECLINE AND DISAPPEARANCE
OF JEWISH CHRISTIANITY

I T WOULD be of much interest if any monuments were to be found
of the early Jewish Christian Church which had its center in
Jerusalem. In 1945 a chamber tomb was discovered and excavated near the Talpioth suburb south of Jerusalem beside the road
to Bethlehem, in which were some fourteen ossuaries, rectangular
stone chests for the bones of the dead. A coin of Agrippa I and pottery of late Hellenistic and early Roman style indicate a date around
the middle of the first century A.D. and almost certainly before
A.D. 70. Three ossuaries have Hebrew inscriptions which have been
read as the names Simeon Barsaba, Miriam daughter of Simeon, and
Mattathias in an abbreviated form. Two ossuaries have Greek inscriptions reading Ἰησοῦς ἰού and Ἰησοῦς ἀλώθ, and on the last burial
chest a rough cross, like a plus sign, is marked on each of the four
sides. It has been suggested that this was the tomb of a Jewish family
of Barsabbas, some of the members of which became early followers
of Jesus, and the inscriptions naming Jesus have been interpreted as
lamentations for the death of the founder of Christianity, ἰού being
taken as the interjection of grief in classical Greek, ἀλώθ being derived from a possible Hebrew and Aramaic root meaning "to wail"
or "to lament," and the plus marks being regarded as the Christian
sign of the cross. On this basis it has been suggested that these may

331

be "the earliest records of Christianity in existence."[1] Another interpretation reads the inscriptions as meaning, "Jesus, help," and "Jesus, let (him who rests here) arise,"[2] and this would also definitely connect them with early Christianity.

On the other hand, it may be that the inscriptions have nothing to do with Christianity but are simply Jewish.[3] The occurrence of the name Jesus is not unusual since it is found in at least seven other ossuary inscriptions of that time. It is possible that Ἰησοῦς ἰού means "Jesus, son of Jehu" (since ἰού is a normal transcription of the name Jehu in the Greek Old Testament[4]), or "Jesus, son of Eias" (taking ἰού as the genitive of Ἴας, a name attested in an Egyptian papyrus of the fourth century A.D.); and that Ἰησοῦς ἀλώθ means either "Jesus the Aloes" (explaining this as a nickname from the Hebrew name for the aloe plant), or "Jesus, son of Aloth" (since ἀλώθ appears as a personal name in a papyrus from the Fayum); and thus the references would be to persons other than the founder of Christianity. As for the cross signs, rather than regarding them as Christian symbols, one suggestion is that, since they appear on the sides of an ossuary otherwise marked only with the name on the top, they were simply intended to show to anyone viewing the receptacle from the side that it was already in use.[5] Another suggestion is that these were magical marks of protection.[6] Yet again it has been observed that in early Hebrew script the last letter of the Hebrew alphabet, Taw, was written with a cross sign either upright + or lying on its side ×. The word Taw also means "mark" or "sign," and occurs in Ezekiel 9:4 where those who are faithful to the Law of the Lord are marked with this sign on their foreheads to protect them from judgment. Thus it might be that the cross sign was used on some Jewish graves to signify that the one buried there was a follower of the Law and would be protected by the Lord in the judgment.[7] In view of these alternative explanations, therefore, it remains uncertain whether the Talpioth ossuaries are to be considered as monuments of early Jewish Christianity.

[1] E. L. Sukenik in AJA 51 (1947), pp.351-365.

[2] Berndt Gustafsson in NTS 3 (1956), pp.65-69.

[3] Carl H. Kraeling in BA 9 (1946), pp.16-20; J. Simons in *Jaarbericht No. 11 van het vooraziatisch-egyptisch Genootschap Ex Oriente Lux* (1949-50), pp.74-78.

[4] e.g. I Kings 16:1, LXX ed. Rahlfs, I, p.672.

[5] Harold R. Willoughby in JBL 68 (1949), pp.61-65.

[6] Edwin R. Goodenough, *Jewish Symbols in the Greco-Roman Period.* I (1953), pp.130-132.

[7] Erich Dinkler in ZTK 48 (1951), pp.148-172.

Recently another ancient cemetery has been discovered by chance on the Mount of Olives. This is in the vicinity of the Franciscan chapel known as *Dominus flevit* which marks the traditional place where Jesus wept over Jerusalem (Luke 19:41), and the tombs have been investigated by P. Bellarmino Bagatti.[8] It is indicated that this burial place was in use in the first century A.D. as well as later in the third and fourth centuries. Some thirty-six ossuaries were found which doubtless belong to the early period since the use of such burial chests is believed to have ceased in the second century A.D. These also have inscriptions, and a number of names are found which occur in the Gospels, Jairus, Martha, Mary, Salome, and Simon Bar-Jonah. On an ossuary bearing the name of "Judah the proselyte of Tyre" there is a monogram composed of the Greek characters Chi and Rho which, being the first two letters of the name Christ, are at least at a later date a well-recognized Christian symbol, the so-called Constantinian monogram (p.469 n.19). Another monogram combines the letters Iota, Chi, and Beta, which could stand for Ἰησοῦς Χριστὸς Βασιλεύς, "Jesus Christ King." And finally there is a carefully drawn cross, analogous to the marks at Talpioth. Again therefore, although alternative explanations may be preferable, the possibility is raised that these remains represent the early Jewish Christian community at Jerusalem.

At any rate the fate of Jewish Christianity was sealed with the fall of Jerusalem in A.D. 70. Already the church at Jerusalem had seen Stephen stoned (Acts 7:59), James the son of Zebedee beheaded (Acts 12:2), and James the brother of the Lord thrown from the pinnacle of the Temple, stoned and beaten to death with a club.[9] Then at the time of the Jewish war a revelation was received by the church to leave Jerusalem and migrate to Pella in Transjordan (p.309).[10] This was a Gentile city, hated by the Jews and laid waste by them at the beginning of the war,[11] but it offered refuge to the Christians. Jewish Christianity survived here for a time, as did different kinds of Jewish sects which also, for various reasons, had taken refuge east of the Jordan, and Christian bishops of Pella are mentioned as late as the fifth and six centuries A.D.[12] But the land east of the Jordan was apart from the main streams in which the history of

---

[8] RB 61 (1954), pp.568-570.
[9] Eusebius, *Ch. Hist.* II, xxiii.
[10] *Ch. Hist.* III, v, 2f.
[11] Josephus, *War.* II, xviii, 1.
[12] M. LeQuien, *Oriens Christianus.* (1740) III, pp.698f.

the future was to flow. In the isolation of its lonely deserts Jewish Christianity sank quietly into oblivion.[13]

2. THE WORK OF PAUL

THE wider world was to be won by that true and universal Christianity which found no room for distinctions of Jew or Greek but saw all as one in Christ Jesus (Galatians 3:28). It was Paul who recognized most clearly this universal character of Christianity and labored most effectively to put it into practice by launching a world-wide mission.

TARSUS

To follow the footsteps of Paul one must go far afield from Palestine. Tarsus of Cilicia is named in the book of Acts (9:11; 21:39; 22:3; cf. 9:30; 11:25) as the home of Paul. Tarsus was a meeting place of East and West. The two chief trade routes from the East, one coming from the Euphrates over the Amanus Pass and the other coming from Antioch by the Syrian Gates, united fifty miles east of Tarsus and entered the city as a single road. This road then ran northward toward the mountain wall of the Taurus thirty miles away. The road over these mountains is seventy or eighty miles in length. The actual pass, one hundred yards in length, is known as the Cilician Gates,[1] and is a place where dark cliffs narrow to a mere slit, at the bottom of which is a torrent. Engineering work done here, probably as long ago as 1000 B.C., opened the way to central Asia Minor and the West.

Tarsus itself was situated in the Cilician Plain. The "cold and swift" Cydnus River[2] flowed directly through the heart of the city, entered some miles beyond it a lake called Rhegma, and flowed on to the Mediterranean ten miles away. Shipping came at that time all the way up the river to the city,[3] and thus it was an important port as well as a center on the land route.

The history of Tarsus goes back to Hittite times, and the city is mentioned on the Black Obelisk of Shalmaneser III as one of the cities captured by him.[4] Xenophon (c.400 B.C.) found Tarsus "a

---

[13] Karl Pieper, *Die Kirche Palästinas bis zum Jahre 135.* 1938, p.58.
[1] Pliny, *Natural History.* v, 22.
[2] Strabo, *Geography.* XIV, v, 12; cf. Plutarch, *Life of Alexander.* XIX.
[3] Plutarch, *Life of Antony.* XXVI.
[4] ARAB I, §583.

large and prosperous city,"[5] and II Maccabees 4:30f. mentions an insurrection there which Antiochus IV Epiphanes hastened to quiet (c.170 B.C.). In the time of the Seleucids, Tarsus became strongly Hellenized, and in 64 B.C. Pompey made Cilicia a Roman province with Tarsus as the residence of the Roman governor. From the time of Antony and Augustus on it was a free city, densely populated and wealthy. Tarsus was also an intellectual center with a famed university. Strabo said, "The people at Tarsus have devoted themselves so eagerly, not only to philosophy, but also to the whole round of education in general, that they have surpassed Athens, Alexandria, or any other place that can be named where there have been schools and lectures of philosophers."[6] The most famous philosopher of Tarsus was the Stoic, Athenodorus, who was the teacher of the Emperor Augustus. Also Aratus, the Alexandrian poet of the third century B.C. whose *Phaenomena* was quoted by Paul at Athens according to Acts 17:28, was a native of Soli in Cilicia and was doubtless studied with pride in the schools of Tarsus.[7]

The ancient and splendid city of Paul is represented by the modern Tersoos, with 39,622 inhabitants according to the Turkish census of 1955. Beneath the grounds of the American Tarsus College there are enormous vaults which may have belonged to the hippodrome of Roman times, and at the southeastern edge of the town is the large mound of Gözlü Kule where excavations were conducted, beginning in 1934, by Bryn Mawr College.[8] A native factory of about the middle of the second century A.D. was unearthed. Apparently it had catered to the needs of the hippodrome and the theater, for it made terra-cotta figures of victorious charioteers and horsemen, lamps representing chariot races and gladiatorial combats, and theatrical masks. Here and elsewhere in the digging numerous representations of deities came to light, including Artemis, Athena, Apollo, Serapis, Isis, Aphrodite, Zeus, and Hermes. In the lower levels of the mound the excavators penetrated to remains of Hittite and Babylonian times.

Another link with the past is the trade of tent-making which is still carried on, as it was in the time of Paul (Acts 18:3). Goats

[5] *Anabasis.* I, ii, 23. tr. C. L. Brownson, LCL (1921-22) I, p.263.
[6] *Geography.* XIV, v, 13.
[7] Henri Metzger, *St. Paul's Journeys in the Greek Orient.* 1955, pp.47f.; cf. Henry J. Cadbury, *The Book of Acts in History.* 1955, pp.46, 48.
[8] Hetty Goldman in AJA 39 (1935), pp.526-549; 41 (1937), pp.262-286; and *Excavations at Gözlü Kule, Tarsus,* I, *The Hellenistic and Roman Periods, Text, Plates.* 1950.

living on the Taurus Mountains where the snow lies until May, grow magnificent coats whose hair has long been famous for strength and durability. This is spun into thread and woven into a tough fabric which anciently was known from the name of the province as *cilicium*. This fabric, in turn, is made into tents and other necessities.

DAMASCUS

The conversion of Paul to the faith which once he persecuted is intimately connected with the city of Damascus (Galatians 1:17; II Corinthians 11:32; Acts 9:1-25; 22:5-16; 26:12-20). Damascus lies in a fertile plain east of the Anti-Lebanon range, with snowy Mount Hermon filling the western horizon. The river el-Barada, "the Cool," runs through the heart of the city, while el-A'waj descends from the eastern slopes of Mount Hermon to water the southeastern plain. The Barada is doubtless the Abanah and the A'waj may be the Pharpar of II Kings 5:12, which Naaman thought "better than all the waters of Israel." So fertile is the oasis in which Damascus stands that the Arabian poets compared it with Paradise. The scene is indeed one of beauty with the white roofs, the domes, and the minarets of the city standing out against the green of the environing orchards.

Damascus is mentioned in Genesis (14:15; 15:2) as a city which was in existence in the days of Abraham, and in the fifteenth century B.C. was one of the places controlled by Thutmose III. After Alexander the Great, Damascus was possessed first by the Ptolemies and then by the Seleucids. Around 85 B.C. Antiochus XII was killed in the battle with the king of the Nabateans, and Damascus came under the control of the latter.[9] The Nabateans were a people who had established themselves beyond the Dead Sea in the district of Petra,[10] the ancient home of the Edomites, and the Nabatean king who conquered Antiochus XII was Aretas III (c.85-c.60 B.C.). In 64 B.C. Damascus was taken by the Romans under Metellus,[11] and thenceforward presumably belonged to the Roman province of Syria which was constituted soon afterward. At the time when Paul fled from Damascus, however, the city is stated to have been under a governor of Aretas the king (II Corinthians 11:32). This must have been the Nabatean king, Aretas IV, whose original name was Aeneas

[9] Josephus, *Ant.* XIII, xv, 1f.; *War.* I, iv, 7f.
[10] For Petra see William H. Morton in BA 19 (1956), pp.25-36; Peter J. Parr in PEQ 1957, pp.5-16.
[11] *Ant.* XIV, ii, 3; *War.* I, vi, 2.

and who reigned from 9 B.C. to A.D. 40. He is also known to us for his defeat of Herod Antipas in revenge for the divorce of his daughter by the latter (pp.255f.). Apparently, therefore, Damascus had been returned to the control of Aretas IV at the time to which II Corinthians refers. Some confirmation of this fact may be seen in the coins of Damascus, on which the image of Tiberius appears down to A.D. 34. Then in the time of Caligula (A.D. 37-41) and Claudius (A.D. 41-54) no Damascus coins are known which have the image of the Roman emperor. But coins of Nero begin again in A.D. 62. In the interval Damascus may have belonged to the Nabatean king.[12]

According to the census of 1952, Damascus had a population of 345,237. The East Gate (Bab esh-Sherqi) of the city probably dates from Roman times. It was a threefold archway, but two of the three arches are now walled up. The street which runs directly west from this gate through the city is still called Derb el-Mustaqim ("Straight Street") or Suq et-Tawileh ("Long Bazaar") and probably preserves the line of "the street called Straight" of Acts 9:11 (Fig. 121).

ANTIOCH

The Syrian city of Antioch, which is now in Turkey and is called Antakya, played an important part in early Christian history. It was there that "the disciples were for the first time called Christians" (Acts 11:26), and it was from there that Paul and Barnabas were sent out for wider missionary work (Acts 13:1-3).

Antioch lies on the Orontes River, about twenty miles from the Mediterranean, at the foot of Mount Silpius. Much information concerning the history and topography of the city is to be derived from the *Chronicle* of John Malalas (A.D. c.491-c.578), a Byzantine monk who was born and spent most of his life in Antioch. He relates that Seleucus I Nicator wished to build many cities and made a beginning at the sea of Syria. On the seashore at the trading place of Pieria he founded a city which he called Seleucia after his own name. Then "he built Antioch after the name of his son, Antiochus, surnamed Soter." John Malalas also says that Seleucus planted cypresses in Heraclea, which is now called Daphne, and states that "this same city was built outside a grove by the temple of Athena."[13]

Under Antiochus I Soter, Antioch became the capital of the west-

---

[12] SHJP I, ii, pp.357f.

[13] Matthew Spinka, *Chronicle of John Malalas, Books VIII-XVIII, translated from the Church Slavonic.* (1940) VIII, i-ii (pp.13-15).

ern part of the Seleucid Empire. This king also added a second quarter to the city on its eastern side. Later a third quarter was built by Seleucus II Callinicus on an island in the river; and a fourth was built by Antiochus IV Epiphanes on the slopes of Mount Silpius. Strabo says, "Antiocheia is . . . a Tetrapolis, since it consists of four parts; and each of the four settlements is fortified both by a common wall and by a wall of its own."[14]

Antioch fell into the hands of Tigranes of Armenia around 83 B.C., but about twenty years later was taken from him by the Romans and made a free city and the capital of the Roman province of Syria. It was further beautified by the Roman emperors, including Augustus and Tiberius, and Herod the Great paved one of its broad streets and erected colonnades along it.[15] Perhaps this was in appreciation of the very good relations which existed there between the Gentiles and the Jewish inhabitants, for in Antioch Jews were accorded the right of citizenship and "privileges equal to those of the Macedonians and Greeks who were the inhabitants."[16]

Josephus called Antioch the third city of the Roman Empire, only Rome and Alexandria taking precedence.[17] The city was known as "the Beautiful,"[18] but the reputation of its moral life was not good and Juvenal (A.D. c.60-c.140) described the flooding of Rome with the superstition and immorality of the East as a flowing of the Orontes into the Tiber.[19]

The present city of Antakya, with 37,484 inhabitants according to the census of 1955, covers only a fraction of the area of the ancient city and there is therefore excellent opportunity for archeological work. Excavations have been conducted here beginning in 1932 by Princeton University with the cooperation of the Baltimore Museum of Art, the Worcester Art Museum, and the Musées Nationaux de France.[20]

The island on which one of the principal districts of the city was

[14] Geography. XVI, ii, 4.
[15] Josephus, War. I, XXI, 11; Ant. XVI, v, 3.
[16] Ant. XII, iii, 1.   [17] War. III, ii, 4.
[18] Athenaeus (end of 2d cent. A.D.), The Deipnosophists. I, 20. tr. B. Gulick, LCL (1927-41) I, p.87; cf. the oration in praise of Antioch delivered probably in A.D. 360 by Libanius, a native of that city (Leo Hugi, Der Antiochikos des Libanios [1919]).
[19] Satire. III, 62. tr. G. G. Ramsay, LCL (1918), p.37.
[20] Antioch on-the-Orontes, Publications of the Committee for the Excavation of Antioch and Its Vicinity. I, The Excavations of 1932, ed. G. W. Elderkin. 1934; II, The Excavations 1933-1936, ed. Richard Stillwell. 1938; III, The Excavations 1937-39, ed. R. Stillwell. 1941; IV, 1, Ceramics and Islamic Coins, ed. Frederick O. Waagé. 1948.

built had disappeared from sight with the silting up of one of the channels of the Orontes, but in the excavations it was found again, and the wall which Justinian threw around the city in the sixth century was traced. Two ancient cemeteries of the second century A.D. were discovered, and the acropolis of the city was found to be on Mount Stauris instead of on Mount Silpius as was formerly supposed. The location was plotted of the two principal streets of the city, which had been famous in antiquity for their colonnades. The circus, which was one of the largest and most important in the Roman Empire, was found and excavated. It is believed to have been erected originally in the first century B.C. Other discoveries included baths, Roman villas, and a Byzantine stadium belonging to the fifth and sixth centuries.

Commanding the lower Orontes and looming above the sea south of the Gulf of Alexandretta is the mountain called Musa Dagh. The major portion of Antioch's seaport city, Seleucia Pieria, was built on a long, sloping spur of this mountain, and the city's walls ran on down to enclose the harbor, an area which now is largely marshland. Among the structures studied at Seleucia Pieria were the market gate, houses, the Doric temple of Hellenistic times, and the memorial church which will be referred to later along with the church at Kaoussie also near Antioch (pp.539-542).

The suburb of Daphne was on a plateau lying four or five miles southwest of Antioch and rising more than three hundred feet above the average level of the city. There are springs on the plateau, and the system of aqueducts by which their waters were carried to Antioch has been traced and studied. Beautiful pleasure villas were at Daphne, and there was a fine theater which was built in a splendid natural bowl formed by encircling hillsides on the slope of the plateau overlooking the valley of the Orontes. The theater was constructed probably around the end of the first century A.D.

Many sculptured pieces have been found, but doubtless the most spectacular finds at Antioch and its suburbs have been the numerous floor mosaics, many of which have been uncovered fortuitously or by the operation of natural forces. These extend in date from around A.D. 100 to the sixth century, and provide an unequaled wealth of material for the study of Greco-Roman mosaic art. One mosaic, which decorated the floor of the triclinium of a house belonging to the end of the first century A.D., portrays the judgment of Paris, and a drinking contest between Heracles and Dionysus, with the latter the victor. Other subjects include Oceanus and Thalassa in the midst of the fishes of the sea, landscapes, and hunting scenes, and an illustrated calendar in which the months of the year are personified as little figures carrying fruits and other symbols of the months.[21]

CYPRUS

The destination of Paul and Barnabas, when they were first sent out by the church at Antioch, was nearby Cyprus (Acts 13:4), one of the largest islands in the Mediterranean. The first appearance of Cyprus in history is when it was captured by Thutmose III of Egypt.[22] Later the island was colonized by the Phoenicians and the Greeks. About 58 B.C. it was taken from Ptolemy Auletes by Rome and later made a separate province.[23] In 22 B.C. it was transferred to the senate, and its governor therefore had the title of proconsul (cf. p.256 n.13). Acts 13:7 names a certain Sergius Paulus as proconsul when Paul came, and an inscription of the year A.D. 55 has been found at Paphos with the words "in the time of the proconsul Paulus."[24]

THE CITIES OF GALATIA

From Cyprus, Paul and Barnabas went to the mainland of Asia Minor. According to Acts (13:14, 51; 14:6) they preached there in Antioch of Pisidia, Iconium of Phrygia, and Lystra and Derbe of Lycaonia.

Pisidian Antioch[25] was another of the some sixteen Antiochs

[21] In connection with Antioch, the so-called "Chalice of Antioch" must be mentioned which is reported to have been found by natives at or near this city. It consists of an inner plain silver cup held in an outer openwork gilded shell and set on a solid silver base. The openwork holder is decorated with vines, birds, and animals, and twelve seated human figures. The last are divided into two groups, in each of which five persons are placed about one central figure. Evidently the central figure in each of the two groups is Christ and the others are his apostles. A first century date has been advocated vigorously for this remarkable object, with the additional suggestion that the inner cup is nothing other than the Holy Grail (Gustavus A. Eisen, *The Great Chalice of Antioch*. 1933), but on the other hand the authenticity of the chalice has been called in question (C. R. Morey in *Art Studies, Medieval, Renaissance and Modern* 3 [1925], pp.73-80), and the most that can be said is that it may be a piece of early Christian silver from the fourth or fifth century (H. Harvard Arnason in BA 4 [1941], pp.49-64; 5 [1942], pp.10-16).

[22] ARE II, §§493, 511 (Isy = Cyprus).   [23] Strabo, *Geography*. XIV, vi, 6.

[24] Stephen L. Caiger, *Archaeology and the New Testament*. 1939, p.119.

[25] Ptolemy, *Geography*. V, 4. ed. Stevenson, p.116: *Antiochia Pisidiae*. Strabo, *Geography*. XII, viii, 14 (cf. XII, vi, 4): Ἀντιόχεια ἡ πρὸς Πισιδίᾳ καλουμένη. For the designation see William M. Calder, ed., *Monumenta Asiae Minoris Antiqua*, VII, *Monuments from Eastern Phrygia*. 1956, p.xi.

founded by Seleucus I Nicator, and it was made a free city by the Romans about 189 B.C. and a Roman colony by Augustus before 11 B.C. Antioch was in the extreme northeast of the district of Pisidia and on the frontier of the district of Phrygia. The Pisidians and the Phrygians were peoples of less high civilization but Antioch itself was a thoroughly Hellenized and Romanized city.

The site of Antioch was on the lower slopes of a majestic mountain now called Sultan Dagh, and on the right bank of the Anthius River. The place was discovered in 1833 by Francis V. J. Arundell, British chaplain at Smyrna, and is near the modern Turkish town of Yalovach. The ruins show that Antioch was a strongly fortified city, and the remains of the Roman aqueduct which brought water from the foothills of the Sultan Dagh still are to be seen.[26] The principal temple was dedicated to the god Men and was studied by William Ramsay just before the First World War. The great altar and many engraved tablets were uncovered, and the underlying soil was found to be full of the bones of sacrificial animals. An inscription was found which referred to a "Lucius Sergius Paullus the younger," whom Ramsay believed to be the son of Sergius Paulus, proconsul of Cyprus.[27]

Later, more intensive excavations were conducted by the University of Michigan,[28] and the most important remains of the Roman city founded by Augustus were brought to light. The city enjoyed two fine squares, the upper known as the Augusta Platea or Square of Augustus and the lower as the Tiberia Platea or Square of Tiberius. The two were connected by a broad flight of steps, at the top of which stood the three triumphal archways of the propylaea erected in honor of Augustus. The archways were adorned with many relief sculptures and probably were once surmounted with statues in the round as well. The reliefs in the spandrels of the arches portrayed captive Pisidians and commemorated the victories of Augustus on land, while a frieze with Poseidon, Tritons, dolphins, and other marine symbols celebrated his triumphs at sea, especially at Actium.

On the Square of Augustus stood the great temple, which was not Hellenistic as Ramsay believed but also belonged to the age of Augustus. A wonderful frieze of bulls' heads adorned the temple,

[26] W. M. Ramsay, *The Cities of St. Paul.* 1907. Plate facing p.252.

[27] W. M. Ramsay, *The Bearing of Recent Discovery on the Trustworthiness of the New Testament.* 4th ed. 1920, pp.150f.; Egbert C. Hudson in JNES 15 (1956), pp.103-107.

[28] David M. Robinson in AJA 28 (1924), pp.435-444.

the heads being connected by garlands of leaves and all kinds of fruits realistically rendered. The bull's head was the symbol of Men, who was the local god upon whom the prosperity of agriculture was believed to depend. As the god who bestowed all blessings upon the people, it was not difficult also to identify him with the Roman emperor Augustus.

Both the architecture and the sculpture of these first century structures were very impressive. "Nowhere else in the Roman empire has yet been discovered a better combination of superb realistic sculpture with excellent solid architecture in excellent vertical and horizontal rhythm," says David M. Robinson. "Greek refinement and restraint seem here to be combined with Roman luxuriance, Greek simplicity with Roman complexity, Greek beauty with Roman realism and massiveness."[29]

Another monumental structure at Pisidian Antioch was a triple gateway built into the city wall. It bore an inscription, in bronze letters which are preserved, of G(aius) Jul(ius) Asp(er), consul in A.D. 212, and was adorned with sculptures, but of a quality inferior to those of the propylaea and the temple. Other discoveries included numerous terra-cotta pipes through which the spring water brought by the aqueduct was distributed throughout the city; playing-boards, incised with circles and rectangles, where the Romans spent their idle hours in various games; and a Latin edict of Domitian's praetorian legate L. Antistius Rusticus which prescribed measures for preventing profiteering, controlling the price of grain after a severe winter and ensuring sufficient seed for the next season. Also there was a Christian basilica at Antioch which was more than two hundred feet long, and which dates, according to an inscription, in the time of Optimus, who was bishop of Antioch in the last quarter of the fourth century.

Iconium was sixty miles distant from Antioch to the southeast, on the frontier between Phrygia and Lycaonia. Therefore it was sometimes considered as the last city of Phrygia,[30] and was sometimes spoken of as belonging to the neighboring district of Lycaonia.[31] In Acts 14:6 it is regarded as belonging to Phrygia, for it is implied that in fleeing from Iconium to Lystra and Derbe Paul went from Phrygia to Lycaonia.[32]

[29] Robinson in AB 9 (1926-27), p.6.
[30] Xenophon, *Anabasis.* I, ii, 19.   [31] Strabo, *Geography.* XII, vi, 1.
[32] W. M. Ramsay, *A Historical Commentary on St. Paul's Epistle to the Galatians.* 1900, p.215.

The ancient Iconium is now known as Konia or Konya, and is a relatively modern Turkish city with 93,125 inhabitants according to the census of 1955. It is in a plain watered by streams from the Pisidian mountains, and nearby are twin conical hills known as the peaks of St. Philip and St. Thecla. Thecla was the young woman of Iconium who was associated with the apostle Paul in the apocryphal Acts of Paul. The latter is the work which contains the famous description of Paul as "a man of little stature, thin-haired upon the head, crooked in the legs, of good state of body, with eyebrows joining, and nose somewhat hooked, full of grace: for sometimes he appeared like a man, and sometimes he had the face of an angel."[33]

Lystra and Derbe were in the region of Lycaonia, and in the first century the common people still spoke the native Lycaonian language as is indicated in Acts 14:11. Lystra was some twenty-five miles from Iconium, and its site was discovered in 1885 by J. R. Sitlington Sterrett. It was identified by an altar still standing in its original position. This was a stone, about three and one-half feet high and twelve inches thick, with a clearly cut Latin inscription (Fig. 122). The inscription gave the usual Roman spelling of the city's name, Lustra, and indicated that it was a Roman colony.[34]

Derbe was presumably farther east and south in the same district, and has been thought to be represented by the large mound of Gudelisin, which was also first observed by Professor Sterrett.[35] In 1956, however, there was found at Kerti Hüyük, a mound more than thirty miles east and somewhat north of Gudelisin, an inscription dated in A.D. 157 which contains a dedication by the council and assembly of the people of Derbe, and which makes it probable that Derbe was located at this site.[35a]

In New Testament times all four of these cities—Antioch, lconium,

[33] JANT p.273.

[34] Sterrett, *An Epigraphical Journey in Asia Minor.* 1888; Ramsay, *A Historical Commentary on St. Paul's Epistle to the Galatians,* p.224.

[35] Ramsay, *The Cities of St. Paul,* p.452 n.18. The location on our Map 6 corresponds to this identification.

[35a] . . . .] δερβητῶν ἡ βουλὴ κ-

αἰ ὁ δ]ῆμος . . . .

M. Ballance in *Anatolian Studies.* 7 (1957), pp. 147-151. For δερβήτης as the designation of an inhabitant of Derbe see Strabo, *Geography.* XII, vi, 3. In view of the distance from Lystra to the new site for Derbe, it may be noted that Acts 14:20 does not require that Paul and Barnabas went all the way from the one place to the other in one day, rather it is simply stated that on the morrow they went forth from Lystra toward (εἰς) Derbe, that is to go on the trip to Derbe.

Lystra, and Derbe—were included in the Roman province of Galatia. The Roman province took its name from the smaller northern district of Galatia proper which it included. This ethnographical district of Galatia proper was named from three Gallic tribes which entered Asia Minor around 278-277 B.C. and settled permanently in this region. In 64 B.C. they became a client state of the Roman Empire, and in the following years were able to extend their territory to include the whole center of Asia Minor. Amyntas, their last native king, ruled over Galatia, Phrygia-towards-Pisidia, Pisidia, Lycaonia, and part of Pamphylia.[36] Upon the death of Amyntas in 25 B.C. this kingdom was bequeathed to the Romans,[37] and became the Roman province of Galatia. The new province at first included the entire kingdom of Amyntas, but it was somewhat reduced in size in 20 B.C.[38] Thereafter, however, it continued to comprise Galatia proper, Pisidia, and western Lycaonia.[39] Thus Antioch, Iconium, Lystra and Derbe were all within the boundaries of the Roman province of Galatia.[40]

Paul's letter addressed "to the churches of Galatia" (Galatians 1:2) presumably went, therefore, to the churches of Antioch, Iconium, Lystra, and Derbe, which he himself had founded. To address them as "churches of Galatia," meaning the Roman province of Galatia, was entirely correct.[41] Those who insist on confining the word "Galatia" to its strict ethnographical meaning, on the other hand, believe that the letter was intended for otherwise unknown Christian churches in north Galatia proper.[42] This is less probable, and the first time that the existence of a Christian congregation at Ancyra is even

---

[36] CAH p.69.

[37] King Amyntas was taken prisoner and put to death by the brigand tribes of the Taurus known as Homanadenses. Augustus ultimately avenged the death of his subject king by sending out Publius Sulpicius Quirinius as consul to "pacify" the Homanadensians, which was done with characteristically cruel Roman thoroughness perhaps in the years 10-7 B.C. This was the Quirinius who was also governor of Syria (pp.258f.). CAH x, pp.271f.

[38] Eastern Lycaonia, together with Cilicia Tracheia, was transferred to the rule of the king of Cappadocia.

[39] CAH x, p.261.

[40] Ramsay, The Cities of St. Paul, pp.262f., 343, 401. For Paul's journeys in this region see also T. R. S. Broughton in Quantulacumque, Studies Presented to Kirsopp Lake by Pupils, Colleagues, and Friends, ed. by Robert P. Casey, Silva Lake, and Agnes K. Lake. 1937, pp.131-138.

[41] Ramsay, A Historical Commentary on St. Paul's Epistle to the Galatians; and in HDB II, pp.81-89; Edgar J. Goodspeed, The Story of the New Testament. 1916, p.9; Frederic Rendall in The Expositor's Greek Testament. III, p.128.

[42] Paul W. Schmiedel in T. K. Cheyne and J. Sutherland Black, eds., Encyclopaedia Biblica. 1899-1903, cols. 1592-1616; James Moffatt, An Introduction to the Literature of the New Testament. 3d ed. 1918, pp.90-101; and in EB IX, p.972.

mentioned is in A.D. 192.[43] Ancyra was the chief city of north Galatia and the capital of the entire province. The real greatness of this place dated from the time when Constantinople became the Roman metropolis and the location of Ancyra gave it a lasting importance. Today it is the modern Angora or Ankara, the capital of Turkey. Its most important monument is the Augusteum, a white marble temple which the council of the three Galatian tribes erected to Rome and Augustus during the lifetime of Augustus. On its walls is carved a long inscription in Latin and Greek narrating the public life and work of the emperor. The original which is now lost was composed in a dignified style by Augustus himself and was completed in A.D. 14, to be engraved on bronze tablets in front of his mausoleum in Rome. Fragments of other copies of the same text have been found also at Pisidian Antioch and at Apollonia.[44]

EPHESUS

Ephesus was the city of Asia Minor where Paul worked for the longest time (Acts 19:1-20:1). The earliest inhabitants of Ephesus were of Asiatic origin, and early in the first millennium B.C. the Ionian Greeks settled there. In the sixth century B.C. the city fell to Croesus of Lydia and then to Cyrus of Persia. Around 334 B.C. Ephesus came under the control of Alexander the Great, and later was held by the Seleucids of Syria. When the Romans defeated Antiochus III the Great in 190 B.C. they handed over Ephesus to Eumenes II (197-159 B.C.), king of Pergamum. It was Eumenes II who built the great Altar of Zeus at Pergamum which was reconstructed so splendidly in the Berlin Museum. This great structure was erected in celebration of the victory of Eumenes over the Gauls around 180 B.C. and is adorned with a frieze of magnificent sculptures depicting the combat of gods and giants. The remains of the Temple of Rome and Augustus have also been discovered at Pergamum. This temple was founded in 29 B.C. and was the first in the empire to be dedicated to the cult of Roman emperor worship, with which Christianity was to come into such serious conflict. Either the Altar of Zeus or the Temple of Rome and Augustus was probably the "Satan's throne" of Revelation 2:13.[45]

---

[43] EB I, p.893.
[44] *Res Gestae Divi Augusti.* tr. F. W. Shipley, LCL (1924).
[45] *Altertümer von Pergamon.* 10 vols. 1912-37; Hans Erich Stier, *Aus der Welt des Pergamonaltars.* 1932; Heinz Kähler, *Pergamon.* 1949; Arnold Schober, *Die Kunst von Pergamon.* 1951.

In 133 B.C. the last king of Pergamum, Attalus III Philometor, bequeathed Ephesus, together with the rest of the Pergamenian kingdom, to the Romans and thereafter it continued subject to them. At first Pergamum remained the capital of the Roman province of Asia, but eventually this honor passed to Ephesus. Whether it had become the capital in the time of Paul is uncertain. At any rate Ephesus was "the largest emporium in Asia this side of the Taurus,"[46] and ranked along with Antioch in Syria and Alexandria in Egypt as one of the three great cities of the eastern Mediterranean. This prominence it owed very largely to its favorable geographical location, for it was on the main line of communication between Rome and the Orient in general. The city was situated within three miles of the sea, on the left bank of the river Cayster. At that time this river was navigable as far up as the city, although attention was required to keep the city harbor and the channel of the Cayster free from silt. A breakwater was built under the Pergamenian king Attalus Philadelphus (159-138 B.C.), with the intention of contributing to this end but unfortunately it had the opposite result and made the harbor shallower. Around A.D. 65 the governor of Asia took further measures to improve the connection between harbor and sea.[47] In later centuries the engineering work necessary to maintain the harbor was neglected, and now the mouth of the river has been silted up badly and the harbor reduced to a marsh.

From Ephesus, the Cayster Valley offered the shortest route to Pisidian Antioch and the East. The way was relatively steep, but nevertheless was often preferred by travelers on foot because of its shorter distance. This could have been the route taken by Paul in Acts 19:1. The alternative was the longer but more level route on which the heavier traffic moved, which crossed a six-hundred-foot pass to the south of Ephesus and then followed the Meander and Lycus Valleys eastward by Laodicea even as the modern railroad does.[48]

The railroad station nearest to the site of Ephesus today is the small village of Ayasoluk, or Seljuk as the Turks call it. Ayasoluk is a corruption of Agios Theologos, as St. John "the Theologian" was

---

[46] Strabo, *Geography*. XIV, i, 24.

[47] Tacitus, *Annals*. XVI, 23. tr. J. Jackson, LCL (1931-37) IV, p.373.

[48] For Laodicea and neighboring cities, and the Lycus Valley, see Sherman E. Johnson in BA 13 (1950), pp.1-18. And for conditions involved in visiting Pauline sites from Syrian Antioch to Ephesus, and the cities of the Revelation, as they prevailed at the date of the article, see Robert North in CBQ 18 (1956), pp.30-35.

122. Inscription at Lystra

121. Straight Street in Damascus

123. The Theater at Ephesus

124. Air View of Philippi

125. The Temple of Zeus, with the Acropolis in the Background

126. The Altar to Unknown Gods at Pergamum

127. Ruins of the Temple of Apollo at Corinth, with Acrocorinth in the Background

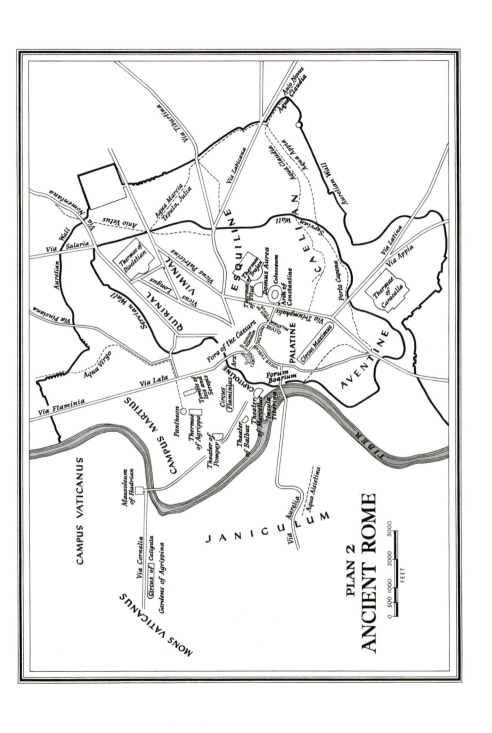

PLAN 2
ANCIENT ROME

CAMPUS VATICANUS

MONS VATICANUS

Via Cornelia
Circus of Caligula
Gardens of Agrippina

Mausoleum
of Hadrian

Via Aurelia

Aqua Alsietina

J A N I C U L U M

TIBER

CAMPUS MARTIUS

Pantheon
Thermae
of Agrippa
Theater
of Pompey
Theater
of Balbus
Theater
of Marcellus
Temple of
Isis and
Serapis
Circus
Flaminius

Via Flaminia

Via Lata

Aqua Virgo

Via Pinciana

Aurelian Wall

Via Salaria

Via Wall

Via Nomentana

Anio Vetus

Aqua Marcia,
Tepula, Julia

Via Tiburtina

Via Labicana

Thermae of
Diocletian

Vicus Longus

Vicus Patricius

QUIRINAL

VIMINAL

Servian Wall

E S Q U I L I N E

Thermae
of Trajan
Domus Aurea
Colosseum
Arch of
Constantine
Thermae
of Constantine

Fora of the Caesars

CAPITOLINE

Arx

CLIVUS

PALATINE

Via Triumphalis

Forum
Boarium

Insula
Tiberina

VICUS TUSCUS

Circus Maximus

A V E N T I N E

C A E L I A N

Servian Wall

Porta Capena

Via Appia

Via Latina

Thermae
of
Caracalla

Aurelian Wall

Aqua Claudia
Anio Novus

Anio Novus
Claudia
Aqua

0 500 1000 2000 3000
FEET

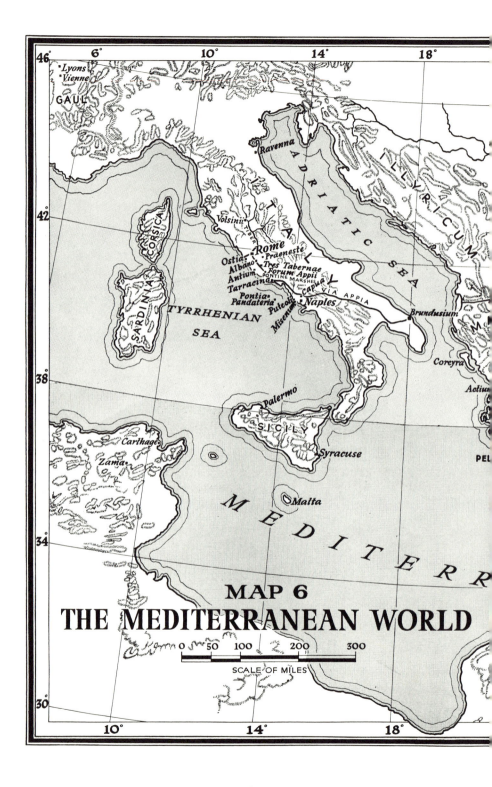

MAP 6
THE MEDITERRANEAN WORLD

0 50 100   200   300
SCALE OF MILES

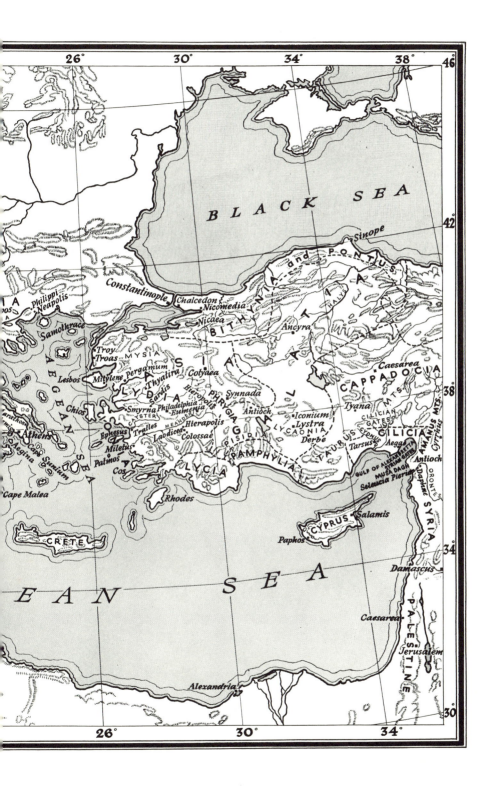

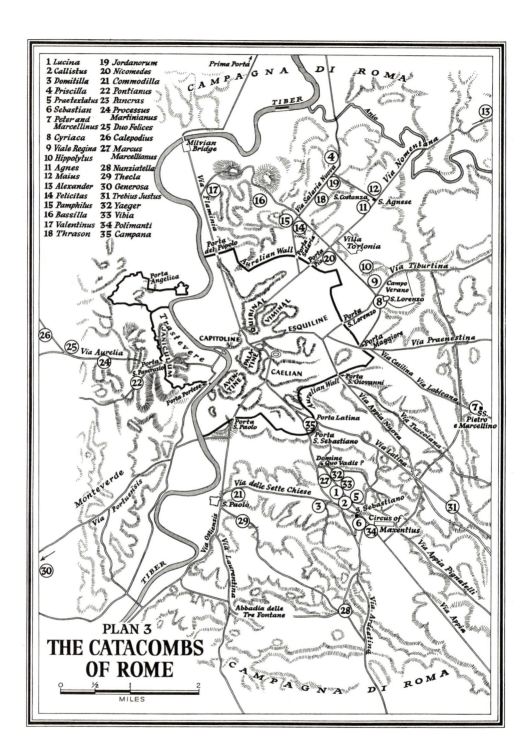

1 Lucina
2 Callistus
3 Domitilla
4 Priscilla
5 Praetextatus
6 Sebastian
7 Peter and Marcellinus
8 Cyriaca
9 Viale Regina
10 Hippolytus
11 Agnes
12 Maius
13 Alexander
14 Felicitas
15 Pamphilus
16 Bassilla
17 Valentinus
18 Thrason
19 Jordanorum
20 Nicomedes
21 Commodilla
22 Pontianus
23 Pancras
24 Processus Martinianus
25 Duo Felices
26 Calepodius
27 Marcus Marcellianus
28 Nunziatella
29 Thecla
30 Generosa
31 Trebius Justus
32 Yaeger
33 Vibia
34 Polimanti
35 Campana

PLAN 3
THE CATACOMBS OF ROME

0   ½   1   2
MILES

128. The Agora at Corinth

129. Nero

130. The Appian Way and the Claudian Aqueduct

131. Caricature of the Crucifixion

132. The Roman Forum

133. The Pyramid of Cestius and the Gate of St. Paul

called, to whom Justinian dedicated here a fine church.[49] The houses of Ayasoluk mostly are made of stones brought from the ruins of Ephesus, a mile or two away to the southwest.

Ephesus was particularly famous for the worship of Artemis and the Artemision or temple of this goddess was accounted one of the seven wonders of the ancient world. The goddess originally had been a Lydian deity of character similar to the Phrygian Cybele and the Phoenician Astarte. The Greek colonists in Ephesus identified her with their own Artemis, who was known to the Romans as Diana. The first systematic exploration of Ephesus was carried out by the English architect, J. T. Wood, whose chief purpose was to find the famous temple of Artemis. The search was begun on May 2, 1863, and after the most persistent endeavor the temple wall was discovered on May 2, 1869. The clue which led to the discovery was a Roman inscription which was found in the course of clearing the theater and which dates in the time of Trajan, that is about fifty years after the time of Paul. This inscription described a number of gold and silver images of Artemis (cf. Acts 19:24), weighing from three to seven pounds each, which were to be presented to the goddess and placed in her temple. According to the inscription, an endowment was provided for the care and cleaning of the images, and instruction given that when they were carried from the temple to the theater for the birthday anniversary of the goddess the procession was to enter the city by the Magnesian Gate and leave it afterward by the Coressian Gate. By finding the site of the two city gates mentioned and then following the road from the Magnesian Gate, Wood finally discovered the temple, which stood more than a mile northeast of the city proper.[50]

Wood continued his work until 1874, and in 1904-1905 further excavations were made and the entire history of the temple studied by David G. Hogarth on behalf of the British Museum.[51] In the meantime in 1896 the Austrian Archaeological Institute began its thorough and long-continued excavations at Ephesus, the results of which have appeared in a series of impressive publications.[52]

[49] Procopius (A.D. c.490-c.562), *Buildings*. v, i, 4-6. tr. H. B. Dewing, LCL VII (1940), pp.317-319.

[50] J. T. Wood, *Modern Discoveries on the Site of Ancient Ephesus*. 1890, pp.37-41, 84.

[51] Hogarth, *Excavations at Ephesus, The Archaic Artemisia*. 1908; and in EB VIII, pp.641-644.

[52] *Forschungen in Ephesos, veröffentlicht vom Österreichischen archaeologischen Institute*. 5 vols. 1906-44. For the excavations as resumed in 1954 see L. Vanden

It is believed that the earliest beginnings of the Artemision go back to a time around the end of the eighth century B.C. At that time only a small shrine was in existence, being little more than an enclosure containing a platform, a sacred tree, and an altar, and perhaps later a wooden image. In the centuries immediately following this shrine was reconstructed at least twice. Later these primitive structures were replaced by a much larger and more splendid temple which was probably begun about 550 B.C., and to which Croesus, the famous king of Lydia, contributed some beautiful columns.[53] The building work continued for 120 years,[54] and the final dedication was around 430 B.C. Herodotus speaks of this temple as standing in his day, and tradition has it that it was burned in 356 B.C. on the night in which Alexander the Great was born.

This temple, in turn, was succeeded by what is known as the Hellenistic temple, the plans for which were drawn by Dinocrates, the famous architect of Alexandria. This structure was begun probably before 350 B.C. and work was continuing on it when Alexander came to Ephesus in 334 B.C. and offered to pay the cost of its completion. It stood on a large platform nearly 240 feet wide and over 400 feet long. The temple itself was 180 feet wide and 360 feet long and boasted more than one hundred columns over fifty-five feet high. This Hellenistic temple endured until A.D. 262, when it was sacked and burned by the Goths. The altar foundations have been discovered, behind which no doubt stood the statue of the goddess. The roof was covered with large white marble tiles, and the building was adorned with sculpture, painting, and gold. The cry, "Great is Artemis of the Ephesians" (Acts 19:28, 34) was fully justified, therefore, by what we know of the external splendor of the cult center.[55]

Berghe and H. F. Mussche, *Bibliographie analytique de l'Assyriologie et de l'archéologie du Proche-Orient,* I, A, *L'Archéologie 1954-1955,* p.23.

[53] Herodotus. I, 92; A. S. Murray in JHS 10 (1889), p.9.

[54] Pliny, *Natural History.* XXXVI, 14.

[55] cf. W. M. Ramsay, *The Church in the Roman Empire before A.D. 170.* 1912, pp.135-139. Referring to the seven wonders of the ancient world ([1] the wall of Babylon; [2] the statue of Zeus at Olympia; [3] the hanging gardens of Babylon; [4] the pyramids; [5] the temple of Artemis at Ephesus; [6] the Colossus of Rhodes; [7] the Mausoleum of Halicarnassus), Antipater of Sidon (first century B.C.) praised the temple of Artemis as supreme among them all: "I have set eyes on the wall of lofty Babylon on which is a road for chariots, and the statue of Zeus by the Alpheus, and the hanging gardens, and the colossus of the Sun, and the huge labor of the high pyramids, and the vast tomb of Mausolus; but when I saw the house of Artemis that mounted to the clouds, those other marvels lost their brilliancy, and I said, 'Lo, apart from Olympus, the Sun never looked on aught so grand.'" *The Greek Anthology.* IX, 58. tr. W. R. Paton, LCL III (1948), p.31.

Yet today the site of the temple of Diana which was built originally on marshy soil[56] has become but a stagnant pond, inhabited by myriads of frogs, and is permanently flooded.

The theater of Ephesus is also of special interest as having been the scene of the tumult which was aroused by the work of Paul (Acts 19:29). The site of the theater, which is shown in Fig. 123, was in the hollow of a hill from which one looked out over the busiest parts of the city. The theater had an imposing façade with aediculae and niches and was adorned with fine statuary. While the existing remains represent a reconstruction carried out after the period of Paul, the plan of the structure is probably essentially the same as that of the apostle's time.

Another important feature of ancient Ephesus was the agora or marketplace. This was a great rectangular, colonnaded area entered by magnificent gateways and surrounded by halls and chambers. Nearby was the library, built with fine columns and with its walls recessed with niches for bookcases. Other buildings which have been excavated include gymnasia, baths, and burial monuments. One of the city's finest streets ran directly from the theater to the river harbor, being nearly one-half mile long and about thirty-five feet wide, and lined with halls on either side. Also at the harbor there were monumental gateways.

Later Christian times are represented not only by the remains of Justinian's Church of St. John already mentioned (p.347), but also by the very interesting ruins of the double Church of the Virgin Mary, where the Council of Ephesus was held in A.D. 431. This church was built probably around A.D. 350 on the foundations of a pagan building more than eight hundred feet long, probably a school, which had been destroyed in the preceding century. There is an extensive Christian catacomb at Ephesus, too, which dates from the fifth and sixth centuries, and is connected with the legend of the Seven Sleepers of Ephesus. According to the story, these were seven Christian youths at Ephesus who took refuge in a cave outside the city during the persecution under Decius (A.D. 250). By the emperor's command they were sealed up in the cave, but instead of perishing they fell into a sleep from which they were awakened nearly two hundred years later when some stones happened to be removed from the entrance. Thereupon the youths reaffirmed their

[56] Pliny, *Natural History.* XXXVI. 14.

Christian faith before Theodosius II (A.D. 408-450) and Bishop Maximus, and then died.

PHILIPPI

After making the memorable crossing from Troas to what we now know as Europe, Paul preached in Philippi, the first city of that district of Macedonia and a Roman colony (Acts 16:12). This city was founded in the middle of the fourth century B.C. by Philip of Macedon. "In earlier times Philippi was called Crenides," says Strabo, "and was only a small settlement, but it was enlarged after the defeat of Brutus and Cassius."[57] This Battle of Philippi took place in 42 B.C. and to celebrate their victory Antony and Octavian made the city a Roman colony, its name, Colonia Julia Philippensis, honoring the victory of the cause of Julius Caesar. The first citizens appear to have been veterans of this battle, and after the Battle of Actium in 31 B.C. dispossessed adherents of the defeated Antony also were settled here. The victory of Augustus over Antony and Cleopatra was commemorated by the additional title Augusta, so that the full name of the city became Colonia Augusta Julia Philippensis.

The territory of the colony included Neapolis (the modern Kavalla), the seaport at which Paul landed (Acts 16:11), some nine miles distant on the coast. From Neapolis the Via Egnatia, the main overland route from Asia to Rome, ran over Mount Symbolum and directly into Philippi where it passed the whole length of the city's forum, and where the marks of wagon and chariot wheels can still be seen scored to a depth of three and four inches.

The once proud Roman colony is known today as Felibedjik, or "Little Philippi," and its ruins cover many acres of ground (Fig. 124). Excavations were conducted here between 1914 and 1938 by the École Française d'Athènes, which have provided much information concerning the city.[58] The forum, which has been uncovered completely, was a rectangular area over 300 feet long and 150 feet wide. It was entered through five porticoes on three sides, and had

[57] *Geography.* VII, fr. 41.

[58] *Bulletin de correspondance hellénique.* 44 (1920), pp.406f.; 45 (1921), pp.543-547; 46 (1922), pp.527-531; 47 (1923), pp.534-536; 48 (1924), p.501; 49 (1925), p.462; 52 (1928), pp.492f.; 54 (1930), pp.502-506; 55 (1931), pp.499-502; 57 (1933), pp.279-285; 58 (1934), pp.257-261; 59 (1935), pp.285-291; 60 (1936), pp.478-480; 61 (1937), pp.463-468; 62 (1938), pp.1-3; Paul Collart, *Philippes ville de Macédoine depuis ses origines jusqu'à la fin de l'époque romaine.* 2 vols. 1937; Paul Lemerle, *Philippes et la Macedoine orientale a l'époque chretienne et byzantine.* 1945.

on its north side a rectangular podium to which steps gave access on both sides. This was evidently the tribunal from which orators spoke and magistrates dispensed justice. The forum was overlooked by temples at either end, and otherwise surrounded with public buildings. Most of these ruins date from a rebuilding in the second century, but it is probable that the plan of the forum was not radically different in Paul's day. Incidentally, the Roman rain-gutters are so well preserved that they still carry off water.

Other features of Philippi which have been studied by the French archeologists include the acropolis, the Roman baths, the theater dating originally perhaps from the fourth century B.C. and rebuilt in the second century A.D., and the Christian churches whose ruins belong to a much later date.

While most of the extant remains at Philippi belong to a period considerably after that of Paul, one important structure has been identified which is believed to date from the time of the apostle and even to figure in the account of his work given in Acts. This is a colonial archway whose ruins are to the west of the city. It probably was constructed at the time the Roman colony of Philippi was established, and it served to symbolize the dignity and privileges of the city. Also, it may have marked the line of the pomerium within which foreign deities were not permitted. As the Via Egnatia left Philippi and headed west it ran beneath this arch and then, at a distance of a little over one mile from the city, it crossed the river Ganga or Gangites.[59] It seems natural to conclude, therefore, that the "gate" mentioned in Acts 16:13 was this very archway, that the Jews met beyond it because this was required by law, and that the "riverside" where Paul spoke to the assembled women was on the edge of the Gangites.[60]

THESSALONICA

From Philippi Paul proceeded to Thessalonica, seventy miles distant along the Via Egnatia. According to Strabo, this city was founded by Cassander (c.315 B.C.) and named after his wife Thessalonica, the sister of Alexander the Great.[61] Because of its support of Antony and Octavian in the Battle of Philippi, it was rewarded by

---

[59] Appian (2d cent. A.D.), *Roman History, The Civil Wars.* IV, xiii, 106. tr. Horace White, LCL (1912-13) IV, p.319; Hirschfeld in PWRE I (1894), col. 2191.

[60] Collart, *Philippes ville de Macédoine*, pp.319-322, 458-460.

[61] *Geography.* VII, fr. 21.

being made a free city (*civitas libera*). In the time of Strabo, Thessalonica was the most populous city in Macedonia.[62]

Thessalonica is now the modern city of Salonika and an important seaport. In 1951 the population of the city proper was estimated at 217,049. The place enjoys a picturesque location at the head of the Gulf of Salonika and has mountains piled behind it. The course of the Via Egnatia is still represented by the main street of the city on which there also stands the Arch of Galerius (A.D. 305-311). At its western entrance to the city, the Via Egnatia was spanned until 1876 by another Roman arch called the Vardar Gate. This was of special interest since it carried an inscription, now in the British Museum, beginning, "In the time of the Politarchs. . . ." It is probably to be dated somewhere between 30 B.C. and A.D. 143, while several other Thessalonian inscriptions, including one definitely dated in the reign of Augustus, also mention Politarchs. This is of importance since in the Greek of Acts 17:6 the rulers of Thessalonica are called Politarchs. The term is otherwise unknown in extant Greek literature, but Luke's accuracy in the matter is entirely vindicated by the inscriptions.[63]

ATHENS

When Paul came to Athens (Acts 17:15) he was in one of the world's most famous centers of philosophy, architecture, and art, a city in whose ruins are still to be seen today some of the most beautiful things ever made by man. Systematic study of the topography of ancient Athens was begun in the seventeenth century by the French consuls Giraud and Chataignier and by the Capuchin monks, while toward the end of the century descriptions of Greece and Athens were published by the French physician Jacques Spon[64] and the Englishman George Wheeler.[65] The most important studies of the next century were made by James Stuart and Nicholas Revett, who spent three years at Athens (1751-1754) and published four large volumes on *The Antiquities of Athens* (3d ed. 1885). In the nineteenth century the work of W. M. Leake introduced the period of modern research.[66] The scientific investigations of modern times, in which Greek archeologists and the Greek government as well as

[62] *Geography.* VII, vii, 4.
[63] Ernest DeWitt Burton in AJT 2 (1898), pp.598-632.
[64] *Voyage d'Italie, de Dalmatie, de Grèce et du Levant.* 1678.
[65] *Journey into Greece.* 1682.
[66] *The Topography of Athens.* 2d ed. 1841.

at least six foreign archeological schools have participated, have made available a wealth of information concerning ancient Athens. Although the multitudinous details cannot be considered here, it is of much interest to be able to glimpse, little dimmed by time, the beauty of "the city of the violet crown," in which the culture of the ancient world reached its greatest height and where the apostle Paul once stood though but briefly.

The remarkable and precipitous rocky hill (512 feet high) known as the Acropolis was occupied by man as early as Neolithic times. In the seventh century B.C. the city of Athens emerged from obscurity and in the wars with Persia after 500 B.C. became the natural leader of Greece. Under the administration of Pericles around 443-429 B.C. Athens reached its golden age. The friend of Pericles, the sculptor Phidias (d. c.432 B.C.), superintended the adornment of the city with a magnificent array of temples, public buildings, and works of art. From the spoils of Marathon, Phidias made a colossal bronze statue of Athena Promachos, the goddess who fights in front, which was erected on the Acropolis and towered so high that mariners rounding the promontory of Sunium could see the sunlight flashing on her spear and helmet.[67] Then the incomparable Parthenon was built and a great gold and ivory statue of Athena by Phidias erected within (c.438 B.C.). Later came the completion of the stately entrance, the Propylaea, and of the beautiful temples, the Erechtheum and the shrine of Athena Nike, the goddess of victory. Of the Parthenon-crowned Acropolis J. P. Mahaffy wrote, "There is no ruin all the world over which combines so much striking beauty, so distinct a type, so vast a volume of history, so great a pageant of immortal memories. . . . All the Old World's culture culminated in Greece—all Greece in Athens—all Athens in its Acropolis—all the Acropolis in the Parthenon."[68]

Along the southern base of the Acropolis ran the colonnaded precinct of Asclepius, the god of healing. Just to the east and partly hollowed out from the declivity of the Acropolis was the lovely Theater of Dionysus. The earlier wooden structures of this theater were replaced by stone under the administration of Lycurgus around 337-323 B.C. Farther east was the Odeum of Pericles where musical contests were held, and beyond was the small circular Monument of

[67] Pausanias, *Description of Greece*. i, xxviii, 2. tr. W. H. S. Jones, LCL (1918-35) i, p.147.
[68] *Rambles and Studies in Greece*. 1878, p.83. For the buildings of the Acropolis see Nicolas Balanos, *Les monuments de l'Acropole, relèvement et conservation*. 1936.

Lysicrates, dedicated about 335 B.C. Southeast of the Acropolis stood the colossal temple of Olympian Zeus (Fig. 125). Measuring 354 feet by 135 feet at its base and towering to a height of over ninety feet, this was the largest temple in Greece and one of the largest in the ancient world. Begun by the Athenian ruler Pisistratus about 530 B.C., it stood unfinished for several centuries. Then the work was resumed by Antiochus IV Epiphanes, king of Syria, who employed the Roman architect Cossutius on the project. Even then the temple was not finished entirely, and it remained for the Emperor Hadrian to complete certain details, probably including the interior colonnades and the roof. For the most part the extant remains probably represent the work of Cossutius.[69]

After the sacred precinct of the Acropolis, the most important part of ancient Athens was the agora or marketplace which was the center of the city's civic and commercial life. According to the book of Acts (17:17) it was "in the agora" as well as in the Jewish synagogue that Paul "argued . . . every day with those who chanced to be there." The agora was some distance to the north of the west end of the Acropolis and covered a large area. The western portion of this region is recognized as having been the Hellenic agora, while the space to the east represents an enlargement of the marketplace probably financed by Julius Caesar and Augustus and hence known as the Roman agora. Early agora excavations were conducted by the Greek Archaeological Society, and by the German Archaeological Institute under Professor Wilhelm Dörpfeld. Then between 1931 and 1940 very large-scale excavations, which involved the moving of around 250,000 tons of earth, were undertaken in the western or specifically Greek section of the agora by the American School of Classical Studies at Athens under the leadership of T. Leslie Shear.[70]

On the eastern side of the Greek agora stood a colonnaded portico known as the Stoa of Attalos, which, together with the near-by so-called Stoa of the Giants, had been uncovered by the Greek Archaeological Society. Along the south side ran two large parallel stoas and on the west were a number of important buildings all of which have been unearthed by the American archeologists. The structures excavated on the west side of the agora include from north to south the

[69] Charles H. Weller, *Athens and Its Monuments*. 1924, pp.161-165.

[70] Shear in *Hesperia*. 2 (1933), pp.96-109, 451-474; 4 (1935), pp.311-339, 340-370; 5 (1936), pp.1-42; 6 (1937), pp.333-381; 7 (1938), pp.311-362; 8 (1939), pp.201-246; 9 (1940), pp.261-307; 10 (1941), pp.1-8. For Paul in the agora see Suzanne Halstead in *Quantulacumque*, pp.139-143.

Stoa of Zeus Eleutherios, the last name having been applied to Zeus because he delivered the Athenians from the Persian menace; the Temple of Apollo Patroos (the Father); the Sanctuary of the Mother of the Gods; the Bouleuterion, where the Athenian Council of Five Hundred assembled; and the circular Tholos, where the executive sections of the Council were maintained. Other buildings found in the agora are the Temple of Ares, the Odeum or Music Hall in which poets and musicians contended for prizes, and the Library dedicated to Trajan and located just south of the Stoa of Attalos.

Overlooking the agora from the west is the hill called Kolonos Agoraios, on which are the well preserved ruins of a temple now identified as that of Hephaistos, the god of fire and metal-working. To the east in the region of the Roman agora are the ruins of numerous shops and arcades, and just beyond is the Horologium popularly called the Tower of the Winds. The latter was an octagonal marble structure with sun dials on the exterior and probably a water-clock on the inside. It served as a public timepiece for the city of Athens and therefore was near the chief trading center. Like the Roman agora, the Horologium was probably constructed in the second half of the first century B.C.[71]

In view of the address by Paul reported in Acts 17:22-31, special interest attaches to the Areopagus. Areopagus or Hill of Ares is the name of a bare, rocky hill, about 377 feet high, immediately north-west of the Acropolis and separated from it by a narrow declivity now largely filled in. Steps cut in the rock lead to the top where rough, rock-hewn benches, forming three sides of a square, can still be seen. In ancient times this was the meeting place of the Areopagus court. This court or council was composed of city fathers and in early times had supreme authority in both political and religious matters. In the time of Pericles the council became largely a criminal court, but in Roman times was charged again with the care of religion and of education. From its place of assembly the court itself was called the Areopagus, and in Acts 17:34 we find one of its members referred to as an Areopagite. The word Areopagus in Acts 17:19, 22 might be interpreted, therefore, either as referring to the hill or (v. 19 ASV. margin) to the court. In either case, however, it remains probable that the place of Paul's speech was on this hill, since it was the customary meeting place of the court.[72]

[71] Henry S. Robinson in AJA 47 (1943), pp.291-305.
[72] Walther Judeich, *Topographie von Athen* (in Walter Otto, ed., *Handbuch der Altertumswissenschaft*. III, ii, 2, 2d ed. 1931), p.299; Oscar Broneer in BA 21 (1958), p.27 n.4.

It is true that the Areopagus court seems to have met at times in the Stoa Basileios or Royal Stoa, and if this happened to be the case when Paul was in Athens then the place of his address would have to be sought in this stoa. The stoa in question is identified by some with the already mentioned Stoa of Zeus Eleutherios at the northwest corner of the agora as now excavated,[73] but is believed by others to have lain yet farther north. The point cannot be decided at present since the excavations did not reach the northern limits of the agora. As a matter of fact, work in this northern region may be long delayed because of the presence of an important modern street and also of a railway line.[74]

In his Areopagus address Paul is reported (Acts 17:23) to have referred to an altar with the inscription, "To an unknown god," or "To the unknown god."[75] Not far from the time when Paul was in Athens, the city was visited by Apollonius of Tyana. This remarkable wandering Neo-Pythagorean philosopher, whose career parallels that of Paul's in some regards, was born at Tyana in Cappadocia, around the beginning of the Christian era, and died at Ephesus, probably in A.D. 98. After studying in Tarsus and in the temple of Asclepius at Aegae on the Gulf of Iskanderun, he traveled into all parts of the known world, at one time enduring trial and imprisonment in Rome. The last ten years of his life were spent in Greece. The biography of Apollonius was written by Flavius Philostratus (A.D. c.170-c.245) at the request of Julia Domna, the wife of the Emperor Severus, but not published until after her death in A.D. 217. Philostratus was able to draw upon a collection of letters by Apollonius and upon a travel journal by the Assyrian Damis, the disciple and companion of Apollonius. Nevertheless he added large amounts of legendary and miraculous material so that the *Life* resembles an historical novel. The biography is of interest to us, however, because it contains a remark of Apollonius to the effect that it is a proof of wisdom "to speak well of all the gods, especially at Athens, where altars are set up in honour even of unknown gods."[76]

[73] Homer A. Thompson in *Hesperia.* 6 (1937), pp.5-77. Wilhelm Dörpfeld (*Alt-Athen und seine Agora* [Heft 2, 1939], pp.146-167) thinks that the Stoa Basileios was the building immediately south of the Stoa of Zeus which the Americans called the Temple of Apollo Patroos.

[74] T. Leslie Shear in *Hesperia.* 4 (1935), p.354; 6 (1937), p.360.

[75] The article is absent in the Greek, but since this is common in inscriptions, either translation is permissible.

[76] ἀγνώστων δαιμόνων βωμοί. Philostratus, *The Life of Apollonius of Tyana.* vi, 3. tr. F. C. Conybeare, LCL (1912) II, p.13.

Another remarkable traveler who visited Athens at a somewhat later date than Apollonius was the geographer Pausanias. Born in Lydia, he had already traveled in Palestine and Egypt before he came to Greece. He visited Athens in the period between A.D. 143 and 159 and then devoted the first thirty chapters of his *Description of Greece* to an extensive and accurate topographical account of Athens as he saw it. He says that on the road from the Phaleron Bay harbor to the city he had noticed "altars of the gods named Unknown, and of heroes,"[77] and also mentions "an altar of Unknown Gods"[78] at Olympia.

Although no such altar now remains at Athens, a comparable one was discovered in 1909 at Pergamum in the sacred precincts of the temple of Demeter (Fig. 126). A corner of the stone is broken and a portion of the inscription is lost but it is probably to be read:

> To unknown gods,
> Capito,
> torch-bearer.[79]

A somewhat similar altar stands on the Palatine Hill at Rome and dates from about 100 B.C. Its inscription begins, *Sei deo sei deivae sac[rum]*, "Sacred to a god or goddess."[80]

After the time of Paul the Emperor Hadrian (A.D. 117-138) added to the city of Athens with lavish benefactions. About A.D. 143 a wealthy Roman resident, Herodes Atticus, rebuilt the old stadium, making it into an immense marble structure which would accommodate 44,000 spectators. The same man also later built a theater at the southwestern base of the Acropolis, known as the Odeum, in memory of his wife. In Byzantine times Athens sank into the position of a provincial town and was robbed of many of its works of art. The Athena Promachos and the Athena Parthenos were taken away to adorn Constantinople, and other spoliation took place when the church of Hagia Sophia was rebuilt in the sixth century. The Parthe-

---

[77] βωμοὶ δὲ θεῶν τε ὀνομαζομένων Ἀγνώστων καὶ ἡρώων. I, i, 4.

[78] Ἀγνώστων θεῶν βωμός. v, xiv, 8.

[79] Adolf Deissmann, *Paul.* tr. William E. Wilson. 2d ed. 1926, pp.288-291.

[80] Hammerton, *Wonders of the Past.* I, p.524. Although it is possible to give exact literary and epigraphic attestation only to the plural form "to unknown gods," it would have been quite possible even in a polytheistic environment for someone to have felt a sense of gratitude "to *an* unknown god." Therefore it is unnecessary to argue with E. Norden (*Agnostos Theos* [1913], p.121) that the author of the Areopagus address first changed the plural form to the singular in order to obtain the text for a monotheistic sermon.

non, the Erechtheum, and other temples, however, were converted into Christian churches and thus preserved throughout the Middle Ages. When the Acropolis was taken by the Turks in 1458 the Parthenon was transformed into a mosque, and a minaret was built at its southwestern corner. The Turkish commandant used the Propylaea as a residence and employed the Erechtheum for his harem. In 1687 the Venetians bombarded the Acropolis where the Turks were entrenched, and a bomb from a mortar struck the Parthenon and blew up a powder magazine in it, damaging the building severely.[81] The Turks remained in possession of the Acropolis until 1833, when Athens became the capital of the independent kingdom of Greece. At that time it was only a village of 5,000 inhabitants, but in 1951 the population of Athens proper was estimated at 565,084.

Eventually philosophers like Justin Martyr (A.D. c.100-c.165) were to recognize that in Christ the true Word had become manifest, only fragments of which had been laid hold of by the search and speculation of Socrates and the other thinkers of the past, and thus the Greek tradition was to be brought into relation to the Christian message.[82] But the sophisticated Athenians (cf. Acts 17:21) of Paul's time gave little serious attention to his message,[83] and Paul apparently went on soon to Corinth, convinced that "the wisdom of this world is folly with God" (I Corinthians 3:19), and seeking hearers to whom the foolishness of the preaching would seem a wisdom greater than that of men (cf. I Corinthians 1:21, 25).

CORINTH

In going from Athens to Corinth (Acts 18:1) Paul was moving from the intellectual center of Greece to its most splendid commercial city. Whereas Athens was situated on the Greek mainland near the southern end of the great plain of Attica, Corinth was just across the narrow isthmus which connects central Greece with the Peloponnesus. This isthmus was a natural meeting place for trade from East and West. Ships from Asia Minor, Syria, and Egypt put in to the

[81] Theodor E. Mommsen in AJA 45 (1941), pp.544-556.
[82] *Apology.* II, 10 (ANF I, p.191); cf. Paul Elmer More, *Christ the Word* 1927, pp.9-11.
[83] Compared with the wealth of evidence concerning pagan Athens, there are few traces of the Christian community in this city during the first five centuries, the chief material being simple epitaphs from humble tombstones, dating perhaps in the fourth century and later. See John S. Creaghan and A. E. Raubitschek, *Early Christian Epitaphs from Athens.* 1947.

port of Cenchreae (cf. Romans 16:1) on the eastern side of the isthmus, while those of Italy, Sicily, and Spain docked at Lechaeum, the harbor on the western side. The distance between these two ports was less than ten miles, and while the cargoes of the larger vessels were transshipped, the smaller boats were hauled across bodily on a sort of tramway. Otherwise, the circumnavigation of stormy Cape Malea,[84] requiring a detour of two hundred miles, was necessary. Naturally enough the desirability of cutting a canal across the isthmus was recognized by many men including Alexander the Great, Julius Caesar, and Nero. In A.D. 66 Nero went so far as to dig the first dirt of such a canal with a golden spade, and to set at the task of excavating it six thousand young Jews recently captured by Vespasian in the Jewish War which had just begun. But this and all the other similar projects of antiquity were abandoned[85] and it was not until A.D. 1881-1893 that the present canal was cut. This canal runs straight across the isthmus at its narrowest point and is four miles in length. It is crossed by the 170-foot-high iron bridge of the Athens and Corinth railway. Situated but one and one-half miles south of this isthmus and commanding the ports on either side of it, the city of Corinth obviously was destined for commercial greatness. Pindar called the Isthmus of Corinth "the bridge of the sea,"[86] and Strabo summed up the situation accurately when he said, "Corinth is called 'wealthy' because of its commerce, since it is situated on the Isthmus and is master of two harbors, of which the one leads straight to Asia, and the other to Italy; and it makes easy the exchange of merchandise from both countries that are so far distant from each other."[87]

The site of Corinth was occupied as anciently as in the Neolithic and Chalcolithic ages,[88] and in Greek mythology the city was the home of Medea, Sisyphus, and Bellerophon. From early times the distinctive cult associated with Corinth was that of the worship of Aphrodite. In the eighth and seventh centuries B.C. Corinth estab-

[84] cf. Strabo, *Geography.* VIII, vi, 20: "But when you double Malea, forget your home."

[85] Philostratus (*Life of Apollonius.* IV, 24) records the report that Nero stopped the work of cutting the canal "because Egyptian men of science explained to him the nature of the seas, and declared that the sea above Lechaeum would flood and obliterate the island of Aegina."

[86] Pindar (c.522-c.448 B.C.), *The Nemean Odes.* VI, 40. tr. John Sandys, LCL (1915), p.373.

[87] *Geography.* VIII, vi, 20.

[88] John G. O'Neill, *Ancient Corinth, with a Topographical Sketch of the Corinthia,* Part I, *From the Earliest Times to 404 B.C.* 1930, pp.60f.; Saul S. Weinberg in *Hesperia.* 6 (1937), pp.487-524.

lished colonies at Syracuse and Corcyra, and under the tyrants Cypselus (c.657-c.629 B.C.) and Periander (c.629-c.585 B.C.) rose to great prominence and prosperity. She dominated extensive trade routes, and Corinthian bronze and pottery were exported widely over the Mediterranean. About 146 B.C. Corinth warred with Rome and upon defeat was completely destroyed, probably because of commercial jealousy. The inhabitants were sold into slavery and for one hundred years the site of the city lay desolate. Then in 46 B.C. Julius Caesar refounded the city as the Colonia Laus Julia Corinthiensis, and peopled it with Italian freedmen and dispossessed Greeks.[89] Its commercial prosperity was recovered rapidly, and Augustus made Corinth the capital of Achaia and seat of its proconsul (cf. Acts 18:12). After the time of Paul, Hadrian beautified the city with public works. In the Middle Ages it continued to be a flourishing place until captured by the Sicilians in 1406 and the Turks in 1458. In 1858 the ancient city suffered a terrible earthquake and the survivors built New Corinth on a new site three and one-half miles northeast of the old city. This city, too, was almost wholly destroyed by earthquake in 1928, but was rebuilt and thereafter attained a population of some 10,000.

The excavation of ancient Corinth has been conducted over a period of many years, beginning in 1896, by the American School of Classical Studies at Athens.[90] The city spreads out over two terraces, one about one hundred feet higher than the other, while in the southwestern background a towering mountain, Acrocorinth,[91] rises 1,500

[89] Strabo, *Geography*. VIII, iv, 8; vi, 23; XVII, iii, 15.

[90] See AJA 34 (1930), pp.403-454; 37 (1933), pp.554-572; 39 (1935), pp.53-75; 40 (1936), pp.21-45, 466-484; 41 (1937), pp.539-552; 42 (1938), pp.362-370; 43 (1939), pp.255-267, 592-600; O. Broneer in BA 14 (1951), pp.78-96; and various volumes of *Corinth, Results of Excavations Conducted by the American School of Classical Studies at Athens*, including I, 1, Harold N. Fowler and Richard Stillwell, *Introduction, Topography, Architecture*. 1932; I, 2, R. Stillwell, Robert L. Scranton, and Sarah E. Freeman, *Architecture*. 1941; I, 3, R. L. Scranton, *Monuments in the Lower Agora and North of the Archaic Temple*. 1951; II, R. Stillwell, *The Theatre*. 1952; III, 1, Carl W. Blegen, R. Stillwell, Oscar Broneer, and Alfred R. Bellinger, *Acrocorinth, Excavations in 1926*. 1930; III, 2, Rhys Carpenter and Antoine Bon, *The Defenses of Acrocorinth and the Lower Town*. 1936; IV, 1, Ida Thallon-Hill and Lida S. King, *Decorated Architectural Terracottas*. 1929; IV, 2, O. Broneer, *Terracotta Lamps*. 1930; V, T. Leslie Shear, *The Roman Villa*. 1930; VI, Katharine M. Edwards, *Coins 1896-1929*. 1933; VII, 1, Saul S. Weinberg, *The Geometric and Orientalizing Pottery*. 1943; VIII, 1, Benjamin D. Meritt, *Greek Inscriptions 1896-1927*. 1931; VIII, 2, Allen B. West, *Latin Inscriptions 1896-1926*. 1931; IX, Franklin P. Johnson, *Sculpture 1896-1923*. 1931; X, O. Broneer, *The Odeum*. 1932; XI, Charles H. Morgan II, *The Byzantine Pottery*. 1942; XIV, Carl Roebuck, *The Asklepieion and Lerna*. 1951; XV, 1, Agnes N. Stillwell, *The Potters' Quarter*. 1948.

[91] Strabo, *Geography*. VIII, iv, 8; vi, 21.

feet above the city and 1,886 feet above the sea. In the center of the city was a large agora or marketplace, surrounded with colonnades and monuments. On the north side the road from Lechaeum entered the agora through a stately gateway or propylaea. Just east of this was the famous fountain of Pirene, and from the southern side of the marketplace the road to Cenchreae departed. West of the Lechaeum road and north of the marketplace, on a low hill was the temple of Apollo. It was built probably in the sixth century B.C.,[92] and seven of its fine Doric columns still stand. A corner of this temple is shown in Fig. 127, with Acrocorinth looming in the background. Some distance away to the northwest was the theater of Corinth, built in the Greek period and repaired under the Romans. On the summit of Acrocorinth was a temple of Aphrodite.

Among the shops opening onto the agora at Corinth were ones which had clearly been used for the sale of meat and other foodstuffs. Interestingly enough, each was provided with a well connecting with a subterranean channel through which flowed fresh water. Evidently this arrangement provided the shops not only with a source of water but also with a means of cooling perishable products.[93] An inscription found there, belonging to the last years of Augustus or to the reign of Tiberius, calls one of these shops a "market," using in the Latin exactly the same word which Paul employs in the Greek in I Corinthians 10:25.[94] Another Corinth inscription mentions a certain Erastus who may very well be identified with the Erastus named as a friend of Paul's in Romans 16:23, II Timothy 4:20, and Acts 19:22.[95]

On the Lechaeum road in Corinth, at the foot of the marble steps leading to the propylaea, a stone was found in 1898 which once formed the lintel over a doorway. It bears an inscription in Greek and although the stone is broken at the right and damaged at the left the inscription clearly reads "Synagogue of the Hebrews."[96] The inscription is usually dated somewhere between 100 B.C. and A.D. 200.[97] Consequently it may once have stood over the entrance to the synagogue in which Paul preached (Acts 18:4), or have marked a

[92] Benjamin Powell in AJA 9 (1905), pp.44-63; Saul S. Weinberg in *Hesperia.* 8 (1939), pp.191-199.

[93] Oscar Broneer in *The Lutheran Companion.* Nov. 12, 1942, p.1306.

[94] Macellum, μάκελλον. H. J. Cadbury in JBL 53 (1934), pp.134-141; Gerhard Kittel, ed., *Theologisches Wörterbuch zum Neuen Testament.* (1933-), IV, pp.373f.

[95] H. J. Cadbury (in JBL 50 [1931], pp.42-58) questions the identification, but see C. C. McCown in AJA 50 (1946), p. 426.

[96] First published by Benjamin Powell in AJA 7 (1903), pp.60f.

[97] DLO p.12 n.8.

later building on the same site. The letters, which are two and one-half to three and one-half inches high, are poorly cut and suggest that the synagogue was not wealthy. This would accord with Paul's characterization of the Corinthian Christians in his letter to them (I Corinthians 1:26). Since the stone is of considerable weight it may be presumed that it was found not far from the place where the synagogue stood, and if this is correct then the synagogue was on or near the road to Lechaeum and not far from the marketplace. The west side of the Lechaeum road was lined with colonnades and shops close under the hill where the temple of Apollo stood, and the more probable location of the synagogue was therefore on the east side of the street. This area was in the main a residential district, as the many remaining house walls indicate, and consequently the house of Titus Justus could easily have been "next door" (Acts 18:7).

In the agora one of the prominent features is an elevated platform which once served as an outdoor speaker's platform. It is mentioned in an inscription by the Latin name *rostra* which is the equivalent of the Greek word by which the "judgment-seat" (ASV) or "tribunal" (RSV)[98] at Corinth is referred to in Acts 18:12-17, and is doubtless to be identified with the very place where Paul stood before Gallio. In the photograph reproduced in Fig. 128 the marketplace is viewed from the east and the ruins of the rostra appear to the left of the center of the picture. In the distance at the extreme left are the slopes of Acrocorinth and at the right is the temple of Apollo.

The Gallio who was proconsul of Achaia when Paul was in Corinth (Acts 18:12) was the elder brother of the philosopher Seneca and is mentioned by Tacitus[99] and Dio Cassius.[100] An important inscription has been found which makes it possible to date Gallio's arrival in Corinth as proconsul quite accurately. It was discovered at Delphi, which was on the other side of the Gulf of Corinth some six miles inland. The inscription begins: "Tiberius Claudius Caesar Augustus Germanicus, Pontifex Maximus, of tribunican authority for the 12th time, imperator the 26th time, father of the country, consul for the 5th time, honorable, greets the city of the Delphians." The emperor then goes on to say that he has long been well disposed to the city of Delphi, and that he has observed the religious ceremonies of the Pythian Apollo that were held there. The actual business with which

[98] τὸ βῆμα.
[99] *Annals.* xv, 73.
[100] *Roman History.* LXI, XXXV, 2.

the communication deals is lost in the broken places in the inscription, but it is possible to make out further along the words, "as Lucius Junius Gallio, my friend, and the proconsul of Achaia wrote. . . ." This inscription therefore provides testimony to the fact that Gallio did serve as proconsul of Achaia. Furthermore, at the time the emperor's letter was written to Delphi, Gallio had evidently been in office long enough to have given Claudius information of importance concerning the Delphians. Since the reference to the 12th tribunican year and the 26th imperatorship of Claudius dates this communication between January and August of the year A.D. 52, Gallio must have arrived in Corinth not later than the year 51. Dio Cassius reports a decree of Claudius that new officials should start for their provinces by the first day of June,[101] and therefore Gallio must have entered upon his proconsulship in Corinth in the summer, probably around July 1, in A.D. 51. The impression given by the book of Acts is that Gallio had arrived in Corinth only shortly before the time when the Jews brought Paul into his presence. Since at that time the apostle had been in the city a year and six months (Acts 18:11), we can date Paul's arrival in Corinth with considerable confidence at the beginning of the year 50.[102]

ROME

Already upon his last visit to Achaia Paul was purposing to go to Rome (Romans 15:23-28; Acts 19:21). That intention was achieved, though hardly in the way he might have wished, when the apostle was taken to Rome as a prisoner in the charge of Julius the centurion (Acts 27:1; 28:16). After the sea voyage, on which he suffered shipwreck,[103] Paul landed finally at Puteoli (Acts 28:13), the modern Puzzuoli, on the northern shore of the Bay of Naples.

Fifteen miles east of Puteoli was the town of Herculaneum, lying at the foot of the volcano Vesuvius, by which it was to be destroyed in A.D. 79. A discovery was made at Herculaneum in 1938 which may have connection with early Christianity and with Paul. In an upper

[101] *Roman History.* LVII, xiv, 5.
[102] Deissmann, *Paul*, pp.265-283; cf. Lemerle, *Philippes et la Macedoine orientale a l'époque chretienne et byzantine*, pp.18f.
[103] For the shipwreck voyage see Edwin Smith in Tom Davin, ed., *The Rudder Treasury.* 1953, pp.55-66, who reckons that a ship hove-to and drifting before the northeaster (Acts 27:14), would make about thirty-six miles in twenty-four hours, or 477 miles in thirteen and one-quarter days, which agrees almost exactly with a measured distance of 476.4 miles from a point under the lee of Clauda to the entrance of St. Paul's Bay on Malta.

room of the so-called "Bicentenary House" a stucco wall panel was found which contained a somewhat irregular depression roughly in the form of a Latin cross. There were nail holes in this depression and also elsewhere in the panel. On the floor beneath was a piece of wooden furniture. It seemed possible that a wooden cross had once been affixed to the wall at this point and then been torn off and a wooden covering nailed over the area. Likewise the piece of furniture might have been a sort of altar. If this is the correct interpretation of the evidence, then the room may have been a small chapel used by some early Christian or Christians and the use of the cross may even reflect the preaching of the cross by Paul (cf. I Corinthians 1:18, etc.) during his seven-day stay at nearby Puteoli. The removal of the cross and the covering over of the panel containing its impression could have been done by the Christians themselves in a time of persecution such as that by Nero in A.D. 64.[104] On the other hand, the irregularity of the cross-shaped depression and the many nail marks scattered over the area lead some to advance the alternative explanation that it was simply some practical object, such as a wall cabinet, which was anchored to the wall at this place and upon removal left these marks.[105]

At Pompeii, twenty-five miles east of Puteoli, a rudely scrawled inscription was found on the wall of a room, which may have contained a disparaging remark about Christians. This graffito is in Latin characters, and the word *Christianos* seems unmistakable. Otherwise the text is difficult to interpret. It has been suggested that it is actually in the Aramaic language, although transliterated in Latin letters, and on that basis the whole sentence has been translated: "A strange mind has driven A. and he has pressed in among the Christians who make a man a prisoner as a laughingstock." In that case the inscription might have been an expression of pagan opinion of Christian missionary work, and this might have been the very room in which some early Christian missionary of about the time of Paul taught. On this basis the text has been called the first known non-Christian reference to Christians. At all events the date of the inscription must be before A.D. 79 since, like Herculaneum, Pompeii was destroyed at that time.[106]

[104] Amadeo Maiuri in *Rendiconti della Pontificia Accademia Romana di Archeologia.* 15 (1939), pp.193-218; cf. William L. Holladay in JBR 19 (1951), pp.16-19; Parrot, *Golgotha and the Church of the Holy Sepulchre,* p.117.

[105] L. de Bruyne in RAC 21 (1945), pp.281-309; Erich Dinkler in ZTK 48 (1951), pp.158f.

[106] H. Leclercq in DACL VI, cols. 1482-1484; W. R. Newbold in AJA 30 (1926), pp.291-295; A. T. Olmstead in JNES 1 (1942), p.41.

From Puteoli Paul presumably went on to Capua, twenty miles away, to reach the Via Appia, the main highway to Rome. "The worn and well-known track of Appia, queen of the long roads," as this highway was described by Statius (A.D. c.45-c.96),[107] was built from Rome to Capua by the censor Appius Claudius Caecus in about 312 B.C. and was later extended until by around 244 B.C. it reached Brundisium (modern Brindisi), the important harbor 350 miles away on the southeastern coast. From Capua it was 132 miles to Rome. At Tarracina (modern Terracina) the Via Appia touched the coast, then ran for the final fifty-six miles almost as straight as an arrow across the Pontine Marshes and the Alban Hills to Rome. The Forum Appii or Market of Appius (Acts 28:15), where the first of "the brethren" met Paul, was a post station forty-three miles from Rome, and is mentioned by Horace (65-8 B.C.) as the usual halt at the end of the first day's journey from Rome.[108] Tres Tabernae or Three Taverns (Acts 28:15) was a village nearly ten miles farther on toward Rome, and is mentioned by Cicero (106-43 B.C.) as the point where a branch road from Antium joined the Appian Way.[109]

Rome itself, with Nero (Fig. 129) then on the throne (A.D. 54-68), was at that time approaching the height of its imperial greatness, and Martial (A.D. c.40-c.102) was soon to hail the proud capital of the world as "Rome, goddess of earth and of the nations, that has no peer and no second."[110] We shall seek to gain a swift glimpse of the city as it was when Paul entered it, in the midst of Nero's reign and before the great fire of A.D. 64. For the purpose of such an inquiry there is available an immense wealth of notices in ancient literature, inscriptions, and archeological monuments, all of which have been the object of intensive study by scholars of many nations, by the Roman Catholic Church, and by the Italian government.

Nearing Rome, the Via Appia crossed what is known as the Campagna di Roma, the low plain surrounding the city. Nearby ran the great aqueduct Claudia which was completed by the Emperor Claudius in A.D. 50 (Fig. 130). The water which it brought from more than forty miles away was carried across the Campagna on arches 110 feet high, the remains of which are yet very impressive.[111]

[107] *Silvae.* II, ii, 12. tr. J. H. Mozley, LCL (1928) I, p.97.
[108] I, v, 3-6. tr. H. R. Fairclough, LCL (1926), p.65.
[109] *Letters to Atticus.* II, xii. tr. E. O. Winstedt, LCL (1913-19) I, p.143.
[110] *Terrarum dea gentiumque Roma,*
    Cui par est nihil et nihil secundum.
Epigrams. XII, viii, 1f. tr. W. C. A. Ker, LCL (1925-27) II, p.325.
[111] cf. Pliny, *Natural History.* XXXVI, xxiv.

This was but one of eight or nine conduits and aqueducts which at that time brought water to Rome from distant springs and rivers.[112] Of them Sextus Julius Frontinus, their keeper at the close of the first century A.D., remarked, "With such an array of indispensable structures carrying so many waters, compare, if you will, the idle Pyramids or the useless though famous works of the Greeks!"[113]

On the Campagna, the Via Appia began to penetrate the suburbs of the city. The plain was dotted with houses, gardens, and magnificent villas. Nearing the city the houses naturally became closer together and smaller in size. Deep within the city of the first century A.D. was the old Servian Wall, through which the Via Appia entered by the Porta Capena. This ancient wall is named for King Servius Tullius (c.578-c.534 B.C.) but was actually built by order of the republican Senate between 378 and 352 B.C. After the Punic Wars of the third and second centuries B.C. it was allowed to fall into decay and the city spread far beyond its limits. Some portions of it still exist, and the remains of the Porta Capena have been found near where the Via di San Gregorio now unites with the Via di Porta San Sebastiano. In the third century A.D. the approach of the barbarians led to the building of a new wall. It was begun by the Emperor Aurelian (A.D. 270-275) and completed by the Emperor Probus (A.D. 276-282). Restored by later emperors and popes, the Aurelian Wall still surrounds the city on the left bank of the Tiber. The wall on the right bank of the Tiber dates mainly from the time of Pope Urban VIII (1623-1644).[114]

The main part of the city, which was attained when one reached the Porta Capena, was built upon a famous group of seven hills (cf. Revelation 17:9), past which the Tiber River sweeps in three great

---

[112] (1) The first, the Appia, was constructed about 312 B.C. by Appius Claudius Caecus, who also built the Via Appia. It was a ten-mile covered tunnel from springs east of the city. (2) The Anio Vetus, built around 272 B.C., brought water 41 miles from the river Anio in the Apennines. (3) The Marcia was built about 145 B.C. by Marcius the praetor. It was 58 miles long, the last seven miles being on arches high enough to carry the flow to the summit of the Capitol. (4) The Tepula of around 127 B.C. was small and short. (5) The Julia and (6) the Virgo were built by Agrippa in 33 B.C. and 20 B.C. respectively. (7) The Alsietina was constructed by Augustus. (8) The Claudia was started by Caligula in A.D. 36 and finished by Claudius. An archway of the Claudia was made by Aurelian into one of the gates of his city wall, and is now the Porta Maggiore. (9) The Anio Novus also was begun by Caligula but only completed in A.D. 86. Esther B. Van Deman, *The Building of the Roman Aqueducts.* 1934; Thomas Ashby, *The Aqueducts of Ancient Rome.* 1935.

[113] *The Aqueducts of Rome.* I, 16. tr. C. E. Bennett, LCL (1925), pp.357-359.

[114] I. A. Richmond, *The City Wall of Imperial Rome.* 1930; G. Säflund, *Le mura di Roma reppublicana.* 1932.

curves. Standing at the Porta Capena, the Aventine hill was on the left, the Caelian on the right, and the Palatine directly ahead. Beyond the Palatine was the Capitoline, which rises near the inner curve of the Tiber and the island in the river. Ranged north of the Caelian hill were the Esquiline, Viminal, and Quirinal hills. The plain west of the Quirinal and enclosed in the outward curve of the Tiber was the Campus Martius. Across the Tiber, on its right or western bank, was the commanding height of the hill of Janiculum, and beyond it at the northwestern end of Rome the Ager Vaticanus or Vatican district. The latter included a low eminence known as Mons Vaticanus and a plain beside the river called the Campus Vaticanus.

The Via Appia and the other highroads which led into Rome, such as the Via Ostiensis and Via Latina on the south, the Via Labicana and Via Tiburtina on the east, and the Via Nomentana, Via Salaria, Via Pinciana, and Via Flaminia on the north, were good thoroughfares, fifteen to twenty feet in width. In many cases these highways continued directly into the heart of the city in the form of fine avenues, and frequently the streets of modern Rome follow their lines exactly. The Via Flaminia, for example, which was constructed by the Roman statesman Caius Flaminius Nepos about 200 B.C., continued as the Via Lata directly to the foot of the Capitoline hill. It is represented by the splendid central avenue of modern Rome, the Corso Umberto Primo, beneath which at a depth of fifteen or twenty feet the lava paving blocks of the ancient street are still found.[115]

Within the old Republican Wall and on the Seven Hills, however, many of the streets were narrow, steep, and crooked. They were usually called *vici*, as for example the Vicus Longus and the Vicus Patricius. In cases where they made steep ascents and descents they were frequently known as *clivi*, as for example the Clivus Capitolinus and the Clivus Palatinus. It was required that they be at least nine and one-half feet wide to allow for projecting balconies. In many parts of the inner city they formed an inextricably tangled labyrinth. It was said that if they could have been straightened out and laid end to end they would have reached for more than sixty miles.[116] They were often defiled by refuse and were quite unlighted by night. By day they were jammed with pedestrians, horsemen, litters, and carrying chairs, and by night they were filled with the noise of trans-

[115] Rodolfo Lanciani, *Ancient and Modern Rome*. 1925, p.145.
[116] Pliny, *Natural History*. III, ix, 67.

port carts of all sorts, such wheeled vehicles being permitted within the city only between dusk and dawn.[117]

In the residential districts the dwellings were of two chief types. The *domus* was the home of the wealthy. It spread out horizontally in a series of halls, and had its doors and windows opening on its interior courts. The *insula* was the residence of the masses. It was an apartment house, filling a square or block, and rising vertically to surprising heights. Augustus found it necessary to place a limit of seventy feet on the height of structures on the public streets,[118] but this still allowed apartment houses of three, four, five, and six stories to be common. In external appearance these apartment houses, the finest of which were adorned with balconies and brightened with window gardens, would have seemed quite modern. Their conveniences within were strictly limited, however. Light and heat were inadequate. Water from the aqueducts seems to have been conveyed only to the ground floors, which alone were connected with Rome's excellent network of sewers.[119] Often, too, builders and landlords sought to increase their profits by cheap construction and poor repair even though the lives of the renters were imperiled by the frequent collapses of the buildings which ensued. In his satire on life at Rome Juvenal cried, "Who at cool Praeneste, or at Volsinii amid its leafy hills, was ever afraid of his house tumbling down? . . . But here we inhabit a city propped up for the most part by slats: for that is how the landlord patches up the cracks in the old wall, bidding the inmates sleep at ease under a roof ready to tumble about their ears."[120]

Thus Rome was a teeming metropolitan center at the time when Paul came to it. The population of the city in the first century A.D. has usually been estimated at about 1,200,000, or substantially the same as the modern population which in January 1939 was 1,284,600. In 1941, however, the discovery of an inscription at Ostia was announced with statistics indicating that in A.D. 14, the year in which Tiberius began to reign, the city of Rome had a population of 4,100,-000 inhabitants.[121] Statistics from 250 years after the time of Paul

[117] A. Grenier in Ch. Daremberg and Edmond Saglio, eds., *Dictionnaire des antiquités grecques et romaines d'après les textes et les monuments.* (1877-1919), v, cols.861-863.

[118] Strabo, *Geography.* v, iii, 7.

[119] The central collector for the system of sewers was the Cloaca Maxima, the mouth of which still can be seen opening into the Tiber, and which was in use until very recently. Pliny, *Natural History.* XXXVI, xxiv.

[120] *Satire.* III, 190-196.   [121] AJA 45 (1941), p.438.

list 1,797 *domus* and 46,602 *insulae*, or blocks of apartment houses, in the city.[122]

The great city was fortunate in the possession of many parks and gardens. It has been calculated that one-eighth of the total area of the city was given over to parks and open spaces, whereas in modern London, for example, only one-tenth of the total area is so used.[123] In the Campus Martius numerous garden porticoes were to be found, many of which had been built by Augustus and his wealthy friends. These were large parallelograms of green enclosed by a colonnade. For the enjoyment of the public, the twelve largest of these porticoes protected an area of 28,000 square yards from sun and rain. Under such shelter it was possible to walk all the way from the Forum Boarium, which was between the Palatine hill and the Tiber, to the opposite end of the city where Hadrian's mausoleum was built. There were imperial gardens also in the Vatican district. The elder Agrippina, the wife of Germanicus (15 B.C.-A.D. 19), possessed a villa on the north slope of the Janiculum, and her son Caligula built his famous Circus in the plain beneath. To the east were the gardens of Domitia, Nero's aunt. After her death the entire district became a single domain, known as Horti Neronis or Nero's Gardens.

The buildings erected for purposes of amusement and recreation were among the most impressive structures in Rome. These included not only circuses but also theaters, amphitheaters, and baths, which were frequented avidly by a populace whose leisure time included no less than 159 holidays in the year. Ninety-three of these holidays were devoted to games and performances held at public expense.[124] The games par excellence at Rome in the time of Paul were the chariot races of the circus.[125] The characteristic plan of the circus was a long rectangle rounded off at one end into a semicircle, and with a low wall called the spina or "backbone" running lengthwise in the center. Of them all the Circus Maximus[126] was the oldest and largest. It was situated in the hollow between the Aventine and the Palatine, and Paul must have seen it soon after passing through the Porta

[122] These figures are from the *Regionaries*, which are two descriptions of Rome, one called the *Curiosum* and the other the *Notitia*, and both deriving from a lost original which probably was compiled in the reign of Constantine between A.D. 312 and 315. Jérôme Carcopino, *Daily Life in Ancient Rome*. 1940, pp.23,287f.

[123] A. G. Mackinnon, *The Rome of Saint Paul*. 1930, p.168.

[124] Carcopino, *Daily Life in Ancient Rome*, p.205.

[125] cf. Juvenal, *Satire*. x, 77-81, "The public has long since cast off its cares; the people . . . now . . . longs eagerly for just two things—Bread and Circuses!"

[126] PATD pp.114-120.

Capena. This circus had been used for centuries, but was greatly enlarged and improved by Caesar in 46 B.C., and later was adorned with the obelisk of Ramses II which Augustus brought from Heliopolis and which today is to be seen in the Piazza del Popolo. The Circus was 1,800 feet in length and seated 150,000 spectators.[127] After enlargements by Nero it seated 250,000.[128] The walls of the Circus Maximus have now disappeared almost entirely, but the form is still distinctly traceable. The Circus Flaminius[129] was built about 221 B.C. by the censor Caius Flaminius Nepos who also constructed the Via Flaminia (p.367). It stood on the site of the present Palazzo Caetani, and was 1,300 feet in length. The Circus of Caligula[130] (A.D. 37-41) was built on the west side of the Tiber in the Ager Vaticanus as was mentioned above (p.369). It was intended as a private course for chariot racing and was relatively small in size, being about six hundred feet long. On the spina Caligula erected an obelisk which he brought from Heliopolis, this being a monolith of red granite without hieroglyphics. The circus in the Vatican was a favorite place for the sports and orgies of Claudius (A.D. 41-54) and Nero (A.D. 54-68), and is often known as the Circus of Nero.

The theaters to which Romans went at that time to enjoy plays included the Theater of Pompey (55 B.C.) seating about 10,000,[131] the Theater of Balbus (13 B.C.) seating around 7,700,[132] and the yet well preserved Theater of Marcellus (11 B.C.) accommodating some 14,000.[133]

The chief development of the amphitheater, to whose cruel spectacles the Romans became so addicted, came after the time of Paul. One permanent amphitheater had been built in the southern part of the Campus Martius in 29 B.C., and was standing when Paul came to Rome.[134] The great Flavian amphitheater or Colosseum[135] in which the gladiators were to be sent to their work of mutual massacre and the Christians were to be thrown to the wild beasts, was not yet built. It was first begun by Vespasian, on a site which had formerly been occupied by an artificial lake at Nero's palace (p.372), and was completed by Titus and decorated by Domitian. A tremendous elliptical structure, measuring nearly one-third of a mile in circumference and built of hard travertine stone, the Colosseum has survived the cen-

[127] Dionysius of Halicarnassus (c.54-c.7 B.C.), *Roman Antiquities.* III, lxviii, 2f. tr. E. Cary, LCL (1937-) II, pp.241-243.
[128] Pliny, *Natural History.* XXXVI, xxiv.   [129] PATD pp.111-113.
[130] PATD pp.113f.,370f.   [131] PATD pp.515-517.   [132] PATD p.513.
[133] PATD pp.513-515.   [134] PATD p.11.   [135] PATD pp.6-11.

turies to loom up still in Rome in gloomy grandeur. In its midst now rises a cross, in memory of the Christian martyrs who died there and in silent protest against the barbarism which cost so many lives before the spirit of Christianity abolished it.[136]

More in accord with the Greek spirit, although a distinctively Roman development, were the *thermae* or baths. These were public institutions where the ideal of "a sound mind in a sound body"[137] was cherished and where gymnasium, bath, and library provided for exercise, cleanliness, and culture. In 33 B.C. when Augustus' son-in-law Agrippa was aedile there were already 170 public baths in Rome, and by Pliny's time he found them to be so numerous that he gave up trying to count them.[138] Remains of the Thermae which Agrippa built during his aedileship are still to be seen in the Campus Martius,[139] which is where the Thermae of Nero[140] also were erected. The most famous baths and those whose ruins are most impressive today, however, were built after the time of Paul. These included the Thermae of Titus[141] now destroyed, the Thermae of Trajan[142] on the Esquiline just southeast of the present church of San Pietro in Vincoli, the magnificent Thermae of Caracalla[143] on the Via Appia outside the Porta Capena, the extensive Thermae of Diocletian[144] which loom up so impressively as one emerges from the railway station in Rome and which today house the National Roman Museum, the Church of Saint Mary of the Angels, and the Oratory of Saint Bernard, and the Thermae of Constantine[145] on the Quirinal.

In the very midst of the city were the Capitoline and Palatine hills, with the Forum lying in the valley between. The outstanding feature of the Capitoline hill was the great temple of Jupiter[146] on the southwestern summit. This temple was originally built by Tarquinius Superbus, the last of the kings, and was dedicated in 509 B.C., the first year of the Republic. It was burned down in 83 B.C., rebuilt,

---

[136] Carcopino, *Daily Life in Ancient Rome*, pp.244-247. Gladiatorial combats were stopped by the Emperor Honorius in A.D. 404 (Theodoret, *Ecclesiastical History*. v, 26 [NPNFSS III, p.151]).

[137] Juvenal, *Satire*. x, 356.   [138] *Natural History*. XXXVI, XXIV.

[139] Karl Baedeker, *Rome and Central Italy*. 16th ed. 1930, p.280.

[140] cf. Martial, *Epigrams*. VII, XXXIV, 4f.:
  What was worse than Nero?
  What is better than Nero's warm baths?

[141] PATD pp.533f.   [142] PATD pp.534-536.

[143] PATD pp.520-524. They were begun by Septimus Severus in A.D. 206, inaugurated by Antoninus Caracalla before being finished, and finally completed by Severus Alexander between 222 and 235.

[144] PATD pp.527-530.   [145] PATD pp.525f.   [146] PATD pp.297-302.

burned again in A.D. 69, and finally reconstructed most splendidly by Domitian. The marble fragments which have been found in excavation of its ruins are probably from the time of Domitian, but even in Paul's time the temple of the chief god of the Romans must have been very impressive. The northern summit of the Capitoline hill was the citadel (Arx) of early Rome and the site later of the temple of Juno Moneta (the Warner). The Arx and north slope of the Capitol are occupied now by the enormous Monument of Victor Emmanuel II, while the site of the temple of Juno is taken by the church of Santa Maria in Aracoeli. On the side of the Capitoline, commanding the Forum, was the Tabularium, erected after the fire of 83 B.C. to provide a fireproof hall of records for the state. It was probably the first attempt at such a building which was to be absolutely impervious to the accidents of the elements, and its walls are well preserved although much rebuilt in the Palazzo del Senatore, which is the modern council chamber of Rome.

The Palatine hill was the residence of the Roman emperor. Augustus, Tiberius, and Caligula all built there until the imperial palace covered a large part of the hill. The house of Livia, the wife of Augustus, still remains on the hill, its walls containing excellent murals. Also the substructures of the palace of Tiberius (Domus Tiberiana) are to be seen occupying a large part of the northwest corner of the Palatine. The ruins which are in the center of the hill are usually called the Domus Augustiana but actually are mostly a reconstruction by Domitian. These structures now appear as great masses of brickwork with arched roofs, but in Paul's day they were splendidly encased in marble and presented a magnificent appearance.[147] The Palatine itself could not content the extravagant Nero, however, and so he built a palace extending from the Palatine to the Esquiline, northeast of where the Colosseum now stands. Shortly after its completion this building was burned in the great fire of A.D. 64 and upon being rebuilt received the name Golden House (Domus Aurea). Suetonius described it as follows: "Its vestibule was large enough to contain a colossal statue of the emperor a hundred and twenty feet high; and it was so extensive that it had a triple colonnade a mile long. There was a pond too, like a sea, surrounded with buildings to represent cities, besides tracts of country, varied by tilled fields, vineyards, pastures, and woods, with great numbers

---

[147] Augustus boasted of Rome that "he had found it built of brick and left it in marble." Suetonius (A.D. c.100), *Augustus*. 28. tr. J. C. Rolfe, LCL (1914) I, p.167.

of wild and domestic animals. In the rest of the house all parts were overlaid with gold and adorned with gems and mother-of-pearl."[148]

On the southwest side of the Palatine, near the Circus Maximus, was a building now known as the Paedagogium, which probably belonged to the offices of the imperial palace. Some of its rooms are thought to have been used as prisons. The walls are still covered with rudely scratched drawings and inscriptions. One of these drawings, which was discovered by Garrucci in 1856 and is now in the Museo Kircheriano in Rome, is the famous "caricature of the crucifixion" (Fig. 131). This crude graffito shows a man's body with an ass's head, on a cross. The feet are supported on a platform and the outstretched arms fastened to the transverse bar of the cross. To the left is a smaller figure of a boy or young man with one hand raised in an attitude of adoration. The inscription reads, "Alexamenos worships his god." Presumably this represents the mockery to which some young Christian in the imperial palace was subjected. This graffito is to be dated perhaps 150 years after Paul was in Rome, or at the beginning of the third century, but it shows vividly how the word of the cross was foolishness to many (I Corinthians 1:18).

The Palatine was the site not only of the imperial palace but also of at least two important temples. One was the Temple of Apollo, which was erected by Augustus, and whose identification among the ruins on the Palatine is now difficult. The other was the Temple of the Magna Mater, or Cybele, the great mother deity of the Phrygians. This goddess, in the form of a meteoric stone, was brought to Rome in response to an oracle in 204 B.C. when Hannibal was threatening the city.[149] Another temple where an imported oriental religion was already entrenched in Rome was that of Isis and Serapis. The sanctuary of these Egyptian gods was on the Campus Martius not far from the famous Pantheon,[150] and was erected probably about A.D. 39. It was a vast structure, the central part being 420 feet long, and approached by a long colonnaded court lined with lions and sphinxes. The site of the temple is now occupied by part of the Church of

---

[148] *Nero*, 31.

[149] Livy (59 B.C.-A.D. 17), *History of Rome*. XXIX, 10-14. tr. Cyrus Edmonds, *Bohn's Classical Library*. III (1878), pp.1244-1250; cf. Samuel Dill, *Roman Society from Nero to Marcus Aurelius*. 1925, p.548.

[150] The best preserved ancient edifice in Rome today, the Pantheon ("all-holy"), originally was built by Agrippa, the son-in-law of Augustus, and was given its present circular form and beautiful dome by Hadrian. It was made into the church Sancta Maria ad Martyres in A.D. 609 when twenty-eight wagonloads of the bones of the martyrs were brought there from the catacombs, and is now known as Santa Maria Rotonda.

Sant' Ignazio, a section of the Collegio Romano, the apse of the Church of Santa Maria sopra Minerva, and the Via del Piè di Marmo. The famous sculptures of the Nile (now in the Vatican Museum) and the Tiber (now in the Louvre in Paris) probably belonged to this temple, as did several obelisks including those now in front of the Pantheon (Piazza della Rotonda), Santa Maria sopra Minerva (Piazza della Minerva), and the Railway Station (Piazza delle Terme).

If Julius the centurion led Paul the prisoner directly to the Forum, the party would have skirted the eastern edge of the Palatine and then have begun to tread the Via Sacra at the point where the Arch of Constantine later was built and now stands. From there the Via Sacra ascended to the summit of the Velia, a low hill running across between the Palatine and Esquiline where the Arch of Titus was to be erected not many years afterward (p.329), and then traversed the great Forum area along its longitudinal axis from southeast to northwest. In front of where the Basilica of Constantine later was to stand the street was lined with the elegant shops of goldsmiths, bronze-workers, jewelers, and dealers in oriental pearls. Beyond were the Palace of the Vestal Virgins (Atrium Vestae) with many of its walls and a few of its statues remaining today, the Temple of Vesta (Aedes Vestae) in which the sacred fire was kept ever alight, and the Regia, an office building with historical lists of the Roman magistrates carved on its marble walls (Fasti Consulares). Then came the Triumphal Arch of Augustus (19 B.C.), of which only the foundations now exist, and on its left the Temple of Castor and Pollux and on its right the Temple of Julius Caesar. The temple to the twin gods, Castor and Pollux, is the most prominent ruin in the Forum today, and if, as is probable, the three beautiful columns which are still standing belong to a reconstruction in the reign of Augustus,[151] they were seen by the eyes of the apostle Paul. The Templum Divi Juli, of which only the concrete substructures now remain, was erected by Augustus to the deified Julius Caesar and dedicated in 29 B.C. Thus the worship of the deceased emperor was established in Rome in the same year in which in the province of Asia the worship of the living emperor was instituted (p.345). By the time Paul was in Rome a temple to Augustus had also been erected there. This Templum Divi Augusti was founded by Tiberius and completed by Caligula, later (after Nero's fire) being restored magnificently by Domitian. It has

---

[151] Baedeker, *Rome and Central Italy*, p.331.

often been identified with ruins lying south of the Temple of Castor and Pollux on the Vicus Tuscus, but this is uncertain. Later than the time of Paul but of interest because of the excellent preservation of its portico is the Temple of Faustina not far northeast of the Temple of Julius Caesar and now incorporated in the church of San Lorenzo in Miranda. It was dedicated by Antoninus Pius in A.D. 141 to his deified wife, the elder Faustina, and then was given an additional dedication to the emperor himself after his own death. Ten beautiful columns of the portico are still standing, and above them is the inscription, the first line of which was added after the death of Antoninus:

"To the deified Antoninus and
to the deified Faustina by the decree of the Senate."[152]

Finally one reached the Forum Romanum proper, the center of the ancient city and in Paul's day the center of the world. New fora had already been erected in the larger plain to the north, the Forum Julium, begun by Caesar and completed by Augustus, and the Forum of Augustus; and yet others would be constructed, the Forum of Vespasian, the Forum Transitorium begun by Domitian and finished by Nerva, and the magnificent Forum of Trajan with Trajan's marvelous Column, which still stands.[153] But nothing could replace the original Forum in the affections of the city, and the glorious traditions connected with it were commemorated with columns, statues, bronzes, marbles, and other works of art. Just to the northwest of the Forum, beyond the rostra or orators' platform and near where the Arch of Severus (A.D. 203) now stands, was the Umbilicus Urbis Romae, the ideal center of the city. Just to the southwest of the Forum, near the Arch of Tiberius (A.D. 16) and in front of the Temple of Saturn, was the Miliarium Aureum, a gilded column erected by Augustus and giving the names and distances of the chief towns to which highroads radiated from Rome. These included points no less distant than Londinium (ancient London) on the west and Jerusalem on the east. When Paul, the world-minded, reached here he

[152] *Divo Antonio et*
divae Faustinae ex S.C.
The initials S.C. are the customary abbreviation for *Senatus consulto.*

[153] The Column is adorned with a spiral frieze over 650 feet in length, depicting military campaigns of Trajan. The emperor's ashes were deposited in the base upon his death in A.D. 117. His bronze statue which once stood on the summit, was replaced by a statue of Saint Peter in the sixteenth century.

had indeed reached the center from which the gospel he preached might spread to the uttermost parts of the earth.

A general view of this central part of ancient Rome is shown in Fig. 132. The eight columns standing in the left foreground belong to the Temple of Saturn which was dedicated originally around 497 B.C. and restored about 44 B.C. Beside and below them is the Forum Romanum proper and glimpsed through the last two of the eight columns is the portico of the Temple of Faustina. Beyond the trees in the right foreground and only partially hidden by them are the three columns of the Temple of Castor and Pollux. Just to the left of these columns and much farther beyond them is the Arch of Titus, while on the horizon appears the Colosseum.

On either side of the Forum stood great basilicas, or quadrangular courts surrounded by colonnades and containing court chambers and public shops. On the north was the Basilica Aemilia, built originally around 179 B.C. by the censors Aemilius Lepidus and Fulvius Nobilior and reconstructed about 54 B.C. by Aemilius Paullus. In the latter year on the other side of the Forum, Julius Caesar began the Basilica Julia, which he dedicated in 46 B.C. although it was not altogether completed until A.D. 12. Both of these vast and splendid structures, of which extensive remains are yet to be seen, are of interest in connection with Paul. It was probably within the colonnaded courts of the Basilica Julia that Paul eventually heard the sentence of death pronounced upon him. It was from the Basilica of Aemilius Paullus that the Roman prefect Probianus in A.D. 386 took twenty-four beautiful columns of Phrygian marble to adorn the Church of Saint Paul which was being erected outside the walls of the city—an event of which the condemned prisoner little could have dreamed.[154]

A short distance northwest of the Forum Romanum and beneath the present church of San Giuseppe de' Falegnami is the prison known as the Carcer Mamertinus. Built in the side of the Capitoline hill, it has an upper vaulted chamber, and a lower chamber or dungeon originally accessible only through a hole in its ceiling. The lower chamber was probably an old springhouse and hence was called Tullianum from the early Latin word *tullius*, meaning "spring." This was where noted prisoners like Jugurtha, the Catilinarian conspirators, and Vercingetorix were kept before execution. In telling of the execution of Catiline's confederates, the Roman historian Sal-

---

[154] Mackinnon, *The Rome of Saint Paul*, pp.33f.; Dorothy M. Robathan, *The Monuments of Ancient Rome*. 1950, pp.64-70.

lust (86-34 B.C.) describes the Tullianum almost exactly as it now exists: "In the prison . . . there is a place called the Tullianum, about twelve feet below the surface of the ground. It is enclosed on all sides by walls, and above it is a chamber with a vaulted roof of stone. Neglect, darkness, and stench make it hideous and fearsome to behold."[155]

3. THE MARTYRDOM OF PAUL AND PETER

ACCORDING to tradition which goes back at least to the fifth century, the Mamertine prison is the place where both Paul and Peter were confined before their execution under Nero.[1] Whether this is correct or not is difficult to determine, but the fact seems certain that the two great apostles suffered martyrdom in Rome under Nero.[2] In the case of Paul, the last statement of the book of Acts is that he lived two whole years in his own hired dwelling in Rome, preaching freely to all who came to him (Acts 28:30f.). Whether his martyrdom followed at the close of these two years, as the further silence of Acts might seem to imply,[3] cannot now be said with certainty. Perhaps he was set free at the expiration of that period and enabled to achieve his cherished purpose of preaching in Spain (Romans 15:24, 28), before eventually suffering death in Rome.[4] In the case of Peter there is a veiled reference to his death in John 21:18: "when you are old, you will stretch out your hands, and another will gird you and carry you where you do not wish to go."

Then, before the end of the first century we find a writer at Rome referring at some length to the impressive example set by Peter and

---

[155] *The War with Catiline.* LV, 3f. tr. J. C. Rolfe, LCL (1921), p.115.

[1] A. S. Barnes, *The Martyrdom of St. Peter and St. Paul.* 1933, p.67.

[2] For arguments that Peter never went to Rome but died in Jerusalem in A.D. 44 see Donald F. Robinson in JBL 64 (1945), pp.255-267; and Warren M. Smaltz in JBL 71 (1952), pp.211-216.

[3] cf. B. W. Bacon (in AJT 22 [1918], p.15), "But as to Paul the reader is *not* really left in ignorance. His fate *is* made known, but made known with that chaste reticence which the Greek poets employ when they only report through others the tragedies enacted behind the scenes. In the great Farewell Discourse of Acts 20:17-38 the martyr takes his leave. In Acts 28:17-31 the tragedy itself is veiled behind the triumph of the cause."

[4] I Clement 5, which is quoted more fully just below, gives support to this view for it speaks of Paul as "having come to the farthest bounds of the West," which to one writing in Rome as Clement did surely would have meant Spain. The Muratorian Fragment (middle of the 2d century A.D.) also refers to "the departure of Paul from the city (i.e. Rome) on his journey to Spain" (ASBACH p.118).

Paul in their martyrdom. The passage is to be found in a letter which Clement, the bishop of Rome (A.D. c.88-c.97), wrote to the Corinthians around A.D. 95. Since there was disharmony in the Corinthian church which had its roots in envy and jealousy, Clement pictured the evil results which had followed upon such attitudes both in ancient and in recent times. As a recent illustration, he cited the persecution and martyrdom of Peter and Paul. Clement said:[5]

"But to leave the ancient examples, let us come to the champions who lived nearest our times; let us take the noble examples of our generation. On account of jealousy and envy the greatest and most righteous pillars of the church were persecuted, and contended even unto death. Let us set before our eyes the good Apostles: Peter, who on account of unrighteous jealousy endured not one nor two, but many sufferings, and so having borne his testimony, went to his deserved place of glory. On account of jealousy and strife Paul pointed out the prize of endurance. After he had been seven times in bonds, had been driven into exile, had been stoned, had been a preacher in the East and in the West, he received the noble reward of his faith; having taught righteousness unto the whole world, and having come to the farthest bounds of the West, and having borne witness before rulers, he thus departed from the world and went unto the holy place, having become a notable pattern of patient endurance."

Clement then proceeded immediately to group with Peter and Paul a large number of Christians, including both men and women, who were persecuted fiendishly and put to death:

"Unto these men who lived lives of holiness was gathered a vast multitude of the elect, who by many indignities and tortures, being the victims of jealousy, set the finest examples among us. On account of jealousy women, when they had been persecuted as Danaïds and Dircae,[6] and had suffered cruel and unholy insults, safely reached the goal in the race of faith and received a noble reward, feeble though they were in body."

That is an unmistakable reference to the persecution of the Christians at Rome by Nero, as it is more fully known to us through the Roman historian Tacitus (A.D. c.55-c.117). Although Tacitus was not an eyewitness of the persecution, he had very good opportunities for obtaining accurate information and his account is regarded as entirely trustworthy. In the fifteenth book of his *Annals* he tells of the terrible conflagration which broke out at Rome on the eighteenth day of July in the year 64. Raging for six days and driven by the

[5] I Clement, 5f. (ASBACH pp.7f.).

[6] That is, they were forced to play the part of the daughters of Danaüs who, according to Greek mythology, suffered in the underworld, and of Dirce who was tied by the hair to a wild bull and dragged to death.

wind, the fire swept irresistibly through the labyrinth of Roman streets and when finally it was stopped only four of the city's fourteen districts were standing entire.[7] Whether the fire started accidentally or was set deliberately by Nero,[8] public suspicion turned upon the emperor as its instigator. Thereupon Nero cast the blame upon the hated Christians and subjected them to the most atrocious tortures. This persecution is described vividly by Tacitus:

"Nero put in his own place as culprits, and punished with most ingenious cruelty, men whom the common people hated for their shameful crimes and called Christians. Christ, from whom the name was derived, had been put to death in the reign of Tiberius by the procurator Pontius Pilate. The deadly superstition, having been checked for awhile, began to break out again, not only throughout Judea, where this mischief first arose, but also at Rome, where from all sides all things scandalous and shameful meet and become fashionable. Therefore, at the beginning, some were seized who made confessions; then, on their information, a vast multitude was convicted, not so much of arson as of hatred of the human race. And they were not only put to death, but subjected to insults, in that they were either dressed up in the skins of wild beasts and perished by the cruel mangling of dogs, or else put on crosses to be set on fire, and, as day declined, to be burned, being used as light by night. Nero had thrown open his gardens for that spectacle, and gave a circus play, mingling with the people dressed in a charioteer's costume or driving in a chariot. From this arose, however, toward men who were, indeed, criminals and deserving extreme penalties, sympathy, on the ground that they were destroyed not for the public good, but to satisfy the cruelty of an individual."[9]

This description by Tacitus agrees remarkably well with the intimations of Clement's letter and fills out the details of the indignities and tortures heaped upon the Christians at Nero's circus play. Both accounts evidently refer to the same events, and the close agreement between Tacitus and Clement is strong reason for regarding the year 64 as the date of the death of the two great apostles.

Around A.D. 200 Tertullian likewise refers to the death of Peter and Paul as having taken place at Rome under Nero and correctly interprets John 21:18 as a reference to Peter's crucifixion: "At Rome Nero was the first who stained with blood the rising faith. Then is Peter girt by another, when he is made fast to the cross. Then does

---

[7] Tacitus, *Annals.* xv, 38, 40.

[8] Suetonius (*Nero*, 38) states that the city was set on fire openly by Nero, who pretended to be disgusted with the ugliness of Rome's old buildings and the narrow and crooked streets.

[9] *Annals.* xv, 44.

Paul obtain a birth suited to Roman citizenship, when in Rome he springs to life again ennobled by martyrdom."[10] On another occasion Tertullian incidentally indicates the manner of both martyrdoms by comparing the death of Peter to that of Jesus and the death of Paul to that of John the Baptist:[11] "How happy is its church, on which apostles poured forth all their doctrine along with their blood! Where Peter endures a passion like his Lord's![12] where Paul wins his crown in a death like John's!"[13]

Also Eusebius relates in his *Church History* that Peter and Paul suffered martyrdom at about the same time in Rome under Nero. The *Church History* was published in A.D. 326, but Eusebius derived his information in this regard from authorities who had lived much earlier. He cites Caius, who probably lived in Rome in the time of Pope Zephyrinus about A.D. 199-217, and Dionysius, who was bishop of Corinth at the same time that Soter was bishop of Rome around A.D. 166-174. The entire passage, with the quotations from the two earlier sources, is as follows:[14]

[10] *Scorpiace.* 15 (ANF III, p.648).

[11] *On Prescription against Heretics.* 36 (ANF III, p.260).

[12] The martyrdom of Peter is narrated with apocryphal elaboration in the Acts of Peter (JANT pp.333f.), which is probably to be dated around A.D. 200-220. In this work is found the famous and beautiful *"Domine quo vadis?"* legend, according to which Peter was warned to leave Rome and went forth but met Jesus coming into the city. "And as he went forth out of the city, he saw the Lord entering into Rome. And when he saw him, he said: Lord whither goest thou here? And the Lord said unto him: I go into Rome to be crucified. And Peter said unto him: Lord, art thou being crucified again? He said unto him: Yea, Peter, I am being crucified again. And Peter came to himself: and having beheld the Lord ascending up into heaven, he returned to Rome, rejoicing, and glorifying the Lord, for that he said: I am being crucified: the which was about to befall Peter." When Peter was crucified he insisted that it should be "with the head downward and not otherwise" and so it was done. Eusebius also states, on the authority of Origen, that Peter was crucified head-downward (see below, n.14).

[13] Mark 6:27. That Paul should have been put to death by the sword was to be expected since he was a Roman citizen (Acts 16:37; 22:27f.; 23:27). Both crucifixion and condemnation *ad bestias* appear to have been methods of execution usually reserved for persons of lower standing than Roman citizens. D. W. Riddle (*Paul, Man of Conflict.* 1940, pp.140f.) suggests the possibility that Paul was thrown to the wild beasts, since Ignatius (A.D. c.110-c.117) who was to die that way (Romans 4. ANF I, p.75) said that he wanted to "be found in (*literally* under) the footsteps of Paul" (Ephesians 12. ANF I, p.55). Ignatius, however, well may have been referring simply to the fact of martyrdom, since in another place he hopes that by fighting with beasts at Rome he "may indeed become the disciple of Jesus" (Ephesians 1 [ANF I, p.49]). Riddle regards the ascription of Roman citizinship to Paul by Acts as a tendentious and therefore unreliable statement, but that Saul who bore the eminent Roman cognomen Paul actually was a Roman citizen is entirely probable.

[14] *Ch. Hist.* II, xxv; cf. III, i, where Eusebius says, "Peter appears to have preached in Pontus, Galatia, Bithynia, Cappadocia, and Asia to the Jews of the dispersion. And at last, having come to Rome, he was crucified head-downwards; for he had requested

"When the government of Nero was now firmly established, he began to plunge into unholy pursuits, and armed himself even against the religion of the God of the universe. . . . He was the first of the emperors who showed himself an enemy of the divine religion. The Roman Tertullian is likewise a witness of this. He writes as follows: 'Examine your records. There you will find that Nero was the first that persecuted this doctrine, particularly then when after subduing all the east, he exercised his cruelty against all at Rome. We glory in having such a man the leader in our punishment. For whoever knows him can understand that nothing was condemned by Nero unless it was something of great excellence.' Thus publicly announcing himself as the first among God's chief enemies, he was led on to the slaughter of the apostles. It is, therefore, recorded that Paul was beheaded in Rome itself, and that Peter likewise was crucified under Nero. This account of Peter and Paul is substantiated by the fact that their names are preserved in the cemeteries of that place even to the present day. It is confirmed likewise by Caius, a member of the Church, who arose under Zephyrinus, bishop of Rome. He, in a published disputation with Proclus, the leader of the Phrygian heresy, speaks as follows concerning the places where the sacred corpses of the aforesaid apostles are laid: 'But I can show the trophies of the apostles. For if you will go to the Vatican or to the Ostian way, you will find the trophies of those who laid the foundations of this church.' And that they both suffered martyrdom at the same time is stated by Dionysius, bishop of Corinth, in his epistle to the Romans, in the following words: 'You have thus by such an admonition bound together the planting of Peter and of Paul at Rome and Corinth. For both of them planted and likewise taught us in our Corinth.[15] And they taught together in like manner in Italy, and suffered martyrdom at the same time.' "[16]

This passage in Eusebius is of particular interest because of the quotation which it contains from Caius. As a presbyter in the Roman

---

that he might suffer in this way. What do we need to say concerning Paul, who preached the Gospel of Christ from Jerusalem to Illyricum, and afterwards suffered martyrdom in Rome under Nero? These facts are related by Origen in the third volume of his Commentary on Genesis."

[15] The mention of a "Cephas" party at Corinth in I Corinthians 1:12 makes it probable that Peter did work there as Dionysius states.

[16] "At the same time" (κατὰ τὸν αὐτὸν καιρόν. ed. E. Schwartz, *Kleine Ausgabe.* 3d ed. 1922, p.73), allows some margin and does not necessarily imply on the very same day. In his *Chronicon* (ed. Scaliger. 1606, p.192, cf. p.162) Eusebius places the deaths of Peter and Paul together in the fourteenth year of Nero, which would be A.D. 67-68. But in the very same connection Eusebius describes Nero's persecution of the Christians in Rome and assigns it likewise to Nero's fourteenth year. It must be concluded, therefore, that Eusebius made an error as to the date of the Neronian persecution, which is definitely known to have taken place in the summer of A.D. 64. It should be noted that a date around A.D. 67 for the martyrdom of Peter and Paul does have the support of a statement by Jerome that Seneca (c.4 B.C.-A.D. 65) died two years before the apostles (Orazio Marucchi, *Pietro e Paolo a Roma.* 4th ed. 1934, p.21), but since this involves separating their death by several years from the fire and persecution of A.D. 64 it seems less probable.

church at the beginning of the third century, he was involved in a disputation with Proclus, the leader of the sect of the Montanists. As is evident from a later passage in the *Church History*, Proclus had supported his position by an appeal to the existence of the tombs of Philip and his four daughters at Hierapolis in Asia.[17] This latter passage reads: "And in the Dialogue of Caius which we mentioned a little above, Proclus, against whom he directed his disputation, in agreement with what has been quoted, speaks thus concerning the death of Philip and his daughters: 'After him there were four prophetesses, the daughters of Philip, at Hierapolis in Asia. Their tomb is there and the tomb of their father.' "[18]

Over against the claims of Proclus, Caius appealed to the existence in Rome of the glorious last resting places of Peter and Paul, who had taught there and laid the foundations of the Roman church. "But," said he in reply to Proclus, "I can show the trophies of the apostles.[19] For if you will go to the Vatican or to the Ostian Way, you will find the trophies of those who laid the foundations of this church." The Greek word "trophy" which is used here, originally meant the memorial of a victory which was raised on the field of battle. Thus, for example, the armor or weapons of the defeated enemy might be fixed to a tree or upright post, with an accompanying inscription and dedication. In similar fashion when a Christian hero fell on the field of martyrdom, a marker at that place or above his grave might appropriately enough be referred to as a "trophy." Since Proclus had appealed, on his side, to the existence of the tomb of the apostle Philip at Hierapolis, Caius in answering him must have been using the word "trophies" to refer to grave-monuments at the last resting places of the two famous martyrs in Rome.

The Vatican, to which Caius pointed as the place of the tomb of Peter, was the Ager Vaticanus, where "Nero's Circus" and "Nero's Gardens" were (pp.369f.), and where so many other Christians also perished in Nero's frightful exhibition of cruelty (p.379). There on the outskirts of Nero's Circus, as near as possible to the place of his triumph in death, was the grave of Peter. According to the first chapter of the Liber Pontificalis[20] the exact location was

[17] A city about five miles north of Laodicea, and mentioned in Colossians 4:13.
[18] *Ch. Hist.* III, xxxi.
[19] *Ch. Hist.* II, xxv, 7: ἐγὼ δὲ τὰ τρόπαια τῶν ἀποστόλων ἔχω δεῖξαι. ed. Schwartz, p.73.
[20] The Liber Pontificalis is a series of biographies of the popes and was compiled in the text in which we have it in the seventh century from earlier papal annals. While

between the Via Aurelia and the Via Triumphalis, near a temple of Cybele which by popular error was later called a shrine of Apollo.

The Ostian Way, to which Caius referred as the place of the tomb of Paul, was the ancient Via Ostiensis. This road led from Rome to the port city of Ostia, some fourteen miles distant at the mouth of the Tiber.[21] It departed from the southern side of Rome at a point some distance west of the Via Appia by which Paul had first entered the city. As Paul was led forth to die his eyes must have fallen upon one monument which still stands today upon the Via Ostiense. This is the Pyramid of Cestius at the present Porta San Paolo (Fig. 133). It was a tomb which was erected in Egyptian pyramidal form for a certain Caius Cestius Epulo who died before 12 B.C. One hundred and sixteen feet high and covered with marble slabs, the pyramid was enclosed by Aurelian within his city wall but extricated in 1660 by Pope Alexander VII, and looms up today exactly as it did when Paul passed. The last resting place of the great apostle was some one and one-quarter miles farther out the Via Ostiensis.[22]

Thus, as Caius is witness, the graves of Peter and of Paul at the Vatican and on the Ostian Way respectively, were perfectly well-known martyr-memorials in Rome around A.D. 200. Nor could these graves have been recent inventions of pious credulity as if they first had been arbitrarily "discovered" say around A.D. 170. By that time the Christian custom of burial in the catacombs was fully established, and if one had wished to invent the graves of Peter and of

---

a considerable part is obviously legendary it also contains much valuable historical material. Louis Duchesne, *Le liber pontificalis, texte, introduction et commentaire*. 2 vols. 1886-92; LLP pp.ix-x.

[21] The city derived its name from the *ostium* or mouth of the river.

[22] The place of Paul's execution is believed to have been yet another one and one-quarter miles out on the Via Laurentina at the Abbey of the Three Fountains (Abbadia delle Tre Fontane). There are three springs here which anciently were known as the Aquae Salviae, and according to the apocryphal Acts of Peter and Paul (R. A. Lipsius and M. Bonnet, *Acta Apostolorum Apocrypha*. I [1891], p.214) Paul was beheaded at a place of this name and under a pine tree. The late legend that when the apostle's head struck the earth it bounced three times and at each place one of the springs welled forth, is of course as worthless as the other story that when his head was struck off, milk came forth (Carl Schmidt, ed., *Praxeis Paulou: Acta Pauli.* 1936, pp.68f.). But the location of the execution at this place also has the authority of Pope Gregory I the Great (A.D. 590-604) and may be not incorrect. The old abbey which stood here was virtually abandoned for a long time owing to malaria but around 1867 was entrusted to French Trappist monks. It is an interesting fact that when the Trappists were doing some digging in connection with one of their buildings in 1875 they unearthed a mass of coins of Nero together with several fossilized pine-cones. R. Lanciani, *Wanderings through Ancient Roman Churches*. 1924, p.169.

Paul it would have been most natural to place them in or near some of these recognized Christian cemeteries where undisturbed veneration of the holy places would have been possible. Instead both graves are remote from all Christian cemeteries and in fact lie amidst pagan cemeteries of the first and second centuries. This fact has been established by excavations which have revealed pagan burial places in the immediate neighborhood of the graves of both Peter and Paul. No one would have "invented" the holy graves in such unholy surroundings.[23]

In the light of history it is eminently fitting that Peter's grave should be hard by Nero's Circus to proclaim that the tyrant's triumph was transient but the apostle's was everlasting. And it is likewise appropriate that Paul who had traveled so far for Christ should be buried at last beside a highway as if to signify that his strong heart was still eager for the preaching of the gospel in distant places. Both graves are truly trophies of victory.

[23] Hans Lietzmann, *Petrus und Paulus in Rom.* 2d ed. 1927, pp.246f.; and cf. below pp.515f.

VII
Manuscripts Found in the Sand

A S EXTENSIVELY as Paul himself traveled, his letters traveled even farther. Occasionally his correspondence was addressed to cities and churches where his face had never been seen (cf. Colossians 2:1), and some of his letters were passed on from one church to another (Colossians 4:16). Moreover, within twenty-five years after his death, copies of his letters appear to have been gathered from the various churches to which he had sent them, and published as a collection.[1] From A.D. 90 on these collected letters of Paul were known widely, and their language and ideas were reflected frequently in other Christian writings.[2] In II Peter 3:16 this collection is referred to and is already regarded as "scripture."

In this manner the letters of Paul were preserved to become known down through the centuries and around the world. The influence of a single one of them, that to the Romans, for example, has been nothing less than world-transforming. The conversion of Augustine came when he took up "the volume of the Apostles" and read Romans 13:13-14.[3] The sudden enlightenment of Martin Luther

---

[1] E. J. Goodspeed (*Christianity Goes to Press.* 1940, pp.49-62) thinks that the collection was made first at Ephesus, possibly by Onesimus, who had been the slave of Philemon and around A.D. 110 became bishop of Ephesus.

[2] A. E. Barnett (*Paul Becomes a Literary Influence.* 1940) finds that Pauline influence was strong in I Peter, Hebrews, I Clement, the Johannine writings, Ignatius, and Polycarp; that it subsided, perhaps due to an anti-Marcionite reaction, in James, Jude, Hermas, Barnabas, the Didache, II Clement, the Martyrdom of Polycarp, and the Apology of Aristides; and that it revived again in II Peter, Tatian's Address to the Greeks, Justin, Melito, Athenagoras, and the Pastoral Epistles.

[3] *Confessions.* VIII, 12 (NPNF I, p.127).

came when he was reading the epistle to the Romans in his monastery cell. The decisive experience in the life of John Wesley came from hearing Luther's preface to the Commentary on Romans read in a little meeting in Aldersgate Street, London. Twentieth century theology has been influenced by the endeavor of Karl Barth to see modern life through the lens of Paul's conception of faith, and the writing by Barth of his first book on *The Epistle to the Romans*.[4] Certainly this single writing of Paul's has been a *Schicksalsbrief*, a "letter of destiny," in the history of Christianity.

Many other writings were also produced in the early Christian community and, of these, four Gospels, the book of Acts, and various other letters and books were eventually joined together with the letters attributed to Paul to constitute the canonical New Testament.[5] The discovery and study of ancient copies of all of these documents is part of the work of archeology,[6] and through such research we may come closer to the original text of the New Testament. In what follows something will be told of the nature of this work, and special reference will be made to manuscripts of the letters of Paul since these are recognized as providing the best place to begin the study of the New Testament text.[7] First, however, we must notice the writing materials and practices of the early Christian centuries.

1. WRITING MATERIALS AND PRACTICES
IN THE ANCIENT WORLD

IN addition to the stone and clay which, as we have seen, were so abundantly used to write on particularly in Egypt and Mesopotamia respectively,[1] two other materials were widely used in the ancient world, namely papyrus and leather.

PAPYRUS

In the Mediterranean world of the first century A.D. it was undoubtedly papyrus which was the most commonly employed mate-

---

[4] *Der Römerbrief*. 1919. tr. Edwyn C. Hoskyns, 1933.

[5] For early lists of the canon see F. W. Grosheide, ed., *Some Early Lists of the Books of the New Testament* (Textus Minores, 1). 1948.

[6] Kenneth W. Clark in BASOR 122 (Apr. 1951), pp.7-9.

[7] Hans Lietzmann, *Einführung in die Textgeschichte der Paulusbriefe* (in *An die Römer, Handbuch zum neuen Testament*. 8 [4th ed. 1933]), p.1.

[1] Reference has also already been made to the early development of writing in Mesopotamia (p.26), Egypt (p.84), and Sinai-Palestine (pp.148f.).

rial, even as it is the term from which the modern word "paper" is derived.[2] It in turn took its name from the plant from which it was made. This was a reed or sedge called papyrus[3] which grew abundantly in Egypt and was also found in adjoining lands.[4] The papyrus plant appears frequently in Egyptian art, from the earliest times. A particularly delightful example is the wall painting representing a wildcat in a papyrus thicket (Fig. 134) from the famous tomb of Khnumhotep (Twelfth Dynasty) at Beni Hasan (pp.92f.). Another scene, in the tomb of Puyemre (Eighteenth Dynasty), shows the papyrus plant being harvested and split for papermaking (Fig. 135).

The process of making writing material from the papyrus plant has been described, although not with complete clarity, by Pliny in his *Natural History:*[5]

"Papyrus grows either in the marshes of Egypt, or in the sluggish waters of the river Nile, when they have overflowed and are lying stagnant, in pools that do not exceed a couple of cubits [about three feet] in depth. The root lies obliquely, and is about the thickness of one's arm; the section of the stalk is triangular, and it tapers gracefully upwards towards the extremity, being not more than ten cubits [about fifteen feet] at most in height. . . .[6]

"Paper is made from the papyrus, by splitting it with a needle into very thin leaves, due care being taken that they should be as broad as possible. That of the first quality is taken from the center of the plant, and so in regular succession, according to the order of division. . . .

"All these various kinds of paper are made upon a table, moistened with Nile water; a liquid which, when in a muddy state, has the peculiar qualities of glue. This table being first inclined, the leaves of papyrus are laid upon it lengthwise, as long, indeed, as the papyrus will admit of, the jagged edges being cut off at either end; after which a cross layer is placed over it, . . . When this is done, the leaves are pressed together, and then dried in the sun; after which they are united to one another, the best sheets being always taken first, and the inferior ones added afterwards. There are never more than twenty of these sheets to a roll."

In other words, single sheets of paper were made out of thin vertical and horizontal strips of papyrus glued together, and a number of such sheets were glued together, side by side, to form a con-

---

[2] Greek, πάπυρος; Latin, *papyrus*; German, *Papier*; French, *papier*; English, *paper*.

[3] Linnaeus, *Cyperus papyrus*.

[4] Strabo, *Geography.* xvii, i, 15. The plant now is practically extinct in Lower Egypt, but is found in Nubia, Ethiopia, at Syracuse in Sicily, and at Lake Huleh in Palestine (for the last place see Walter C. Lowdermilk, *Palestine Land of Promise.* 1944, p.145).

[5] xiii, 11f.

[6] cf. Theophrastus (c.372-c.287 B.C.), *Enquiry into Plants.* iv, viii, 3. tr. A. Hort, LCL (1916) i, pp.347-349.

tinuous roll. They could also, as we shall see, be used in the form of a codex.

Even as Egypt was the place in which the papyrus plant grew most abundantly, so it was in Egypt that papyrus probably first came into use as a writing material. The representation of scribes writing on papyrus is found in Egyptian art from very ancient times. The statuette of a scribe shown in Fig. 137 comes from the Third Dynasty and may be the earliest such figure that has ever been found. The scribe is seated cross-legged and holds upon his lap a roll of papyrus. The unrolled portion of the papyrus is grasped by the left hand and the free end of the roll lying across the lap is held down by the right hand which is in a position to write. The expression upon the face is that of one waiting to take dictation. Similar examples are to be found in the statue of Henka the scribe (Fourth Dynasty) in the Berlin Museum, in that of the Scribe Accroupi (Fifth Dynasty) in the Louvre at Paris, and in that of Haremhab (Eighteenth-Nineteenth Dynasties) already mentioned (pp.112f., Fig. 48). Another interesting representation is that of the limestone relief carving from the Eighteenth Dynasty shown in Fig. 138. Here four scribes are standing and bending forward attentively, each with his papyrus roll and pen.

The oldest actual specimen of a papyrus manuscript yet discovered dates from the Fifth Dynasty,[7] and from that ancient time papyrus continued in use on down through the Greek and Roman periods and well into the days after the occupation of Egypt by the Arabs in A.D. 641. Extant papyri are written not only in the language of ancient Egypt, but also in Greek,[8] Latin,[9] Hebrew,[10] Aramaic,[11]

[7] F. G. Kenyon, *The Palaeography of Greek Papyri.* 1899, p.14. The statement of the Roman antiquarian, Varro (c.116-c.27 B.C.), which is quoted by Pliny (*Natural History.* xiii, 11) that the use of papyrus for writing was discovered first in the time of Alexander the Great is entirely incorrect and was doubted by Pliny himself (xiii, 13).

[8] Greek was the official language of Egypt from the founding of the Ptolemaic Dynasty until the Arab invasion, and by far the largest number of extant papyri are written in Greek.

[9] Latin was used chiefly for military and legal business and in private correspondence between Roman officials, and papyri written in this language are not numerous.

[10] Hebrew papyri are rare in Egypt. The Nash Papyrus, already mentioned (p.27) as containing the Ten Commandments and the Shema (Deuteronomy 6:4ff.) and written probably in the second or first century B.C., was found in Egypt (W. F. Albright in JBL 56 [1937], p.145 n.2).

[11] The best known Aramaic papyri are those from Elephantine which have already been mentioned (pp.239f.). On Aramaic in general see Raymond A. Bowman in JNES 7 (1948), pp.65-90.

Coptic,[12] and Arabic.[13] Thus, this amazing writing material was in continuous and demonstrable use in Egypt for a period of three or four thousand years.[14]

From Egypt the use of papyrus spread to many other lands. Its use in Palestine at least as early as the sixth century B.C. was already proved by the finding at Lachish of a clay seal of Gedaliah with the impression on its back of the papyrus document to which it had originally been attached (p.195), and is now further shown by the discovery in Cave II at Wadi Murabba'at of an actual Hebrew papyrus believed to have been written in the sixth century (p.279). Among the Qumran manuscripts there are various papyrus fragments inscribed in Hebrew, Aramaic, and Greek.[15] At Masada, the Dead Sea fortress destroyed in the war with the Romans in A.D. 73, a small piece of papyrus has been found with traces of Hebrew writing.[16] And at Nessana in the Negeb important though relatively late papyri have been unearthed (pp.429f.). Since in much of Palestine the dampness of the climate is not conducive to the preservation of papyrus, it is probable that it was used even earlier and more widely than we are now able to demonstrate. In Mesopotamia the use of papyrus is attested by fragments of this material which were discovered at Dura-Europos and which date in the third century B.C.[17]

Among the Greeks papyrus was in use at least in the fifth century B.C.[18] and probably much earlier. In the century and a half after the birth of Christ it was the usual writing material, and it continued to be employed as late as the sixth and seventh centuries A.D. The Romans were using papyrus in the third century B.C. and continued to employ it until the seventh century A.D. Thus, as Caspar René Gregory has said of the period in which the New Testament was written, papyrus "was the common writing material, the paper, of that day, whether at Alexandria or at Antioch or at Rome. If a man put a handbill up at Rome, he wrote it on a big piece of coarse

[12] The Copts were the native Egyptians, descended from the ancient inhabitants of the land, and large numbers of Coptic papyri have been found.

[13] C. H. Becker, *Papyri Schott-Reinhardt.* I (1906). After the Arab conquest Greek continued for some time to be employed officially alongside Arabic and then gradually died out.

[14] Wilhelm Schubart, *Das alte Ägypten und seine Papyrus.* 1921, p.6.

[15] DJD I, pp.47,148f.,155.

[16] IEJ 7 (1957), p.60.

[17] C. B. Welles in *Münchener Beiträge zur Papyrusforschung und antiken Rechtsgeschichte.* 19 (1934), pp.379-399.

[18] Herodotus. v, 58.

papyrus. If he wrote a delicate note to his wife or his mother, he wrote it on a little piece of fine papyrus. Papyrus was their paper."[19]

LEATHER, PARCHMENT, AND VELLUM

Leather, parchment, and vellum were also used as writing material. In Egypt the use of leather is attested, for example, by the fact that the victory of Thutmose III at Megiddo "was recorded upon a roll of leather in the temple of Amun."[20] According to Herodotus,[21] the Greeks of Ionia had formerly, when papyrus was scarce, written on the skins of goats and sheep, a custom which was continued by the barbarians in his own day. The Jews employed leather for writing from an early time.[22] When Jeremiah dictated his prophecies to his secretary Baruch (Jeremiah 36:4), they may have been written upon a roll of leather, since King Jehoiakim later used a knife to cut the roll in pieces when he wanted to burn it (Jeremiah 36:23).[23] In the Talmud we find that the Law was written upon the skins of animals,[24] and this doubtless reflects an ancient tradition. The Letter of Aristeas and Josephus state that the copy of the Law which was sent from Jerusalem to Egypt for the making of the Septuagint translation was written on leather skins ($\delta\iota\phi\theta\acute{\epsilon}\rho\alpha\iota$).[25] Most of the Dead Sea Scrolls were written on leather and parchment.[26]

When skins are given a special treatment to prepare them for writing, the material is known as parchment. Whereas leather is tanned, parchment is made by soaking the skin in limewater, scraping off the hair on the one side and the flesh on the other, stretching and drying in a frame, and rubbing with chalk and pumice stone, thus producing a fine material capable of receiving writing on both sides. The skins of sheep, goats, and other animals are used for parchment, but the finest kind of all is prepared from calfskins. This is properly called

---

[19] *Canon and Text of the New Testament.* 1907, p.317.

[20] ARE II, §433.

[21] v, 58. For other ancient references see G. R. Driver, *Semitic Writing.* rev. ed. 1954, pp.81f. See also R. J. Forbes, *Studies in Ancient Technology.* v (1957), pp.1-77.

[22] L. Löw, *Graphische Requisiten und Erzeugnisse bei den Juden.* (1870-71) I, p.114.

[23] The knife employed was a "scribe's knife" (LXX [ed. Swete, III, p.328], τῷ ξυρῷ τοῦ γραμματέως), such as a scribe used for making erasures on leather. On the other hand it can be held that the king would have been more apt to throw papyrus than leather into the fire in his brazier to burn.

[24] *Makkoth.* 11a. SBT p.71.

[25] *Letter of Aristeas.* 3, 176. ed. H. G. Meecham. 1935, pp.5,25,174; Josephus, *Ant.* XII, ii, 11.

[26] Sukenik, *The Dead Sea Scrolls of the Hebrew University*, p.25.

"vellum,"[27] but the name vellum is now used also less discriminatingly to include the other kinds of skins as well, when prepared with particular care to receive writing. The chief marks of vellum are its semitransparent fineness and the striking beauty of its polish.[28]

The Latin expression for parchment was *membrana*, while the Greeks continued to employ the term διφθέρα, meaning leather, or borrowed the word μεμβράνα from the Romans. The word περγαμηνή, *pergamena*, or "parchment,"[29] appears first in an edict of Diocletian in A.D. 301, and apparently is derived from the city of Pergamum in Asia Minor. According to Pliny,[30] Varro stated that parchment was invented at Pergamum. His story was that rivalry existed between King Eumenes II (197-159 B.C.) of Pergamum and King Ptolemy of Egypt over their respective libraries. Since Ptolemy feared that the library at Pergamum might come to surpass the library of Alexandria, he endeavored to retard the literary progress of the rival city by prohibiting the export of papyrus from Egypt. Consequently, the people of Pergamum were driven to the invention of parchment. This account can hardly be historical, but it is doubtless true that a high quality of parchment was developed at Pergamum and that the city was famous for its manufacture and export.[31]

The statement of Herodotus already cited that it was the barbarians who wrote on the skins of goats and sheep, suggests that in the Mediterranean world in general parchment was not at that time as much used as papyrus. In the first century B.C. Roman writers make occasional references to parchment,[32] but it still appears to have been generally regarded as inferior to papyrus. Likewise in the first century A.D. Quintillian (A.D. c.35-c.100), for example, mentions the use of parchment notebooks in the law courts, but himself preferred to write on wax tablets rather than parchment because the latter, "although of assistance to the eye, delays the hand and interrupts the stream of thought owing to the frequency with which the pen has to be supplied with ink."[33] In an interesting passage in II Timothy 4:13 a request is made for the bringing of "the books,

[27] French, *vélin*; from Latin *vitellus*, diminutive of *vitulus*, a calf.
[28] G. Peignot, *Essai sur l'histoire du parchemin et du vélin.* 1812, p.28.
[29] cf. German, *Pergament*; French, *parchemin*.
[30] *Natural History.* xiii, 21.
[31] Theodor Birt, *Kritik und Hermeneutik nebst Abriss des antiken Buchwesens* (*Handbuch der klassischen Altertumswissenschaft.* 1913), p.280.
[32] Cicero, *Letters to Atticus.* xiii, xxiv; Horace ii, iii, 2.
[33] *Institutio Oratoria.* x, iii, 31. tr. H. E. Butler, LCL (1921-22), iv, p.109.

and above all the parchments" (τὰ βιβλία, μάλιστα τὰς μεμβράνας).[34] The "books" would have been in the first instance papyrus rolls, while the "parchments" could have been vellum rolls of the Old Testament, although it is also possible that both the papyrus and the parchment were yet to be written on.[35] A fragment now in the British Museum shows that an oration of Demosthenes was copied on vellum, probably in the second century A.D.,[36] while a vellum fragment of Tatian's Diatessaron has been found at Dura-Europos, a town which was destroyed about A.D. 256.[37] There are also some vellum fragments of the *Iliad*[38] and the *Odyssey*[39] which are believed to have been written at least by around A.D. 300.

THE ROLL

Even as there were two chief writing materials in the early centuries of the Christian era, papyrus and parchment, so also there were two chief forms in which written documents were prepared, the roll and the codex.

In Pliny's description of the manufacture of papyrus already quoted (p.387), it may be remembered that this author said papyrus was made in sheets and the sheets were united to one another to make a roll. The single sheet[40] could, of course, be made in a variety of sizes, and papyri are extant which vary in size from less than two inches to over fifteen inches. A sheet of average size probably ran about nine to eleven inches in height and six to nine inches in width. For a brief letter or other document a single such sheet might suffice, and New Testament writings such as Philemon and II and III John probably each occupied a single sheet.[41] For a longer writing, as Pliny shows, the sheets were glued together to

[34] cf. F. F. Bruce, *The Books and the Parchments, Some Chapters on the Transmission of the Bible*. 1950.

[35] Mackinnon (*The Rome of St. Paul*, pp.87,146) thinks that Paul's mention of parchment implies that he used this material for his own letters which he knew to be of permanent value, but the "occasional" character of Paul's correspondence may make this supposition open to question.

[36] Kenyon, *The Palaeography of Greek Papyri*, p.113.

[37] C. H. Kraeling, *A Greek Fragment of Tatian's Diatessaron from Dura*. 1935.

[38] E. M. Thompson, *An Introduction to Greek and Latin Palaeography*. 1912, pp.198f., 201.

[39] A. S. Hunt, *Catalogue of the Greek Papyri in the John Rylands Library*. I (1911), p.91.

[40] The sheet was called a κόλλημα because the strips of papyrus of which it was made up were glued together (κολλᾶν). Papyrus which was prepared for writing but not yet written upon was called χάρτης as in II John 12. HPUM p.6 n.29, 30.

[41] F. G. Kenyon, *Books and Readers in Ancient Greece and Rome*. 1932, pp.49f.

form an extended strip and this was rolled up for convenience in handling.

When Pliny said that a papyrus roll never consisted of more than twenty of these sheets, he must have been referring to the length of the papyrus rolls as they were customarily placed on the market. With individual sheets not usually running over nine inches in width, a roll such as Pliny refers to, composed of twenty sheets, would have attained a length of fifteen feet at the maximum. Of course if the work of an individual writer did not extend to this length he could cut off a portion, or if it was of greater length he could glue a second roll onto the first. A normal Greek literary roll probably did not exceed thirty-five feet, but Egyptian ceremonial copies of the Book of the Dead were often fifty or one hundred feet in length. The longest papyrus known is a panegyrical chronicle of the reign of Ramses II called the Harris Papyrus, which is 133 feet in length and seventeen inches in height.[42] An average roll in New Testament times, however, would have been probably thirty or thirty-five feet in length, and when rolled up upon itself would have appeared as a cylinder perhaps ten inches in height and one or one and one-half inches in diameter. A book such as the Gospel according to Luke would have filled an ordinary papyrus roll thirty-one or thirty-two feet long, while the book of Acts by the same author would have required a second such roll, and it has been surmised that this is one of the reasons why Luke-Acts was issued in two volumes (Acts 1:1). Likewise if Paul's ten collected church letters (including Philemon) were issued in this form they would probably have filled two papyrus rolls. The papyrus roll (Greenfield Papyrus) shown in Fig. 136 is considerably larger than the average since it measures nineteen inches in height. Other and smaller rolls both open and sealed are shown in Fig. 139.

A sheet or roll of papyrus was ordinarily written on only one side, that where the papyrus fibers ran in the horizontal direction naturally being preferable and being used for the front or right side which is known as the *recto* in speaking of a manuscript. The other side or *verso*, meaning reverse or left, where in the case of a papyrus sheet the component strips were running vertically, could also be used, however, and a roll written on both front and back is called an opisthograph. It is a book of this sort which is described in Revelation 5:1, "a scroll written within and on the back, sealed with seven

---

[42] ARE IV, §§151-412.

seals." The text was written in a column or series of columns (σελίδες), each of which was usually two or three inches wide. In the case of a roll, these columns were not correlated with the sheets of papyrus and the writing frequently ran over the juncture of two sheets. Except in the more elegant books the margins were not large and the columns were close together.

It is obvious that the roll form could also be used with leather or parchment as well as with papyrus, and in the Dead Sea Scrolls we have seen numerous examples of Old Testament and also of non-canonical writings in this form.[43]

How widely used the roll form and the papyrus material were is shown by the fact that the ordinary Greek word for "book" etymologically meant a papyrus scroll. The fibrous part of the papyrus plant (πάπυρος) from which paper was made was known as βύβλος or βίβλος, and this word, preferably in the form βίβλος and indeed most frequently in the diminutive form βιβλίον, was the usual word for "book."[44] These words may be seen in their ordinary Greek usage, for example, in Herodotus[45] where Egyptian priests recite from a book (βύβλος) the names of their kings, and in Aristotle[46] where this author refers to his book (βιβλίον) on meteorology, and in each case it was presumably a papyrus roll which was meant. Although etymologically the word implied papyrus it was also used for a written roll of leather or parchment, as may be seen in Luke 4:17 where "the book (βιβλίον) of the prophet Isaiah" must have been, in accordance with ordinary Jewish usage and as illustrated almost contemporaneously at Qumran, a leather scroll. Also in the passage already cited (pp.391f.), II Timothy 4:13, where request is made to bring "the books, and above all the parchments" (τὰ βιβλία, μάλιστα τὰς μεμβράνας), the manner of expression makes it seem that the word βιβλία is inclusive of the parchments as well as of the papyri. Likewise although βιβλίον usually referred to a roll it could presumably be used for a book or written document even in some other form. Thus the paper (βυβλίον) sealed up in a fish of which Herodotus[47] tells, and the certificate (βιβλίον) of divorce mentioned in Matthew 19:7 = Mark 10:4 might not necessarily have been in the form of rolls.

[43] For the roll form in the Old Testament cf. Psalm 40:7; Ezekiel 2:9; Zechariah 5:1.

[44] In Latin the word for a book in the form of a scroll was *volumen*, from the verb *volvere*, "to roll."

[45] II, 100.   [46] *On Plants.* II, ii, 1.   [47] I, 123.

As seen in the quotation from II Timothy 4:13, the plural of βιβλίον is βιβλία. In I Maccabees 12:9 the plural word occurs in the phrase τὰ βιβλία τὰ ἄγια, "the holy books," no doubt referring to books of the Old Testament. In II Clement 14:2 it is stated that "the books and the apostles" (τὰ βιβλία καὶ οἱ ἀπόστολοι) show that the church is not of the present but from the beginning or from above (ἄνωθεν), and here again τὰ βιβλία certainly refers to holy books, perhaps to ones of the Old Testament (with οἱ ἀπόστολοι referring to New Testament books), or perhaps even to ones of the New Testament. Thus τὰ βιβλία, that is "the books" par excellence, came to be the name for the scriptures. In Latin the word was *biblia* and eventually this plural noun came to be regarded as singular and so the name "Bible" emerged.

THE CODEX

The other chief form of book was the codex. In spite of how widely and long it was used, the roll was after all a relatively inconvenient form. The reader had to employ both hands, unrolling with one hand and rolling up with the other as the reading proceeded. Moreover, there was no simple way to give a reference to a specific passage within a longer roll, and to find a given section might necessitate unrolling the scroll to the very end. Consequently it was inevitable and desirable that the roll should be superseded by a more readily usable form of book. This was found in the codex, where the leaves of the manuscript were fastened together as in a modern book.

The Latin word *caudex* or *codex* meant originally the trunk of a tree, and then a block of wood split up into leaves or tablets.[48] It was possible to write on such a leaf directly, or to cover it with wax and thereby to have a readily erasable writing surface. There is reference to writing on tablets, presumably of wood, in Isaiah 8:1; 30:8; and Luke 1:63. In Rome these wooden tablets, used either plain or with a covering of wax, were known as *tabellae*, and there are actual examples of them extant from Pompeii with dates corresponding to A.D. 53 and 55.[49] When several of these were bound together a convenient notebook was produced which was commonly called a *pugillaris* (sc. *libellus*), literally a "fist (book)," or a handbook. From this point it was an easy step to employ leaves of papyrus or parchment instead of wood, and when this was done the flexibility and utility of the codex form of book were greatly improved. Thus finally the

[48] George Milligan, *The New Testament and Its Transmission*. 1932, p.15.
[49] David Diringer, *The Hand-Produced Book*. 1953, p.33.

word "codex" could designate any leaf book, whether of papyrus, parchment, or other material.

In the centuries just before and after the turn of the era, the Dead Sea Scrolls show us that the roll was the prevailing form for Jewish writings, and at the same time the same was true for works of literature in the pagan world. According to a recent enumeration, 476 non-Christian literary papyrus manuscripts have been found in Egypt dating from the second century A.D., and of these 465 or more than 97 per cent are in the form of the roll.[50] But already at least in the first century A.D. the codex was also being used even for pagan literature. In about A.D. 85 the Latin writer Martial composed a number of verses to accompany presents such as the Romans gave to their friends at the Saturnalia. Found in Book XIV of his Epigrams, these poems contain references to what we may call "pocket editions" in the form of parchment (*membrana*) codices of Homer, Virgil, Cicero, and Livy. Concerning a parchment codex edition of Virgil (*Vergilius in membranis*), Martial remarks on how much such a small parchment book would hold.[51] Similarly he recommends a parchment codex of Cicero (*Cicero in membranis*) as a handy traveling companion.[52]

Interestingly enough, particularly in Christian circles the codex seems to have been specially favored and used from a very early date. From the second century A.D., when 97 per cent of the non-Christian literary papyri were in the roll form, we have by recent enumeration eight Christian biblical papyri and all of these are in the form of the codex. In the entire period extending to shortly after the end of the fourth century, we have 111 biblical manuscripts or fragments from Egypt, of which 99 are codices.[53] Some of the New Testament papyri will be listed a little later in this chapter and it will be seen that almost all of them are from codices. Likewise the great parchment manuscripts of the fourth century and onward, Codex Vaticanus, Codex Sinaiticus, and so on, are, as these names indicate, in the same form.

Since the examples we are fortunate enough to possess will hardly

---

[50] C. H. Roberts in PBA 40 (1954), p.184; cf. C. C. McCown in BA 6 (1943), p.27.
[51] XIV, 186.
[52] XIV, 188. In itself the word *membrana* simply means skin prepared for writing, or parchment, and it can be used of parchment rolls, but in most cases where it appears in classical Latin it is in a context which requires or permits the meaning of notebook or codex (Roberts in PBA 40 [1954], p. 174).
[53] C. C. McCown in HTR 34 (1941), pp.219-250; Roberts in PBA 40 (1954), pp.185-191.

have been the first of their kind, it appears very possible that the codex was used for Christian books even in the first century A.D. at which time, as we have seen from Martial, this form of book was definitely available. The correspondence of the books of Luke and Acts to the length of an ordinary papyrus roll each, has already been noted (p.393) as a possible indication that these works were composed in that form. There is a possible intimation, on the other hand, that the Gospel according to Mark might have been written originally in a codex in the fact that its original ending seems to be missing and could have been lost by wear and tear: in a codex the last leaf is most likely to suffer damage; in a roll the destruction is most apt to be at the beginning. Like the numerous papyrus communications now known from the everyday life of the ancient world and to be illustrated later in this chapter, it may be supposed that the letters of Paul were written originally on papyrus, Philemon on a single sheet, longer letters on rolls. When Paul's letters were collected, however, probably in the latter part of the first century, the codex form was available and, since the purpose of the collection was to make it possible to consult these writings and this could be done much more readily in a codex than in a roll, the collection may well have been made in that form,[54] even as our oldest copy of the collection, namely $\mathfrak{p}^{46}$, is a codex.

By the fourth century A.D. both the codex form and the parchment material were in supreme use for New Testament and biblical manuscripts. In A.D. 332 the Emperor Constantine instructed Eusebius to have fifty parchment manuscripts of the Bible prepared for the churches in his new capital, Constantinople. The letter of the emperor to Eusebius read in part: "I have thought it expedient to instruct your Prudence to order fifty copies of the sacred Scriptures, the provision and use of which you know to be most needful for the instruction of the Church, to be written on prepared parchment in a legible manner, and in a convenient, portable form, by professional transcribers thoroughly practiced in their art."[55]

"Such were the emperor's commands," reports Eusebius, "which were followed by the immediate execution of the work itself, which we sent him in magnificent and elaborately bound volumes of a threefold and fourfold form."[56] The expression "threefold and fourfold" (τρισσὰ καὶ τετρασσά) probably means "having three columns

[54] G. Zuntz, *The Text of the Epistles.* 1953, p.15.
[55] *Life of Constantine.* IV, 36 (πεντήκοντα σωμάτια ἐν διφθέραις).
[56] *ibid.*, IV, 37.

and four columns" and indicates that the pages were written respectively in three columns and in four columns.[57] Furthermore, two great vellum codices of the Bible, dating probably about the middle of the fourth century A.D., are still extant, Codex Vaticanus and Codex Sinaiticus. Although the probability seems to be that they were copied in Egypt and thus would hardly have been among the manuscripts ordered by Constantine, it is interesting to find that they have three and four columns of writing per page respectively. We also learn that about the middle of the same century the famous library of Origen (d. A.D. c.254) and Pamphilus (d. A.D. 309) at Caesarea had fallen into decay and was restored by two priests, Acacius and Euzoius, who replaced what were probably damaged papyrus rolls with copies written on parchment (*in membranis*) and presumably in codices.[58] From this time on, parchment or vellum remained the chief writing material until the general establishment of the use of paper in the fourteenth century; and the codex was retained permanently as the prevailing form of books.

Like modern books the ancient codices were bound in quires. A sheet of papyrus was folded once in the middle, thus forming two leaves or folios[59] of equal size. By fastening together a number of such two-leaf quires a codex was made. Or a more extensive quire could be made by laying a larger number of sheets one upon another, these forming, when folded, a correspondingly larger number of leaves. In the case of $\mathfrak{p}^{46}$ fifty-two sheets of papyrus were laid together, recto side on top, and the whole pile was folded in the middle to make 104 folios. The bulk of so many sheets folded together in such a single-quire book made difficulty, however, in that the middle pages were pushed out and might even have to be trimmed at the edge of the book, thus reducing the area of the inner pages. Accordingly the multiple-quire book was ultimately the preferred form. Also instead of laying the sheets of a quire all with the recto side on top, it was often the custom to place alternately uppermost the recto and the verso, so that when the book was opened a recto page would face a recto page, and a verso a verso. If the same principle was followed in the quires of a parchment or vellum codex, the flesh side of each sheet was laid upon the flesh side of another, and the hair side upon a hair side, so that when the book was opened the pages

[57] J. H. Ropes in F. J. Foakes Jackson and Kirsopp Lake, *The Beginnings of Christianity*, Part I, *The Acts of the Apostles*. III (1926), p.xxxvii.
[58] Jerome, *Epistle*. 34 (141); MPL XXII, col. 448; cf. F. G. Kenyon in HDB IV, p.947.
[59] From Latin *folium*, leaf.

which faced each other were of similar kind. In order to guide the writing, lines were drawn on the hair side with a sharp instrument and allowed to show through on the flesh side.

The adoption of the codex also led gradually to a change in the style of columns employed. In the roll form of book it had been convenient to write in narrow columns of short lines, and the first great vellum manuscripts, especially Codex Sinaiticus, reflect their inheritance from the roll in the narrow columns of writing which they use. With the codex it became desirable to write in wider columns of longer lines, and eventually the prevailing practice was that of having only one or two columns on each page.[60]

PEN AND INK

Writing was done with pen and ink. In a room at Qumran which was evidently the scriptorium of the community centered at that place, there were long, narrow writing tables, and in the debris two actual inkwells were found, one of bronze and the other of terra cotta, one still containing some dried ink.[61] In the New Testament pen and ink are mentioned in III John 13, and ink also in II John 12 and II Corinthians 3:3.[62] The Greek word for pen is κάλαμος which also means reed, and a pen of this sort was made from a thoroughly dried reed stalk, the end of which was sharpened to a point and split into two parts. The word for ink is μέλαν which also means "black." Two kinds of ink were in common use, one made from lampblack, gum, and water, and the other from nutgalls, green vitriol, and water. The former was very black and unfading, the latter turned in the course of time into a handsome rusty brown color.[63]

STYLES OF HANDWRITING

In the Roman period manuscripts of a literary character were generally written in a relatively handsome, regular "bookhand," while other documents and letters were often written in a nonliterary script of "cursive" type. In the latter case the letters were characterized by their roundness and relative continuity of formation, the pen being carried on to some extent from one character to another. The literary

[60] HPUM pp.17-19; McCown in HTR 34 (1941), p.228.

[61] R. de Vaux in RB 61 (1954), p.212 Pls. IXa, Xb. On the book trade in the Roman empire see Felix Reichmann in *The Library Quarterly*. 8 (1938), pp.40-76.

[62] In the Old Testament the pen is mentioned in Jeremiah 8:8 and Psalm 45:1; and ink in Jeremiah 36:18. See Driver, *Semitic Writing*, pp.84-86.

[63] HPUM pp.13-15.

and nonliterary scripts were sometimes used side by side, and their forms also varied a great deal from one period to another, occasionally almost approximating one another and again diverging widely. The appearance of any given manuscript depended, of course, largely upon the skill and neatness of the individual or individuals who wrote it, and at all times there was both poor writing and good.[64]

Writings such as those of Paul, which have every appearance of genuine letters rather than literary productions, were probably written originally in the nonliterary script. These letters, however, were often dictated to Christian helpers who, since they rendered this service for Paul, were probably practiced in the art of penmanship. The use of such secretarial assistants is shown in Romans 16:22 where the scribe interjects, "I Tertius, the writer of this letter, greet you in the Lord," and is also indicated by Paul's custom of adding the closing part of the letter in his own handwriting (II Thessalonians 3:17). In Galatians 6:11 Paul refers to his own writing as being with "large letters." This probably means that as a man more accustomed to manual labor (cf. I Thessalonians 2:9; Acts 18:3) than to the fine art of penmanship, Paul made relatively large, stiff, square characters which contrasted with the flowing cursive script of his scribe. It may be presumed, therefore, that the main body of a Pauline letter was written originally in a relatively careful and practiced hand of the nonliterary type. When the New Testament writings came to be regarded as literature, however, they were naturally copied in the literary bookhand. This style of handwriting developed into the handsome form which is found in the vellum codices and to which the term "uncial" is customarily applied. "Uncial characters" are mentioned by Jerome[65] (A.D. c.340-420) in connection with elegant manuscripts of his time, and since the Latin word *uncia* means "the twelfth part" it is thought that an uncial character may have been one occupying about one-twelfth of a line.[66] This would fit the case of Codex Sinaiticus, for example, where there are approximately twelve letters per line. The New Testament codices from the fourth to the ninth centuries were written in uncial characters.

The uncial style of writing was quite slow and cumbersome, however, and the need was felt for a script which could be written

---

[64] H. Idris Bell in EB XVII, p.97; Wilhelm Schubart, *Griechische Palaeographie* (in Walter Otto, ed., *Handbuch der Altertumswissenschaft*. I, iv, 1. 1925), p.19.

[65] *Preface to Job* (NPNFSS VI, p.492).

[66] HPUM p.22 n.5.

more easily and swiftly and yet be of sufficient legibility and beauty to be employed appropriately for literary and sacred writings. The rapid nonliterary cursive script which we met with in Roman times had continued in use in various forms during the Byzantine period (A.D. c.300-c.650) but did not have the dignity demanded by the Bible and works of literature. From it there was developed, however, a truly calligraphic script which could still be written at a relatively high speed. This is known as minuscule script and is characterized by smaller, differently formed letters, many of which are connected without the raising of the pen. Coming into use in the ninth century, the minuscule hand gradually superseded the uncial characters and thereafter was never supplanted but continued in use as long as books were copied by hand. Thus, numerically speaking, the great mass of New Testament manuscripts are minuscules.[67]

By careful study of these various styles of handwriting and the many intermediate changes of form which they underwent, paleographers are able to establish at least approximate dates for manuscripts upon the basis of the character of the writing which they display.[68]

PUNCTUATION

In the first century, manuscripts were usually written practically without punctuation and with the words following each other in an unbroken succession of letters, as if one should begin to copy Paul's Letter to the Romans in the English in this manner:

PAULASERVANTOFJESUSCHRISTCALLEDTO

BEANAPOSTLESEPARATEDUNTOTHEGOSPE

LOFGODWHICHHEPROMISEDAFORETHROU

GHHISPROPHETSINTHEHOLYSCRIPTURES

Those who were accustomed to such writing could read it rapidly, but even so the possibility of error and misunderstanding was present owing to the absence of punctuation and the lack of division between words. There was, therefore, a gradual increase in the employment of punctuation marks and other aids to the reader.

In the second century papyrus fragment of the Gospel according to John designated as $\mathfrak{p}^{52}$ the words sometimes appear to be slightly

[67] F. G. Kenyon, *Handbook to the Textual Criticism of the New Testament.* 2d ed. 1912, p.124; and see HFDMM.

[68] cf. Thompson, *An Introduction to Greek and Latin Palaeography*, pp.144-147; and see C. H. Roberts, *Greek Literary Hands 350 B.C.-A.D. 400.* 1956.

separated, but there is still no punctuation, although a dieresis is placed over the initial letter Iota. In the Chester Beatty Papyrus of the Letters of Paul ($\mathfrak{p}^{46}$) there are occasional slight intervals between words to mark pauses in sense, initial Iota and Upsilon are marked with a dieresis, and Greek breathings and accents are employed. Also a single point is occasionally used to mark a division in the text. Such use of a point or dot became more frequent in later centuries and high, middle, and low points were differentiated to indicate respectively what would now be signified by a period, a comma, and a semicolon. Eventually a comma proper, a colon, and a question mark written like a modern semicolon, as well as some other marks came to be employed.

Brief headings to the various books are found as early as the Chester Beatty Papyrus of Paul's Letters ($\mathfrak{p}^{46}$), where there are also subscriptions giving the number of stichoi (στίχοι) contained, the latter being standard lines probably of a standard number of letters or syllables used in the measurement of the length of a manuscript.[69] Later the superscriptions and subscriptions of the New Testament books were expanded to contain more data of a traditional character concerning their origin.

To facilitate reference the pages of a codex and also the columns of a scroll could be numbered as may be seen, for example, in $\mathfrak{p}^{46}$ and $\mathfrak{p}^{13}$ respectively.[70] The convenience of the readers was served further by the making of divisions in the text. In $\mathfrak{p}^{64}$ (p.418), fragmentary though it is, there is evidence that the text was divided into sections. In Codex Vaticanus the Gospels are divided into a large

[69] Charles Graux in *Revue de Philologie.* 2 (1878), pp.97-143; J. Rendel Harris, *Stichometry.* 1893; and in NSH XI, pp.91-94; Jack Finegan in HTR 49 (1956), pp.97-101.

[70] The letters of the Greek alphabet were used for numerals as follows:

Alpha	α′	1	Omicron	ο′	70
Beta	β′	2	Pi	π′	80
Gamma	γ′	3	Koppa	ϙ′	90
Delta	δ′	4	Rho	ρ′	100
Epsilon	ε′	5	Sigma	σ′	200
Vau	ϝ′	6	Tau	τ′	300
Zeta	ζ′	7	Upsilon	υ′	400
Eta	η′	8	Phi	φ′	500
Theta	θ′	9	Chi	χ′	600
Iota	ι′	10	Psi	ψ′	700
Kappa	κ′	20	Omega	ω′	800
Lambda	λ′	30	Sampi	ϡ′	900
Mu	μ′	40		α	1,000
Nu	ν′	50		′	etc.
Xi	ξ′	60			

number of sections and Paul's letters are divided into chapters which are numbered continuously throughout as if all the letters formed one book. In Codex Alexandrinus there are also chapters (κεφάλαια) with summary headings (τίτλοι) describing their contents.[71] On the basis of earlier work by Ammonius of Alexandria, Eusebius of Caesarea divided the Gospels into sections (the "Ammonian Sections") and prepared tables (the "Eusebian Canons") of parallel and independent passages,[72] while the so-called "Euthalian Apparatus" supplied tables of chapters, tables of Old Testament quotations, and other introductory materials for Acts and the Epistles.[73] The system of chapter divisions now found in the New Testament was the work of Cardinal Hugo de S. Caro in 1238, while the modern verses were introduced by Robert Étienne (Stephanus) in 1551.

NOMINA SACRA

Another interesting feature of the biblical manuscripts is the employment of abbreviations for the sacred names (*nomina sacra*) and for certain other words. Instead of writing the name in full, the scribe would save time and space by writing only a few of the letters, usually the first and last, and drawing a line above them thus:

KC	XC XPC	ΠΝΑ
κύριος	χριστος	πνεῦμα
Lord	Christ	Spirit
ΘC	ΠΡ ΠΗΡ	ΑΝC ΑΝΟC
θεός	πατήρ	ἄνθρωπος
God	Father	man
IC IHC IH	YC	CTC CPC CTPC
Ἰησοῦς	υἱός	σταυρος
Jesus	Son	cross

ΠΡΟΦΑC
προφήτας
prophets

Such abbreviations appear in the fragments of an unknown Gospel dating probably around the middle of the second century A.D.

[71] Kirsopp Lake, *The Text of the New Testament*. 6th ed. rev. by Silva New, 1928, pp.55f.

[72] These tables as well as the letter of Eusebius to Carpian in which he describes the plan of his work are printed regularly in the preface to Nestle's *Novum Testamentum Graece*. 16th ed. 1936.

[73] Ernst von Dobschütz in NSH IV, p.215.

(p.413), in $\mathfrak{p}^{64}$ of the latter part of the second century (p.417f.), in $\mathfrak{p}^{46}$ (p.420) and $\mathfrak{p}^{66}$ (p.425) both of around A.D. 200, and in many other manuscripts down to the latest times.[74] It is probable that the practice of making contractions of this type was borrowed by the Christians from the Jews. When the Jews translated the Tetragrammaton YHWH into Greek they represented the holy name by Lord or God, written in the abbreviated forms shown above. The Christians naturally adopted this practice and extended it to the specifically Christian names and to other words as well.[75]

2. THE MODERN DISCOVERY
OF ANCIENT PAPYRI

Now we may turn to the story of the actual recovery of ancient manuscripts, and first of all those written on papyrus. The first papyri to reach Europe, so far as is known, were one Greek and two Latin fragments which were given to the library at Basel about the end of the sixteenth century by the theologian Johann Jakob Grynaeus. In 1752 the charred remains of a library of Greek philosophical works were found in the ruins of Herculaneum, and in 1778 an unknown European dealer in antiquities purchased a papyrus roll from Egyptians who had already burned fifty other ancient rolls because they enjoyed the aromatic odor![1] Since that first discovery Egypt has proved to be an almost inexhaustible storehouse of ancient papyri. In its dry climate and buried beneath its drifted sands the fragile papyri have resisted the ravages of time as effectively, and endured as indestructibly, as the pyramids.

During the nineteenth century an increasing number of papyri found their way to the museums of Europe, as the *fellahin* of Egypt awakened to the fact that they could obtain money for these ancient fragments. Many papyri were found accidentally by persons digging

---

[74] Gregory, *Canon and Text of the New Testament*, p.335. No sacred names appear on the tiny second century fragment of the Gospel according to John (p.417; Fig. 142), so it cannot be told whether abbreviations were employed in this manuscript. The earliest literary attestation of the abbreviation IH for the name of Jesus appears around A.D. 130 in the *Letter of Barnabas* (9 [ANF I, p.143]).

[75] Ludwig Traube, *Nomina Sacra, Versuch einer Geschichte der christlichen Kürzung.* 1907, p.31. Gunnar Rudberg (in *Skrifter utgifna af Kungl. Humanistiska Vetenskaps-Samfundet i Uppsala.* 17 [1915], No. 3) proposes the less plausible theory that the practice was taken over from the use of short forms of the names of the Roman emperors.

[1] DLO p.23; Ulrich Wilcken, *Die griechischen Papyrusurkunden*, p.10.

in the ancient mounds for *sebakh,* or nitrous earth which is used for fertilizer. Others were unearthed by Egyptian antique dealers and also by illicit plunderers. In 1877 a great mass of papyri was discovered in the site of Arsinoë, which earlier was Crocodilopolis, in the Fayum, but probably half of it was lost through carelessness.[2]

Before the end of the nineteenth century, however, the Fayum became the scene of truly scientific and highly rewarding work in the recovery of papyri. This district, in which such important finds have been made, is a sunken oasis in the Libyan desert west of the Nile, its capital, Medinet el-Fayum, being about eighty miles south-south-west of Cairo. In ancient times the famous Lake of Moeris[3] occupied a large part of this depression and still is represented by the Birket Qarun. The Egyptian name for this lake was *Shei,* "the lake," and later *Piom,* "the sea," whence the name Fayum is derived. The capital and most important city of the district was situated on this lake, and was a center of worship of the crocodile god, Sebek. The city was known to the Greeks as Crocodilopolis, or Arsinoë,[4] and its ruins are represented by mounds north of the present capital, Medinet el-Fayum. There were other towns and villages in the district, and just south of the oasis was the important city of Oxyrhynchus, the modern Behnesa. It was only about ten miles from the Nile, and on the chief canal (Bahr Yusef) which brought water to the Fayum. In ancient times Oxyrhynchus was the capital of the Oxyrhynchite nome, and in the fourth and fifth centuries A.D. was famous for the number of its churches and monasteries, Christianity apparently having found a place there at a relatively early date.

In the winter of 1889-1890, Professor Flinders Petrie excavated a Ptolemaic cemetery at Gurob, near the mouth of the Fayum, and found a quantity of papyrus manuscripts which had been used as cartonnage in making the inner coffins of mummies. Professor Petrie, of course, fully realized the value of such finds and patiently recovered from their unusual place of preservation all the papyri possible. Then, in the winter of 1895-1896, the Egypt Exploration Fund sent out under the leadership of Drs. B. P. Grenfell, A. S. Hunt, and D. G. Hogarth the first expedition definitely undertaken for the discovery of papyri. The work which was done that year, and continued by

---

[2] James Baikie, *Egyptian Papyri and Papyrus Hunting.* 1925, pp.230f.
[3] Herodotus. ii, 149; Strabo, *Geography.* xvii, i, 35.
[4] Strabo, *Geography.* xvii, i, 38.

Grenfell and Hunt during a number of subsequent seasons, was amazingly successful.[5]

At Tebtunis papyri were found in a resting place even stranger than the human mummy cases at Gurob. Here, there was a crocodile cemetery in which sacred crocodiles had been buried ceremonially. One after another of the mummified crocodiles was turned up, until finally a workman, who was hoping for far better finds, in disgust smashed one of the burials in pieces. It broke open, revealing that the crocodile had been wrapped in the same kind of papyrus cartonnage as the Gurob mummies, and in several instances papyrus rolls were found stuffed into the animals' mouths or other cavities in their bodies.

Oxyrhynchus was no doubt the most rewarding site of all, and the publication of the papyri from this one place has filled a whole series of volumes.[6] In what follows, Oxyrhynchus papyri will be cited a number of times. All together, Grenfell and Hunt recovered from the sands of Egypt many thousands of manuscripts and fragments of papyrus, while other workers who followed them have made many important additions to the vast mass of material now available for papyrological research.

EARLY PAPYRUS LETTERS

Since much of the New Testament and particularly the part connected with the name of Paul was written in the form of letters, it will be of special interest to notice the numerous pagan letters on papyrus which we have from about the same time. On June 17, 1 B.C., an Egyptian laborer Hilarion, who had gone to Alexandria to work, wrote a short letter to his wife Alis, who had remained at home in Oxyrhynchus. The letter (Fig. 140) sounds amazingly modern at most points, yet reflects the pagan custom of exposure of children. It reads:

"Hilarion to Alis his sister, heartiest greetings, and to my lady Berous and to Apollonarion. Know that we are still even now in Alexandria. Do not worry if when all the others return I remain in Alexandria. I beg and beseech of you to take care of the little child. And as soon as we receive wages I will send them to you. If—good luck to you!—you bear a child, if it is a boy, let it live; if it is a girl, expose it. You told Aphrodisias, 'Do not forget me.' How can I forget you? I beg you, therefore, not to worry."[7]

[5] Grenfell, Hunt, and Hogarth, *Fayum Towns and Their Papyri.* 1900.
[6] OP 1898ff. For Oxyrhynchus in Roman times see E. G. Turner in JEA 38 (1952), pp.78-93.
[7] OP IV, No.744; Wilhelm Schubart, *Ein Jahrtausend am Nil.* 2d ed. 1923, pp.65f.; DLO pp.134-136.

At the bottom is the date, "In the 29th year of Caesar, Pauni 23," corresponding to June 17, 1 B.C.,[8] and on the back side is the address: "Hilarion to Alis, deliver." The greeting of Alis as "sister" may be only a tender form of address but perhaps is to be taken literally since marriages of brother and sister were not uncommon in Egypt. Berous, who is courteously called "lady"[9] may have been the mother of Alis, and Apollonarion perhaps was the child of Alis and Hilarion. On the whole the letter is written rather crudely and contains a number of grammatical errors, such as the use of the accusative when the dative is required,[10] which are not shown in the translation above.

On September 13, A.D. 50, an Egyptian olive planter named Mystarion sent a letter to a chief priest named Stotoëtis in order to introduce a certain Blastus who was to perform an errand and return quickly:

"Mystarion to his own Stotoëtis many greetings. I have sent unto you[11] my Blastus for forked sticks for my olive-gardens. See then that you do not stay him. For you know how I need him every hour.
"Farewell
"In the year 11 of Tiberius Claudius Caesar Augustus Germanicus Imperator in the month Sebastos 15."[12]

The address was written on the back: "To Stotoëtis, chief priest, at the island. . . ." This note was penned at the very time when the first of Paul's letters were being written and is an example of letters of introduction such as Paul himself mentions and writes (I Corinthians 16:3; II Corinthians 3:1; Romans 16:1). But the letter of Mystarion is of special interest because the closing "Farewell" and the lengthy date are written in a hand different from the careful scribal hand in which the body of the letter and the address on the back are penned. Evidently Mystarion himself took the pen at the close to add a final personal touch, just as Paul said he did in every letter (II Thessalonians 3:17; cf. Galatians 6:11; I Corinthians 16:21; Colossians 4:18).

The timeless woes of human life are reflected poignantly in a tiny[13]

[8] For the months see the table in George Milligan, *Selections from the Greek Papyri.* 1910, p.xviii.
[9] The same polite form of address is found in II John 1 and 5.
[10] In line 8 of the Greek text.
[11] The grammar is exactly the same as in I Corinthians 4:17 and similar passages.
[12] Fritz Krebs, *Ägyptische Urkunden aus den Königlichen Museen zu Berlin, Griechische Urkunden.* I, No.37; DLO pp.136-139.
[13] The actual size of the papyrus is about three inches square.

second century letter from Irene to Philo and Taonnophris, a married couple who have lost a son in death. Irene, who is evidently a friend of the sorrowing mother (since the latter is named before the father in the salutation), and who has already gone through the experience of losing her own loved one, Didymas, writes to the bereaved parents as follows:

"Irene to Taonnophris and Philo, good cheer.

"I am as much in grief and weep over the blessed one as I wept for Didymas. And everything that was fitting I did and so did all of mine, Epaphroditus and Thermuthion and Philion and Apollonius and Plantas. But truly there is nothing anyone can do in the face of such things. Do you therefore comfort one another.

"Farewell. Athyr 1."[14]

The letter is addressed on the back, "To Taonnophris and Philo."[15]

In the second century a young man named Apion from the small Egyptian town of Philadelphia in the Fayum entered the Roman navy and sailed to Misenum, the naval harbor near Naples. When the voyage became stormy and dangerous Apion was in peril but he prayed to the lord Serapis and was delivered. Upon reaching port he received three pieces of gold as pay, was given a new Roman name, Antonis Maximus, in keeping with his new Roman service, and was assigned to the company Athenonica. Like a modern youth in the service he had his picture made in his new uniform to send home, and then he wrote the following letter to his father:

"Apion to Epimachus his father and lord, many greetings. Before all things I pray that you are in health and that you prosper and fare well continually together with my sister and her daughter and my brother. I thank the lord Serapis that, when I was in peril in the sea, he saved me immediately. When I came to Miseni[16] I received as journey-money from the Caesar three pieces of gold. And it is well with me. I beseech you therefore, my lord father, to write me a little letter, firstly of your health, secondly of that of my brother and sister, thirdly that I may look upon your handwriting with reverence, because you have taught me well and I therefore hope to advance rapidly, if the gods will. Salute Capito much and my brother and sister and Serenilla and my friends. I am sending you by Euctemon a little picture of me. Moreover my name is Antonis[17] Maximus. Fare you well, I pray.

"Centuria Athenonica."[18]

[14] The date is equivalent to October 28.
[15] OP I, No.115; Milligan, *Selections from the Greek Papyri*, pp.95f.; DLO pp.143-145.
[16] This is the plural form of the name of the harbor generally called Misenum.
[17] Antonis is a short form of the name Antonius.
[18] Paul Viereck, *Ägyptische Urkunden aus den Königlichen Museen zu Berlin*. II, No.423; DLO pp.145-150.

The companions of Apion wanted him to include their greetings and since there still was room along the side of the papyrus sheet Apion added: "There salute you Serenus the son of Agathus Daemon, and . . . the son of . . . and Turbo the son of Gallonius and D . . . nas the son of. . . ." The letter was to go by military post to the garrison of the Apamenians in Egypt and through the office of the paymaster of that company be forwarded to the father. This address was written on the back, "To Philadelphia for Epimachus from Apion his son," with the instruction, "Give this to the first cohort of the Apamenians to Julianus . . . the Liblarios, from Apion so that he may send it to Epimachus his father." The lines of address and instruction were divided in the middle by two heavy X-marks which indicate the place for tying up the letter.

Not only does the letter of Apion sound as if it could have been written in the twentieth century instead of the second, but it contains a number of expressions similar to ones found in New Testament letters. "I pray that you are in health" is the same polite and standard formula of greeting that appears in III John 2. Apion's word of thanks to the lord Serapis, the Egyptian god whose worship was widespread throughout the Roman Empire, reminds one of Paul's almost constant habit of beginning his letters with thanks to God (I Thessalonians 1:2; II Thessalonians 1:3; I Corinthians 1:4; Romans 1:8; Philippians 1:3; Colossians 1:3; Philemon 4; cf. Ephesians 1:3,16). The phrase "in peril in the sea" is nearly identical with Paul's words in II Corinthians 11:26, although the Roman soldier's grammar is not quite as excellent as Paul's. Likewise "Salute Capito much" is very similar to the form of greeting in I Corinthians 16:19.

Interestingly enough we have a second letter from the same Apion to his sister, written probably years later when his father was dead and he himself had children of his own.[19]

Also filled with human interest is another second century letter, which a prodigal son wrote to his mother. Addressed on the back, "To . . . his mother from Antonius Longus her son," the pathetic epistle reads:

"Antonis Longus to Nilus his mother many greetings. Continually I pray for your health. Supplication on your behalf I direct each day to the lord Serapis. I wish you to know that I had no hope that you would come up to the metropolis. On this account neither did I enter into the city. But

[19] Krebs, *Ägyptische Urkunden aus den Königlichen Museen zu Berlin.* II, No.632; DLO pp.150-153.

409

I was ashamed to come to Karanis,[20] because I am going about in rags. I write to you that I am naked. I beseech you, mother, be reconciled to me. But I know what I have brought upon myself. Punished I have been every way. I know that I have sinned. I hear from Postumus[21] who met you in the Arsinoïte nome, and unseasonably related all to you. Do you not know that I would rather be a cripple than be conscious that I am still owing anyone an obol? . . . come yourself . . . I have heard that . . . I beseech you . . . I almost . . . I beseech you . . . I will . . . not . . . do otherwise."[22]

Not only is the grammar here similar to that of the New Testament at several points, including the expressions, "I wish you to know" (cf. Philippians 1:12) and "I beseech you" (Philemon 10, etc.), but the youth himself was almost a living example of the lost son in the parable told by Jesus.

Many other letters and documents of all sorts could be cited from these very same times, including a letter saying "Do not lose heart about the rent, for you will certainly get it,"[23] a letter regarding funeral expenses, a boy's letter, an invitation to dinner, a public notice, a contract of apprenticeship, a report of a lawsuit, a marriage contract, a deed of divorce, a deed of adoption, a warrant for arrest, a tax receipt, a census return, a lease of a perfumery business, a will, a magical incantation, and many others.[24] But already it is clear that the papyri have provided much information about the daily and amazingly modern life of the ancient world, as well as affording the possibility of fresh comparisons with the writings of the New Testament.

The longer papyrus letters generally have an opening address or greeting, a thanksgiving and prayer, special contents, and closing salutations and valediction. These are exactly the main features which in a more elaborate form are found in the letters of Paul.[25] Also the language of the papyri is in many ways similar to that of the New Testament. In both grammar and vocabulary there are

[20] A village in the Fayum, and probably the home of the writer.
[21] The reading of the name is not certain.
[22] Krebs, *Ägyptische Urkunden aus den Königlichen Museen zu Berlin.* iii, No.846; Milligan, *Selections from the Greek Papyri*, pp.93-95; DLO pp.153-158.
[23] C. M. Cobern, *The New Archaeological Discoveries and their Bearing upon the New Testament and upon the Life and Times of the Primitive Church.* 9th ed. 1929, pp.93f.
[24] See Milligan, *Selections from the Greek Papyri*; A. S. Hunt and C. C. Edgar, *Select Papyri.* 2 vols. LCL (1932-34); E. J. Goodspeed and E. C. Colwell, *A Greek Papyrus Reader.* 1935.
[25] G. Milligan, *The New Testament Documents, their Origin and Early History.* 1913, p.93.

134. Wildcat in a Papyrus Thicket

135. Gathering and Splitting Papyrus for Papermaking

136. Papyrus Roll before Opening

137. Statuette of an Early Egyptian Scribe

138. Four Scribes with Pens and Rolls

139. Papyrus Rolls Open and Sealed

140. Letter from Hilarion to Alis

141. The Sayings of Jesus Found at Oxyrhynchus

142. Papyrus Rylands Gk. 457

143. A Page from the Chester Beatty Papyrus of Paul's Letters

144. A Papyrus Fragment with the Opening of Paul's Letter to the Romans

145. The First Page of the Letter to the Romans in Codex Vaticanus

146. The Monastery of Saint Catherine at Mount Sinai

147. The Appearance of Codex Sinaiticus before Binding

148. The First Page of the Letter to the Romans in Codex Sinaiticus

149. The First Page of the Letter to the Romans in Codex Alexandrinus

150. A Page in Codex Ephraemi Rescriptus

151. A Double Page in Codex Claromontanus

152. The First Page of Romans in a Minuscule Manuscript Written in A.D. 1045

153. An Illustration in the Minuscule Manuscript of A.D. 1045

many differences between the Greek of the New Testament and classical Greek. All together the New Testament language is doubtless influenced in part by the Hebrew and Aramaic of Palestine and the Old Testament, in part by the Greek of the Septuagint translation, and in part by the *Koine* or Common Greek then widely used in the Mediterranean world. This relatively simpler Greek is found in a literary variety in writers of the time like Strabo and Josephus, and in a nonliterary form in the papyri of which we have been speaking. The similarity of the New Testament language with that of the papyri was first recognized by Adolf Deissmann, Privatdozent at Marburg and later Professor of New Testament at Friedrich-Wilhelms-Universität at Berlin. Through his work and that of others much material has been collected from the papyri to illustrate the contemporary usage and meaning of words which occur in the New Testament.[26]

EARLY CHRISTIAN PAPYRI

Not only documents of everyday life in general but also ones recognizably related to the Christian faith have been recovered from the sands of the past. Apart from manuscripts of the canonical New Testament to be described in the next section, these discoveries include such writings as the following.

On January 11, 1897, Grenfell and Hunt began to dig in the rubbish mounds of ancient Oxyrhynchus, and on the second day unearthed a tattered papyrus leaf, nearly four by six inches in size, of which the verso is shown in Fig. 141.[27] In the upper right-hand corner of the verso was a numeral which was clearly a page number and showed that this leaf had been a part of a papyrus codex. In the case of this particular leaf the verso had been uppermost in the codex. The first indication of the character of the contents of the leaf came with the recognition of the word κάρφος, or "mote," which at once reminded Dr. Hunt of Jesus' saying concerning the mote and the beam (Matthew 7:3-5 = Luke 6:41f.). When the entire fragment was read it was found that it actually did contain a series of sayings of Jesus as follows:

". . . and then shalt thou see clearly to cast out the mote that is in thy brother's eye.

[26] See MMVGT. For the Koine, Semitic, and Christian elements in the language of the New Testament and the individual characteristics of the several books see Bruce M. Metzger in IB VII, pp.43-59.
[27] Grenfell and Hunt, *Sayings of Our Lord*. 1897; OP I, No.1; cf. Leon E. Wright in JBL 65 (1946), pp.175-183.

"Jesus saith, Except ye fast to the world, ye shall in no wise find the kingdom of God; and except you make the sabbath a real sabbath, ye shall not see the Father.

"Jesus saith, I stood in the midst of the world, and in the flesh was I seen of them, and I found all men drunken, and none found I athirst among them, and my soul grieveth over the sons of men, because they are blind in their heart, and see not.

". . . poverty.

"[Jesus saith,] Wherever there are two, they are not without God, and wherever there is one alone, I say, I am with him. Raise the stone, and there thou shalt find me, cleave the wood, and there am I.

"Jesus saith, A prophet is not acceptable in his own country, neither doth a physician work cures upon them that know him.

"Jesus saith, A city built upon the top of a high hill and established, can neither fall nor be hid.

"Jesus saith, Thou hearest with one ear [but the other ear thou hast closed]."

This papyrus is probably to be dated in the third century A.D., and shows the kind of collection of Jesus' sayings that was being read by Christians in Egypt at that time. A second fragment containing sayings of Jesus was found by Grenfell and Hunt at Oxyrhynchus in 1903.[28] It was a piece of a papyrus roll, which was probably written slightly later in the third century than the fragment first found. In it the words of Jesus have lost yet more of their original freshness and simplicity, and have taken on still more of the complexity of the later age.

In a large group of papyri purchased for the John Rylands Library in Manchester, England, by J. Rendel Harris in 1917 was a part of a double leaf of a papyrus codex, written in a hand of probably the fourth century A.D., which contained verses from different parts of the Septuagint.[29] Two other fragments belonging to the same codex are in Oslo. The Old Testament texts used include portions of the "Messianic" passages in the fifty-second and fifty-third chapters of Isaiah, and in general are such as could be applied to Christ and Christianity.[30] It is believed, therefore, that the work represented by these surviving fragments originally comprised a collection of "pro-

[28] Grenfell, L. W. Drexel, and Hunt, *New Sayings of Jesus and Fragment of a Lost Gospel.* 1904.

[29] C. H. Roberts, *Two Biblical Papyri in the John Rylands Library, Manchester.* 1936, pp.47-62.

[30] The combined texts contain quotations from the following verses: Isaiah 42:3f.; 66:18f.; 52:15; 53:1-3, 6f., 11f.; Genesis 26:13f.; II Chronicles 1:12; Deuteronomy 29:8 (9), 11 (12).

phetic" passages from the Old Testament which were used as witnesses to the truth of Christianity.[31]

In another collection of papyri purchased from a dealer around 1935 were two imperfect leaves and a scrap of a third from a papyrus codex dating probably not later than the middle of the second century. Now designated as Papyrus Egerton 2, these fragments contain an account of four different incidents in the life of Jesus, namely a dispute with the rulers of the people who attempt to stone him, the healing of a leper, a question about paying dues to kings, and a miracle of some sort on the bank of the Jordan. The document is believed to depend upon sources other than the canonical Gospels, and perhaps to have been intended for private use by individual Christians. It may be noted that the writer employed abbreviations for Lord, God, Jesus, prophets, as shown on p. 403, and some other words.[32]

In 1946 an accidental discovery at the ancient Sheneset-Chenoboskion in the region of Nag Hammadi thirty-two miles north of Luxor brought to light thirteen papyrus codices, all remarkably well preserved, nine with leather covers still about them.[33] They were all written in Coptic, most in the Upper Egyptian dialect called Sahidic, and are probably to be dated between the middle of the third and the middle of the fourth century A.D. Most or all are believed to rest on Greek originals. The thirteen codices contain some forty-four different treatises including literature of the nature of gospels, epistles, apocalypses, and prayers, and discussions of cosmogony and dogmatics. In some cases the material purports to be what was divulged by Jesus to his disciples during his ministry or after his resurrection,

[31] Such works are otherwise known, as for example in the collection of *Testimonies against the Jews* made by Cyprian about A.D. 248, and consisting of extensive quotations from the Old Testament arranged under various headings (*Treatise.* XII. ANF V, pp.507-557). J. Rendel Harris even believed that such an assemblage of "testimonies" directed against the Jews was the first Christian book to be written and that its influence could be traced throughout the New Testament as well as in the church fathers (J. R. Harris and V. Burch, *Testimonies.* 2 vols. 1916-20; cf. D. Plooij in *Verhandelingen der Koninklijke Akademie van Wetenschappen te Amsterdam, Afdeeling Letterkunde, Nieuwe Reeks Deel.* XXXII, 2 [1932]). We now know that collections of texts expressive of Messianic hope were made among the Jews too, since a page of *testimonia* was found in Cave 4 at Qumran (see above p.278).

[32] H. Idris Bell and T. C. Skeat, *Fragments of an Unknown Gospel and Other Early Christian Papyri.* 1935, pp.1-41; H. Idris Bell, *Recent Discoveries of Biblical Papyri.* 1937, pp.17-20; Goro Mayeda, *Das Leben-Jesu-Fragment Papyrus Egerton 2 und seine Stellung in der urchristlichen Literaturgeschichte.* 1946; Bruce M. Metzger in JBL 68 (1949), pp.73-75; Sherman E. Johnson in JNES 5 (1946), p.46.

[33] Victor R. Gold in BA 15 (1952), pp.70-88.

and all of it is intended for those initiated in the doctrines of the sect to which the literature belonged, evidently a group of Egyptian Gnostics. As an example of what is contained, one of the works is the Apocryphon or Secret Book of John. Three copies were found at Chenoboskion and another was already known in the fifth century Berlin Coptic Codex 8502.[34] The contents of the book are supposed to have been given by Jesus to John on the Mount of Olives with a warning to reveal these things only to those who are worthy. In brief the teaching is that the true God, the highest being in the world of light, created various divine beings, among them Barbelo the image of the invisible One, and Sophia or Wisdom. The latter had an evil son, Yaldabaoth, who is the God of the Old Testament and the creator of this world. Since it is the constant endeavor of Yaldabaoth to keep the divine spark which is in man from returning to the world of light from whence it came, it was necessary for Christ to come into the world and bring the knowledge of the truth through which those who are able to receive it can be delivered. This truth, it is evident, is of the sort contained in this book and taught by the Gnostics. In his work *Against Heresies*,[35] Irenaeus (A.D. c.180) describes Gnostics who were evidently akin to those represented at Chenoboskion since they too recognized Barbelo as a high divine being, and after outlining their teachings the Christian apologist says, "Such are the falsehoods which these people invent."[36]

3. NEW TESTAMENT MANUSCRIPTS

LIKE the documents of which we have just been telling, the oldest known copies of any parts of the New Testament are written upon papyrus, and after that come the parchment or vellum manuscripts, first those written in uncial letters and then those in minuscule script. There are so many of these documents all together that some kind of brief designation and also of comprehensive listing is necessary.

[34] This papyrus, which contains not only the Apocryphon of John, but also the Gospel of Mary, and the Wisdom of Jesus Christ, is edited by Walter C. Till, *Die gnostischen Schriften des koptischen Papyrus Berolinensis 8502* (TU 60). 1955.

[35] I, xxix. ANF I, pp.353f.

[36] Another Coptic manuscript which contains Gnostic texts is the Codex Jung, a papyrus of probably the fourth century A.D. It contains a copy of the Gospel of Truth, probably the work of that title attributed by Irenaeus (*Against Heresies*. III, xi, 9) to the Gnostics who followed Valentinus. See Henri-Charles Puech, Gilles Quispel, and W. C. van Unnik, *The Jung Codex*. 1955; Michel Malinine, H.-C. Puech, and G. Quispel, *Evangelium Veritatis*. 1956; cf. R. McL. Wilson in NTS 3 (1957), pp.236-243; Floyd V. Filson in BA 20 (1957), pp.76-78.

In 1751-1752 Johann Jakob Wettstein published in Amsterdam a critical edition of the Greek New Testament,[1] in the prolegomena of which he listed by letters of the alphabet and by numbers some 125 manuscripts. Beginning with the uncial manuscripts available at that time, A was Codex Alexandrinus, B Codex Vaticanus, C Codex Ephraemi Syri rescriptus, and so on. Continuing with the available minuscule manuscripts, these were numbered 1, 2, 3, and so on.

In the latter part of the nineteenth century Constantine Tischendorf (1815-1874) published his *Novum Testamentum Graece*.[2] Having discovered Codex Sinaiticus and having a very high regard for its importance, Tischendorf put it at the head of his list of manuscripts, labeling it with the first letter of the Hebrew alphabet, Aleph. The number of uncials known also extended now beyond the letter Z, and Tischendorf continued his list with capital letters of the Greek alphabet, Γ, Δ, Θ, and so on.

Like Wettstein and Tischendorf, in the first volume of his *Textkritik des Neuen Testaments*, published in 1900, Caspar René Gregory listed the uncials by capital letters and the minuscules by numbers. The letter Aleph was still used for Codex Sinaiticus, but it was noted that some wished to avoid the introduction of a Hebrew letter in the series and proposed alternatively to employ here the letter S.[3] Even by using letters from the Hebrew, Latin, and Greek alphabets, however, there was a limit to how many manuscripts could be so designated, and accordingly in the third volume of the *Textkritik*, published in 1909,[4] Gregory employed another system in which the uncial manuscripts were designated by numbers. To distinguish these numbers from those used for the minuscule manuscripts they were preceded by 0 and printed in boldface type. Although the familiar letter designations were still used for the earlier known uncials, these manuscripts were also included in the new system and so Codex Sinaiticus was shown as א or **01**, Codex Alexandrinus as A or **02**, Codex Vaticanus as B or **03**, Codex Ephraemi Syri rescriptus as C or **04**, and so on. The numbers ran at that time to **0165**. After the uncials Gregory listed the papyri, of which fourteen were then

---

[1] Ἡ Καινὴ Διαθήκη. 2 vols.   [2] Editio octava critica maior. 2 vols. 1869-72.

[3] *Textkritik des Neuen Testaments*, I, p.122. S is used instead of א for Codex Sinaiticus by Hans Lietzmann, *Einführung in die Textgeschichte der Paulusbriefe*, p.6, by Burton H. Throckmorton, Jr., ed., *Gospel Parallels, A Synopsis of the First Three Gospels*. 2d ed. 1957, p.viii, and by others (cf. Merrill M. Parvis in JR 27 [1947], p.216), and is used in the present book. Otherwise S designates the relatively unimportant Vatican manuscript Gr. 354.

[4] cf. also his *Die griechischen Handschriften des Neuen Testaments*. 1908.

known. For these he used an Old German ℊ with a superior number, thus ℊ¹, ℊ², and so on. The minuscules in turn ran at this time from 1 to 2304. Lectionaries were designated with numbers preceded by a small letter l, thus l 3, l 707, and the like. When these and also the versions such as Syriac, Armenian, and Latin translations were included, Gregory's catalogue must have included over four thousand items.

The work of Gregory in assigning numbers and listing manuscripts was continued by Ernst von Dobschütz, and hundreds of manuscripts more were added to the catalogue.[5] By the time installment IV of his list was published in 1933, without including versions in other languages the total of the Greek manuscripts was approximately 4,230. Upon the death of von Dobschütz in 1934 the *Kirchenväter Kommission der Preussischen Akademie der Wissenschaften* entrusted the same responsibility to Walther Eltester, and more recently the list has been continued by Kurt Aland.[6]

In the meantime, Hermann Freiherr von Soden (1852-1914) undertook to make an entirely new listing and new assignment of numbers.[7] In this system, Codex Vaticanus became δ1, Codex Sinaiticus δ2, Codex Ephraemi Syri rescriptus δ3, Codex Alexandrinus δ4, and so on. In spite of the large volume of the work he did, the system of von Soden was not most widely accepted.

With several systems of identification thus in existence, it is useful to have a concordance of the several listings.[8] In practice the earlier known uncials are still usually cited by the letters as found in Tischendorf and in the first volume of Gregory's *Textkritik*; the later known uncials and the minuscules by their respective series of numbers as listed by Gregory, von Dobschütz, Eltester, and Aland; and the papyri by the ℊ series of the same authorities. In 1957 in Aland's continuation list vi the papyri extended to ℊ⁶⁸, the uncials to 0241, the minuscules to 2533, and the lectionaries to l 1838, making a total of 4,680 items.[9]

---

[5] E. von Dobschütz in zNW 23 (1924), pp.248-264; 25 (1926), pp.299-306; 26 (1927), p.96; 27 (1928), pp.216-222; 32 (1933), pp.185-206; cf. J. Schmid in zNW 34 (1935), pp.308f.; 39 (1940), pp.241f.

[6] Hans Lietzmann in zNW 35 (1936), p.309. K. Aland in zNW 45 (1954), pp.179-217; 48 (1957), pp.141-191; cf. in TL 82 (1957), col. 167 n.11.

[7] *Die Schriften des Neuen Testaments.* Teil i, 2d ed. 1911; Teil ii, 1913.

[8] Benedikt Kraft, *Die Zeichen für die wichtigeren Handschriften des griechischen Neuen Testaments.* 3d ed. 1955.

[9] K. Aland in TL 82 (1957), col. 161 n.3; and in zNW 48 (1957), pp.141-191.

PAPYRI

As has already been stated the earliest known copies of any portions of the New Testament are papyrus fragments and manuscripts.[10] The oldest of these belong to the second century, and at present the very earliest that is known is a tiny piece of papyrus leaf with a small portion of the Gospel according to John. This was discovered in 1935 in the John Rylands Library in Manchester, England, among papyri acquired in Egypt in 1920 by B. P. Grenfell.[11] In that library the fragment is catalogued as Papyrus Rylands Gk. 457, and in the international listing it is $\mathfrak{p}^{52}$. The actual size of the papyrus, shown somewhat enlarged in Fig. 142, is 3.5 by 2.3 inches. The recto is at the left, the verso at the right. The recto contains John 18:31-33, the verso John 18:37-38, and thus the fragment is almost certainly from a codex. According to its style of handwriting the papyrus is dated in the first half of the second century A.D., probably about A.D. 125. As far as it goes the text agrees with Codex Vaticanus, Codex Sinaiticus, and Codex Ephraemi Syri rescriptus.[12] In comparison with the relatively irregular handwriting in an everyday papyrus such as the Letter from Hilarion to Alis (Fig. 140), the writing in $\mathfrak{p}^{52}$ seems like a rather carefully executed literary script. There is no punctuation, although the dieresis is placed over initial Iota, and the words appear to be slightly separated. No *nomina sacra* appear, so it cannot be established whether abbreviations were employed.

Our second oldest manuscript, as presently known, is $\mathfrak{p}^{64}$.[13] This consists of three small fragments of a codex leaf, purchased in Luxor in 1901 and preserved in the Library of Magdalen College at Oxford. The handwriting is regarded as an early predecessor of the later uncial script, and the date is believed to be in the latter part of the second century. The writing is in two columns to the page, and on the verso and recto are contained parts of Matthew 26:7, 10, 14-15, 22-23, 31, 32-33. *Nomina sacra* in abbreviated form are found

[10] For the papyri see also Georg Maldfeld in znw 42 (1949), pp.228-253; 43 (1950-51), pp.260f.; Kurt Aland in znw 45 (1954), p.187; and in nts 3 (1957), pp.261-286.

[11] C. H. Roberts, *An Unpublished Fragment of the Fourth Gospel in the John Rylands Library*. 1935. For the date of the fragment cf. Roberts in bjrl 36 (1953), p.98; Kurt Aland in tl 82 (1957), col. 162.

[12] Textual affinities of the papyri are given by Maldfeld in znw 42 (1949), pp.239, 242-253; and by Kraft, *Die Zeichen für die wichtigeren Handschriften des griechischen Neuen Testaments*, pp.48f.

[13] Colin Roberts in htr 46 (1953), pp.233-237; Aland in tl 82 (1957), col. 164.

in verses 23 and 31, the line above the abbreviations not being visible because of damage to the papyrus but presumably having once stood there. In verse 31 the first letter of the word αὐτοῖς ("to them") projects into the left margin. The line which is marked in this way is the first complete line of the section of texts which begins, "Then Jesus said to them," and this same section division is also recognized in Codex Alexandrinus; therefore the section divisions used in the latter codex must have originated at least as early as the present papyrus. In verse 14 "twelve" is written with a numerical symbol (ι]β) rather than with the word; in verse 22 the damaged text probably read "to say one after another to him," which is a unique word order; and in verse 32 Galilee is misspelled (γαλεγλαιαν); thus the text, brief as it is, shows how variations entered.

Coming to the end of the second century or the beginning of the third, say about A.D. 200 as the date is usually given, we find two papyrus manuscripts which are still relatively very early and are also, in contrast with the tiny fragments thus far mentioned, of very considerable extent, thus are extremely important documents. These are 𝔭⁴⁶ and 𝔭⁶⁶, and will be described next.

𝔭⁴⁶ is one of a group of papyrus manuscripts which became known in 1931. These were found and marketed by diggers and dealers in Egypt, and the greater part of the collection was purchased by Mr. A. Chester Beatty, an American living then in London and now in Dublin, while some portions of the find were acquired by the University of Michigan and by other individuals. The entire assemblage comprises no less than eleven codices, which date from the second to the fourth century and presumably represent the library of some early Christian church. The codices contain portions of nine Old Testament and fifteen New Testament books as well as the Book of Enoch and a homily by Melito of Sardis. The part of the collection with which we are concerned at this point is a codex of the letters of Paul. It is designated as 𝔭⁴⁶, and is believed to date around A.D. 200.[14] This means that it is 150 years older than the major manuscripts such as Codex Vaticanus upon which we have otherwise previously been dependent for the text of Paul's letters, and that it is removed from the time of the origin of the Pauline collection by little more than a century and from the time of the composition of the originals by 150 years in round numbers.

Eighty-six leaves of this notable codex survive, of which thirty

[14] U. Wilcken in AP 11 (1935), p.113.

belong to the University of Michigan and the remainder to Mr. Beatty.[15] Seven leaves are missing at the beginning, which implies that an equal number are lost at the end, while four other leaves near the beginning and end also are missing. Thus the original codex must have consisted of 104 leaves. It was formed by laying fifty-two sheets of papyrus one upon another, each having the recto side uppermost, and then folding the entire stack in the middle.[16] None of the extant leaves is preserved perfectly, but most of them have lost only a few lines at the bottom. The maximum size of the present leaves is approximately nine by six inches, and the original column of writing was normally around eight inches high by four and three-quarters inches wide.

The codex contains the letters of Paul in the following order: Romans, Hebrews, I and II Corinthians, Ephesians, Galatians, Philippians, Colossians, I Thessalonians. The last leaf which is extant contains the conclusion of I Thessalonians, but, as was pointed out just above, seven leaves have been lost from the end of the codex. Of these the first two doubtless contained II Thessalonians, with which book the codex seems to have closed. It is believed that the remaining five leaves were left blank, for ten more leaves instead of five would have been required if I and II Timothy, Titus, and Philemon had been included.[17] If this is true, then it appears that at this time the standard Pauline collection included his church letters but not the four letters to individual persons, although a small letter like Philemon might have been included. The place of Hebrews immediately following Romans is almost unique but is in agreement with Egyptian opinion which at that time ascribed Hebrews to Paul.[18] At the same time the Muratorian Canon, representing the usage of Rome about A.D. 200, does not include Hebrews among Paul's letters,[19] and the doubt of its Pauline authorship relegated it

[15] The entire manuscript is edited by Frederic G. Kenyon, *The Chester Beatty Biblical Papyri.* Fasciculus III. Text 1934, Supplement Text 1936, Supplement Plates 1937. See also H. A. Sanders, *A Third Century Papyrus Codex of the Epistles of Paul.* 1935; cf. Ernest C. Colwell in JR 16 (1936), pp.96-98.

[16] Consequently in the first half of the manuscript the verso side of the leaf precedes the recto, and in the second half the recto precedes the verso. The change comes at folio 53.

[17] Frederic Kenyon, *Our Bible and the Ancient Manuscripts.* 1958, p.188 n.1.

[18] Clement of Alexandria (A.D. c.200) said that Hebrews was the work of Paul (Eusebius, *Ch. Hist.* VI, xiv) and repeatedly quoted it as Pauline (e.g. *Stromata.* IV, 16, 20 [ANF II, pp.427f., 432]).

[19] *The Muratorian Fragment* (ASBACH p.119); E. J. Goodspeed, *The Formation of the New Testament.* 1926, pp.187f.

afterward to a place following II Thessalonians,[20] and finally, when the Pastorals and Philemon were accepted fully, to a place on the borderland between the Pauline epistles and James. Aside from the inclusion of Hebrews, and also the reversal of the order of Galatians and Ephesians, the Chester Beatty Papyrus lists Paul's church letters in exactly the order which became accepted generally and is used now in our printed Bibles. The principle of arrangement seems to be in the order of length, with letters which have the same address placed together.

Since the first seven leaves of the manuscript have been lost, Romans 1:1-5:17 is missing. Folio 8 contains Romans 5:17-6:14 but more than half of the leaf is broken away. Folios 9 and 10 again are missing, but beginning with folio 11 (Romans 8:15ff.) the remainder of Romans is substantially preserved. Folio 11 verso, containing Romans 8:15-25, is reproduced in Fig. 143. The text is broken away slightly at the left, but the missing words or portions of words are easily restored. At the bottom of the page four lines have been lost. The scribe wrote a large, flowing hand of calligraphic character, with the individual letters upright and square in formation and well spaced. Another hand put in the page numeration, the Greek letter κ at the top of this page being equivalent to number 20. Probably this latter hand is responsible also for the rather thick oblique stroke above the line which marks the ends of clauses as in lines 3, 5, 8, 10, 15, 20, and 22. The original scribe occasionally used a high dot for punctuation, as in line 3, and generally marked initial Upsilon and Iota with a dieresis, as in lines 1, 5, 11, and 23.[21] The scribe also abbreviated some words including the sacred names.

The text of this page reads as follows, the translation and punctuation being made in the style of the American Standard Version for convenience in comparison.

> Ye received the spirit of adoption, whereby we cry,
> Abba, Father. The Spirit itself beareth witness with
> our spirit, that we are children of God: and if children,
> then heirs of God and joint-heirs with Christ;
> if so be that we suffer, that we may be glorified with him. For
> I reckon that the sufferings of this present time are not worthy
> to be compared with the glory which shall

---

[20] This is the position it has in Codex Sinaiticus. Hebrews also follows Thessalonians in the present arrangement of Codex Vaticanus, but the paragraph numbers indicate that in an older division of this manuscript Hebrews stood between Galatians and Ephesians. Gregory, *Canon and Text of the New Testament*, pp.336, 344.

[21] Medial Iota also has the dieresis in line 9.

be revealed to us-ward. For the earnest expectation
of the creation waiteth for the revealing of the sons
of God. For the creation was subjected to vanity,
not of its own will but by reason of him who
subjected it, in hope that the creation itself also shall be delivered from the bondage of
corruption into the liberty of the glory of the
children of God. For we know that the whole creation
groaneth and travaileth in pain together until now.
And not only so, but we who have
the first-fruits of the Spirit also ourselves groan within ourselves, waiting for the redemption
of our body. For in hope were we saved:
but hope that is seen is not hope:
for who hopeth for that which he seeth? But if we hope for
that which we see not, then do we with patience wait for it.

Even a rapid reading of the above passage indicates that the Chester Beatty Papyrus of the Letters of Paul presents substantially the same text with which we are familiar in the best modern versions of the Bible. Indeed this very fact is the most significant thing about the manuscript. Here is our oldest copy of Paul's letters, and it emphatically confirms the accuracy and soundness of the general textual tradition.[22]

When manuscripts are copied many times, however, mistakes and alterations both unintentional and intentional creep in. Intentional alterations which are found include the simplification of a difficult passage, the addition of a lacking word or a desired quotation, and even changes made for dogmatic reasons. Far more frequent are unintentional alterations, which include writing a word once when it should be repeated, writing a word twice when it should appear only once, omitting a word or line when the eye skips to a second word or line ending similarly, and other errors of like kind. It is not surprising that such mistakes occurred in the laborious copying by hand of ancient manuscripts, for the same types of errors are perfectly familiar to modern stenographers, and even appear in printed books whose proofs have been carefully examined and re-examined. Thus, an edition of the English Bible printed in 1653 omitted the word "not" in I Corinthians 6:9 and made the passage read, "Or know ye not that the unrighteous shall inherit the king-dom of God?" The famous "Printer's Bible" gave Psalm 119:161 in

[22] Hans Lietzmann, *Zur Würdigung des Chester-Beatty-Papyrus der Paulusbriefe* (*Sitzungsbericht der Preussischen Akademie der Wissenschaften Phil.-Hist. Kl. 1934. xxv*), pp.3f.

the form "Printers have persecuted me without a cause" instead of "Princes have persecuted me without a cause," and an edition printed in 1717 became known as the "Vinegar Bible" because it misprinted "Vinegar" for "Vineyard" in the headline to the twentieth chapter of Luke. It is no wonder, therefore, that Irenaeus (A.D. c.180) thought it necessary to add the following note at the close of one of his writings: "I adjure thee who mayest copy this book, by our Lord Jesus Christ, and by his glorious advent when he comes to judge the living and the dead, to compare what thou shalt write, and correct it carefully by this manuscript, and also to write this adjuration, and place it in the copy."[23]

Rufinus (A.D. c.345-c.410) included an even longer adjuration and entreaty in the prologue to his translation of Origen's *De Principiis*:

"And, verily, in the presence of God the Father, and of the Son, and of the Holy Spirit, I adjure and beseech every one, who may either transcribe or read these books, by his belief in the kingdom to come, by the mystery of the resurrection from the dead, and by that everlasting fire prepared for the devil and his angels, that, as he would not possess for an eternal inheritance that place where there is weeping and gnashing of teeth, and where their fire is not quenched and their worm dieth not, he add nothing to Scripture, and take nothing away from it, and make no insertion or alteration, but that he compare his transcript with the copies from which he made it, and make the emendations and distinctions according to the letter, and not have his manuscript incorrect or indistinct, lest the difficulty of ascertaining the sense, from the indistinctness of the copy, should cause greater difficulties to the readers."[24]

And in his Preface to the Vulgate Translation of the Four Gospels (A.D. 383), Jerome spoke of "the mistakes introduced by inaccurate translators, and the blundering alterations of confident but ignorant critics, and further, all that has been inserted or altered by sleepy copyists."[25]

As a very early manuscript, the Chester Beatty Papyrus of Paul's letters is free from many alterations which appear in later codices. An instance of this may be seen in line 12 of the page reproduced in Fig. 143. Here in Romans 8:20f. it is probable that Paul wrote exactly as the papyrus reads, "by reason of him who subjected it, in hope that[26] the creation itself also shall be delivered. . . ." Codex Vaticanus, Codex Alexandrinus, and Codex Ephraemi rescriptus all

---

[23] Irenaeus, *On the Ogdoad*; quoted by Eusebius, *Ch. Hist.* v, xx.
[24] ANF IV, p.238; cf. Revelation 22:18f.
[25] NPNFSS VI, p.488.   [26] $\dot{\epsilon}\phi'$ $\dot{\epsilon}\lambda\pi\dot{\iota}\delta\iota$ $\ddot{o}\tau\iota$.

agree that this is the correct reading. But in Codex Sinaiticus, Codex Claromontanus, and Codex Boernerianus a slight alteration is found whereby the sentence is made to read, "by reason of him who subjected it, in hope, because[27] the creation itself also shall be delivered. . . ." At many other points also the Chester Beatty Papyrus clearly preserves what Paul wrote originally. In Romans 6:8 he wrote, "But if we died with Christ, we believe that we shall also live with him." Later scribes changed the last word "him" into "the Christ" in order to remove any possible ambiguity, but the papyrus preserves the original "him."[28] In Romans 9:31 Paul wrote "but Israel, following after a law of righteousness, did not arrive at the law,"[29] just as the papyrus has it. But some scribe thought that Paul should have used the same phrase in both parts of his sentence, and so changed the conclusion to read "did not arrive at the law of righteousness,"[30] and this appears in the mass of the later manuscripts. In Romans 10:15 Paul wrote, "How beautiful are the feet of them that bring glad tidings of good things!" and that is the way the Chester Beatty Papyrus has it.[31] This was a quotation, however, from Isaiah 52:7 and later manuscripts added from the Septuagint, "How beautiful are the feet of them that bring glad tidings of peace,[32] of them that bring glad tidings of good things."

In a number of instances, however, alterations have already crept into the text of the Chester Beatty Papyrus. Examples may be seen in lines 17-20 and 22 of the page illustrated in Fig. 143. In Romans 8:23 Paul wrote originally, "but also ourselves, who have the first-fruits of the Spirit, we also ourselves groan within ourselves, waiting for the adoption, the redemption of our body."[33] This was an involved and complicated sentence, as many of Paul's sentences are. In the papyrus the first "also ourselves" was omitted and so was the word "adoption" with the result that the sentence emerged in simplified form but with Paul's tumultuous manner of speech and richness of thought considerably modified: "but we who have the first-fruits of the Spirit also ourselves groan within ourselves, waiting for the redemption of our body." Codex Claromontanus and Codex Boernerianus later did the same as the papyrus in the omission of

[27] ἐφ' ἐλπίδι διότι.

[28] αὐτῷ p⁴⁶ SABC sa bo; τῷ Χριστῷ DG Latt.

[29] νόμον p⁴⁶ SAB sa bo DG. [30] νόμον δικαιοσύνης Latt Koine.

[31] p⁴⁶ SABC sa bo. [32] + τῶν εὐαγγελιζομένων εἰρήνην DG Latt.

[33] ἀλλὰ καὶ αὐτοὶ τὴν ἀπαρχὴν τοῦ πνεύματος ἔχοντες ἡμεῖς καὶ αὐτοὶ ἐν ἑαυτοῖς στενά-ζομεν υἱοθεσίαν ἀπεκδεχόμενοι, τὴν ἀπολύτρωσιν τοῦ σώματος ἡμῶν SAC.

the word "adoption," but handled the first part of the sentence differently: "but also ourselves, who have the first-fruits of the Spirit, ourselves groan within ourselves, waiting for the redemption of our body." Codex Vaticanus, on the other hand, did nothing but omit the original "we."

In Romans 8:24 the Chester Beatty Papyrus again seems to have slightly changed and simplified an originally more complex Pauline sentence. The papyrus reads, "for who hopeth for that which he seeth?"[34] Other forms in which the sentence is found are: "for what a man seeth, why doth he hope for?"[35] "for what a man seeth, why doth he yet hope for?"[36] "for who yet waiteth for that which he seeth?"[37] and "for what a man seeth, why doth he yet wait for?"[38] Of these the last is probably the original form since it is more probable that a scribe would change the verb "wait for" into "hope for" which appears so frequently in the rest of the passage, than that someone would invent the new expression "wait for."

Elsewhere in the papyrus appear errors, changes in words, and attempted corrections. For example there is a grammatical error in Romans 6:13 made through carelessness,[39] a word changed in 9:27 to make a quotation agree more exactly with the Septuagint,[40] and an omission of two words in 11:17 in order to simplify Paul's grammar where three genitives follow one another in unbroken succession.[41]

As the preceding examples have shown and as may also be seen by detailed study of the entire papyrus, $\mathfrak{p}^{46}$ agrees most often with the manuscripts of the Alexandrian family, sABC, but also not infrequently with those of the Western family, including D and G.[42] As a very early codex it is free from many alterations which appear in later manuscripts, yet it also shows how changes and errors had already been introduced. Doubtless this papyrus is typical of many other codices which were in existence in the second and third cen-

---

[34] ὅ γὰρ βλέπει τίς ἐλπίζει $\mathfrak{p}^{46}$ B.   [35] ὅ γὰρ βλέπει τις, τί ἐλπίζει DG Latt.

[36] ὅ γὰρ βλέπει τις, τί καὶ ἐλπίζει C Koine   [37] ὅ γὰρ βλέπει τις καὶ ὑπομένει S.

[38] ὅ γὰρ βλέπει τις, τί καὶ ὑπομένει A.   [39] ζῶντες $\mathfrak{p}^{46}$ DG instead of ζῶντας.

[40] κατάλιμμα $\mathfrak{p}^{46}$ DG instead of ὑπόλειμμα SAB.

[41] τῆς ῥίζης τῆς πιότητος τῆς ἐλαίας ("of the root of the fatness of the olive tree") SBC; "of the root" is omitted by $\mathfrak{p}^{46}$ DG; another attempt to make the sentence more readable is represented by the addition of "and" in A Koine, "of the root and of the fatness of the olive tree."

[42] Kenyon, *The Chester Beatty Biblical Papyri*, Fasciculus III Supplement Text, pp.xv-xvii. (These terms are explained later in this chapter: Alexandrian, p.432, Western p.441, and Caesarean, p.446.)

turies A.D., no two of which were exactly alike and in each of which numerous variations were to be found.

$\mathfrak{p}^{66}$ is a codex which is in the Bibliothek Bodmer in Geneva where it is known as Papyrus Bodmer II.[43] Upon its publication in 1956 it was recognized to be of significance comparable to $\mathfrak{p}^{46}$ upon grounds of both age and extent. As to its date, a time around A.D. 200 is probable and some think that it may be even somewhat earlier. As to its extent, the codex preserves for us approximately two-thirds of the Gospel according to John. There is an unwritten leaf at the outset which provides a front cover. Beginning with the first written page, the pages are numbered. They run consecutively from page a' (page 1) to page $\lambda\delta'$ (page 34) which ends in the eleventh verse of the sixth chapter of John; then pages 35-38 are missing; and after that the manuscript continues from page $\lambda\theta'$ (page 39), beginning in the thirty-fifth verse of chapter six, to page $\rho\eta'$ (page 108), ending with the twenty-sixth verse of the fourteenth chapter of the Gospel. Except for the two missing leaves (pages 35-38), the intact character of this part of the manuscript is amazing. The leaves are nearly rectangular and quite small, being about five and one-half inches wide and a little over six inches high. Individually the leaves are so well preserved that there are rarely more than a few letters missing on a page. In addition to this part of the manuscript, however, there are said to be portions of the balance of the codex which still await publication which are extremely fragmentary.

The handwriting of $\mathfrak{p}^{66}$ is an excellent, upright, regular, quadratic literary script. There is rudimentary punctuation with a high point at the end of sentences and a double point at the end of sections. The dieresis is used frequently over Iota and Upsilon. The words $\theta\epsilon\delta s$, $'I\eta\sigma o\hat{v}s$, $\kappa\dot{v}\rho\iota o s$, and $X\rho\iota\sigma\tau\delta s$ are always abbreviated, and so also sometimes are $\ddot{a}\nu\theta\rho\omega\pi o s$, $\pi a\tau\dot{\eta}\rho$, $\pi\nu\epsilon\hat{v}\mu a$, and $\upsilon\iota\delta s$. There are numerous errors in the manuscript, but most of these have been corrected, many of the corrections perhaps having been made by the scribe himself during the course of his work. This, it has been thought, may suggest that the manuscript was written by a commercial copyist. As to the text, in fashion similar to $\mathfrak{p}^{46}$, there are many variants and

---

[43] Victor Martin, *Papyrus Bodmer II, Evangile de Jean, chap. 1-14* (Bibliotheca Bodmeriana v). 1956; cf. Georg Maldfeld in NTS 3 (1956-57), pp.79-81; K. Aland in TL 82 (1957), cols. 161-184; and in NTS 3 (1956-57), pp.280-284; J. Ramsey Michaels in *The Bible Translator.* 7 (1956), pp.150-154; Floyd V. Filson in BA 20 (1957), pp.54-63; M.-E. Boismard in RB 64 (1957), pp.363-398; C. K. Barrett in *The Expository Times.* 68 (1956-57), pp.174-177.

the manuscript does not agree consistently with any of the major texts established later. John 5:4 and John 7:53-8:11 are omitted, passages which other manuscript evidence had already suggested were not a part of the Gospel according to John in its original form.[44]

Continuing now on into the third century A.D. we may note the following papyri. $\mathfrak{p}^{45}$ is another of the Chester Beatty Papyri, with a fragment of the same manuscript in the Österreichische National-bibliothek in Vienna.[45] There are thirty leaves of this codex, often poorly preserved, and the content extends, with many gaps, from the twentieth chapter of Matthew to the seventeenth chapter of Acts. The date is probably in the early part of the third century. The text is mixed, being mainly Caesarean in Mark but Alexandrian and Western in the other parts.

$\mathfrak{p}^{53}$ is the designation of two fragments at the University of Michigan of a codex which probably like the foregoing one also contained the four Gospels and the book of Acts, since the extant portions have most of the verses of Matthew 26:29-40 and Acts 9:33-10:1.[46] The date is probably about the middle of the third century. The text shows agreements with the Alexandrian, Western, and Caesarean families of manuscripts.

$\mathfrak{p}^{37}$ is a codex leaf at the University of Michigan with Matthew 26:19-52.[47] It was probably written in the second half of the third century, and the text has resemblances to the Caesarean. $\mathfrak{p}^{5}$ designates two Oxyrhynchus papyri in the British Museum which came from the same codex and contain parts of John 1, 16, and 20.[48] They were probably written in the second half of the third century, and the text resembles the Alexandrian and the Western. $\mathfrak{p}^{22}$ is also a papyrus from Oxyrhynchus and is in the University Library at Glasgow.[49] In this case the copy was a roll rather than a codex, and parts of two columns are preserved with portions of John 15 and 16. The date is probably toward the end of the third century; the text often agrees with S but sometimes also with D.

[44] John 5:4 is found in AG but is omitted in SBCD. John 7:53-8:11 is found in D but is omitted in SABC (A and C are actually imperfect at this point but calculation of space shows that they cannot have contained the passage; see Marcus Dods in The Expositor's Greek Testament. I, p.770).

[45] Frederic G. Kenyon, The Chester Beatty Biblical Papyri. Fasciculus II, The Gospels and Acts, Text 1933, Plates 1934.

[46] Henry A. Sanders in Quantulacumque, pp.151-161.

[47] Henry A. Sanders in HTR 19 (1926), pp.215-226; HPUM Pl. XIII.

[48] OP II, No.208; XV, No.1781; HPUM Pl. VIII.

[49] OP X, No.1228; HPUM Pl. VII.

𝔭²⁷ designates two fragments of a codex leaf from Oxyrhynchus, now in the Cambridge University Library, with portions of Romans 8 and 9.[50] The date is probably in the third century. The text agrees generally with B, and there are some readings like the Western text. 𝔭⁴⁹ is a codex leaf in three pieces in the possession of Yale University.[51] It contains Ephesians 4:16-29 and 4:31-5:13, and was probably written in the third century. The text shows agreements with B and 𝔭⁴⁶. 𝔭³² is a codex leaf in the John Rylands Library with Titus 1:11-15 on the recto and Titus 2:3-8 on the verso.[52] The date is in the third century; the text agrees with S and also with Western manuscripts. 𝔭³⁰ is two leaves of a codex from Oxyrhynchus, now in the Bibliothèque Universitaire in Ghent, containing I Thessalonians 4:12 to II Thessalonians 1:2 with breaks.[53] Page numbers 207 and 208 are preserved, and if the codex contained Paul's collected letters the usual order from Romans to I Thessalonians would exactly account for the preceding 206 pages. The date is probably late in the third century. The text shows agreements with the Alexandrian manuscripts but also divergences.

𝔭⁴⁷ is another part of the Chester Beatty Papyri and consists of ten leaves of a codex containing Revelation 9:10-17:2.[54] The date is probably in the latter part of the third century. The text agrees generally with A, C, and S.

Belonging to the third or fourth century is 𝔭¹, a codex leaf found at Oxyrhynchus only a day or two after the first discovery of the sayings of Jesus (OP No. 1; see above pp.411f.) and in nearly the same place.[55] Now at the University of Pennsylvania, it contains most of Matthew 1:1-20. The text is similar to S and B.

Continuing on in the fourth century we note the following papyri. 𝔭⁴ designates four fragmentary codex leaves in the Bibliothèque Nationale in Paris which are from a lectionary (1943) and contain portions of the first six chapters of Luke.[56] The date is fourth century, and the text is Alexandrian. 𝔭²⁸ is a codex leaf from Oxyrhynchus, now in the Palestine Institute of Archeology at Pacific School of Religion, with John 6:8-12, 17-22.[57] The date is the early or middle fourth century; the text agrees with B. 𝔭⁵⁰ is two codex leaves at Yale

[50] OP XI, No.1355.　　　　　　　　　　　[51] Maldfeld in ZNW 42 (1949), p.250.

[52] HPUM Pl. III (where it is numbered 𝔭³¹).

[53] OP XIII, No.1598.

[54] Kenyon, *The Chester Beatty Biblical Papyri.* Fasciculus III. Text 1934; Plates 1936.

[55] OP I, No.2; HPUM Pl. XI.　　　　　　　　[56] RB 47 (1938), pp.5-22.

[57] OP XIII, No.1596.

University, containing Acts 8:26-32 and 10:26-31.[58] The date is fourth century; the text agrees mostly with B.

$\mathfrak{p}^{13}$ is a portion of a papyrus roll from Oxyrhynchus, now in the British Museum, with an unusually interesting history.[59] The roll was written originally in the third century A.D. as an epitome in Latin of the history of Rome by Livy.[60] Probably in the first half of the fourth century the back (verso) of the roll was used to copy at least part of the New Testament. The extant portion contains eleven broad columns with parts of Hebrews 2-5 and 10-12. The columns are numbered at the top, the preserved numbers being 47-50, 63-65, and 67-69; thus some other part of the New Testament presumably occupied the preceding part of the roll. The text tends generally to agree with B, but also has agreements with D.

$\mathfrak{p}^{10}$ (Fig. 144) is an individual leaf from Oxyrhynchus, now in the Semitic Museum at Harvard University.[61] At the top, Romans 1:1-7 is copied in eleven lines of rough, large letters. There are several mistakes in spelling and part of verse six is left out. From the carelessness of the copying and the rudeness of the uncial letters, Grenfell and Hunt thought that this was a schoolboy's exercise. At the bottom of the leaf are two lines of cursive writing, and Adolf Deissmann suggested that the entire leaf might have served as an amulet for the Aurelios Paulos who is named there.[62] The cursive writing is such as occurs in the first half of the fourth century, and the papyrus was actually found tied up with a contract dated in A.D. 316, so an early fourth century date is confirmed. In the copying the following divine names are all abbreviated: Christ Jesus (line 1), God (lines 2, 9, 10), Son (line 3), Son of God (line 5), Spirit (line 5), Jesus Christ (lines 6, 8), Lord (line 6), Father (line 10) and Lord Christ Jesus (lines 10-11). The text is mainly Alexandrian. In verse 1, $\mathfrak{p}^{10}$ and Codex Vaticanus are the chief witnesses for the characteristic Pauline "Christ Jesus" (instead of "Jesus Christ") in verse 1, while $\mathfrak{p}^{10}$ is quite alone in the same order in verse 7 (lines 10-11) and in reading "the name of Jesus Christ" instead of "his name" in verse 5 (line 8).

$\mathfrak{p}^{15}$ is a codex leaf from Oxyrhynchus, now in Cairo, containing I Corinthians 7:18-8:4.[63] Written also in a good-sized uncial hand, the date of the papyrus is probably in the second half of the fourth century. With some exceptions, the text agrees with BSA.

[58] Carl H. Kraeling in *Quantulacumque*, pp.163-172.   [59] OP IV, No.657.
[60] OP IV, No.668.   [61] OP II, No.209.   [62] DLO p.203 n.4.   [63] OP VII, No.1008.

Moving on into the fifth century A.D., we note these examples: 𝔭²¹ is a fragmentary codex leaf from Oxyrhynchus, now in Muhlenberg College, Allentown, Pennsylvania.[64] It contains several verses of the twelfth chapter of Matthew. The rather large uncials point to a date in the fifth century. Textually there are agreements with D and with a corrector of S. 𝔭¹¹, now in Leningrad, consists of six or seven fragments which probably came from a papyrus codex but were later used for some kind of a book cover.[65] They contain parts of I Corinthians 1-2 and 6-7. The date is probably fifth century, and the text is Alexandrian.

In the sixth century we note these papyri: 𝔭³ is a fragment of a lectionary (1 348), now in the Österreichische Nationalbibliothek, Vienna, with Luke 7:36-45; 10:38-42.[66] The date is sixth century, and the text is Alexandrian. 𝔭³⁶ is two codex leaves, now in the Bibliotheca Laurenziana in Florence, containing John 3:14-18, 31-32.[67] The date is probably sixth century; the text is Alexandrian and Western.

Coming to the end of the sixth or beginning of the seventh century we find such a papyrus as 𝔭⁴⁴. This is three leaves of a codex, now in the Metropolitan Museum of Art, New York City, with portions of Matthew 17, 18, and 25, and John 9, 10, and 12.[68] The text is Alexandrian, agreeing particularly with B. 𝔭³⁵ is probably to be dated sometime in the seventh century. This is a codex leaf, now in the Bibliotheca Laurenziana in Florence, which contains Matthew 25:12-15, 20-22.[69] The text is Alexandrian and Western.

Finally toward the end of the seventh century we find several fairly extensive papyri which have only recently been published. These were found at Nessana in the Negeb in southern Palestine by the Colt Archaeological Expedition, under H. Dunscombe Colt, which worked at this place in 1936 and 1937. Nessana was a stopping point on the caravan route from Aqabah to Gaza, was fortified as early as the second century B.C., flourished in the sixth and seventh centuries A.D., and is the location of a small settlement named 'Auja-el-Hafir at the present time. The papyri found here had been buried in the collapse of a room annexed to a small church. Since southern Palestine is relatively dry, and since the church was on the top of a hill where such rain as fell ran off rapidly, conditions were fairly favorable for the preservation of the papyri. All together

[64] OP X, No.1227.
[66] ibid., pp.242f.   [67] ibid., p.247.
[65] Maldfeld in ZNW 42 (1949), p.244.
[68] ibid., p.249.   [69] ibid., p.247.

there were found not only the New Testament papyri about to be mentioned but also a copy of the apocryphal correspondence between Abgar and Christ, a version of the legend of St. George, a portion of the Twelve Chapters on Faith ascribed, perhaps incorrectly, to Gregory Thaumaturgus, and classical, legal, and nonliterary documents. These are now in New York University.[70]

The New Testament papyri from Nessana are $\mathfrak{p}^{59}$, $\mathfrak{p}^{60}$, and $\mathfrak{p}^{61}$. $\mathfrak{p}^{59}$ and $\mathfrak{p}^{60}$ are probably from the latter part of the seventh century, $\mathfrak{p}^{61}$ is slightly later, either at the end of the seventh or the beginning of the eighth century. $\mathfrak{p}^{59}$ consists of fourteen leaves, two complete, the others fragmentary, with parts of John 1, 11, 12, 17, 18, and 21. $\mathfrak{p}^{60}$ is made up of twenty consecutive leaves, half or two-thirds intact, with text extending from John 16:29 to 19:26. $\mathfrak{p}^{61}$ consists of seven fragmentary leaves with small portions of Romans, I Corinthians, Philippians, Colossians, I Thessalonians, Titus, and Philemon. Since, as far as can be determined, these books stood in the order just given, it appears likely that the complete codex contained the entire Pauline collection and in the usual order. Determination of the character of the text of the Nessana papyri awaits further study.

Such are some representative and interesting examples of the papyri of the New Testament. While many are only fragments, they doubtless give us a more realistic impression of how many of the New Testament writings appeared originally than do the relatively elegant vellum manuscripts of which we shall soon speak. Including all of the more than sixty papyri thus far known, only seven out of the twenty-seven books of the New Testament are not represented, namely I and II Timothy, and I and II Peter, II and III John, and Jude.[71] All together also the known papyri contain a good 50 per cent of the entire New Testament text, and in the case of the Gospel according to John they preserve 88 per cent of it.[72] Naturally the individual papyri must be individually evaluated as to age and text form.[73]

In the analysis above of a section of $\mathfrak{p}^{46}$ it was seen that on the whole the text of this papyrus was very good and agreed frequently with the oldest parchments such as Codex Vaticanus, Codex Sinaiticus, and Codex Alexandrinus, but that it also contained readings

---

[70] *Excavations at Nessana*, ii, *Literary Papyri*, by Lionel Casson and Ernest L. Hettich. 1950. For the *Non-Literary Papyri* see Vol. iii by Casper J. Kraemer, Jr. 1958.
[71] Maldfeld in zNw 42 (1949), p.239.
[72] Maldfeld in nts 3 (1956), p.80.
[73] Kurt Aland in *Forschungen und Fortschritte.* 31 (1957), p.51

which seemed to be errors and changes from what Paul probably wrote originally. Likewise the other papyri cited from the second and third centuries usually manifested texts of a mixed character. In the fourth and later centuries, however, we have observed many papyri the text of which is much more strictly Alexandrian. This suggests that the very existence of many different copies of New Testament writings in the second and third centuries, each with its own variants, led to the desire for a better text and that, probably in the fourth century, a more nearly standard text was wrought out. This hypothesis will be referred to again in what follows.

PARCHMENTS

We turn next to early copies of the New Testament, or portions of the New Testament, written on parchment or vellum. The earliest of these presently known belong probably to the third century A.D. and thus are about a century later in date than the earliest known New Testament papyri. By the fourth century, as we have seen (pp.397f.), parchment became the chief material for New Testament manuscripts although, as we have also just seen, copies on papyrus are also found for yet a number of centuries.

As far as known at the present time, the oldest parchment containing New Testament material is 0212, a fragment in the possession of Yale University.[74] It is a little over three and one-half by four inches in size, and may have been part of a scroll rather than a codex. The fifteen lines of writing which are preserved provide a text in which the four Gospels are woven together to make a single narrative in the manner of the well-known Diatessaron. The material contained is Matthew 27:56-57; Mark 15:40, 42, 43; Luke 23:49-51, 54; John 19:38. The date is probably in the first half of the third century.

The next oldest parchment and the first with text which is directly from a New Testament book as known in the regular canon is 0220.[75] This is a fragment obtained in Cairo in 1950 by Dr. Leland C. Wyman of Jamaica Plain, Massachusetts, and said to have come from Fustat, northeast of Old Cairo and near the site of the Roman fortress of Babylon. It is about three and one-half by four and one-half inches in size and contains Romans 4:23-5:3 on the recto and Romans 5:8-13 on the verso. The writing suggests a date in the latter part of the

[74] Aland in ZNW 45 (1954), p.188; and in TL 82 (1957), cols. 161f.
[75] William H. P. Hatch in HTR 45 (1952), pp.79-85.

third century. As far as it goes the text is mostly like the Alexandrian, although it is no doubt pre-Hesychian. There is an important reading in 5:1 where the indicative $\check{\epsilon}\chi o\mu\epsilon\nu$ is found instead of the subjunctive $\check{\epsilon}\chi\omega\mu\epsilon\nu$ which is in BSACD[p] and other manuscripts. This confirms the conclusion already drawn on grounds of the context that Paul meant to affirm that "we have peace," rather than to exhort, "let us have peace."[76]

THE ALEXANDRIAN TEXT

We come now to the theory already suggested, that the existence in the second and third centuries of many different manuscripts with many different readings led to the desire to obtain a more nearly standardized text, freed from as many as possible of these changes and errors. The hypothesis is that in the fourth century the scholars at Alexandria brought together a number of the better manuscripts, such as the Chester Beatty Papyri, and endeavored to strike out their variants and thus arrive at a good average text.[77] At any rate the next few manuscripts to be mentioned form a sort of family whose text well might have arisen in this very way. In each of these several manuscripts there are still individual corrections, changes, and errors, but the group has such decided similarities that it is commonly referred to as representing the Egyptian or Alexandrian text. Since this characteristic text may go back to the Egyptian bishop and martyr Hesychius (d. A.D. c.311),[78] whose work on the text of the Gospels is mentioned by Jerome,[79] it is also called the Hesychian recension (𝔥). Four great vellum Bibles, written in uncial characters, constitute the chief witnesses to the Egyptian text. These are Codex Vaticanus, Codex Sinaiticus, Codex Alexandrinus,[80] and Codex Ephraemi Syri rescriptus.

CODEX VATICANUS

Codex Vaticanus, designated as B or 03, is a fine parchment codex containing almost the entire Greek Bible. It was already in the possession of the Vatican Library at Rome before the first catalogue of

---

[76] Lietzmann, *An die Römer*, p.58.

[77] Lietzmann, *Zur Würdigung des Chester-Beatty-Papyrus der Paulusbriefe*, p.10.

[78] Eusebius, *Ch. Hist.* VIII, xiii.

[79] Preface to the Vulgate Translation of the Four Gospels, addressed to Pope Damasus, A.D. 383 (NPNFSS VI, p.488); cf. Lietzmann, *Einführung in die Textgeschichte der Paulusbriefe*, p.13.

[80] It must be noted, however, that while the text of Codex Alexandrinus is Alexandrian in the letters of Paul it is Byzantine in the Gospels.

432

that library was made in 1475. Napoleon carried the manuscript to Paris as a prize of war, and it remained there from 1809 until it was returned to Rome in 1815. While at Paris the manuscript was studied by Leonhard Hug, a Roman Catholic professor from Tübingen, and its great age and true value were recognized for the first time. In 1843 Constantine Tischendorf was able to study the manuscript in Rome, but only under very restricted circumstances, and full and accurate knowledge was not available to the scholars of the world until a complete photographic facsimile was published in Rome in 1889-1890.

The codex must have originally contained about 820 leaves, of which 759 are preserved, 142 of these belonging to the New Testament. Each leaf measures about ten and one-half by ten inches, and there are three columns of text to the page with forty-two lines to a column. The writing is in perfectly simple and unadorned uncials, smaller letters sometimes being crowded in at the ends of lines. The words are written continuously without separation. There is almost no punctuation, although initial Iota and Upsilon are marked with a dieresis and sacred names are abbreviated. Old Testament quotations are marked with a horizontal caret (>). One scribe copied the entire New Testament, although a different scribe wrote the Old Testament. Two correctors have made corrections in the manuscript, one being almost contemporary with the original scribes, and the other being as late as the tenth or eleventh century. The later corrector retraced the pale letters, omitting only the letters and words which he believed to be incorrect, and also added the breathings and accents. The style of handwriting and almost complete absence of ornamentation indicate a date for Codex Vaticanus in the middle of the fourth century A.D., and the place of writing may have been in Alexandria.[81]

As far as the letters of Paul are concerned, then, in this manuscript we have a copy which was made, in round numbers, only 150 years later than the Chester Beatty Papyrus and three hundred years after the originals. The opening page of Paul's Letter to the Romans, with its simple title, "To the Romans," is reproduced in Fig. 145.

CODEX SINAITICUS

Codex Sinaiticus (‮א‬, S, or 01)[82] derives its name from Mount Sinai

[81] Lake, *The Text of the New Testament*, pp.14f.
[82] For the designation cf. above p.415.

where it was found in the Monastery of Saint Catherine (Fig. 146). The traditional region of Mount Sinai (cf. p.151) was one of the places sought out by hermits and anchorites upon the inception of the Christian monastic movement in the third and fourth centuries. These hermits settled in the caves of Jebel Serbal, and eventually churches and convents were built in the neighboring valley of Pharan (now the Wadi Feiran), which became the seat of the Bishop of Pharan. Other hermits established themselves twenty-five miles away at a place where a bush was shown as the Burning Bush of Exodus 3:2-4. This was in a desolate valley of nearly four thousand feet altitude at the foot of Jebel Musa and nearby Jebel Catherine. It is believed that St. Helena built a church here to enshrine the Burning Bush and also a tower of refuge for the hermits who were under attack by Arab raids. Such interest on the part of Helena is not improbable since we know that she visited Jerusalem about A.D. 327 and was interested in the erection of churches in the Holy Land (p.532). About A.D. 460 the region was visited by the Spanish nun and pilgrim Etheria. She was received at a certain monastery and energetically climbed various mountains including a middle one to which the name of Sinai was especially attached, but whether this was at Jebel Serbal or Jebel Musa is difficult to make out. Her travel journal reads:

"We reached the mountain late on the sabbath, and arriving at a certain monastery, the monks who dwelt there received us very kindly, showing us every kindness; there is also a church and a priest there. We stayed there that night, and early on the Lord's Day, together with the priest and the monks who dwelt there, we began the ascent of the mountains one by one. These mountains are ascended with infinite toil, for you cannot go up gently by a spiral track, as we say snail-shell wise, but you climb straight up the whole way, as if up a wall, and you must come straight down each mountain until you reach the very foot of the middle one, which is specially called Sinai."[83]

In A.D. 530, since the attacks of the Arabs were continuing, the Emperor Justinian built a massive wall around St. Helena's church and tower. At about this time the Church of the Burning Bush was rebuilt on a larger scale and renamed the Church of the Transfiguration. When the settlement at Pharan broke up under Arab raids the Bishop of Pharan took refuge in the Monastery of the Burning Bush, and after A.D. 630 his successors had the title of Bishop of Sinai. The

[83] *The Pilgrimage of Etheria.* tr. M. L. McClure and C. L. Feltoe in *Translations of Christian Literature.* Series III Liturgical Texts, pp.3f.

Archbishop of Sinai now resides in Cairo. Saint Catherine, by whose name the Monastery of the Burning Bush later became known, was a martyr in Alexandria under the Roman ruler Maximinus (A.D. 305-313). According to legend her body was transported by angels to Mount Sinai, where some five centuries later her bones were discovered and where, at least in part, they are still preserved. Curiously enough, the monastery enclosure now includes also a mosque with a square minaret which rises beside the bell tower of the church. The story told concerning this is that centuries ago a Turkish general was marching against the monastery with troops which were thirsting for the conquest. He was met by a deputation of monks and dissuaded from his purpose, but fearing that his troops could not be restrained, he advised the hasty erection of the mosque. When the troops arrived the minaret appeared beside the church tower, and the Muslims spared the place where it appeared that their Prophet was known.[84]

Such is the story of the famous monastery in which one of the greatest manuscript discoveries of all time was made. The discoverer was the unrivaled critic and decipherer of ancient manuscripts, Dr. Constantine Tischendorf. He told the story of the great discovery in his own words as follows:

"It was at the foot of Mount Sinai, in the Convent of St. Catherine, that I discovered the pearl of all my researches. In visiting the library of the monastery, in the month of May, 1844, I perceived in the middle of the great hall a large and wide basket full of old parchments; and the librarian, who was a man of information, told me that two heaps of paper like these, mouldered by time, had been already committed to the flames. What was my surprise to find amid this heap of papers a considerable number of sheets of a copy of the Old Testament in Greek, which seemed to me to be one of the most ancient that I had ever seen. The authorities of the convent allowed me to possess myself of a third of these parchments, or about forty-three sheets, all the more readily as they were destined for the fire."[85]

Tischendorf was allowed to take the forty-three leaves to Leipzig where he edited them under the title *Codex Friderico Augustanus* (1846) in acknowledgment of the patronage of the king of Saxony. In 1853 Tischendorf returned to Sinai but could find nothing more of

[84] H. V. Morton, *Through Lands of the Bible*. 1938, p.347.
[85] *Codex Sinaiticus, the Ancient Biblical Manuscript now in the British Museum, Tischendorf's Story and Argument Related by Himself*. 8th ed. 1934, pp.23f. The quotations from this book are made by permission of the Lutterworth Press, Redhill, Surrey, England.

the manuscript. Once again in 1859 he came back, this time with the approval of the emperor of Russia for systematic researches in the East, but still there was no trace of the great treasure. He was on the point of leaving when the steward of the convent invited him to his cell. Tischendorf relates that the monk "took down from the corner of the room a bulky kind of volume, wrapped up in a red cloth, and laid it before me. I unrolled the cover, and discovered, to my great surprise, not only those very fragments which, fifteen years before, I had taken out of the basket, but also other parts of the Old Testament, the New Testament complete, and, in addition, the Epistle of Barnabas and a part of the Pastor of Hermas."[86]

After complex transactions it became possible for Tischendorf to place the great manuscript in the hands of the emperor of Russia and for himself to prepare a facsimile edition of it. Payment of some $6,750 was made to the monks by the emperor for the manuscript. Acclaim came to Tischendorf from throughout the Christian world for his notable discovery. Relating the recognitions which he received, Tischendorf said:

"The two most celebrated universities of England, Cambridge and Oxford, desired to show me honour by conferring on me their highest academic degree. 'I would rather,' said an old man—himself of the highest distinction for learning—'I would rather have discovered this Sinaitic manuscript than the Koh-i-noor of the Queen of England.'

"But that which I think more highly of than all these flattering distinctions is the fact that Providence has given to our age, in which attacks on Christianity are so common, the Sinaitic Bible, to be to us a full and clear light as to what is the real text of God's Word written, and to assist us in defending the truth by establishing its authentic form."[87]

Codex Sinaiticus remained in Leningrad until it was purchased from the Soviet government by the British Museum for some $500,000. When the valuable manuscript arrived at the British Museum December 27, 1933, its appearance was still much as when Tischendorf first saw it at Sinai, a large pile of loose quires and leaves, lacking both beginning and end and having no covers or binding (Fig. 147). It has been carefully bound by the British Museum in two volumes, Old Testament and New Testament.

Whereas originally the Sinaitic manuscript probably had at least 730 leaves, only 390 (including those at Leipzig) remain today—242 in the Old Testament and 148 in the New Testament. The leaves

[86] *ibid.*, p.26.　　　　　　　　[87] *ibid.*, pp.31f.

are about fifteen inches high by thirteen and one-half or fourteen inches broad, and the text is written in four columns to the page, with forty-eight lines to the column. The words are written continuously without separation and there are no accents or breathings, although high and middle points and colon are used for punctuation, initial Iota and Upsilon have the dieresis and sacred names are abbreviated. The codex was written by three scribes, known as A, B, and D, of whom Scribe A wrote almost all of the New Testament. The three hands are very much alike, but they show individual peculiarities, particularly in the matter of spelling; it is largely on the basis of spelling that the three are differentiated. Many corrections have been made in the manuscript not only by the original scribes but also by a series of correctors from the fourth to the twelfth century.[88] No less than 14,800 places are enumerated in Tischendorf's edition where some alteration has been made to the text.[89] The dignified simplicity of the elegant capital letters in which the manuscript was originally written is comparable to that of Codex Vaticanus, and both manuscripts were probably written at about the same time around A.D. 350, the Vatican manuscript being perhaps a little the older of the two.[90] The place where the Codex Sinaiticus was written is uncertain but at least there is nothing to contradict an Egyptian origin although Caesarea or Palestine are also regarded as possibilities. Since Codex Vaticanus and Codex Sinaiticus are written in three and four columns respectively it has sometimes been believed that they are two of the fifty vellum Bibles ordered by Constantine from Eusebius of Caesarea in A.D. 332 but, as we have already noted (p.398), there are also arguments against this supposition. The first page of Paul's Letter to the Romans in Codex Sinaiticus is shown in Fig. 148.[91]

[88] H. J. M. Milne and T. C. Skeat, *Scribes and Correctors of the Codex Sinaiticus.* 1938, pp.22f., 40-50.

[89] Milne and Skeat, *The Codex Sinaiticus and the Codex Alexandrinus.* 1938, p.19.

[90] Schubart, *Griechische Palaeographie*, p.155.

[91] In 1949-1950 a Mount Sinai Expedition, for which Kenneth W. Clark was general editor, surveyed 3,300 manuscripts in six languages in the Monastery of Saint Catherine at Mount Sinai and copied more than 1,600 of them on microfilm. These include over five hundred manuscripts of biblical text in five languages, 175 of them of Greek New Testament text. The oldest Greek text is a seventh-century lectionary with readings from the Gospels and Letters of Paul. The same expedition also studied 2,400 manuscripts in eleven languages in the library of the Patriarchate of the Greek Orthodox Church at Jerusalem, and yet others in the library of the Armenian Patriarchate at Jerusalem. Over one thousand of these manuscripts were photographed on microfilm, including 270 biblical texts, ninety of the Gospels in Greek. A complete New Testament in Greek, written in the eleventh century and not previously noted

CODEX ALEXANDRINUS

Codex Alexandrinus (A or 02) was given by Cyril Lucar, patriarch of Constantinople, to Sir Thomas Roe, the English ambassador to the Sublime Porte, to be presented to the king of England, and is first mentioned in a letter by Roe dated January 20, 1624 (i.e. January 30, 1625) as "an autographall bible intire, written by the hand of Tecla the protomartyr of the Greekes, that liued in the tyme of St. Paul; and he doth auerr yt to be true and authenticall, of his owne writing, and the greatest antiquitye of the Greeke church."[92] The codex arrived in England in 1628 and was placed in the Royal Library, which in 1757 was incorporated in the British Museum.

Cyril Lucar had been patriarch of Alexandria before assuming the same position in Constantinople in 1620, and probably brought the codex with him from Alexandria when he came to Constantinople. The earlier Alexandrian location of the manuscript is also indicated by an Arabic note written at the bottom of the first page of Genesis: "Made an inalienable gift to the Patriarchal Cell in the City of Alexandria. Whosoever shall remove it thence shall be accursed and cut off. Written by Athanasius the humble."

This Athanasius who calls himself "the humble" was probably the Melchite patriarch who died in A.D. 1308. Another Arabic note of the thirteenth or fourteenth century is written at the back of the Table of Books and gives the tradition alluded to in Sir Thomas Roe's letter that the manuscript was written by the martyr Thecla, but this is probably only a legend. The close connection of the codex with Alexandria makes it probable that that city was its place of origin. In point of time Codex Alexandrinus was presumably somewhat later than the Vatican and Sinaitic manuscripts, generally being ascribed to the first half of the fifth century.[93]

The manuscript originally contained perhaps 820 leaves, of which 773 are extant, 630 in the Old Testament, and 143 in the New Testament. The vellum leaves measure approximately twelve and five-eighths by ten and three-eighths inches. The quires were of eight leaves, numbered in Greek characters in the center of the top margin

---

by outside scholars, was found. The microfilms are in the Library of Congress. See Kenneth W. Clark in BA 16 (1953), pp.22-43; *Checklist of Manuscripts in St. Catherine's Monastery, Mount Sinai.* 1952; *Checklist of Manuscripts in the Libraries of the Greek and Armenian Patriarchates in Jerusalem.* 1953; Aziz Suryal Atiya, *The Arabic Manuscripts of Mount Sinai.* 1955.

[92] Milne and Skeat, *The Codex Sinaiticus and the Codex Alexandrinus,* p.28.
[93] *ibid.,* p.31.

of each first page. A fourteenth century Arabic numeration is written in the lower outer corner of the verso of the leaves, while Patrick Young, librarian to Charles I, made the modern ink foliation and chapter notation. The text is written in two columns per page with from forty-six to fifty-two lines to the column. The words are written continuously without separation and there are no accents and only rare breathings. High and middle points are used, initial Iota and Upsilon have the dieresis, sacred names are abbreviated, and Old Testament quotations are marked.

While in general this manuscript still has the air of simplicity which is characteristic of the oldest uncials, a small amount of ornamentation has been introduced. At the beginning of each book a few lines are written in red, and the paragraphs are marked by larger letters set in the margin. It is not necessarily the first letter of the first word of the new paragraph which is thus enlarged. Rather, the new paragraph begins in the line wherever it may happen to fall, and then the first letter which strikes the next line is placed in the margin. Also, there are panel-shaped tailpieces or colophons at the end of the various books. Two scribes are distinguishable in the Old Testament, and the first of these seems also to be responsible for the New Testament, except perhaps in Luke 1 to I Corinthians 10:8 where a smoother, lighter hand may indicate the work of yet a third scribe.[94] There are also many corrections, but most of them are of an early date. The appearance of the opening page of Romans in Codex Alexandrinus is shown in Fig. 149.

CODEX EPHRAEMI SYRI RESCRIPTUS

Codex Ephraemi Syri rescriptus (C or 04) was in the possession of Cardinal Ridolfi of Florence, a member of the de' Medici family, in the sixteenth century, and later in the same century through Catherine de' Medici, wife of Henry II of France, was brought to Paris, where it is now in the Bibliothèque Nationale.

The codex is what is technically known as a palimpsest, or rewritten manuscript. Originally it was written in the fifth century as a manuscript of the Greek Bible. In the twelfth century, when vellum was scarce, the original writing was erased and many of the sheets were used over again to receive a Greek translation of the discourses of Ephraem Syrus, the latter having been a prominent theologian of the Syrian church in the fourth century A.D. The underlying

[94] *ibid.*, p.32.

writing was not destroyed entirely, however, although it did appear impossible that it could ever be read again. Several attempts to make it out, including one in which chemical reagents were employed, had failed or met with very limited success, when the task was undertaken by Tischendorf. In 1840 the man who was to study the Vatican manuscript in 1843 and to discover the Sinaitic treasure in 1844 had just habilitated as a Privatdozent in the theological faculty at Leipzig. During 1841-1842 he attempted the decipherment of the famous palimpsest and was able in 1843 to publish a complete edition of the New Testament.[95] Today it has been found possible to use ultra-violet rays to read such manuscripts, but this device was not available to Tischendorf.

Only 209 leaves remain of the original codex, but of these 145 are in the New Testament and they contain portions of every New Testament book except II Thessalonians and II John. The leaves measure twelve and one-half by nine and one-half inches and the text is written in a single column of forty to forty-six lines to the page. The words are written continuously without separation and there are no accents or breathings but high and middle points are employed. Two correctors, perhaps of the sixth and of the ninth centuries respectively, have worked on the manuscript, the second of whom inserted a cross after the high point. The original writing is generally believed to belong to the fifth century, and perhaps to be a little later than Codex Alexandrinus. A page from Codex Ephraemi rescriptus (Matthew 20:16-34) is shown in Fig. 150.

Such are the four great uncial manuscripts which, together with the Sahidic (sa) and Bohairic (bo) versions,[96] and church fathers like Clement of Alexandria and Origen, are the chief witnesses to the Alexandrian text.[97] With this type of text the Chester Beatty Papyrus of Paul's letters is most often in agreement,[98] as is shown in the examples cited above (p.424), although sometimes the papyrus goes its own way and sometimes agrees with the Western

[95] C. Tischendorf, *Codex Ephraemi Syri rescriptus sive fragmenta Novi Testamenti.* 1843.

[96] These are third and fourth century translations into the native Egyptian language known as Coptic, Sahidic being the dialect spoken in Upper Egypt and Bohairic that spoken in Lower Egypt. For the early New Testament versions see Arthur Vööbus, *Early Versions of the New Testament* (Papers of the Estonian Theological Society in Exile, 6). 1954.

[97] It has already been noted (p.432 n.80) that in the Gospels the text of Codex Alexandrinus is Byzantine.

[98] The preponderance of agreement is with B and next with SAC. Kenyon, *The Chester Beatty Biblical Papyri.* Fasc. III. Suppl. Text, pp.xvi-xvii.

text. On the whole the Alexandrian text is the best and most dependable which we have, but nevertheless it has to be compared constantly with as many other early manuscripts as possible.

THE WESTERN TEXT

Even as the manuscripts just described seem to represent a text which probably originated in Egypt, so other groups of manuscripts may be recognized which represent texts which prevailed in other areas. The Western text (𝔐) is represented by several manuscripts now to be described which are written in both Greek and Latin, by the Old Latin versions, and by quotations in Latin church writers such as Cyprian. The fact that these authorities are all from the West suggests that this text originated there, perhaps in North Africa, and if this is the case the customary naming of the text as "Western" may be taken in the natural geographical sense of the word. Some think, however, that it originated in some other place, perhaps Asia Minor, and if this should be correct then "Western" would have to be understood as a technical rather than a geographical designation. Since some of the Western manuscripts such as W and *k* perhaps come from Africa, and some such as D and *a* from Europe, it is possible to speak of African and European branches of the text.[99]

CODEX BEZAE

Codex Bezae (D or 05),[100] one of the bilingual manuscripts just referred to, was given to the University of Cambridge in 1581 by Calvin's friend and successor at Geneva, Theodore Beza, who said that the manuscript had been found in 1562 in the monastery of Irenaeus at Lyons. It is believed to have been written in the fifth or sixth century. The manuscript now has 406 leaves and probably originally had at least 510. The pages measure about ten by eight inches in size, and each page has only a single column of writing, Greek on the left-hand page which is the place of honor, Latin on the right-hand page. The lines are short sense-lines, which make it more easily possible to keep the Greek and Latin parallel, and the Greek uncial letters are shaped somewhat like the Latin letters. The words are not separated and there are no accents or breathings on

[99] See *An Introduction to the Study of the New Testament*, by A. H. McNeile, 2d ed. rev. by C. S. C. Williams. 1953, pp.378, 441.

[100] *Codex Bezae Cantabrigiensis Quattuor Evangelia et Actus Apostolorum complectens Graece et Latine Sumptibus Academiae phototypice repraesentatus*. 1899; cf. HPUM Pl. XXII.

the Greek. Initial Iota and Upsilon are marked with the dieresis, and there is some punctuation. Sacred names are abbreviated. A number of correctors, from the sixth century to the twelfth, have made corrections in both the Greek and the Latin. The manuscript contains the four Gospels in the order, Matthew, John, Luke, and Mark, and the book of Acts. Also just ahead of the book of Acts the Latin has III John 11-15, which suggests that once the codex also contained the Catholic Epistles.

CODEX CLAROMONTANUS

Codex Claromontanus (D^p or **06**)[101] is a sixth century vellum manuscript of the letters of Paul (including Hebrews, added at the end), which was acquired between 1565 and 1582 by Theodore Beza, who stated that it was found in the monastery at Clermont in Beauvais. In 1656 the codex was purchased by Louis XIV, and it is now in the Bibliothèque Nationale, Paris. The manuscript comprises 533 leaves, each measuring nine and three-quarters by seven and three-quarters inches and having wide margins. The Greek text is written in a single column on the left-hand page and the corresponding Latin on the right-hand. There are twenty-one lines to the page, the lines being divided according to pauses in the sense and the first letter of a new section being thrust into the margin. The words are written continuously without separation and there is no punctuation. Initial Iota and Upsilon have the dieresis, but the accents and breathings have been added by one of the numerous later correctors. The first three lines of each letter are written in red, and so are the quotations from the Old Testament. The Greek and Latin columns of the manuscript do not always agree, and the Latin translation was not just made from this Greek text but doubtless is one of the Latin translations already in existence before Jerome. A double page from this manuscript (Romans 16:23-27) is shown in Fig. 151.

Codex Augiensis (F^p or **010**) was once in the monastery of Reichenau on an island in the Lake of Constance, and in 1786 was presented to the Library of Trinity College, Cambridge.[102] The manuscript consists of 136 leaves of vellum, and contains the Pauline letters including Hebrews. Each page has two columns of text, Greek in the inner column, the Latin of the Vulgate in the outer column. Hebrews

---

[101] C. Tischendorf, *Codex Claromontanus sive Epistulae Pauli omnes Graece et Latine*. 1852.
[102] HPUM Pl. L.

follows Philemon and is preserved only in the Latin. The date is probably in the ninth century.

Codex Boernerianus (G^p or **012**) came into the possession of Professor Christian Friedrich Börner in 1705 and is now in the Royal Library at Dresden.[103] It also is a bilingual manuscript, but in this case the Latin is written interlinearly above the Greek. It contains the Pauline letters, not including Hebrews. The date is also probably in the ninth century.

The Washington Codex (W or **032**) was purchased by Mr. Charles L. Freer in 1906 from an Arab dealer at Gizeh and is in the Freer Gallery of Art in Washington, D.C.[104] This is a Greek manuscript, and was written probably in the fifth century. It contains the four Gospels in the Western order, Matthew, John, Luke, and Mark, and has a Western text in Mark 1:1-5:30. The rest of Mark, however, may be Caesarean; Luke 1:1-8:12 is mainly Alexandrian; and the rest of Luke and Matthew are Byzantine. Thus the entire manuscript contains a remarkable variety of text types.

The Old Latin manuscripts are designated by small italicized letters and are often referred to collectively as the Itala, this being abbreviated as "it." Examples of the manuscripts are: Codex Bobbiensis (*k*), written probably in Africa not later than A.D. 400, once belonged to the monastery of Bobbio in North Italy and is now in Turin; it contains Mark 8-16 and Matthew 1-15, and the text is almost identical with the quotations of Cyprian. Codex Vercellensis (*a*) is preserved in the cathedral at Vercelli in North Italy, and is traditionally said to have been written by Eusebius, the bishop of Vercelli who was martyred in A.D. 371; it contains the four Gospels, with breaks, in the Western order, Matthew, John, Luke, and Mark, and at least in Luke is practically identical with the text regularly cited by Jerome.[105] For the letters of Paul, Old Latin texts are found in two commentaries, one preserved in the works of Ambrose (A.D. c.340-397) but written by an unknown author of the time of Pope Damasus (A.D. 366-384), and the other written by Pelagius (c.400).[106] A revision of the Old Latin versions was carried out by Jerome at

[103] *Der Codex Boernerianus der Briefe des Apostels Paulus . . . in Lichtdruck Nachgebildet.* 1909.

[104] Henry A. Sanders, *The New Testament Manuscripts in the Freer Collection.* 2 vols. 1912-18; HPUM Pl. XXI.

[105] *An Introduction to the Study of the New Testament*, by McNeile, rev. by Williams, pp.391, 393f.; *The Text and Canon of the New Testament*, by Alexander Souter, 2d ed. rev. by C. S. C. Williams. 1954, pp.34f., 38.

[106] Lietzmann, *Einführung in die Textgeschichte der Paulusbriefe*, p.9.

the suggestion of Damasus, the Gospels being published in A.D. 383 and the rest of the Bible in 405. This is known as the Vulgate (vg). Also, as already mentioned, Latin church writers such as Cyprian (A.D. c.200-258) are witnesses to the Old Latin text. They are sometimes referred to by the abbreviation Latt.[107]

The Western type of text is very old and was the basis for Marcion's revision before A.D. 150.[108] Nevertheless, when judged by inner criteria, it is found to contain numerous alterations. Quotations are supplemented according to the Septuagint, corrections are made which result in a smoother style or clearer sense, and unintentional alterations are introduced through mistakes in copying. In general the Western text is characterized by many interpolations, and hence was regarded by Westcott and Hort as of greatest weight in its omissions. That is, its omissions are not omissions so much as non-interpolations.

THE EASTERN TEXT

An Eastern text may also be recognized and, just as the Western text has two branches, African and European, so this has two forms, namely the Old Syriac, sometimes also called the Antiochene, and the Caesarean.[109]

THE OLD SYRIAC TEXT

The Old Syriac has agreements with the Western text and used to be considered a part of it, but now is often treated as an independent text. It is represented by two manuscripts. The Sinaitic Syriac (sy[s]) is a manuscript in the Monastery of Saint Catherine at Mount Sinai, and was discovered there in 1892 by Mrs. A. S. Lewis and Mrs. M. D. Gibson.[110] It is a palimpsest or rewritten manuscript. The upper writing is a Syriac treatise dated in A.D. 778; the text underneath is that of the four Gospels in the usual order, and was probably written not later than the early fifth century. The Curetonian Syriac (sy[c]) was brought in 1842 from the Convent of St. Mary Deipara in the Nitrian desert west of Cairo to the British Museum and was there recognized in 1847 and published in 1858 by William Cureton. It contains portions of the four Gospels in the unusual order, Matthew, Mark, John, and Luke, and was probably written

[107] *ibid.*, p.10. [108] *ibid.*, p.14.
[109] *An Introduction to the Study of the New Testament,* by McNeile, rev. by Williams, p.378.
[110] cf. R. V. G. Tasker in HTR 41 (1948), p.74.

in the middle of the fifth century.[111] Although these manuscripts are relatively late, the Old Syriac text which they preserve is probably much older, and it has been held that it was originally a translation made about A.D. 200 of the Greek text of the Gospels current at that time at Antioch.[112]

The Syrians called this version the *Evangelion da-Mepharreshe*, meaning the "Gospel of the Separated Ones," to distinguished it from the Diatessaron of Tatian which they spoke of as the *Evangelion da-Mehallete* or "Gospel of the Mixed Ones." The latter was a harmony of the four Gospels arranged in one narrative, a work which Tatian, the disciple of Justin Martyr, may have made in Greek[113] at Rome and then brought with him when he returned in about A.D. 173 to the East, where it was soon translated into Syriac.[114] The Greek text underlying the Diatessaron was closely related to that of Codex Bezae (D) and the Old Latin, therefore since the Diatessaron was probably known by those who made the *Evangelion da-Mepharreshe* it may be the influence of the Diatessaron which accounts for Western readings found in the Old Syriac.[115]

It was probably in order to displace the Diatessaron and provide a standard text of the separate four Gospels that Rabbula, the bishop of Edessa from A.D. 411 to 435, made a revision of the Old Syriac. This, if the hypothesis just stated is correct, accounts for the origin of the Peshitta, the "Simple" version which thereafter was supreme in the Syrian churches. The Peshitta also contained the other New Testament books, except that II and III John, II Peter, Jude, and Revelation were not included, and its text agrees with the Byzantine.[116] Two more revisions were also made, intended to make the Syriac render the Greek more literally, one in A.D. 508 by Philoxenus, bishop of Mabug or Hierapolis in eastern Syria, which is extant only in the books lacking in the Peshitta, namely II and III John, II Peter, Jude, and Revelation; and the other in A.D. 616-617 by Thomas of Heraclea or Harkel in Mesopotamia. There is also a Palestinian Syriac version, as it is called, known from various lectionaries and frag-

[111] F. Crawford Burkitt, *Evangelion da-Mepharreshe*. 2 vols. 1904.

[112] *ibid.*, II, pp.5f., 209.

[113] A Greek fragment of the Diatessaron found at Dura-Europos has already been mentioned (p.392).

[114] cf. J. Hamlyn Hill, *The Earliest Life of Christ Ever Compiled from the Four Gospels, Being the Diatessaron of Tatian [circ. A.D. 160], Literally Translated from the Arabic Version and Containing the Four Gospels Woven into One Story*. 1894.

[115] Burkitt, *Evangelion da-Mepharreshe*, II, pp.5f., 206, 210.

[116] *The Text and Canon of the New Testament*, by Souter, rev. by Williams, pp.55f.

ments, whose language is a Western Aramaic that is believed to be much like the Aramaic spoken in Galilee in the time of Jesus, but the version itself is probably a translation from Greek, perhaps made at Antioch, and not older than the sixth century.[117]

Of the Peshitta version there are several hundred manuscripts. One of these is the Yonan Codex. This takes its name from the Yonan family of a Christian community near Lake Urmia in Azerbaijan, is in the possession of Mr. Norman Yonan of Washington, D.C., and in 1955 was on loan to the Library of Congress for exhibition. The codex contains 227 leaves and extends from Matthew to Hebrews. The text appears to be that of the standard Peshitta Syriac, and the writing to be of the seventh century at the earliest.[118]

THE CAESAREAN TEXT

Some other manuscripts have been believed to form a recognizable group which might have centered around Caesarea. The Koridethi Codex (Θ or 038) once belonged to a monastery at Koridethi at the eastern end of the Black Sea, was discovered in 1853 in the Caucasus, and was finally placed in the Georgian Museum at Tiflis.[119] It contains the four Gospels in the usual order, and has been assigned to a date from the seventh to the ninth century. The so-called Lake Group or Family 1, also designated λ, is a group of minuscules which was identified by Kirsopp Lake and which includes the manuscripts numbered 1, 118, 131, and 209. Codex 1, which heads the group, is in the University Library at Basel and is dated in the tenth to twelfth centuries.[120] While this manuscript contains Acts, the Catholic Epistles, and the Pauline letters including Hebrews, as well as the four Gospels, it is only the Gospels which have the Caesarean text, while the other books are Western. The Ferrar Group or Family 13, also designated φ, includes the minuscules 13, 69, 124, and 346, which were edited by W. H. Ferrar and T. K. Abbott, and others which were added to the group later. Codex 13, which heads the group, is in the Bibliothèque Nationale at Paris.[121] It contains the four Gospels and was probably written in the twelfth or thirteenth century.

The reason for connecting the text represented by the foregoing manuscripts with Caesarea is that Origen, who came from Alexandria to Caesarea in A.D. 231, seems to have used this text at the latter

[117] F. C. Burkitt in JTS 2 (1901), pp.174-185.
[118] Bruce M. Metzger in *The Christian Century*. Feb. 22, 1956, pp.234-236.
[119] HPUM Pl. XLIV.   [120] HFDMM Pl. LX.
[121] HFDMM Pl. LXVII.

place.[122] Two other manuscripts already mentioned, however, also have at least in part a "Caesarean" text, namely $\mathfrak{p}^{45}$ (p.426) which is mainly Caesarean in Mark, and W (p.443) which is Caesarean in Mark 5:31-16:20. Since $\mathfrak{p}^{45}$ was found in Egypt, and since Origen may in fact have used a "Caesarean" text in Alexandria as well as at Caesarea,[123] it is possible that this text originated in Egypt. It may also be that the entire text is not as clear-cut and homogeneous as sometimes supposed.[124]

THE BYZANTINE OR KOINE TEXT

If the foregoing textual families have been rightly recognized there were then, broadly speaking, an Alexandrian text, a Western text with manuscripts both from Africa and Europe, and an Eastern text with both Syriac and Caesarean manuscripts.[125] There was, however, yet another revision of the New Testament text, and the purpose of this seems to have been to make the text as full and smooth as possible. Even as the Alexandrian text may have been the work of Hesychius, so this one may have been carried out by Lucian, a presbyter of the church at Antioch and a martyr at Nicomedia under Maximinus in A.D. 312. The reason for pointing to him is that both Eusebius[126] and Jerome[127] speak of his learning and Jerome says that even in his time there were copies of the Scriptures which bore the name of Lucian. That Antioch was the place where this text arose is rendered likely by the fact that the Syrian Peshitta of the next century has a very similar text. From Antioch, if this is where it originated, the text under discussion spread to Constantinople and became the text generally accepted throughout the Byzantine church. For this reason it is known as the Byzantine text, or the Koine ($\mathfrak{K}$), that is the Common text.

As has already been mentioned, the Byzantine text is found in Codex Alexandrinus in the Gospels (see above p.432 n.80), and in the Washington Codex in Matthew and most of Luke (p.443). For the letters of Paul it is represented by three ninth century uncial manuscripts, Codex Angelicus (L or **020**), Codex Porphyrianus (P or **025**), and Codex Mosquensis (K or **018**). Likewise this text is

---

[122] Burnett H. Streeter, *The Four Gospels.* 1925, pp.92-102.

[123] Kirsopp Lake, Robert P. Blake, and Silva New in HTR 21 (1928), pp.207-404.

[124] *An Introduction to the Study of the New Testament,* by McNeile, rev. by Williams, p.389.

[125] *ibid.*, pp.378f.   [126] *Ch. Hist.* VIII, xiii, 2; IX, vi, 3.

[127] *Lives of Illustrious Men.* 77. NPNFSS III, p.378.

found in most of the other late uncials and in the great mass of minuscules. The minuscule manuscripts (cf. p.401) are scattered in many different libraries, and extend in date from the ninth to the sixteenth century. In some cases the manuscripts bear dates, and as far as known the oldest definitely dated one is Codex 461. This is in the Public Library in Leningrad, contains the four Gospels, and was written in A.D. 835.[128] The second oldest dated minuscule has only recently became known and bears the number 2500. It was written in A.D. 891, and is in the Akademiebibliothek in Leningrad.[129] A sample page of yet another of the many minuscules is shown in Fig. 152. This manuscript is in Paris where it is known as Cod. Gr. 223.[130] It contains the Pauline letters and Acts with commentary, and is dated in the year 1045. On another page of the same manuscript is an illustration showing the apostle Paul dictating to his secretary (Fig. 153).

In addition, the Byzantine text is found in the Peshitta (p.445) and Gothic versions,[131] and the writings of church fathers such as Chrysostom (A.D. c.390), Basil of Caesarea in Cappadocia (d. A.D. 380), and Ephraem Syrus (d. A.D. 373).

The Koine is now clearly recognized as a late and secondary text. Interpolations and corrections are numerous in it. Often it combines Alexandrian and Western readings and thus retains them both. For example in Romans 1:29 the Alexandrian text reads "wickedness, covetousness, maliciousness," although these three words stand in different order in different manuscripts.[132] The Western text changed "wickedness" into "fornication," these two words having a very similar appearance in the Greek.[133] The Byzantine text then combined the Alexandrian and Western readings and the result was a list including "fornication, wickedness, covetousness, maliciousness."[134]

THE DEPENDABILITY OF THE NEW TESTAMENT TEXT

At first, European translations of the New Testament were based

[128] HFDMM Pl. I.

[129] Aland in TL 82 (1957), col. 162; and in ZNW 48 (1957), pp.141, 161.

[130] Kirsopp and Silva Lake, *Monumenta Palaeographica Vetera*, First Series, *Dated Greek Minuscule Manuscripts to the Year 1200*, IV, *Manuscripts in Paris*. Part I (1935), Pl. 267.

[131] A translation by Bishop Ulfilas, A.D. c.350.

[132] πονηρίᾳ πλεονεξίᾳ κακίᾳ B; πονηρίᾳ κακίᾳ πλεονεξίᾳ SA; κακίᾳ πονηρίᾳ πλεονεξίᾳ C bo sa.

[133] κακίᾳ πορνείᾳ πλεονεξίᾳ DG.

[134] πορνείᾳ πονηρίᾳ πλεονεξίᾳ κακίᾳ L; πορνείᾳ πονηρίᾳ κακίᾳ πλεονεξίᾳ Peshitta. Lietzmann, *An die Römer*, pp.13, 35.

simply upon the Latin Vulgate. Then men sought to go back to the Greek text, but only manuscripts of the less accurate Byzantine type were available. This was still the case when the Authorized Version was made under King James (1611), for the value of Codex Vaticanus was not yet realized at that time nor was Codex Sinaiticus even discovered. The scholars who have made the American Standard Version and the Revised Standard Version have had the advantage of the use of these and many other important manuscripts, and therefore these translations are more accurate than former ones could be. But every scrap of biblical parchment or papyrus recovered from the sands of the past adds to the vast amount of material available for the work of textual criticism, and the task of painstaking comparison of all the witnesses to the original text is an unending labor.[135]

The total number of New Testament manuscripts is very impressive. As we have already seen (p.416), even without counting the versions in other languages, the listed Greek papyri, uncials, minuscules, and lectionaries now total 4,680, and of these it may roughly be estimated that over two thousand contain the text of the Gospels, over seven hundred the text of Paul.[136] No other Greek book has anything like this amount of testimony to its text. It is true that there are numerous textual variations among these different New Testament manuscripts, but the majority of them are of a relatively minor character, as has appeared in the examples given in this chapter. As a matter of fact, it has been estimated that there are substantial variations in hardly more than a thousandth part of the entire text.[137]

The close relationship in time between the oldest New Testament manuscripts and the original texts is also nothing less than amazing. The proximity of the Chester Beatty Papyrus of the letters of Paul to the time when the apostle wrote those letters, and of Papyrus Bodmer II to the time when the Gospel according to John must have been written, and for that matter the closeness of Codex Vaticanus and Codex Sinaiticus to the period of the composition of the New Testament, can be appreciated properly only by contrast with most of the rest of the literature of the Greco-Roman world. For our knowledge of the writings of most of the classical authors we are dependent upon manuscripts the oldest of which belong to a time between

---

[135] Merrill M. Parvis and Allen P. Wikgren, *New Testament Manuscript Studies, The Materials and the Making of a Critical Apparatus.* 1950.
[136] Kenneth W. Clark in BA 16 (1953), p.42.
[137] Gregory, *Canon and Text of the New Testament,* p.528.

the ninth and eleventh centuries A.D., or in other words are a thousand years removed from their originals.[138] Thus it is that the certainty with which the text of the New Testament is established exceeds that of any other ancient book. The words which the New Testament writers addressed to their world and time have crossed the further miles and centuries to us substantially unchanged in form and certainly undiminished in power.

[138] Hans Lietzmann in *Die Antike, Zeitschrift für Kunst und Kultur des klassischen Altertums.* 11 (1935), pp.142-146.

VIII
Exploring the Catacombs and Studying the Sarcophagi

Less than one hundred years after Paul wrote his Letter to the Romans, or by the middle of the second century A.D., the Christians of Rome are known to us through their remarkable places of burial, the catacombs.

Cremation was the normal practice of pagan Rome in the first century A.D.,[1] and the cinerary urns were placed in the niches of vaults constructed for this purpose and known as columbaria. Not until the time of Hadrian (A.D. 117-138) did cremation give way to inhumation among the pagan population of Rome. Then their interments were made in and beneath the columbaria and also in sarcophagi. But from the first the Christians seem to have avoided the burning of the bodies of the deceased, and no trace of early Christian cremation has been found. Rather, the first Christians followed the practice of the Jews who were living in Rome and buried their dead in underground sepulchral chambers and galleries.

1. THE CHARACTER OF THE CATACOMBS

THE development of such subterranean burial places was specially favored at Rome by the underlying geological formation. The great plain surrounding the city is composed of materials of volcanic

[1] A. D. Nock in HTR 25 (1932), p.232.

451

origin. There is sand (*pozzolana*), there is stone (*tufa litoide*), and there is granular tufa (*tufa granolare*). The sand is too soft to permit excavations unless the walls are faced with brick, and the stone is so hard that it is quarried for building purposes, but the granular tufa is relatively easy to cut, yet is strong and holds up satisfactorily. Also, it is porous and drains well. The existence of this tufa facilitated the digging of the catacombs.[1] The actual excavation was done by a sort of guild of workers known as *fossores* or "diggers." Their title appears in inscriptions on their own tombs in the catacombs and they are depicted in the wall paintings, holding pick and spade, the tools of the trade.[2]

The characteristic form of a catacomb is that of a network of interconnected corridors and chambers containing burial niches in the walls. The corridors are usually approximately three feet in width and have a normal height of a little over six feet. This corresponds to a man's height, with a bit of additional room for the *fossor* to swing his pick. In their simplest form the graves were square-cornered, horizontal recesses, known as *loculi*, cut in the walls of the galleries and chambers. The corpses were laid here wound in wrappings, in accordance with Jewish custom, and the openings were closed with bricks or marble slabs. A more elaborate form of grave was that known as an *arcosolium*, where a semicircular recess was cut in the wall, and the body was placed in a coffin-like space closed from above by a horizontal slab.

When additional space was needed for more graves the corridor was often deepened. By digging the floor of the gallery some three feet deeper two more rows of graves could be accommodated, and this process was sometimes continued until there were as many as a dozen tiers of graves one below the other. As a moment's consideration of the work involved will indicate, this was an entirely feasible procedure, but to have attempted to *heighten* the corridor would have necessitated extremely awkward manipulation of pick and shovel. Thus in such corridors the highest graves are normally the oldest and the lowest are the newest. Also entire second, third, or more stories of galleries and chambers often were laid out. While the uppermost corridors are some twenty or twenty-five feet below the surface of the earth, the lowest may be forty or fifty feet deeper.

[1] cf. G. de Angelis D'Ossat, *La Geologia delle Catacombe Romane.* 1938-.
[2] L. von Sybel, *Christliche Antike, Einführung in die altchristliche Kunst.* I (1906), p.102.

The oldest catacombs seem to have been excavated within privately owned and therefore relatively small and limited areas and thus characteristically assumed a sort of gridiron pattern. When later catacombs were excavated in more extensive properties owned by the church, their corridors branched out and out almost endlessly. Whereas at first sight the catacombs now appear to be inextricably tangled networks, an appreciation of the process of their excavation enables the scientific investigator to retrace the course of their development and understand their earlier forms.

2. THE REDISCOVERY OF THE CATACOMBS

THE rediscovery of the catacombs at Rome dates from 1578 when some workmen accidentally happened upon one of the long-lost subterranean cemeteries. The pioneer investigation of the catacombs was undertaken by Antonio Bosio, who devoted thirty-six years to the task, and whose *Roma Sotterranea* was published in 1632, three years after his own death. Not until the nineteenth century was Bosio's work worthily resumed, most notably by Giovanni Battista de Rossi (d. 1894).[1] He was assisted by his brother, Michele Stefano de Rossi, who had the knowledge of a geologist and an engineer, and was followed in the work by his pupils, Josef Wilpert[2] and Orazio Marucchi.[3] More recently Professor Paul Styger[4] has applied the most rigorously scientific techniques to a fresh investigation of the catacombs, with results necessitating many revisions of the earlier conclusions.

3. THE JEWISH CATACOMBS

BEFORE proceeding to describe the oldest and most important Christian catacombs, a word should be said about the Jewish catacombs. It was noted above that the Christians were probably following a Jewish custom in adopting catacombs for burial places, and some half-dozen ancient Jewish cemeteries of this sort have been found in Rome.

[1] *La Roma Sotterranea Cristiana*. 1864-77.
[2] *Die Malereien der Katakomben Roms*. 1903.
[3] *Le Catacombe Romane, opera postuma*. 1932.
[4] SRK.

The beginnings of the Jewish community in Rome, like those of the later Christian community, are little known. In 161 B.C. an embassy of Judas Maccabeus came to Rome seeking assurances of support in the struggle against the Seleucids, and in 139 B.C. Simon, the last of the sons of Mattathias, renewed relations with Rome and obtained ratification of a treaty between Rome and the now independent Jewish state. In the same year that the embassy of Simon was received in honor by the Roman Senate and sent away with the promise of friendship, Hispalus, the praetor peregrinus, who was the magistrate having jurisdiction in cases involving foreigners, banished the Chaldeans and the Jews from Rome and Italy within a period of ten days. But the Jews returned, and in the first half of the first century A.D. the Jewish population of Rome is estimated at about twenty thousand.[1]

It was always the custom of the Jews to practice inhumation, and in Palestine many graves were hewn in the native rock.[2] At Rome the soft tufa formation made it easily possible to dig more extensive corridors and halls to receive the graves. The oldest catacomb of the Jews now known was discovered by Bosio in 1602 but was lost to knowledge again and rediscovered only in 1904. The other Jewish catacombs have also become known only since the middle of the nineteenth century and later. The oldest Jewish catacomb just mentioned lies near Monteverde, before the Porta Portese in Trastevere, and burials were probably begun there in the first century A.D.[3] One of the inscriptions of this catacomb, probably belonging to the second century, is shown in Fig. 154. It reads, simply and pathetically, "Here lies Leontia, 20 years old." The seven-armed lampstand is a characteristic mark in all the Jewish catacombs.

Two other Jewish catacombs are on the Via Appia before the Porta San Sebastiano, one in the Vigna Randanini and the other in the Vigna Cimarra. A fourth is on the Via Appia Pignatelli, a fifth under the Via Labicana east of the Esquiline, and the sixth, most recently discovered, is in the Villa Torlonia (onetime residence of Benito Mussolini), before the Porta Pia in the northeast part of the city.

[1] Hermann Vogelstein, *Rome* (1940. tr. from rev. ed. of *Geschichte der Juden in Rom*), pp.9f., 17.
[2] For the remarkable Jewish catacombs at Beth She'arim in Galilee, dating from the second to the fourth century A.D., see N. Avigad in *Archaeology.* 8 (1955), pp.236-244; 10 (1957), pp.266-269; and in IEJ 5 (1955), pp.205-239; 7 (1957), pp.73-92, 239-255.
[3] N. Müller, *Die jüdische Katakombe am Monteverde zu Rom, der älteste bisher bekannt gewordene jüdische Friedhof des Abendlandes.* 1912, p.120.

Numerous rooms in the catacomb of the Villa Torlonia are adorned with paintings, and as usual the ruling motif is the seven-armed lampstand. One of the frescoes is reproduced in Fig. 155. On the right is the scroll of the Law, on the left the ethrog, and in the middle the seven-armed lampstand. The scroll of the Law is rolled around a rod whose knobs are indicated by heavy points. A small triangular piece of parchment is to be seen above at the right. In reality this was glued to the roll and contained the title of the work. The perspective is primitive and shows both ends of the roll at once. The ethrog is a citron, which was used along with the lulab or festive palm branch in the Feast of Tabernacles, and hence was a symbol of Judaism.[4] The seven-armed lampstand likewise was a notable symbol of the Jewish religion. The prototype was the golden lampstand in the temple at Jerusalem which Titus carried off in triumph (p.329) but similar lampstands burned also in the synagogues and in the homes of the Jews at the reading of the Law and at other religious ceremonies. So instead of seeking in the symbol of the seven-armed lampstand some mysterious astral-eschatological significance as certain scholars have done, it is correct to interpret it far more simply. Wherever it appears it signifies, "Here a Jew worships his God," and when it is found upon graves it means, "He was a faithful Jew."[5]

4. THE CHRISTIAN CATACOMBS

THE great development of catacombs, however, was carried out by the Christians. Michele Stefano de Rossi estimated that the catacombs known in 1867 covered a surface area of 615 acres and, basing his calculations upon the average development of the galleries under a given area, he computed that the total length of their corridors was over five hundred miles.[1] Today thirty-five or more separate Christian catacombs are known at Rome (see Plan 3). They are for the most part in a circle outside the city, some three miles from its center, the reason being that Roman law prohibited burial or cremation within the walls and forbade dwelling in the neighborhood of a sepulchral monument. Like the pagan tombs which were built along

[4] This was in accordance with Leviticus 23:40, the citron being held to be "the fruit of goodly trees" (cf. JE v, pp.261f.).

[5] Hermann W. Beyer and Hans Lietzmann, *Die jüdische Katakombe der Villa Torlonia in Rom.* 1930, p.18.

[1] Karl Baedeker, *Central Italy and Rome.* 15th ed. 1909, p.453.

all the public roads leading out from Rome, so the catacombs also were chiefly on the main roads like the Via Appia and others.

According to Professor Styger's researches into their origins, the oldest of the catacombs belong to a time around the middle of the second century.[2] Although no Christian catacombs earlier than this have been found, it is possible that such did exist. The catacombs of the middle of the second century manifest a fully developed system of construction which not only reflects Jewish models but suggests that the Christians themselves had learned by actual experience in earlier excavations. If such earlier catacombs did exist they of course had to be outside the Wall of Servius, but could still have been considerably nearer the center of the city than the later ones were. The city was growing rapidly at that time and seldom, if ever, was there more building done here than in the first half of the second century, particularly in the reign of Hadrian. The areas of suburban extension on all sides are clearly shown by the line which the Aurelian Wall had to follow in A.D. 270-275. This rapid suburban development must constantly have pushed the burial zone farther out from the center of the city to where it is represented by the now known catacombs. If there were earlier catacombs it may be that they had to be abandoned and were destroyed as the city grew. The four oldest catacombs now known are those of Lucina, Callistus, Domitilla, and Priscilla, all of which belonged originally to the middle of the second century.

THE CRYPTS OF LUCINA

On the edge of the Via Appia, a little more than a mile outside the Porta San Sebastiano, are the impressive remains of a tomb which probably belonged to some prominent Roman of the first century. Connected with the monument was a piece of ground beneath which, at about the end of Hadrian's reign (A.D. 117-138), a Christian cemetery was excavated. Whether the owner of the tomb had himself become a Christian, or simply had allowed his Christian slaves and freedmen to make their burials on his property, remains unknown. The first excavation consisted of entrance steps leading down to a long passageway about six feet in height, from which two other passageways branched off. From this earliest period only empty loculi remain, perhaps fifty in number.

A decade or two later the subterranean cemetery was extended

---

[2] SRK p.319.

by the digging of steps to a passageway at a deeper level and also by the excavation of several chambers opening off from the original passageways. Paintings, datable to about the middle of the second century,[3] remain in some of these chambers. The finest is the ceiling painting in the chamber known as "Y" (Fig. 156), in which the motifs in part are still those of classical Roman interior decoration. The field is divided by lines into circles and sections, while the figures are represented in an almost statuary way and with an exaggerated thinness. The representations include little winged persons, women with arms uplifted in prayer, and the Good Shepherd who carries a lamb upon his shoulders. In the center stands Daniel between two lions.

Toward the end of the second century additional room was gained in the cemetery by deepening the passageways, and early in the third century other extensive work was done on a series of galleries at a lower level. At about the end of the third century, the remains of Pope Cornelius, who had died in exile in 253, were buried in one of the chambers. Later accounts state that this was done by a certain Saint Lucina (p.458), but since several persons of the same name are mentioned in sixth century legends it is difficult to establish for certain any historical facts concerning the woman whose name the area has come to bear.[4]

THE CATACOMB OF CALLISTUS

Somewhat farther back in the same field in which the Crypts of Lucina were located, another Christian cemetery was begun at about the middle of the second century. The area in which it was excavated may have belonged to the church by purchase or gift. Two main corridors, each entered by its own steps, were driven lengthwise along the two longer sides of this area. Later these were connected at the far end of the field by a cross corridor, and additional cross galleries began to give the whole a sort of gridiron plan. At first the place was known simply as Coemeterium or "sleeping chamber," which was the name generally applied by the early Christians to their burial places. Pope Zephyrinus (c.198-c.217) placed the cemetery under

[3] Here and elsewhere in this chapter the dates that are given for the Christian catacombs at Rome and also for their paintings, are those of Styger. The paintings are dated somewhat later by Fritz Wirth who believes that no Christian catacomb paintings in Rome are earlier than the third century A.D. (*Römische Wandmalerei vom Untergang Pompejis bis ans Ende des dritten Jahrhunderts.* 1934, p.226). Wirth ascribes the ceiling painting in the Lucina catacomb which is mentioned in the text above, to a time around A.D. 220 (*ibid.*, pp.168f.).

[4] SRK pp.21-33.

the administration of Callistus, who at that time was a priest and was to become the next pope (c.217-c.222). This is narrated by Hippolytus, who states that Zephyrinus entrusted Callistus with the management of the clergy and "appointed him over the cemetery."[5] A notable extension of the cemetery was carried out under the leadership of Callistus, and thereafter the catacomb retained his name although he had not been its founder nor was buried there himself. The old passageways were deepened at this time, new cross corridors were made, and a number of larger burial chambers were excavated.

Of these the most important was a large double chamber which became a burial place for the Roman popes and hence is known as the Crypt of the Popes (Fig. 157). Up to this time most of the popes had been buried, like Peter himself, in the Vatican. The Liber Pontificalis lists fourteen men who headed the Roman church between Peter and Zephyrinus and indicates burial at the Vatican for all but two of them. The two exceptions are Clement I, who is said to have been buried in Greece, and Alexander who is stated to have been buried on the Via Nomentana. Otherwise the typical statement concerning each of these popes is, "He also was buried near the body of the blessed Peter in the Vatican." But for Zephyrinus and his successors the burial notices in the Liber Pontificalis run as follows:

> Zephyrinus (d. c.217) "He also was buried in his own cemetery near the cemetery of Calistus on the Via Appia."
> Callistus I (d. c.222) "in the cemetery of Calipodius on the Via Aurelia at the third milestone"
> Urbanus I (d. 230) "in the cemetery of Pretextatus on the Via Appia"
> Pontianus (d. 235) "in the cemetery of Calistus on the Via Appia"
> Anteros (d. 236) "in the cemetery of Calistus on the Via Appia"
> Fabianus (d. 250) "in the cemetery of Calistus on the Via Appia"
> Cornelius (d. 253) "And his body was taken up at night by the blessed Lucina and the clergy and was buried in a crypt in her own garden, near the cemetery of Calistus on the Via Appia."
> Lucius (d. 254) "in the cemetery of Calistus on the Via Appia"
> Stephen I (d. 257) "in the cemetery of Calistus on the Via Appia"
> Xystus II (d. 258) "in the cemetery of Calistus on the Via Appia"
> Dionysius (d. 268) "in the cemetery of Calistus on the Via Appia"
> Felix I (d. 274) in the cemetery of Callistus (according to earlier lists)[6]

[5] *The Refutation of All Heresies (Philosophumena)*. IX, vii (ANF V, p.130).
[6] LLP p.33 n.1; SRK p.48.

Eutychianus (d. 283) "in the cemetery of Calistus on the Via Appia"

Gaius (d. 296) "in the cemetery of Calistus on the Via Appia"

Marcellinus (d. 304) "on the Via Salaria in the cemetery of Priscilla"

Marcellus (d. 309) "in the cemetery of Priscilla on the Via Salaria"

Eusebius (d. c.310) "in the cemetery of Calistus on the Via Appia"

Miltiades (d. 314) "in the cemetery of Calistus on the Via Appia"

Sylvester (d. 335) "in the cemetery of Priscilla on the Via Salaria, three miles from the city of Rome."

Of these popes who are stated by the Liber Pontificalis to have been buried "in the cemetery of Calistus," at least some found their last resting place in the simple niches of the double chamber under consideration. This is certain for Pontianus, Anteros, Fabianus, Lucius, and Eutychianus, whose grave inscriptions have been found there and who are mentioned in prayers scratched on the walls by pious visitors of ancient times, and it is probable for Stephen I, Xystus II, Dionysius, and Felix I, although their actual epitaphs are now lost. Several of these popes were martyrs, including Xystus II who perished on August 6, 258 in Valerian's persecution, when he and four deacons were taken by surprise in the catacomb and killed.

The papal crypt was enlarged in later times, and the wall between the two halves of the double chamber gave way to two simple marble columns, but the original plan is still clearly recognizable. Pope Damasus (366-384), who everywhere was zealous to honor the martyrs, placed one of his monumental inscriptions here. As is well known, these inscriptions were composed in poetic style by Damasus, lettered by his secretary and artist Furius Dionysius Filocalus, and placed in a large number of Rome's most venerated tombs. While most of the originals have perished, the text of many of them is preserved in copies which were made by pilgrims.[7] The marble slab which bore the inscription of Damasus in the crypt of the popes was broken into over one hundred fragments, but has been restored and replaced in its original location as may be seen in Fig. 157. The inscription reads: "Here if you inquire, lies crowded together a throng of the righteous, the venerable tombs hold the bodies of the saints, their lofty spirits the palace of heaven took to itself. Here the

---

[7] C. M. Kaufmann, *Handbuch der altchristlichen Epigraphik.* 1917, pp.338-365.

companions of Xystus who bore trophies from the enemy; here a number of the leaders who ministered at the altars of Christ; here is placed the priest who lived in long peace; here the holy confessors whom Greece sent; here young men and boys, old men and their pure descendants, who chose to keep their virgin modesty. Here, I confess, I Damasus wished to deposit my body, but I feared to disturb the holy ashes of the righteous."[8]

It was probably in the fourth century that the further chamber beyond the Crypt of the Popes was excavated; it is known as the Tomb of Cecilia. By the middle of that century it was adorned with marble and mosaic work. Having been damaged perhaps at the time of the Goths (410) and Vandals (455), it was restored toward the end of the fifth century and some of the mosaics were replaced by paintings. The name of the chamber is connected with Saint Cecilia, whose remains are said to have been discovered by Pope Paschal I (817-824). She is represented, along with Pope Urban (222-230) and with Christ, in the frescoes of the main wall, which are dated by their style in the ninth century. At the same time pilgrims have scratched on the walls their appeals to the famous martyr and saint. Definite information concerning Saint Cecilia is no longer available, however, since the existing late fifth century account of her life is full of contradictions and improbabilities, and the date of her martyrdom is unknown.

Under the administration of Callistus the entire cemetery increased greatly in size, many of the common Christians of Rome as well as the clergy and martyrs no doubt now being buried there. On the other side of the main corridor from the papal crypt, three large chambers were excavated in the time of Callistus, and to these yet three more were later added. The six chambers have received the name of Sacrament Chapels since, when first discovered, their frescoes were believed to be symbolical representations of the sacraments of baptism, the Eucharist, confirmation, and confession.[9] Actually, it is probable that these chambers served not only as burial places but also as rooms in which the survivors held meals in honor of the deceased. Therefore they were adorned especially with numerous paintings for which place was found on the ceilings and on the walls between the graves. The paintings of the first chamber are now destroyed almost

[8] Walter Lowrie, *Monuments of the Early Church.* 1901, pp.74f.
[9] J. Wilpert, *Die Malereien der Sacramentskapellen in der Katakombe des hl. Callistus.* 1897.

completely, but those which remain in the other rooms include the following subjects: the Fossor, the Woman with Arms Uplifted in Prayer, the Shepherd, a Meal Participated in by Seven Persons, Abraham's Sacrifice of Isaac, Moses' Miracle of Bringing Water from the Rock, Jonah, the Baptism of Jesus, the Healing of the Paralytic, and the Resurrection of Lazarus.

The first three chambers are believed to belong to the time of Callistus, and the style of the paintings which remain in them is in agreement with a date at the beginning of the third century. In the middle of the second century the classical tradition still prevailed and tall figures stood in statuary repose, with all details carefully worked out, but here the forms are relatively coarse, the faces are but masks, and details, such as the number of fingers, are neglected.[10]

THE CATACOMB OF DOMITILLA

The Catacomb of Domitilla is some distance from that of Callistus on the Via delle Sette Chiese where anciently ran the Via Ardeatina. It has been known as Coemeterium Domitillae at least since the seventh century and doubtless since its origin. The Domitilla whose name it preserves was probably the Flavia Domitilla who is described in Dio's *Roman History* as a relative of the Emperor Domitian and wife of the consul Flavius Clemens. In A.D. 95 both she and her husband were condemned on account of "atheism" and inclination toward Judaism, these being familiar charges against the early Christians, and while he was beheaded she was banished to the island of Pandateria in the Tyrrhenian Sea. Dio's statement is: "And the same year Domitian slew, along with many others, Flavius Clemens the consul, although he was a cousin and had to wife Flavia Domitilla, who was also a relative of the emperor's. The charge brought against them both was that of atheism, a charge on which many others who drifted into Jewish ways were condemned. Some of these were put to death, and the rest were at least deprived of their property. Domitilla was merely banished in Pandateria."[11]

Substantially the same account is recorded by Eusebius, although he probably is wrong in calling Domitilla the niece instead of the wife of Flavius Clemens. He also names a different but nearby island, Pontia, as the place of Domitilla's exile, and explicitly describes her

[10] SRK pp.34-62; cf. G. B. de Rossi, *La Roma Sotterranea Cristiana.* II (1867); E. Josi, *Il Cimiterio di Callisto.* 1933.
[11] *Rom. Hist.* LXVII, xiv, 1f.

as a Christian although he does not mention Flavius Clemens as also having been a Christian martyr. The statement of Eusebius is: "In the fifteenth year of Domitian Flavia Domitilla, daughter of a sister of Flavius Clemens, who at that time was one of the consuls of Rome, was exiled with many others to the island of Pontia in consequence of testimony borne to Christ."[12] Jerome also tells how at the end of the fourth century the widow Paula visited "the island of Pontia ennobled long since as the place of exile of the illustrious lady Flavia Domitilla who under the Emperor Domitian was banished because she confessed herself a Christian," and saw "the cells in which this lady passed the period of her long martyrdom."[13]

It does not appear, however, that the catacomb was constructed in the time of Domitilla herself. Without doubt this area of ground belonged to her, and two heathen inscriptions were found near by which indicated that burials had been made there by the permission of Flavia Domitilla. Evidently she had made a gift of her property or a portion of it for burial purposes, and since the burials there were pagan she must not yet have been converted to Christianity. The pagan possessors of the property developed it into an extensive place of burial. This is indicated by the ruins of columbaria and of an enclosing wall which still exist there, and it is probable that pagan burials continued to be made until around A.D. 140. Up to this time it is extremely unlikely that a Christian catacomb would have been excavated beneath ground while pagan rites and ceremonies were conducted overhead. Meanwhile the area continued to be known by the name of Domitilla. Then shortly before the middle of the second century the owners of the property appear to have accepted Christianity. At any rate the pagan burials ceased above ground and beneath the surface a Christian catacomb came into existence. Whose name should it bear if not that of the earlier owner of the property, Flavia Domitilla, who now long since had become a Christian and a glorious martyr?

The origin of the Christian cemetery only shortly before the middle of the second century is indicated not only by the continuation of pagan burials above ground until about that date, but also by the oldest frescoes in the catacomb itself. These are comparable in style to those in the crypts of Lucina and like them evidently belong to a time near the middle of the second century. They are to be found in

[12] *Ch. Hist.* III, xviii.
[13] *Letter 108 to Eustochium* (NPNFSS VI, p.197).

a region of the catacomb which is generally known as the Hypogeum of the Flavians. This name was given because of the belief that the catacomb was established sometime in the relatively quiet period between Nero and Domitian and was the burial place of members of the Flavian house. This was the view presented originally by G. B. de Rossi, but no Flavian inscriptions have been discovered in the Hypogeum, and Professor Paul Styger finds no historical argument which justifies the first century date.[14]

Another portion of the catacomb whose origins probably go back to the same period at the middle of the second century as the Hypogeum of the Flavians, is the so-called Region of the Aurelians. This area is relatively distinct and is marked by corridors of unusual height. Evidently its owners limited themselves to their own definite area and kept digging their passageways deeper as more burial space was required.

Between these two regions is yet a smaller area where a third group of the owners of the property made their burials. It is a subterranean room containing a number of burial places in the floor and two niches designed to receive sarcophagi. One sarcophagus still remains *in situ*, and De Rossi saw a second of similar type standing there when the place was first discovered in 1854, but the latter has since been purloined. The sarcophagus which remains is of the tub-shaped kind, adorned with rippled marks and lions' heads, which is ascribed to the time of the Antonines in the middle of the second century. Since there is nothing distinctively Christian about this sarcophagus and since Roman custom did change to inhumation in the immediately preceding time of Hadrian, it is possible that it was a pagan who was buried here. But even if that is the case, the subterranean room must have become a Christian burial place very soon afterward, that is around the middle of the century, when the portions of the same property on either side were so employed, for Christians and pagans would not have shared an almost common cemetery. Later the upper part of this subterranean room was destroyed by the building of a basilica directly above it. This was the Basilica of Saint Petronilla, which was in use from the fifth to the eighth centuries, and the area which we have described beneath it is known as the Hypogeum under the Basilica.

The hypothesis that the property of Domitilla was made available to a group of pagans for a burial ground in the first century, and that

14 SRK p.78.

about the middle of the second century their heirs accepted Christianity and established the three underground burial places just described, is substantiated by the inscriptions found in the debris in these regions. These are both Christian and pagan in character, and it is presumable that the heathen inscriptions belonged originally to the heathen burial area within the enclosing wall above ground. The older Flavian inscriptions are almost entirely pagan, but the inscriptions from the time of the Antonines are not only pagan but also frequently Christian. It was, therefore, at this time that Christianity was being accepted by those to whom the former property of Domitilla belonged.

Two other areas of the cemetery of Domitilla have often been regarded as of great antiquity, but more recent research places them at the end of the third century or in the fourth century. These are the region with the painted chamber at the foot of the great stairway by the Tor Marancia, and the region of the grave of Ampliatus.[15] These sections are outside the old wall which surrounded the original pagan burial area, and eventually many other areas were excavated in yet other directions also. Evidently in its later development the catacomb could be extended quite freely and was not limited to a precisely defined area. Thus there developed in the fourth century a vast system of subterranean galleries and rooms, connecting with the three most ancient regions and branching off in all directions. To the entire mighty complex the name of Domitilla continued to belong.[16]

THE CATACOMB OF PRISCILLA

The Catacomb of Priscilla is on the other side of Rome from the catacombs thus far described, on the Via Salaria Nuova. Its extent and complexity surpass anything met hitherto, but three chief component parts of the entire cemetery can be clearly distinguished. Evidently these three areas originally were separate, privately owned burial places.

The first is the so-called Hypogeum of the Acilians, which was excavated and studied by De Rossi in 1880, and which lies beneath the Basilica di San Silvestro. It has been believed that this was the burial place of Manius Acilius Glabrio who was consul in the year 91, and in 95 was condemned to death by Domitian on account of Christian

---

[15] P. Testini (in RAC 28 [1952], pp.77-117) claims a date in the middle of the second century A.D. for the crypt of Ampliatus.

[16] SRK pp.63-99.

faith at the same time that Domitilla was exiled and Titus Flavius Clemens was executed. No trace of his grave has been found, however, and on the contrary the style of the oldest painting here is that of the middle of the second century. The Priscilla whose name the entire catacomb preserves may well have been a member of the same senatorial family. The catacomb bore her name at least from the fifth century and probably from the beginning. A third century inscription found in the debris mentions a certain Priscilla in connection with a Manius Acilius, both of whom are called "most illustrious." Perhaps the connection of the original Priscilla with this catacomb is comparable to that of Domitilla with the cemetery previously considered.

The Hypogeum is entered by a subterranean stairway, which leads to a wide corridor running first to the northwest and then to the southwest. This corridor originally was vaulted, and traces of the paintings which adorned its walls still remain. The schematic division of field by red, green, and brown lines and the classical elegance of birds and flowers which are still recognizable in these paintings indicate a date around the middle of the second century. In later years the Hypogeum was extended to include a number of further passageways and rooms.

The stairway which leads down to the Hypogeum also gives access to a complex of corridors in a near-by area. These are laid out on a regular plan of the gridiron type as in Lucina and Callistus, and probably also belong to the middle of the second century. While in the Hypogeum there are sarcophagus niches for relatively well-to-do persons, the corridors here have only simple loculi and presumably served for the poor. On the graves were marked the anchor, the palm, and the dove.

A second major area of the catacomb likewise belongs in its origin to the middle of the second century. This is known as the Region of the Cryptoporticus and includes the famous Cappella Greca. Here again a common entrance gives access on the one hand to a large hall with chambers and niches for rich graves and on the other hand to an unadorned corridor whose simple arcosolia and loculi were for the poor. The most important and best preserved room is the so-called Cappella Greca (Fig. 158) which opens off from the large hall just mentioned. The "Greek Chapel" is a relatively small room around the sides of which runs a masonry bench with two simple graves underneath it. It has been believed that this room was intended for the celebration of the Eucharist in solemn church assembly, but since not more than ten people could find comfortable seats in it at once it may have served only for the holding of meals in honor of the dead. A neighboring room, which has a water drain of lead piping, has been interpreted wrongly as a baptistery,[17] but was probably the place where these meals were prepared.

The Cappella Greca is adorned with the greatest series of early Christian paintings which is preserved in any single room of the catacombs. In general the elegance of the tall, statuary figures, the conscientious reproduction of the features, the exact treatment of the garments, and the plastic handling of light and shade represent a style comparable to that in the oldest paintings of the Crypts of Lucina on the Via Appia and of the Hypogeum of the Flavians on the Via Ardeatina and indicate a date around the middle of the second century. This date is confirmed by the coiffure of the half-veiled woman in the painting of the meal scene which will be mentioned in a moment. She wears the braid of hair on the crown of the head in the same way as that worn by the Empress Faustina, wife of Antoninus Pius (138-161), as seen on some well-known coins bearing her likeness, while the daughter, Faustina Junior, wife of Marcus Aurelius (161-180) changed the style.

On the wall at the end of the chamber is painted a meal scene, showing seven persons provided with fish and baskets full of bread to eat (Fig. 159). Elsewhere in the chamber are a number of biblical scenes, including Noah in the Ark, Abraham's Sacrifice, the Miracle of the Water in the Wilderness, the Three Youths in the Fiery Furnace, Daniel between the Lions, the Story of Susanna, the Adoration of the Magi, the Healing of the Paralytic, and the Resurrection of Lazarus.

The painting of the Resurrection of Lazarus is now almost effaced but it is still possible to recognize that on one side is depicted a small building containing a mummy and, on the other, the sister of Lazarus standing with arms upraised. In the middle Christ is shown, facing toward the tomb and with the right hand uplifted in a gesture of speech. He is represented in the Roman type, and is dressed in tunic

---

[17] If the drain pipe had been shut off water could have stood in this room only to a depth of about four inches. Moreover, it is unlikely that the Roman Christians were baptized in the catacombs at all. The *Teaching of the Twelve Apostles* (7 [ANF VII, p.379]), written about the beginning of the second century, calls for baptism in running water, and at Rome this was probably in the Tiber where, according to Tertullian (*On Baptism*. 4 [ANF III, p.671]), Peter himself baptized.

and pallium, the left hand holding the garment. He is youthful and beardless, with short hair and large eyes. The left portion of this picture, showing Christ in the center and the sister of Lazarus at the left, is reproduced in Fig. 160. Although it is now only barely recognizable, this picture is of great interest since it is the oldest representation of Jesus that is preserved anywhere.

In part the Region of the Cryptoporticus lies in an area where there had been a sand quarry. The third major region of the Catacomb of Priscilla arose in farther reaches of this abandoned quarry whose subterranean galleries could be readily employed to receive Christian graves. In general this part of the cemetery (Fig. 161) is simple and little adorned and appears to have served largely for the burial of the poorer Christians. A date around the end of the second or beginning of the third century is probable for the origin of this burial place. Some of the graves have bricks with which they were originally closed, still remaining in place, and stamps on these indicate a time under the Severan house of emperors.

In the neighborhood of some stamped bricks of this date, and at the end of one of the quarry galleries there are a number of badly damaged paintings. They are grouped around the highest loculus on the right wall of the corridor and all were produced at the same time. On the ceiling in painted stucco relief are two shepherds with lambs, represented amidst olive trees. One of these pictures, with the Good Shepherd standing between two lambs and carrying another on his shoulders, is reproduced in Fig. 163. To the right, on the ceiling, is a painting (Fig. 162) showing a mother, seated and holding her child, and with a star above her head. Standing beside her is a man dressed in a pallium, holding a roll in his left hand and pointing upward with his right hand. This is believed to be a representation of Isaiah prophesying the birth of the Messiah (Isaiah 7:14), with the fulfillment of the prophecy indicated at the same time in the Madonna. On the wall of the corridor to the left of the loculus are three figures of the deceased, a man, a woman, and a child, with uplifted arms, while at the right is another standing figure of a man together with traces of a feminine figure.

When compared first with the earliest frescoes in Lucina and Domitilla, and then with the later ones in the Callistus chambers, these are clearly seen to be comparable to the latter. The tall, elegant form of the figures in the paintings of classical style does not appear here. Rather the figures are relatively heavy and executed without close attention to detail. A date at the end of the second or beginning of the third century is probable. Thus of the three main areas of the catacomb the two older arose about the middle of the second century, while the newer was established at the end of the second century or beginning of the third. All three evidently were at first private property. Around the middle of the third century they appear to have been used no more. Then, approximately in the time of Constantine, they again came into use, this time as church property, and were connected with one another and further extended.[18]

THE CATACOMB OF PRAETEXTATUS

On an ancient road to the left of the Via Appia and not far from the cemetery of Callistus lies a catacomb which preserves the name of an otherwise unknown founder, Praetextatus. Of the eight distinct areas which are recognizable within the entire complex, the first is known as the Region of the Scala maggiore. It is characterized by the large stairway leading down to a long corridor, with which are connected two chambers and seven branch corridors. The main chamber is adorned with frescoes which represent the scene at Jacob's Well, the Healing of the Woman with an Issue of Blood, the Resurrection of Lazarus, and another incident which may be an illustration of Similitude VIII in the Shepherd of Hermas. The style of these paintings seems to be midway between that of the oldest frescoes in Lucina, Domitilla, and Priscilla, and the early third century paintings in Callistus, and a date toward the end of the second century is indicated. The first excavation probably was done a decade or so before the time of the paintings.

A second area is called the Spelunca Magna in the pilgrim itineraries of the eighth century. This means literally "large cave" but the pilgrims used *spelunca* practically as a synonym for "cemetery." A long corridor some six and one-half feet in height was later deepened to more than eleven feet and elegant burial chambers were established on either side of it. The original excavation here belongs to the middle of the third century, while the later chambers, including the so-called crypt of Januarius, are dated by the style of their frescoes in the middle of the fourth century.

Adjoining the Spelunca Magna is a third area which is designated as the Region Cocorum from a graffito which seems to refer to a col-

[18] SRK pp.100-145.

lective burial place of cooks and bakers. The frequently encountered abbreviation of *Christos* known as the Christ-monogram or the Constantinian monogram probably indicates a fourth century date.[19] At the foot of the entrance to the Spelunca Magna a stairway leads to a fourth area at a lower level, whose numerous chambers likewise seem to belong to the middle of the fourth century. A few steps from the entrance to the Spelunca Magna is another stairway which leads down to a system of subterranean corridors which is laid out in an unusually orderly fashion. This is the Region of the Scala minore and constitutes the fifth area of the cemetery. It belongs to the fourth century.

The sixth area is excavated at an intermediate level and still bears dates from the year A.D. 384. Also to the late fourth century belongs the seventh area which lies beneath the Via Appia Pignatelli. Its corridors are crowded with loculi of the poorest appearance. The eighth region is that where the great arcosolium grave of Celerina was found, with its late fourth century paintings representing the story of Susanna and portraying saints including Liberius and Xystus II.

Thus in the catacomb of Praetextatus the origins of the Region of the Scala maggiore go back into the late second century and of the Spelunca Magna into the middle of the third. The other complexes which were connected with these regions later, belong to the fourth century.[20]

THE CATACOMB OF SEBASTIAN

The cemetery of Sebastian is in a valley on the Via Appia. This depression was so marked as to give to the region the name Catacumbas, "by the hollow." The Emperor Maxentius (A.D. 306-312) built a circus near by, and a notice in the Roman city calendar of A.D. 354 which states that this circus was built *in catacumbas*, meaning "in the place which is called Catacumbas," is the earliest appearance of the term. The Christian cemetery at this place originally was known, therefore, as Coemeterium Catacumbas, and only later re-

---

[19] This is the symbol (☧) which Constantine is said to have seen in a dream or vision, and to have inscribed on the shields of his soldiers or to have fashioned as a labarum or imperial standard, before his victory at the Milvian bridge (p.251 n.5), and which appears thereafter with frequency on his coins and those of his sons, and in Christian inscriptions. Lactantius (A.D. c.260-c.325), *Of the Manner in Which the Persecutors Died.* 44 (ANF VII, p.318); Eusebius, *Life of Constantine.* I, 28-31; Max Sulzberger in *Byzantion, Revue Internationale des Études Byzantines.* 2 (1925), pp.393-448. For a possible earlier occurrence of a similar symbol see above p.333.
[20] SRK pp.146-174.

ceived the name of Saint Sebastian. By a natural misunderstanding the name "catacombs" now has come to be applied generally to all subterranean burial places of the early Christians throughout Rome and elsewhere in Italy and other lands.

Excavations begun here in 1915 beneath the Church of San Sebastiano have led to the most significant discoveries. At the lowest level to which the digging penetrated, a heathen necropolis was unearthed. No less than sixteen pagan columbaria were found in the precincts of the basilica alone. These were rectangular brick structures dating, according to the style of their inscriptions, stucco paintings and mosaics, in the first and second centuries. Their walls held niches for the urns of cremation. As the custom changed to inhumation, burials were made in the earth beneath, with clay pipes leading down through the floor into the graves for the usual oblations of wine. At the beginning of the second century, three two-story mausoleums were built near by. One of these was constructed to accommodate urns for ashes but the other two were intended exclusively for inhumation. When the first one came into the possession of a certain M. Clodius Hermes, who is known from an inscription at the door, he had the niches for the urns walled in and new frescoes painted. These showed a deceased person being led by Hermes, the conductor of souls, into the presence of Hades, the ruler of the underworld. In the course of the second century the necropolis grew also through the building of assembly rooms for holding meals in memory of the dead. Nowhere at this lowest level was any trace of a Christian monument found. The necropolis was exclusively pagan.

Then the property came into the possession of Christians. Perhaps this was by purchase or gift, but more probably the owners themselves were converted to Christianity at this time. At any rate, about the middle of the third century the heathen necropolis was entirely filled in, rooms for Christian use were built above it, and a Christian catacomb came into existence beneath ground. The level at which the Christian rooms were found in the excavations was above that of the pagan necropolis but still some six feet beneath the floor of the church. The first room now called the Triclia, was supported at the back against an old basalt wall, which probably was the enclosing wall of the heathen necropolis, and at one end rested upon the first century columbaria. At the front, on the slope of the hill, pillars supported a roof and provided an open loggia. Masonry benches ran around the sides of the room. At one corner was a small spring, in the slime of whose drain were found remains of food, bones of fish, chicken, and hare, and bits of broken glass. A fresco showed a bright garden scene, with a reed hedge, vine leaves, and fluttering birds.

The most important discovery was that of the numerous graffiti which had been scratched on the walls of the room by those who visited it (Fig. 164). A great part of the wall with these rough inscriptions is still preserved in its original position, while broken pieces lay on the floor and could be pieced together again. The graffiti are written in both Greek and Latin and in capital as well as in cursive letters. Most of them are short prayers to Paul and Peter for remembrance and intercession, like the following:

> PAULE ET PETRE PETITE
> PRO VICTORE
>
> PAUL AND PETER PRAY
> FOR VICTOR

Others mention *refrigeria* or "refreshments" in honor of the apostles. These were meals held according to ancient custom at famous graves in remembrance of venerated saints. One such inscription reads:

> PETRO ET PAULO
> TOMIUS COELIUS
> REFRIGERIUM FECI
>
> TO PETER AND PAUL
> I TOMIUS COELIUS
> MADE A REFRIGERIUM

In all, the names of the two great apostles are scratched on the wall more than one hundred times.[21] A second room was of somewhat similar character, and also had the names of the apostles, *Petre Paule*, scratched at least once on a brick column.

The style of the painting and the paleographical character of the graffiti point to a date around the middle of the third century for the origin of these rooms. Since not a single visitor scratched on the wall a so-called Constantinian monogram, such as is met at every turn on fourth century monuments, the Triclia cannot have continued in use long after the year 313. Soon after this date, and certainly within the first half of the fourth century, the two rooms, as well as other

[21] As far as the order of the two names is concerned, they are written "Paul and Peter" or "Peter and Paul" without any apparent preference. Lanciani, *Wanderings through Ancient Roman Churches*, p.89.

buildings on this part of the hill, were largely destroyed as the site was leveled up for the building there of a great three-aisled church, the "Basilica of the Apostles." Since the technique of the construction of its walls is similar to that of the nearby Circus of Maxentius (306-312), the basilica must belong to Constantinian times.

The character of the rooms which were frequented so eagerly from the middle of the third to the early part of the fourth century, and which then disappeared so completely beneath the basilica until their recent discovery, is indubitable. They constituted a memorial gathering place, where the Christians honored the memory of Paul and Peter. In the so-called Triclia, common meals were held in remembrance of the two great apostles and the visitors scratched innumerable prayers to them on the walls.[22]

All the evidence points, therefore, to the fact that at this time the bones of Peter and of Paul actually rested here. This is confirmed by an inscription of Pope Damasus I, who as we know was eager to adorn the graves of the martyrs with precious marbles and poetic inscriptions composed by himself. While the original of the inscription in question has perished, it is known from several medieval manuscripts and from a partial thirteenth century copy which stands in the Church of Saint Sebastian, presumably in its original place. This is near the entrance to the crypt of Sebastian, which as we shall see was in the immediate vicinity of the resting place of Peter and Paul. The inscription reads:

> Hic habitasse prium sanctos cognoscere debes,
> Nomina quisque Petri pariter Paulique requiris,
> Discipulos Oriens misit, quod sponte fatemur—
> Sanguinis ob meritum, Christumque per astra secuti
> Aetherios petiere sinus regnaque piorum—
> Roma suos potius meruit defendere cives.
> Haec Damasus vestras referat nova sidera laudes.

> You should know that the saints formerly dwelt here,
> if you are seeking the names of Peter and Paul. The
> Orient sent the disciples, as we freely admit, but on
> account of their bloody martyrdom—they followed
> Christ through the stars and reached the heavenly
> bosom and the realm of the pious—Rome rather has
> won the right to claim them as citizens. This
> Damasus records to your praise, ye new stars.[23]

[22] srk pp.331-345.
[23] Lietzmann, *Petrus und Paulus in Rom*, pp.145f.; Walter Lowrie, SS. *Peter and Paul in Rome*. 1940, pp.87f. A misunderstanding of this inscription appears to have

The inscription of Damasus is in complete agreement with the evidence of the graffiti in the Triclia. Writing in the latter half of the fourth century, Damasus declares that Peter and Paul "formerly dwelt here," which is a poetic way of saying "were formerly buried here." At a time from the middle of the third to the early part of the fourth century, Christians came here in numbers to hold meals in honor of Paul and Peter and to scratch prayers to the two great saints on the walls.

We have seen already that around A.D. 200 Caius pointed to the graves of Peter and of Paul at the Vatican and on the Ostian Way respectively as well-known martyr memorials, and we have concluded that the tradition of the apostles' original interment near the respective places of their martyrdoms is entirely trustworthy (p. 384). It must be concluded, therefore, that at the middle of the third century their remains were transferred temporarily to the Via Appia. As a matter of fact there is further evidence that this was the case. This evidence is to be found in the fourth century Church Calendar for the City of Rome. The latter document constituted a sort of yearbook for the inhabitants of Rome, which was edited in A.D. 354 by Furius Dionysius Filocalus, the calligrapher who later was in the service of Pope Damasus and carried out the making of the latter's poetical inscriptions in honor of the martyrs.[24] The portion of the Calendar with which we are concerned is the Depositio Martyrum. This is a list of the dates of the various festivals which were held in honor of the martyrs during the church year, together with an indication of the places where these observances were celebrated. The notation for June 29 reads:

> III KAL. IUL. Petri in Catacumbas
> et Pauli Ostense Tusco et Basso cons.[25]

A more complete and correct text of the same notice is found in the Martyrologium Hieronymianum as follows:

> Romae Via Aurelia natale[26] sanctorum apostolorum
> Petri et Pauli, Petri in Vaticano, Pauli vero
> in via Ostensi, utrumque in Catacumbas, passi
> sub Nerone, Basso et Tusco consulibus.

given rise to the fifth century legend of an attempt by men from the Orient to carry off the bodies of Peter and Paul (Lipsius and Bonnet, *Acta Apostolorum Apocrypha*, I, pp.220f.).

[24] J. P. Kirsch, *Aus den römischen Katakomben*. 1926, p.15.

[25] Hans Lietzmann, ed., *The Three Oldest Martyrologies*. 1904, p.4.

[26] It is the "birthday" of the heavenly life of the saints that is celebrated.

Thus, according to sources from the middle of the fourth century, at that time the church festivals in honor of the martyrdom of Peter and Paul were celebrated at three different places. The festival in honor of Peter was held at the Vatican, that in remembrance of Paul on the Ostian Way, and a celebration in honor of both of them was held in Catacumbas. What is signified by "Basso et Tusco consulibus"? This is the consular date indicating the year 258. In that year Valerian's brief but terrible persecution of the Christians was raging, when, among other acts of violence which were committed, on August 6 Pope Xystus II and four deacons were taken by surprise in a catacomb and killed (p.459). We conclude naturally that fear was felt for the safety of the bones of the two great apostles hitherto resting at their relatively exposed locations in the Vatican district and on the Ostian Way, and that on June 29, 258, they were transferred to the greater safety of the subterranean cemetery *ad Catacumbas*. When the brief persecution was over, the remains of the two apostles were returned to rest permanently in their original graves at the Vatican and on the Ostian Way where later, under Constantine, the churches of Saint Peter and Saint Paul were built. But the names of Peter and Paul continued to be remembered *in Catacumbas* as well as *in Vaticano* and *in via Ostensi*. Such is at least a possible hypothesis to account for the evidence presented above.[27]

The honoring of Paul and Peter *ad Catacumbas* greatly accelerated the development of an extensive Christian cemetery at this place. Many of the faithful wished to find their last rest in proximity to the spot thus hallowed by the two great saints. So there developed a vast network of subterranean corridors and chambers, constituting one of Rome's largest catacombs. Wide areas of these subterranean complexes continued to be visited by pilgrims throughout the Middle Ages as in the case of no other catacomb, but today a great part is filled up and forgotten beneath the surrounding hills. In corridors

[27] Lietzmann, *Petrus und Paulus in Rom*, p.126; cf. Kirsch, *Aus den römischen Katakomben*, p.36; Lowrie, *SS. Peter and Paul in Rome*, pp.91f. Styger believes that if not both of the apostles at least Peter originally was buried on the Via Appia and only later interred near the place of his martyrdom. But he is then able to give no more convincing explanation of the reference to the year 258 in the Calendar of Filocalus than that it signifies that the two apostles began to be honored *in Catacumbas* around the middle of the third century (SRK p.346). Why not until then if one or both were buried here in A.D. 64, and why is the precise year 258 specified? See also below (p.515) for an item of evidence at the Vatican held by some to indicate that the bones of Peter remained permanently at the Vatican from the time of their original burial there. And see H. Chadwick in JTS 8 (1957), pp.31-52 for alternative explanations of the origin of the memorial *ad Catacumbas*.

156. Painting on the Ceiling of Chamber "Y" in the Crypts of Lucina

154. Inscription and Seven-armed Lampstand in the Jewish Catacomb at Monteverde

155. Fresco in the Jewish Catacomb of Villa Torlonia

157. The Crypt of the Popes in the Catacomb of Callistus

158. The Cappella Greca in the Catacomb of Priscilla

159. The Meal Scene in the Cappella Greca

160. The Oldest Picture of Christ, a Fresco in the Cappella Greca

161. Burial Niches in the Catacomb of Priscilla

162. The Prophet and the Madonna

163. The Good Shepherd as Painted in the Catacomb of Priscilla

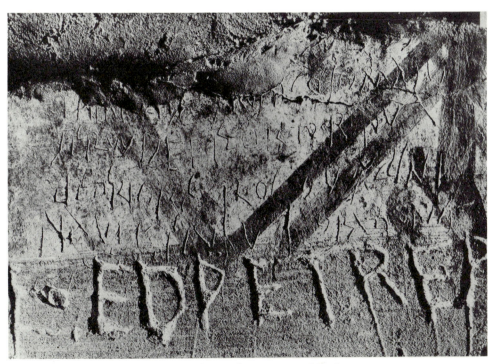

164. Graffiti Invoking Peter and Paul

165. Grave Inscription of Licinia Amias

166. The Deceased Offering Prayer in the Garden of Paradise,
a Painting in the Catacomb of Callistus

167. Statuette of the Good Shepherd

168. Noah in the Ark, a Painting in the Catacomb
of Peter and Marcellinus

169. Wall Paintings in the Catacomb of Domitilla

171. Portrait of Paul in the Catacomb of San Gennaro in Naples

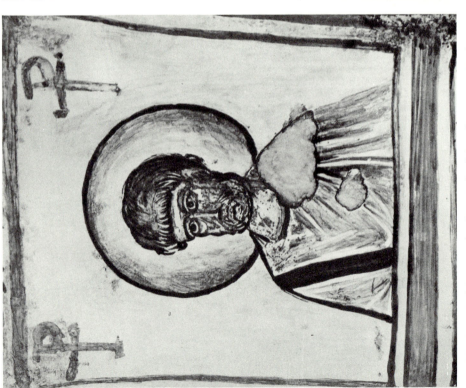

170. Portrait of Peter in the Catacomb of San Gennaro in Naples

172. Early Christian Sarcophagus of the "Philosopher" Type

173. Sarcophagus with the Story of Jonah

174. Sarcophagus of the Latin Frieze Type

175. A "City-Gate" Sarcophagus

176. A "Bethesda" Sarcophagus

177. The Sarcophagus of Junius Bassus

so long trampled by pilgrim feet it is not to be expected that many monuments should remain and as a matter of fact only a few traces of frescoes are to be seen and a few inscriptions with dates in the latter part of the fourth century.

The name by which the entire catacomb is known is that of Sebastian, the saint and martyr. The Roman city calendar of A.D. 354 lists the festival *Sebastiani in Catacumbas* on the date XIII KAL. FEB. or January 10.[28] According to the fifth century *Acts of Saint Sebastian* he was shot with arrows in the Colosseum as a victim of the great persecution by Diocletian and then was buried *ad Catacumbas in initio cryptae iuxta vestigia apostolorum*, "at Catacumbas in the entrance of the crypt near the vestiges of the apostles."[29] Actually the present crypt of Sebastian is found in immediate proximity to the memorial of the apostles at the entrance to the catacomb. The grave was originally in the wall of a simple corridor, and later the opposite wall was removed to provide more room for the numerous visitors. Probably in the time of Constantine, a basilica was built above ground. It was known as the Church of the Apostles and later as the Church of Saint Sebastian.[30] The martyr's grave continued to be accessible by steep steps leading down from within the church. At the beginning of the fifth century two priests, Proclinus and Ursus, rebuilt the crypt of Sebastian, giving it strong brick walls and a new monumental entrance, as well as placing the holy relics in an altar at the same place where the original grave had been.[31]

THE CATACOMB OF PETER AND MARCELLINUS

The Catacomb of Peter and Marcellinus lies on the Via Casilina, as the ancient Via Labicana now is known, and is one of the most extensive complexes of subterranean Rome. It is also notable since no other cemetery possesses so many chambers adorned with frescoes. Before it received the name of Peter and Marcellinus it was known simply by a place-designation as Inter duas Lauros, "Between the two Laurels" (p.522). Three great stairways lead down to as many regions, which were originally independent of one another but developed so extensively as eventually to interconnect. The first stairway led down from the Via Labicana at right angles to the main

[28] Lietzmann, ed., *The Three Oldest Martyrologies*, p.4.
[29] Lietzmann, *Petrus und Paulus in Rom*, p.169.
[30] San Sebastiano was rebuilt in the form it has today in 1612.
[31] SRK pp.177-184; cf. F. Farnari, S. Sebastiano "extra moenia." 1934.

corridor, from which side corridors ran off at regular intervals. Several chambers were excavated in connection with these corridors, and the paintings in the first of them are in the style of the fourth century.

The last corridor attained special significance when the remains of two martyrs (Peter, an exorcist, and Marcellinus, a priest[32]) were interred there in simple wall graves. This took place perhaps in the time of the peace of the church, since at the time of their death under Diocletian in A.D. 304 the two martyrs were buried at the place of their beheading on the Via Cornelia. Since many persons now wished to find a last resting place in the catacomb near the revered saints, numerous burial chambers were laid out in the vicinity. They are adorned with paintings in the style of the advanced fourth century. The excavation in the immediate neighborhood became so extensive that a small, subterranean basilica had to be built for the protection of the graves of the martyrs. Later a Constantinian basilica was built above ground and became the center of a cemetery lying in the open air.

The second stairway led down to another extensive region with numerous chambers. The paintings here belong to the fourth century and include frequent representations of a meal scene. The third stairway gave access to yet a third region of more limited extent. Its most important chamber contains a fresco of the advanced fourth century. Thus this catacomb appears to have undergone its most important development during the later years of that century.[33]

5. THE ART OF THE CATACOMBS

IN DESCRIBING the above Roman catacombs some of the more important paintings on their walls have been mentioned. A brief summary of the development of Christian art in the catacombs can now be given. In the first place, early Christian art did not hesitate to borrow from representations already familiar in pagan art. Christianity was not hostile to ancient culture except where faith or moral principles were endangered. Just as Clement of Alexandria around A.D. 200 held that a Christian should not employ for his signet ring any idolatrous, warlike, or licentious symbol but rather such seals as

[32] Not to be confused with Pope Marcellinus (296-304), who also died later in the same year in the persecution of Diocletian and was buried in the cemetery of Priscilla on the Via Salaria.
[33] SRK pp.198-205.

a dove, a fish, a ship, a lyre, or an anchor,[1] so too the artists of the catacombs freely employed such figures in a decorative way and even gave some of them deeper Christian meaning. The little winged persons, which we noted in the Crypts of Lucina (p.457) and which are known as Erotes or Amoretti, might have seemed less acceptable since actually they came from pagan tombs where they had represented departed souls. But such signification had long since been forgotten and they were employed in a purely decorative way and without offense to Christian taste, along with butterflies, birds, and flowers.

Other representations were interpreted to convey deeper Christian meanings. The fish had already appeared in pagan art, but the Christians soon discovered that in the Greek language the five letters constituting the word "fish" were the initial letters of the phrase "Jesus Christ, the Son of God, the Saviour."[2] Writing about A.D. 200 On Baptism, Tertullian said, "But we, little fishes, after the example of our FISH Jesus Christ, are born in water,"[3] while Augustine (A.D. c.425) said that in the word fish "Christ is mystically understood, because he was able to live, that is, to exist, without sin in the abyss of this mortality as in the depth of waters."[4] Thus the fish might stand symbolically for the name of Christ. In the catacomb of Priscilla there is an inscription reading "ALEXANDER IN," after which a fish is shown, completing the phrase "Alexander in Christ."[5] Or fishes might stand for the Christians themselves. A grave inscription of Licinia Amias from around A.D. 200 (Fig. 165) has the word "Fish" followed by "of the living," which must mean "Jesus Christ, the Son of God, the Saviour of the living," and is adorned with two fishes, which may represent the Christians who are "the living."[6] The initials D.M. which appear on this inscription stand for *Dis Manibus*, meaning "To the spirits of the world of the dead."[7] These initials appeared regularly on pagan graves, and were frequently employed by Christians simply as a conventional form and without further thought of their original meaning.

[1] *The Instructor.* III, 11 (ANF II, p.285).
[2] ΙΧΘΥΣ—'Ιησοῦς Χριστὸς Θεοῦ Υἱὸς Σωτήρ.
[3] *On Bapt.* I (ANF III, p.669).
[4] *The City of God.* XVIII, 23 (NPNF II, p.373).
[5] Orazio Marucchi, *The Evidence of the Catacombs for the Doctrines and Organization of the Primitive Church.* 1929, p.32.
[6] F. J. Dölger, *Ichthys, das Fischsymbol in frühchristlicher Zeit.* I (1910), pp.159-177.
[7] René Cagnat, *Cours d'épigraphie latine.* 4th ed. 1914, p.424.

The representations of a woman with arms uplifted in prayer and of a shepherd with a lamb on his shoulders were also familiar in Hellenistic art. But these figures recur with great frequency in the Christian art of the catacombs from this time on and are invested with special significance. The woman with hands lifted up in prayer is known as an orant[8] and reflects the Hellenistic tendency to personify abstract ideas.[9] Here in the catacombs the orant becomes a distinctive Christian figure, a personification of prayer for salvation and a symbol of Christian devotion. Since such figures occasionally are shown amidst the garden of paradise, and have the names of the departed written nearby, it is clear that they might also be regarded as symbolical representations of the deceased who offer prayer to God in the blessedness of heaven (Fig. 166).[10]

The sight of a shepherd carrying a sheep on his shoulders is familiar in the Middle East today, and the representation of a subject of this type is found not only in Greco-Roman times as for example in Hermes Criophorus, the protector of flocks who carries a ram on his shoulders, but also much more anciently. In Assyria and Syria, reliefs have been found from the eighth and tenth centuries B.C. which portray a man bearing a gazelle upon his shoulders, while the statue from Mari of a man carrying a kid in his arms is as early as the third millennium B.C. (p.56, Fig. 21). These older figures, to be sure, represent worshipers bringing animals for sacrifice, but at least by the time of the ram-bearing Hermes of Greece and perhaps much earlier the thought of the Good Shepherd was introduced.[11] In Christian art the type was conceived anew and filled with Christian meaning.[12] The Good Shepherd now is none other than Christ himself (John 10:11) who carries the lost sheep back to the fold (Luke 15:5f.). The particular appropriateness of such a picture in the catacombs is seen in the conception preserved in a later Latin liturgy: "Lord, let these who are asleep, when they are redeemed from death, freed from guilt, reconciled to the Father, and brought home on the shoulders of the Good Shepherd, enjoy everlasting blessedness in the

[8] C. M. Kaufmann, *Handbuch der christlichen Archäologie*. 3d ed. 1922, p.272.
[9] Charles R. Morey, *Early Christian Art*. 1942, p.63.
[10] H. Leclercq in DACL II, col. 2472.
[11] A. Parrot in *Mélanges Syriens offerts a Monsieur René Dussaud*. I (1939), pp.171-182; G. Ernest Wright in BA 2 (1939), pp.44-48; also for prehistoric antecedents in Egypt see Valentine Muller in JNES 3 (1944), pp.87-90.
[12] Pierre Maranget, *Jésus-Christ dans les peintures des catacombes*. 1932, p.41; J. Wilpert, *Principienfragen der christlichen Archäologie*. 1889, p.15.

train of the eternal king and in the company of the saints."[13] The famous marble statuette of the Good Shepherd (Fig. 167), usually dated in the third century and now in the Lateran Museum in Rome, also once may have stood in a cemeterial crypt. It shows the Shepherd as a young and beardless man whose curly hair falls upon his shoulders. He wears a tucked-up tunic and high stockings, and has a basket slung on a strap. He carries the lost sheep gently on his shoulders holding its front feet in one hand and the rear feet in the other.[14]

The juxtaposition of the orant and the Good Shepherd is found as early as in the painting in the Lucina crypt (p.457; Fig. 156) and recurs frequently thereafter in Christian art. The significance of placing these two symbols in connection with each other is unmistakable. The Christian prayer for deliverance in time of need and death is answered by the Good Shepherd who carries the soul safely home to its fatherland in paradise.[15]

The famous inscription of Abercius[16] casts light on the place held by the Shepherd and the Fish in Christian thought at the end of the second century. Abercius was a Christian of Hieropolis,[17] a small town in Phrygia between Eumenia and Synnada, who at the age of seventy-two composed an epitaph relating his visit to Rome and return by way of Syria and Mesopotamia. He said:

"I, a citizen of an elect city, in my lifetime have erected this monument, to have where to place my body when time shall require it.
"My name is Abercius, a disciple of the holy Shepherd who feeds his sheep upon the hills and plains, whose eyes are large and all-seeing, who taught me the sure learning of life, and sent me to Rome to see the imperial majesty and the queen clad in a golden robe and with golden shoes. There I saw a people who had the gleaming seal. I saw also the plains of Syria and all cities, Nisibis, beyond the Euphrates. Everywhere I had a companion, for Paul sat in the chariot with me; everywhere Faith was my guide, and gave me everywhere for food the Fish from the spring, the great, the pure, which the spotless Virgin caught and ever puts before the friends to eat; she has also delicious wine, and she offers wine mixed with water together with bread. I, Abercius, dictated this to

[13] Hans Lietzmann, *Geschichte de alten Kirche.* II (1936), p.138.
[14] O. Marucchi, *I Monumenti del Museo Cristiano Pio-Lateranense riprodotti in atlante di XCVI tavole, con testo illustrativo.* 1910, p.13.
[15] cf. Cyprian (A.D. c.200-258), *Treatise VII On the Mortality.* 26 (ANF v, p.475): "We regard paradise as our country."
[16] Dölger, *Ichthys.* II (1922), pp.454-507; *Die Eucharistie nach Inschriften frühchristlicher Zeit.* 1922, pp.10-42.
[17] He is probably to be identified with the Avircius Marcellus to whom an anti-Montanist work was dedicated in that region around A.D. 183 (Eusebius, *Ch. Hist.* v, xvi, 3).

be written in my presence, and in fact in the seventy-second year of my life. Let every fellow believer who understands this pray for Abercius.

"No man may lay another in my grave; but if it be done, he must pay to the Roman treasury two thousand gold pieces, and to my dear native city Hieropolis a thousand gold pieces."

The language of Abercius is poetic but he expects fellow Christians to understand. Rome is referred to as "the imperial majesty and the queen clad in a golden robe," in fashion somewhat similar to the symbolism employed in Revelation (17:3-5, 9, 18). The Christians are the people with the "gleaming seal." Abercius had Paul for a companion in the sense that he carried the Pauline letters with him. Even so he describes Christ now as the great Shepherd who cares for his flock upon the hills and plains, and again as the Fish from the spring, caught by the holy Virgin. He says that the Virgin places the Fish before the friends to eat, and offers them wine and bread. The inner meaning of this last language is that the Christians everywhere partake of Christ in the observance of the Lord's Supper. It will be remembered that meal scenes are frequently represented in the catacombs with fish and bread, and sometimes wine, for food. It is not certain whether these scenes depict the meals that were held in honor of the dead, as was also done in pagan custom,[18] or represent the Lord's Supper itself. Perhaps the loaves and fishes reflect the Feeding of the Five Thousand, which was regarded as the prototype of the Lord's Supper because of the interpretation given to it in John 6:54, "He who eats my flesh and drinks my blood has eternal life, and I will raise him up at the last day."[19] At any rate the words of Abercius, combining the Fish with the bread and wine, give some support to the interpretation of the meal scenes of the catacombs in a eucharistic sense.

In the second place, not only pagan but also Jewish art seems to have made its contribution to the Christian art of the catacombs. Some seven Old Testament scenes appear repeatedly among the oldest paintings in Lucina, Domitilla and Priscilla (middle of the second century), and Callistus and Praetextatus (end of the second and beginning of the third century). These seven subjects are: Noah in the Ark, Abraham's Sacrifice of Isaac, Moses' Miracle of Water in the Wilderness, the Story of Jonah, the Three Youths in the Fiery Furnace, Daniel in the Lions' Den, and, from the Old Testament

[18] Morey, *Early Christian Art*, p.64.
[19] Lietzmann, *Geschichte der alten Kirche*. II, p.141.

Apocrypha, the Story of Susanna.[20] It is now known that the Jews used paintings and other artistic representations in their catacombs (p.455) and synagogues (p.497f.) and some of those that have been found reveal the same subjects that appear in the Christian catacombs at Rome. In the synagogue at Dura one of the wall paintings depicts Abraham's Sacrifice of Isaac, in a third-century Palestinian synagogue the floor mosaic shows Daniel between the Lions, and around A.D. 200 the city of Apamea in Phrygia, under the influence of the Jews who lived there, stamped on some of its coins the same type of portrayal of Noah in the Ark that is familiar in the Christian catacombs. Thus it is probable that at least some of the Christian representations of Old Testament events were taken over from the realm of Jewish art.[21]

In the third place, the Christian artists went on to develop their own representations of New Testament subjects. Perhaps this was done first for the decoration of the walls of Christian houses and cult-rooms,[22] and from there the paintings were copied in the catacombs. At any rate some half-dozen New Testament scenes appear repeatedly in the oldest Roman catacombs. These are: the Visit of the Magi, the Baptism of Jesus, the Healing of the Paralytic, the Healing of the Woman with an Issue of Blood, the Samaritan Woman at the Well, and the Resurrection of Lazarus.[23]

These thirteen scenes which have now been mentioned—seven from the Old Testament and six from the New Testament—not only appear frequently in the five oldest Christian cemeteries at Rome but also are repeated over and over again in all the later catacombs. The Old Testament picture of Noah in the Ark reproduced in Fig. 168 is from the Catacomb of Peter and Marcellinus, while the paintings in Fig. 169 are from the Catacomb of Domitilla and include three of the New Testament scenes, the Raising of Lazarus, the Coming of the Magi, and the Walking of the Paralytic with his Bed, as well as a representation of the Bringing of Water from the Rock. Ultra-symbolic interpretations have been advanced for all these subjects, but actually their leading motif is the simple theme of deliverance. As the early Christians faced tribulation and death, their courage was increased by the remembrance of God's mighty deeds in

[20] SRK p.356.
[21] Lietzmann, *Geschichte der alten Kirche.* II, p.140. See also Heinz-Ludwig Hempel in ZAW 69 (1957), pp.103-131.
[22] cf. the house church at Dura, see below pp.499f.
[23] SRK p.356.

the past on behalf of his children. The wonderful deliverances which had taken place were types of the resurrection to which Christian faith looked forward with confidence. This conception which shines through the earliest art of the catacombs is preserved also in written sources. Thus, for example, in the *Constitutions of the Holy Apostles*, a work belonging probably to the fourth century, the author urges that martyrdom be faced with equanimity because of the certainty of the resurrection, and says: "Now he that brought Jonah in the space of three days, alive and unhurt, out of the belly of the whale, and the three children out of the furnace of Babylon, and Daniel out of the mouth of the lions, does not lack power to raise us up also."[24] Even so, in the prayer for a departing soul which is still in use today in the Roman Catholic Church the words are found: "Deliver, O Lord! the soul of Thy servant, as Thou didst deliver Noah in the flood . . . Isaac from the sacrificing hand of his father . . . Daniel from the lions' den . . . the three children from the fiery furnace . . . Susanna from her false accusers."[25]

From the time of Constantine and the peace of the church on, a large number of other subjects are found among the paintings in the catacombs. More than sixty new scenes appear, including pictures from the Old Testament like those of Job, Adam and Eve, and Moses before Pharaoh; representations from the Gospels like the Annunciation to Mary, the Entry into Jerusalem, and the Women at the Tomb; events from the book of Acts like the Sin of Ananias and Sapphira, and the Raising of Tabitha; and stories from the New Testament Apocrypha like Peter's Miracle of the Water (p.488), and the Healing of Petronilla. In contrast to the constantly repeated thirteen scenes of older times, these new subjects appear far less frequently, over half of them being found but a single time. It is probable that they were copied from the new paintings and mosaics which were being developed to adorn the numerous new churches of Constantinian times.[26]

6. THE INSCRIPTIONS IN THE CATACOMBS

AN additional word should be said about the inscriptions in the catacombs. In the Jewish catacombs at Rome most of the inscriptions

[24] v, i, 7 (ANF VII, p.440).
[25] P. Griffith, compiler, *The Priest's New Ritual, revised in accord with the latest Vatican Edition of the Roman Ritual*. 1939, pp.138-140.
[26] SRK pp.357-360.

are in Greek and some in Latin. Inscriptions in Hebrew are rare, except for the single word Shalom, meaning peace or rest. Very frequently found are the Greek words, "May his [or her] sleep be in peace."[1]

The Christian inscriptions are also more often in Greek than in Latin and thus may indicate the humble and foreign extraction of those on whose graves they are written.[2] The following are typical inscriptions in the Christian catacombs:

> Victorina, in peace and in Christ.
> Julia, in peace with the saints.
> Thou wilt live in God.
> Mayest thou live in the Lord Jesus.
> Mayest thou live in the Holy Spirit.
> Thou wilt live forever.
> May God give thee life.

An epitaph on the grave of a little child reads:

> To Paul, my son, in peace. May the spirit of all the saints receive thee. He lived two years.

Some inscriptions refer to the life beyond as a *refrigerium* or refreshment:

> May God refresh thy spirit.

Some contain a prayer on behalf of the departed one:

> Demetris and Leontia, to their daughter, Sirita. Jesu, be mindful of our child.

Others request the prayers of the departed:

> In thy prayers pray for us, for we know that thou dwellest in Christ.[3]

Not only paintings and inscriptions are found in the catacombs but also many small objects which were left at the graves. These include lamps, pitchers, vases, plates, and the interesting "gold-glasses" within whose glass bottoms medallions made of gold leaf were sealed.[4]

[1] G. M. Bevan, *Early Christians of Rome, their Words and Pictures.* 1927, p.24.
[2] Morey, *Early Christian Art*, p.60.
[3] Bevan, *Early Christians of Rome, their Words and Pictures*, pp.28-32.
[4] Oskar Beyer, *Die Katakombenwelt, Grundriss, Ursprung und Idee der Kunst in der römischen Christengemeinde.* 1927, pp.106-112. For glass in antiquity see R. J. Forbes, *Studies in Ancient Technology.* v (1957), pp.110-231.

7. CATACOMBS IN OTHER CITIES AND LANDS

NUMEROUS catacombs are to be found elsewhere in Italy and in other places including Sicily, Malta, North Africa, Egypt, and Palestine.[1] As a single example we may mention the catacombs at Naples. Six early Christian catacombs exist here whose origins are in the second and third centuries and whose use continued for many centuries thereafter. They are adorned with many paintings, and the development of their art is traceable through several periods. In the first period, in the second and third centuries, it may be seen clearly that the Christian art has arisen out of the decorative painting of the ancient world. Flowers, birds, and leaping animals such as antelopes and panthers are represented, while also such a biblical subject as that of Adam and Eve makes its appearance. In the second period, in the fourth century, the influence of the Roman catacomb art is felt strongly, and the painters at Naples copied Roman models to represent the Story of Jonah, Moses Striking Water from the Rock, and other familiar subjects. Only in the third period, from the fifth to the eighth centuries, did the Christian art of Naples achieve independent significance and attain its high point. Examples of the portraits characteristic of this period may be seen in two fifth century paintings of Peter and Paul. The two apostles are decidedly different in type, Peter (Fig. 170) with his broader face, curling hair, and short beard, and Paul (Fig. 171) with his bald head, lofty brow, long nose, and straight beard. Peter's expression is distrustful or almost sullen, and may reflect the influence of monasticism, while in the companion picture of Paul a Christian thinker and philosopher is depicted.[2]

8. THE LATER HISTORY OF THE ROMAN CATACOMBS

A BRIEF word may be said concerning the later history of the catacombs at Rome. During the third century the persecuted Christians frequently sought refuge in the catacombs and many even suffered martyrdom within them.[1] In that century and the next the venera-

[1] See Leclercq in DACL II, cols. 2442-2450.
[2] Hans Achelis, *Die Katakomben von Neapel*. 1936.
[1] In his edict of A.D. 257, Valerian forbade the Christians to hold assemblies or to enter into the catacombs (Eusebius, *Ch. Hist.* VII, xi, 10) but in A.D. 261 Gallienus again allowed the Christians to use their places of worship inclusive of the cemeteries (*Ch. Hist.* VII, xiii).

tion of the martyrs who were buried in the catacombs became very important and we have already noted (pp.459f., 472) the contributions of Pope Damasus to the beautification of the crypts now so eagerly visited by pilgrims. With the peace of the church under Constantine it became possible to build cemeterial churches above the catacombs and to erect other churches elsewhere. From this time on it became gradually customary to bury the dead no longer in the subterranean rooms of the catacombs but in graves and sarcophagi in and around these churches. As the burials in surface cemeteries became more and more numerous, the catacombs fell into disuse. With the sack of Rome by Alaric in A.D. 410, interments in them ceased entirely. The tombs of the martyrs were still visited after that and kept in repair, but other sections of the catacombs were neglected and often became inaccessible. When the Goths besieged Rome in 537 and the Lombards in 755 the catacombs suffered much destruction and the crypts of the martyrs were damaged badly. The popes of the eighth and ninth centuries found it necessary to bring the bones of the martyrs from their graves in the catacombs to safer resting places in the churches inside the city. Where there are basilicas still standing outside the city today, however, these churches were always kept in use and the remains of the martyrs buried there did not have to be removed.[2] But after the remains of the martyrs were removed from the crypts at the catacombs, the catacombs fell into complete ruin. Their entrances were choked with dirt, the grass of the Campagna covered them, and their very existence was forgotten until their accidental rediscovery in 1578.

9. EARLY CHRISTIAN SARCOPHAGI

OCCASIONALLY in the catacombs and far more frequently in and around the churches above ground there are found the sculptured stone coffins which are known as sarcophagi.[1] These constitute relatively elaborate tombs and reflect the existence of a wealthier group of believers than some of the poor who buried their dead in the humble niches of the catacombs.[2]

The employment of sarcophagi for pagan burials has already been

[2] Kirsch, *Aus den römischen Katakomben*, pp.10-12.
[1] James C. Stout in *Papers of the American Society of Church History*. Second series. 8 (1928), pp.1-15.
[2] Morey, *Early Christian Art*, p.67.

alluded to (pp. 451, 463), and it may be presumed that when Christians first began to use such tombs they were procured directly from the workshops of those who served the population as a whole. In such cases the sarcophagi would not exhibit any marks distinctive of Christianity, but would be adorned like the pagan coffins with lines, animal heads, scenes from the sea and the chase, and other subjects. Themes repugnant to Christian principles, of course, would be avoided in the selection of the sarcophagi.[3]

SARCOPHAGI OF THE THIRD CENTURY

But the time soon came when Christianity developed its own plastic art, and sculptured sarcophagi appear which are unmistakably Christian productions. According to the researches of Friedrich Gerke, the oldest of these are to be dated around the middle of the third century A.D.[4] It was probably at about this time, and particularly under the influence of the philosopher Plotinus who worked in Rome from 244 until 270, that a distinctive type of pagan sarcophagus arose in whose sculptures the deceased was represented in the role of a philosopher with his book.[5] When, therefore, a number of Christian sarcophagi display this very theme, it is a natural conclusion that they are to be dated at about the same time. In the case of the latter productions, however, the orant and the Good Shepherd are characteristically added in the sculptures to show that the content of the true philosophy is the Christian message of immortality.

A Christian sarcophagus of the "philosopher" type, which was found in the Via Salaria in Rome and now is in the Lateran Museum, is shown in Fig. 172. This sarcophagus is of the tub-shaped kind and is adorned at the corners with figures of rams. Two trees serve to divide the sculptures on the front into three groups. At the left sits the deceased man in the guise of a philosopher accompanied by two friends. At the right is his wife, with whom are two companions. Of these, however, the one in front appears as an orant who gazes toward the Good Shepherd in the center. The Shepherd in turn looks toward the orant, and in this unmistakable juxtaposition of the two figures the motif familiar in the catacombs (p.479) appears again.[6] The

---

[3] O. Marucchi, *Manual of Christian Archaeology.* tr. from 4th Italian edition by Hubert Vecchierello, 1935, pp.330f.

[4] F. Gerke, *Die christlichen Sarkophage der vorkonstantinischen Zeit.* 1940, p.316.

[5] Gerhart Rodenwaldt in *Jahrbuch des Deutschen Archäologischen Instituts.* 51 (1936), pp.101-105.

[6] The heads of both the orant and the Good Shepherd are modern restorations, but

prayer for deliverance from death is answered by the Good Shepherd. This theme holds the place of focal importance in the composition and toward this central truth of Christian philosophy the attention of the believers is directed.[7]

In the latter part of the third century another distinctive type of Christian sarcophagus makes its appearance. General symbolism here gives way to specifically biblical composition. The motif in the sculptures is still that of deliverance from death, but the idea now is conveyed through the portrayal of events from the Bible. Obviously the influence of the art of the catacombs continues to be effective, and the stories which are represented include such familiar ones as those of Jonah, Daniel, and the Fiery Furnace.

Of the prominent class of sarcophagi which portray the history of Jonah, an outstanding example now in the Lateran Museum is shown in Fig. 173. Against a unified background of sea and rocky coast, the story of Jonah is unfolded in three consecutive parts. At the left Jonah is being cast out of the ship and received into the mouth of the sea monster. In the scene immediately adjacent the sea monster is shown again, throwing up Jonah on the rocks of the coast. The picture is enlivened at this point with representations of the flora and fauna of the seacoast, including reeds and trees, the snail, the lizard, the crab, and the heron. An angler is drawing a fish from the ocean, and a shepherd is seen with his sheep before a massive sheep stall. The third part of the dramatic history of Jonah is represented just above the seacoast, where Jonah rests beneath the shade of the gourd. Although most of the front of the sarcophagus is occupied by this detailed and extensive portrayal of the story of Jonah, some room remains in which other biblical subjects are introduced. On a bit of open sea between the monster and the coast, Noah floats in his ark, and in an upper panel we see from left to right the Resurrection of Lazarus, the Water Miracle of Moses, and what is probably yet a further scene from the life of Moses.[8]

SARCOPHAGI OF THE FOURTH CENTURY
THE LATIN FRIEZE STYLE

The greatest number of early Christian sarcophagi belong to the fourth century, and in this period it is possible clearly to distinguish

---

sufficient traces of the original heads remain to show clearly that they were represented as gazing at each other.

[7] Gerke, *Die christlichen Sarkophage der vorkonstantinischen Zeit*, pp.246-299.

[8] *ibid.*, pp.38-46.

two main groups among them, namely those of the frieze type and those of the columnar style. In the case of the frieze group the entire front of the sarcophagus is occupied with a continuous series of figures. Such a style of arrangement was customary in the pagan sarcophagus art of the Latin West during the second and third centuries and doubtless provided the pattern for the Christian sculptors. The Christian sarcophagi display a basic difference, however, in that the façade is made to carry not a single unified representation but a half-dozen or more separate scenes crowded together in undivided succession. The purpose clearly is to tell as many stories as possible in the space at hand. The subjects chosen are largely biblical scenes such as were already represented in conveniently abbreviated form in the art of the catacombs.[9]

A sarcophagus executed in the Latin frieze style and now in the Lateran Museum is shown in Fig. 174. Placed side by side upon its front are the representations of no less than nine different events. At the left is the Fall of Man, with Adam and Eve standing on either side of the tree and the Lord laying his hand on Adam's shoulder. Continuing to the right we see the Miracle of the Wine at Cana, the Healing of the Blind, and a Resurrection scene which may represent one of the miracles of Christ or Ezekiel's vision of the valley of dry bones (Ezekiel 37:1-14). In the center Christ is prophesying the Denial of Peter, at whose feet the symbolic cock appears. Farther to the right we find the Healing of the Paralytic, the Sacrifice of Isaac, the Arrest of Peter, and Peter Smiting the Rock to bring water to baptize his jailers. The last scene is similar to that of Moses' Miracle of Water in the Wilderness, but is believed to be derived from some apocryphal incident in the life of Peter.

THE ASIATIC COLUMNAR STYLE

In contrast with the crowded and indiscriminate arrangement of the sculptures of the Latin frieze sarcophagi, a far more orderly composition is exhibited by the so-called columnar sarcophagi. The latter are characterized by the placing of the various figures in an architectural framework which is usually made up of columns and arches. This type of arrangement is known in the pagan sarcophagi of the second and third centuries, and seems to have originated in Asia Minor. The Christian sarcophagi of the columnar group are regarded, therefore, as standing under the direct influence of this

[9] Alexander C. Soper in AB 19 (1937), pp.148-202.

Asiatic style, and it is believed that many of them, although made in the West, were executed by Asiatic artisans.[10]

Since the columnar sarcophagi constitute a numerous group, the general style may be illustrated by two examples in each of which a characteristic modification appears. Fig. 175 shows a sarcophagus which was discovered in the foundation of St. Peter's Church in Rome and is now in the Louvre. Its Asiatic style is unmistakable, and in this case the columns and arches are so arranged as to give the appearance of a series of city-gates. Sarcophagi of this type commonly are spoken of as belonging to the "city-gate" group.[11] We see that in the present case the entire front of the sarcophagus is given over to a single scene, that of the Mission of the Apostles. Christ stands upon the mount, surrounded by the Twelve, and with the two donors of the sarcophagus represented as small figures at his feet. While many of the heads were broken and have been restored, that of Christ is original and shows him as bearded. Christ is giving the scroll of the new law to Peter, who carries a jeweled cross and heads the apostles from the right. Paul occupies the corresponding position on the left.

The sarcophagus shown in Fig. 176, and now in the Lateran Museum, displays the architectural features of the Asiatic style and by virtue of the appearance of the gate of Jerusalem at the extreme right is allied with the "city-gate" sarcophagi. A special modification occurs here, however, in the introduction, near the center, of a double-register scene portraying the Healing of the Paralytic at the Pool of Bethesda. In the lower register, the paralytic lies upon his bed; in the upper, at the command of Christ, he walks away with his bed upon his back. Sarcophagi having this central scene as an identifying feature are commonly designated as belonging to the "Bethesda" type.[12] The other representations which appear on the sarcophagus illustrated include at the left the Healing of Two Blind Men, and the Healing of the Woman with an Issue of Blood, and at the right the Triumphal Entry of Christ into Jerusalem.

THE SARCOPHAGUS OF JUNIUS BASSUS

The influence of the eastern tradition in the West led in many cases to a mingling of the Asiatic and the Latin styles, and some of

---

[10] Marion Lawrence in AB 13 (1931), pp.535f.; 14 (1932), pp.103-185.
[11] *ibid.*, 10 (Sept. 1927-June 1928), pp.1-45.
[12] *ibid.*, 14 (1932), p.121.

the resultant productions were very fine. For a single example we may turn to the sarcophagus of Junius Bassus (Fig. 177), which is believed to have been the work of a Latin artist using various Asiatic models.[13] This magnificent stone coffin, which was found in the Church of St. Peter in 1595, was the tomb of a prefect of Rome who died in A.D. 359. This is indicated by the following inscription upon the sarcophagus: "Junius Bassus, a most illustrious man, who lived forty-two years and two months, and when he was in office as prefect of the city and after he had received baptism went to God on the 25th day of August in the year in which Eusebius and Hypatius were consuls." On the top of the sarcophagus may be scenes from the life of Junius Bassus, which are now difficult to make out, on the ends are representations from ancient nature mythology, but on the front are wholly Christian scenes. Here there are two rows of sculptures, each row in turn being divided by columns into niches in which the various scenes are found. In the upper row the scenes are from left to right (1) Abraham's Sacrifice, (2) the Arrest of Peter, (3) Christ Enthroned above Caelus[14] and bestowing upon Peter and Paul their missions, and (4-5) Christ Led before Pilate. In the lower row are (1) Job, (2) Adam and Eve, (3) Christ's Entry into Jerusalem, (4) Daniel between the Lions,[15] and (5) Paul Led to Execution. In between, in the spandrels of the lower colonnade, lambs play the parts in scenes representing the Three Hebrews in the Fiery Furnace, Peter's Miracle of Water, the Baptism of Christ, the Multiplication of Loaves and Fishes, Moses Receiving the Law, and the Resurrection of Lazarus. The plan of the main sculptures is clear if we may consider that when they were carried out the niches of Abraham and Paul became reversed. Thinking of Abraham as belonging to the lower register we find there a series of Old Testament scenes, with Christ in the center, riding triumphantly through the world of human sin and suffering. Placing Paul in the upper series, we have there the theme of the passion in which Christ is followed in death by his two apostles. On the right, Christ walks slowly between two soldiers toward the judgment place, while Pilate sits upon the magistrate's chair and a servant prepares to pour the water for the symbolic washing of his hands. On the left, Peter stands between two soldiers, calmly

[13] *ibid.*, 14 (1932), p.133.
[14] The god who in Roman art spreads out the veil of the sky, as on the breastplate of Augustus (cf. Fig. 99 and p.250).
[15] The figure of Daniel in the middle is a modern restoration. The lions are accompanied by men holding rods.

awaiting the end, and Paul, in the other niche, bows his head as the officer draws the sword while reeds indicate the marshes of the Tiber where his execution was fulfilled. In the center the heavenly Christ is upon his throne of eternal victory and over the entire sarcophagus there is a calm peace, the peace which the early Christians wished for their deceased when they carved the words *in pace*.[16]

[16] Friedrich Gerke, *Der Sarkophag des Junius Bassus*. 1936.

IX

The Story of Ancient Churches

Tʜᴇ meeting places of the early Christians were in private homes. At Jerusalem the first disciples, being Jews, continued for a time to frequent the Temple (cf. Acts 3:1), but it was doomed to destruction in A.D. 70. In the Gentile world Paul at first went regularly to the synagogue to preach, but Christianity could not remain long within its confines (cf. Acts 13:5,14,45f., etc.). Having, therefore, no other meeting place of their own, the disciples perforce assembled in private houses. Wherever some Christian had the room and desire to invite his fellow believers to gather in his home for worship, there a "house church" arose.

The use of private homes for Christian assemblage is reflected clearly in various New Testament passages. An upper room in a private house in Jerusalem was used by Jesus and the twelve for the Last Supper (Mark 14:15), and the apostles later stayed in an upstairs room (Acts 1:13) in that city, while the house of Mary the mother of John Mark was a place where they gathered for prayer (Acts 12:12). Even so it is said that Saul "laid waste the church, and entering house after house, he dragged off men and women and committed them to prison" (Acts 8:3). When he himself as a Christian preacher was ejected from a synagogue, he frequently went to private homes instead. Paul's experience at Corinth may well have been typical of that which happened at many other places. He preached in the synagogue every Sabbath but his assertion that Jesus was the Christ met with contradiction and abuse, so finally he left the synagogue "and went to the house of a man named Titius Justus, a worshiper of God; his house was next door to the synagogue" (Acts 18:7). At Philippi, Lydia, who as a seller of purple may have been relatively well-to-do, made her house available for Paul and perhaps also for Christian meetings (Acts 16:14f.). At Troas the Christian gathering took place in an upper chamber (Acts 20:8), and at Caesarea the house of Philip the evangelist may have been the Christian center (Acts 21:8). At Rome Paul lived in his own rented house, and preached in it (Acts 28:30f.).

The references in Paul's letters are even more explicit. "Aquila and Prisca, together with the church in their house, send you hearty greetings" (I Corinthians 16:19). "Greet Prisca and Aquila . . . also the church in their house" (Romans 16:3, 5; cf. 14f.). "Give my greetings . . . to Nympha and the church in her house" (Colossians 4:15). "Paul . . . to Philemon . . . and the church in your house" (Philemon 1f.).

Eusebius mentions a tradition that up to the time of Hadrian's siege there existed in Jerusalem a very large Christian church which was constructed by the Jews.[1] Nothing else is known about this church, but it may have been a large assembly room in the house where the heads of the church lived.[2] In the account of the *Martyrdom of Justin Martyr* (d. A.D. c.165) it is related that Rusticus, the prefect of Rome, asked Justin in what place he had his followers assemble, and Justin replied that he lived with a certain Martinus, and that those who wished came there to him to hear his teaching.[3] Similarly, in the *Recognitions of Clement*[4] it is narrated that when Peter was in Tripoli large numbers of people wished to hear him preach. Upon his asking where there was a suitable place for discussion, a certain Maro offered his house saying, "I have a very spacious hall which can hold more than five hundred men, and there is also a garden within the house." "Then Peter said: 'Show me the hall, or the garden.' And when he had seen the hall, he went in to see the garden also; and suddenly the whole multitude, as if some one had called them, rushed into the house, and thence broke through into

[1] *Demonstratio Evangelica.* III, v, 108. ed. G. Dindorf, *Eusebii Caesariensis Opera.* (1867) III, p.188.

[2] J. W. Crowfoot, *Early Churches in Palestine.* 1941, p.1.

[3] *Martyrdom.* 2 (ANF I, p.305).

[4] A fictional work of the early fourth century, probably based upon an earlier and lost Clement romance of A.D. c.260, which describes a journey of Clement of Rome to Palestine where he met and talked at length with Peter and marvelously had his own long lost parents and brothers restored to him (hence the name, *Recognitions*). E. J. Goodspeed, *A History of Early Christian Literature.* 1942, p.127.

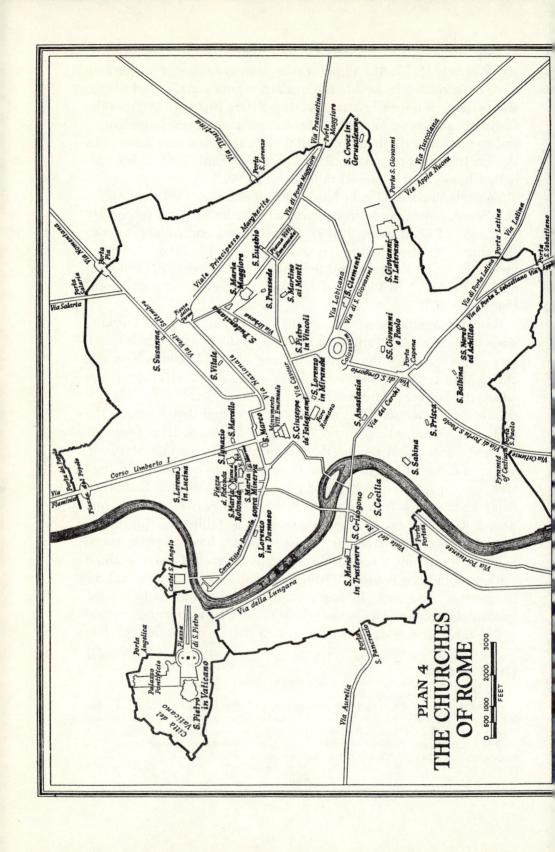

PLAN 4

THE CHURCHES OF ROME

the garden where Peter was already standing, selecting a fit place for discussion."[5]

At this time we also hear of private houses set aside entirely for the work of the church. When Peter was in Antioch, according to the *Recognitions of Clement*, more than ten thousand men were baptized within seven days and thereupon "Theophilus, who was more exalted than all the men of power in that city, with all eagerness of desire consecrated the great palace of his house under the name of a church, and a chair was placed in it for the Apostle Peter by all the people; and the whole multitude assembled daily to hear the word."[6]

It is clear, therefore, that the earliest gathering places of the Christians were in private houses. Having no temple or synagogue of their own, they naturally made use of available rooms in their own homes. When concealment was necessary, as in time of persecution, such meeting places were inconspicuous and relatively secret. When conditions warranted, parts or even the whole of such residences might be dedicated entirely to church use and equipped and adorned for this purpose. Such were the meeting places of the early Christians, as we may reconstruct the situation from literary references.

1. DURA-EUROPOS

IT IS of great interest, therefore, that such an actual house church of the early Christians has now been discovered.[1] We must tell the story of it in some detail. The city of Dura-Europos lies in the Syrian desert on an immemorial caravan route beside the Euphrates. Here, on the site of an earlier settlement known by the Aramaic name of Dura, there was established around 300 B.C. a Seleucid fortress. This took place in the early part of the reign of Seleucus I Nicator, and although the colony was actually established by the king's governor general, Nicanor, Seleucus Nicator was regarded as the founder. Hence the place was renamed Europos after Europos in Macedon, the native city of Seleucus. In the second half of the second century B.C. Dura-Europos became a part of the Parthian Empire and in the years of Partho-Roman peace rose to be an important agricul-

---

[5] *Rec.* IV, 6 (ANF VIII, p.136).   [6] *Rec.* X, 71 (ANF VIII, p.210).

[1] We have already mentioned (p.364) the place at Pompeii where a Christian missionary may have preached, and the upper room at Herculaneum which may possibly have been a small Christian chapel.

tural and caravan city. Although it remained a Parthian city at this time, the prestige of Rome was high in Dura; also the influence of the famous city of Palmyra[2] nearly 150 miles to the west, situated in an oasis in the Syrian desert, was strongly felt. In the second century A.D. there was war between Parthia and Rome, and Dura was taken by the Romans and made a part of the province of Syria. The ancient fortress received a Roman garrison in A.D. 167 and was maintained as an important stronghold on the Euphrates frontier of the Roman Empire.

Yet the end was not far distant. It came in the third century when the Sasanian kings took the offensive against the Roman Empire. The troops of Ardashir (224-241) nearly captured Dura-Europos in A.D. 238, and the final siege came soon after 256. The exact date of the fall of Dura is unknown but it was probably just after the famous battle of Edessa (between 258 and 260), where the Roman emperor Valerian was taken prisoner (p.237) by the Sasanian king Shapur I (241-272). Dura was probably occupied for a short time by the Persians and then abandoned. It reverted swiftly to the desert, and on the expedition in which he was to die fighting against Shapur II (310-379) the Emperor Julian (361-363) hunted lions among its ruins. It was reserved for modern archeologists to rescue the city from oblivion.[3]

The first intimation of what might be waiting beneath the desert sand came by chance in 1921. The British army was operating against the Arabs, and in the course of digging trenches in the ruins of Dura some notable temple paintings came to light.[4] From 1928 on, a series of archeological expeditions was conducted at Dura by Yale University and the French Academy of Inscriptions and Letters under the general supervision of M. I. Rostovtzeff.[5] The house church with which we are concerned here was found in the season of 1931-1932, and the Jewish synagogue which also is to be mentioned came to light in 1932-1933.

[2] Palmyra is the Greek and Latin name of the city which is called Tadmar in the inscriptions of Tiglath-pileser I (ARAB I, §§287, 308). It is mentioned in II Chronicles 8:4 where Solomon is said to have built "Tadmor in the wilderness." But this passage is evidently based upon I Kings 9:18 which says that Solomon built "Tamar in the wilderness," a city in Judah (Ezekiel 47:19; 48:28). The Chronicler may have altered the name to Tadmor to increase the extent of Solomon's kingdom and heighten the glory of his achievements.

[3] M. I. Rostovtzeff, *Dura-Europos and its Art*. 1938, pp.10-30.

[4] J. H. Breasted, *Oriental Forerunners of Byzantine Painting, First-Century Wall Paintings from the Fortress of Dura on the Middle Euphrates*. 1924.

[5] Rostovtzeff, ed., *The Excavations at Dura-Europos*. 1929-.

THE SYNAGOGUE

As a striking air view (Fig. 178) made in 1932 shows, the city was surrounded by a wall against which the desert sand is now heaped heavily. The main gate of the city was on the west side where the wall faces the desert (at the left side of the photograph). A little distance north of this gate, with the city wall at its back and a street in front, was the synagogue.[6] This building was originally a private residence, and may have served as an informal synagogue even before being rebuilt. Later it was enlarged and made into a formal house of worship, this being under the presbytership of Samuel the priest, as an inscription states, and "in the year 556 which is the second year of Philip Caesar." The date is given in the Seleucid era (p.245) and corresponds to A.D. 245. Some years later this building was replaced by a new synagogue, which seems to have been opened for services in about 253, although at that time it was not yet entirely finished. The completion of the synagogue probably was in 255, when the frescoes were added. This was only a very few years before the destruction of Dura.[7]

One entered the synagogue through a courtyard on the east and came into a room of approximately twenty-five by forty feet in size, along the walls of which were benches for the worshipers. The orientation was toward the west, and in the middle of the west wall was a niche where the Ark of the Law was placed during the services. The walls were adorned from top to bottom with paintings, many of which are well preserved and have been removed to Damascus. Around the niche just mentioned are a representation of the shrine in which the Law was kept, a seven-branched lampstand, an ethrog and lulab on the left, and a picture of Abraham's Sacrifice of Isaac on the right. Abraham stands with his back to the viewer, holding a knife in his right hand. Isaac is bound on the altar, but a hand symbolizes the intervention of God and a ram is waiting by the bush behind Abraham. Other wall paintings include scenes from the life of Moses, the Exodus, the Return of the Ark, Ezekiel's Vision of the Valley of Dry Bones, the Story of Job, and other subjects. These subjects seem to have been chosen to illustrate from a variety of incidents the covenant relationship between God and his people as

[6] A. R. Bellinger, F. E. Brown, A. Perkins, and C. B. Welles, *The Excavations at Dura-Europos conducted by Yale University and the French Academy of Inscriptions and Letters.* Final Report VIII, Part I, *The Synagogue*, by Carl H. Kraeling with contributions by C. C. Torrey, C. B. Welles, and B. Geiger. 1956.

[7] AJA 47 (1943), p.335.

it was established with Abraham and as it was yet to be fulfilled in a future messianic era.[8]

The painting of the Return of the Ark (I Samuel 5f.) shows five lords of the Philistines sending away the ark upon a cart drawn by two oxen, while the Philistine temple stands in the background (Fig. 179). Strewn upon the ground are holy vessels, musical instruments, and the broken images not of Dagon but of the principal Palmyrene gods which were worshiped in Dura.[9] In the picture of the story of Job one of the friends rides to visit the afflicted man, and it is at first surprising to note that the friend is represented in kingly splendor. The explanation is found in a midrash which evidently was familiar to the Jews of Dura and which states explicitly that the three friends of Job were kings. A careful comparison of the Vision of Ezekiel, the Finding of Moses, and the Visit to Job in these paintings, and in corresponding miniature paintings in later Christian illustrated manuscripts, has shown that both must go back to an earlier and common Jewish source.[10] Thus again the dependence of early Christian art upon Jewish art is suggested.

THE CHRISTIAN CHURCH

The Christian church was on the same street as the synagogue but to the south of the main city gate. Like the synagogue, it had once been a private house. Probably this house belonged to a citizen of some means and standing for it was somewhat larger than the average home at Dura. Otherwise, however, it conformed in its original plan exactly to the customary arrangement of a private residence at Dura. From the street one entered by a little vestibule which turned into an inner paved court. Around this court was a series of rooms, while a covered stairway led to the flat roof which

[8] Kraeling, The Synagogue (The Excavations at Dura-Europos, Final Report VIII, Part I), p.357. Rachel Wischnitzer (The Messianic Theme in the Paintings of the Dura Synagogue. 1948) interprets the paintings as animated by the messianic idea of return, restoration, and salvation, and thinks that the Jews of Dura considered themselves descendants of the Lost Ten Tribes. See also Comte du Mesnil du Buisson in L'Illustration. 185 (July 1933), pp.454-457; Marcel Aubert in Gazette des Beaux-Arts. 6e période. 20 (1938), pp.1-24; Sukenik, Ancient Synagogues in Palestine and Greece, pp.82-85; Jacob Leveen, The Hebrew Bible in Art (The Schweich Lectures of the British Academy, 1939). 1944, pp.22-65; James A. Fischer in CBQ 17 (1955), pp.189-195; Kurt Weitzmann in AJA 61 (1957), pp.89f.

[9] Comte du Mesnil du Buisson in Gazette des Beaux-Arts. 6e période. 14 (1935 2e semestre), pp.25-203; Lietzmann, Geschichte der alten Kirche. II, pp.35f. For the temple of the Palmyrene gods in Dura cf. Otto Eissfeldt in Der Alte Orient. 40 (1941), pp.134-139.

[10] Gitta Wodtke in ZNW 34 (1935), pp.51-62.

was over fifteen feet high. When the house was being built, or soon afterward, someone pressed into the plaster a graffito which supplies the date of the building, the year A.D. 232-233.

One of the rooms in the house was used, probably from the first, as a Christian chapel. A few years later two other rooms were thrown together to provide a larger meeting place, accommodating about one hundred people and having an elevated rostrum at one end for the speaker. From this time on the larger part of the building, or perhaps all of it, was employed openly and entirely as a church.[11] Of its Christian use there can be no doubt. Three graffiti read, "One God in heaven," "Remind Christ of Proclus among yourselves" (TON XN IN YMEIN MNHCKECΘ[E . . .]OKΛOY), and "Remind Christ of the humble Siseos" (TON XPIC[12] MNHCKETE CICEON TON TAΠINON), the two latter being requests that Proclus and Siseos should be remembered by the congregation in prayer. The greatest interest attaches to the small room known as the chapel. At its west end is a niche set against the wall with an arched roof resting on pillars. This contains a sunken receptacle which may have been a baptismal font.[13] Like the baptistery in the later church at Kaoussie (pp.540f.), this was too small to have permitted the practice of immersion, and if it was really a baptistery it must be assumed that the rite was performed by affusion. Since the more general custom among the early Christians was that of immersion,[14] other explanations have been sought such as that this was the tomb of a martyr.[15]

The chapel was decorated with wall paintings in a fashion very similar to that of the synagogue.[16] At the back of the niche just mentioned are two paintings, the lower depicting Adam and Eve, the upper showing the Good Shepherd. Adam and Eve stand with the tree between them as in similar representations in the West. The

---

[11] *Preliminary Report of Fifth Season of Work October 1931-March 1932 of the Excavations at Dura-Europos conducted by Yale University and the French Academy of Inscriptions and Letters*, pp.237-252 "The Christian Church" by C. Hopkins.

[12] The abbreviation XPIC is unusual (*Preliminary Report of Fifth Season of Work*, p.285), but for a parallel see M. Avi-Yonah, *Abbreviations in Greek Inscriptions (The Near East, 200 B.C.-A.D. 1100)* in QDAP Supplement to vol. 9 (1940), p.112.

[13] C. Hopkins in *Preliminary Report of Fifth Season of Work*, pp.249-252; Rostovtzeff, *Dura-Europos and its Art*, p.131.

[14] cf. Tertullian, *On Baptism*. 7 (ANF III, p.672); Kenneth Scott Latourette, *A History of the Expansion of Christianity*. I (1937), p.259.

[15] P. V. C. Baur in *Preliminary Report of Fifth Season of Work*, p.255.

[16] *Preliminary Report of Fifth Season of Work*, pp.254-283 "The Paintings in the Christian Chapel" by P. V. C. Baur.

Good Shepherd carries a huge ram on his shoulders in the manner with which we are familiar, but whereas in Rome he usually stands in a symmetrical composition between his sheep, here he stands behind his flock. The placing of these two scenes together evidently is meant to show that through Adam came death but through Christ came salvation.

The south wall of the chapel is broken by two doors which give access to the room. Between these two doors and under an arched niche is a painting of David and Goliath, the two characters being identified by their names which are written on in Greek. Goliath is misspelled Golitha. While this scene could be regarded as representing the familiar theme of deliverance (cf. I Samuel 17:37), it does not otherwise occur frequently in early Christian art. At the west end of the same wall the Samaritan woman is shown grasping a rope with both hands to raise a pail from the mouth of a well. Doubtless for lack of space the figure of Christ does not appear. The coiffure of the Samaritan woman is like that of Julia Soaemias who was killed at the same time as her son Elagabalus in A.D. 222, and confirms a date early in the third century for these paintings. In the upper register on the same wall was another scene now so badly damaged that only the traces of a garden can be recognized.

The pictures on the north wall were placed most conspicuously opposite the two entrances to the chapel. In the lower register is a scene showing a structure which has been called a huge sarcophagus and beside which are at least three women. This has been interpreted as a representation of the women at the sepulcher of Christ (cf. Mark 16:1).[17] The coiffure of the two women whose heads still appear in the painting is the same as that used by Julia Mamaea and Orbiana, the mother and wife respectively of the Emperor Severus Alexander (222-235). In the upper register on the north wall are two scenes. On the right is the Miracle of the Lake (Matthew 14:24-31). In a ship which is plowing through the water are seated several men. They look out to sea with gestures of astonishment at two figures walking on the water. Peter is sinking. Christ is walking toward him with outstretched hand which Peter is about to grasp. Christ is clad in a tunic, but the head and shoulders of the figure are destroyed. The figure of Peter, who is shown

[17] It has also been suggested that the same painting may have been continued on the east wall of the room, and that it may have portrayed the parable of the Wise and Foolish Virgins (Joseph Pijoan in AB 19 [1937], pp.592-595).

with beard and thick curly hair, is well preserved and of much interest since it is the earliest representation of that apostle now known.

To the left of the foregoing scene and with no line of demarcation, is the picture (Fig. 180) of the Healing of the Paralytic (Mark 2:1-12). The sick man lies at full length on his left side on a small bed. The bed has a coverlet with red fringes and the man is dressed in a yellow tunic outlined in brown. Above the bed stands Jesus, clothed in tunic and mantle, and in the act of reaching out his right hand toward the paralytic. The second act in the drama is shown at one side. The sick man, now healed, is walking away. He has turned his bed upside down and is carrying it upon his back, holding it by the crisscross lacing. In the West the Healing of the Paralytic is a subject frequently employed, as we have seen (p.481), but the first part of the scene with Christ standing over the bed is usually omitted and only the sequel shown in which the man walks away with his bed. Also in the West the bed is carried with its legs hanging down. The illustration at Dura is of special interest because the picture of Christ is one of the two oldest such representations now known. The almost destroyed painting of Christ in the Catacomb of Priscilla at Rome (pp.466f. and Fig. 160) probably belongs, as we have seen, to the middle of the second century. The painting at Dura is dated even more definitely in the first part of the third century. In both pictures Christ is shown as a young and beardless man with short hair and wearing the ordinary costume of the day. These and similar portrayals are the earliest type of Christ as far as is now known in early Christian art.[18] Later in the third century Christ appears still as youthful but with long, curly hair, and from the fourth century on the more familiar bearded type appears.[19]

Such was the gathering place of the Christians in Dura and similar to this, doubtless, were many other house churches throughout the Roman Empire during the early centuries of Christianity's life.

2. EARLY CHURCHES AT ROME

AT THE same time that the Christians of Dura were meeting in the house church just described, many Christians in Rome were assem-

[18] cf. L. von Sybel, *Christliche Antike.* i, pp.225, 229, 233.
[19] On the representation of Christ in early Christian art see Johannes Kollwitz, *Das Christusbild des dritten Jahrhunderts.* 1953; and in KRAC iii, cols. 1-24.

bling in private buildings which had been transferred to the church for the purpose of public worship. In Rome almost all of these later disappeared beneath new buildings by which they were replaced, but for centuries each of these churches continued to be designated by the name or *titulus* of its former owner and founder. For this reason they are called "title churches." Of the twenty-five churches which are known to have had this designation, eighteen are earlier than Constantine and the majority of these probably go back at least as far as to the middle of the third century or to around the time of the Dura house church.[1]

SAN CLEMENTE

As an example of one of these title churches in Rome we may turn to San Clemente, which according to tradition was built on the site originally occupied by the house of Clement I who suffered martyrdom around A.D. 100. San Clemente is now on the modern Via di San Giovanni, running from the Colosseum to the Lateran, but once stood in the middle of an *insula* or block of buildings, fronting on a public road and with more distant streets on the other three sides. From the Via di San Giovanni one descends a few steps to the level of the present church. This is a structure which was consecrated in 1108 by Pope Paschal II and has been restored frequently since. It is a building oriented on an east-west axis, with a nave ending in a semicircular apse, and flanked by two side aisles likewise terminating in apses. In front is an atrium of oblong shape, surrounded by colonnaded porticoes.

Beneath this church Prior Mulhooly (d.1880) discovered in 1852 a second and older basilica. Like the church above, it was divided by rows of columns into a nave and two aisles. The nave ended in an apse, and in front of the church was an atrium. This lower church was a grander structure than the building afterward superimposed, its nave being as wide as the upper church's nave and right aisle combined. This lower church was probably constructed around A.D. 390.

In turn, beneath this church are the remains of still older Roman buildings. The Roman structure under the main section of the lower church was a rectangular edifice, constructed of heavy tufa blocks, and probably was a part of some public building. It is believed to date from the end of the first or beginning of the second century.

[1] Lietzmann, *Geschichte der alten Kirche.* II, p.256.

Behind this public building and separated from it only by a narrow passage, a large private house was built. The latter is to be dated probably not before the middle of the second century. At a later time, perhaps in the second quarter of the third century, the inner courtyard of this house was transformed into a Mithraeum, or chapel in which Mithras was worshiped.[2]

In approximately the third quarter of the third century, a new brick house was erected above the tufa edifice. It was a large building and contained an extensive hall on the ground floor. This hall was divided by rows of supports in a longitudinal direction, and opened in a series of wide apertures on both sides onto the exterior level. Later this last house was transformed into the existing lower basilica, in which a portion of the adjoining building, where the Mithraeum had been, was also incorporated. This rebuilding involved piercing the west wall of the house with the large hall and constructing an apse which projected into the neighboring house, adding a narthex and atrium at the east end, and erecting two rows of columns in the interior, thus making a nave and two aisles.

The complicated architectural history just outlined is of much interest because it enables us to show clearly that the fourth-century basilica of San Clemente was preceded by a third-century house in which there was a large ground-floor hall appropriate for public gatherings. It is very probable, therefore, that the third-century building was the meeting place of the Christian community before the lower basilica came into being. Whether the house and hall were constructed by the Christians from the very beginning or only purchased by them to serve as a place of meeting, remains uncertain. But at any rate in this hall, which evidently was arranged for relatively large Christian gatherings, we see an important transitional stage between the simple homes in which the earlier believers met and the large basilicas in which the later Christians were privileged to worship.[3]

[2] At Ostia, the remains of seven such Mithraea have been found (Baedeker, *Rome.* 16th ed., p.540).

[3] Richard Krautheimer, *Corpus Basilicarum Christianarum Romae.* I, 2 (1937), pp.117-136; E. Junyent, *Il titolo di San Clemente in Roma.* 1932, p.23, Fig. 1; Louis Nolan, *The Basilica of San Clemente in Rome.* 4th ed. 1934.

3. YEARS OF PERSECUTION AND
YEARS OF PEACE

IN THE same period in which the hall church just described was in use in Rome, many other buildings were probably being erected throughout the empire for Christian assembly. Christianity underwent bitter persecutions in the time of Decius (A.D. 250) and Valerian (A.D. 257-258), but in A.D. 261 the Emperor Gallienus granted toleration in an edict which permitted the Christians again to use their places of worship and their cemeteries and provided that no one should molest them.[1] The final and terrible persecution of Diocletian (A.D. 303) was yet to come, but in the more than forty years intervening Christianity attracted great masses of people, and for their accommodation in services of worship it was necessary to erect buildings specifically planned as churches. This situation is explicitly indicated by Eusebius in the following words: "But how can anyone describe those vast assemblies, and the multitude that crowded together in every city, and the famous gatherings in the houses of prayer; by reason of which not being satisfied with the ancient buildings they erected from the foundation large churches in all the cities?"[2] In connection with an isolated case of martyrdom which took place at this same time, Eusebius incidentally mentions "the church" at Caesarea.[3]

DIOCLETIAN

Over these churches which sprang up during the relatively peaceful last four decades of the third century, a devastating storm was soon to break. This was the great persecution of Diocletian, who ruled in the East as Augustus, Galerius Caesar being his subordinate colleague and Nicomedia his capital. It was largely at the instigation of Galerius that the blow was planned. At dawn on February 23, 303, officers appeared before the Christian church in Nicomedia. The gates were forced open, the church pillaged and the Bibles burned. The church was situated on rising ground within view of the imperial palace where Diocletian and Galerius were standing, watching. Galerius wished to have the building set on fire, but Diocletian feared that the fire might spread to other parts of the city, so

---

[1] Eusebius, *Ch. Hist.* VII, xiii (cf. above p.484 n.1).
[2] *Ch. Hist.* VIII, i, 5.
[3] *Ch. Hist.* VII, xv, 4.

the Praetorian Guards were sent with axes and other instruments of iron, "and having been let loose everywhere, they in a few hours levelled that very lofty edifice to the ground."[4] On the next day an edict went out which was published everywhere. It not only deprived the Christians of all legal rights and called for the burning of the Scriptures but also commanded that the churches should be levelled to the ground.[5] Eusebius was living in Caesarea at this time and gives an eyewitness account of the persecution as it was carried out in Palestine. "We saw with our own eyes the houses of prayer thrown down to the very foundations,"[6] he says, and goes on to tell of the burning of Bibles and the torturing and slaying of martyrs.[7]

How many churches were destroyed before Galerius terminated the persecutions with an edict signed on his deathbed we do not know. Doubtless they were many. If, perchance, some did not fall before the storm they were ultimately replaced by later structures so that they, too, disappeared from sight. Of all the church buildings whose existence we infer in the latter years of the third century, scarcely a trace now survives.[8]

CONSTANTINE

It is first from the time of the Emperor Constantine and the true peace of the church that abundant and material evidence remains concerning early Christian churches. When Constantine and his eastern colleague, Licinius, issued the Edict of Milan in A.D. 313, full legal standing was granted to Christianity, and all confiscated church buildings and properties were returned. The churches which had been destroyed were now rebuilt and new ones were erected, all on a grander scale than had been known hitherto. "We saw," says Eusebius, "every place which shortly before had been desolated by the impieties of the tyrants reviving as if from a long and death-fraught pestilence, and temples again rising from their foundations

[4] This account is given by Lactantius, who was a teacher of rhetoric in Nicomedia at this time and therefore an eyewitness. It is found in his book entitled *Of the Manner in Which the Persecutors Died* (12), in which he shows the evil end to which all of the emperors came, from Nero on, who persecuted the Christians.

[5] Lactantius, *Of the Manner in Which the Persecutors Died*. 13; Eusebius, *Ch. Hist.* VIII, ii, 4 = *Martyrs of Palestine*, Intro.

[6] *Ch. Hist.* VIII, ii, 1.

[7] *Martyrs of Palestine* (a separate work, later appended to Bk. VIII of the *Church History*).

[8] Lietzmann, *Geschichte der alten Kirche*. III (1938), p.43.

to an immense height, and receiving a splendor far greater than that of the old ones which had been destroyed."[9]

THE CATHEDRAL AT TYRE

On the rubbish-covered site of an earlier church at Tyre, a new and elegant cathedral was erected, at the dedication of which around A.D. 316 Eusebius himself delivered an oration. From this address we can gain some idea of the church. The area in which it stood was enclosed by a wall and the main entrance was through a vestibule on the east. Between the outer entrance and the church building proper was a colonnaded court open to the sky with a fountain in the middle. Triple doors gave access to the church itself, which was paved with marble and roofed with cedar. Adjacent to the church were additional rooms and buildings, probably including a baptistery.[10]

THE "BASILICA"

The church at Tyre was evidently built on the plan characteristic of most of the great churches of the fourth and fifth centuries and to which the name basilica is given. The word "basilica" refers literally to a kingly hall,[11] and was therefore applied to a building of grandeur, but came to have a meaning almost as broad as our simple word, hall. Greek and Roman law courts, markets, and meeting halls all were occasionally known by this term basilica (cf. p.376).[12] But the private houses of the Greeks and Romans[13] and the synagogues of the Jews[14] also often exhibited the rectangular, colonnaded form which is the chief characteristic of the basilica and, as we have seen, it is most probably out of such backgrounds that Christian meeting places were developed.[15]

In its most distinctive Christian development the basilica had some or all of the following features. It might stand, as at Tyre, in an area surrounded by a wall or *peribolos*. Also as at Tyre, the entrance was often through a colonnaded court or *atrium*, which

---

[9] *Ch. Hist.* x, ii, 1.

[10] *Ch. Hist.* x, iv, 37-45.   [11] βασιλική i.e. στοά.

[12] Sartell Prentice, *The Heritage of the Cathedral.* 1936, pp.19-28.

[13] Lowrie, *Monuments of the Early Church*, pp.97-101.

[14] Kohl and Watzinger, *Antike Synagogen in Galiläa*, p.219.

[15] For the basilica see H. Leclercq in DACL II, cols. 525-602; E. Langlotz and Fr. W. Deichmann in KRAC I, cols. 1225-1259; *Kunst-Chronik* (Zentralinstitut für Kunstgeschichte). 4 (1951), pp.97-121; L. H. Vincent in *Quantulacumque*, pp.55-70; J. G. Davies, *The Origin and Development of Early Christian Church Architecture.* 1953; cf. H. R. Willoughby in *Religion in Life.* Summer 1953, pp.473-475.

178. Air View of Dura-Europos

179. The Ark Reclaimed from the Philistines

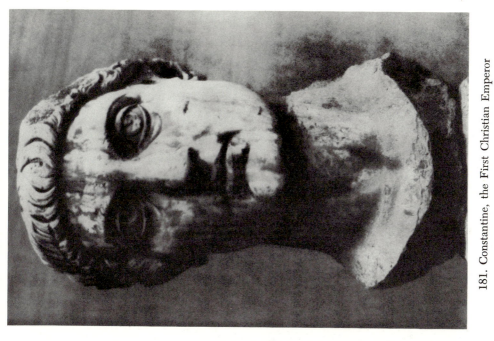

181. Constantine, the First Christian Emperor

180. The Healing of the Paralytic

182. San Pietro in Vaticano, Rome

183. Canopy over the Altar, San Pietro

184. San Paolo fuori le Mura, Rome

185. San Paolo fuori le Mura, Interior

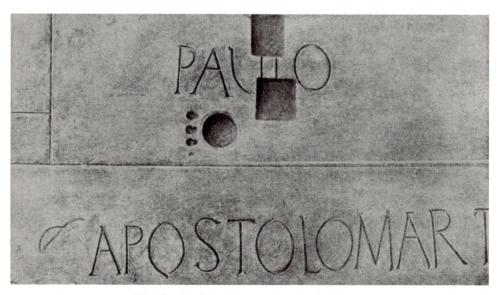

186. The Marble Slab over the Tomb of Paul

187. Apse Mosaic in Santa Pudenziana

188. The Taking of Jericho

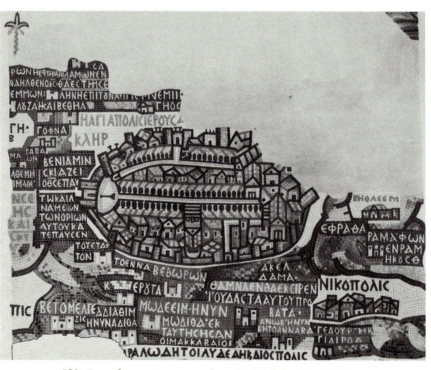

189. Jerusalem as Represented on the Madeba Mosaic Map

190. The Church of the Holy Sepulcher, Jerusalem

191. The Church of the Nativity, Bethlehem

192. Interior of the Church of the Nativity

193. Early Mosaic in the Church of the Nativity

195. Mosaic in the Church of the Prophets,
Apostles and Martyrs at Gerasa

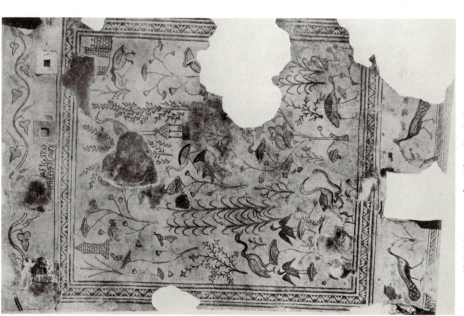

194. Mosaic in the Church of the Loaves
and Fishes at et-Tabgha

196. Air View of the Ruins of the Church at Kaoussie

197. Ruins of the Martyrion at Seleucia Pieria

198. Mosaic in the Martyrion at Seleucia Pieria

199. The West Door of the Church of St. Simeon Stylites

201. A Flask of St. Menas

202. The Baptistery at the Church of St. Menas

200. The Crypt in the Church of St. Menas

203. The Church of Hagia Sophia at Istanbul

204. Interior of Hagia Sophia

protected the worshipers from the noise of the streets and contained the fountain (*cantharus*) where the hands were washed symbolically before entering.[16] The basilica proper was a long, rectangular hall, which might be entered through a vestibule or *narthex*. The main, longitudinal area within the basilica was known as the *nave*, a word probably derived from the Latin word for ship (*navis*), to which the church was often likened. On each side of the nave were one or two rows of columns, which formed side aisles. These aisles had relatively low roofs, while the roof of the nave was much higher. The part of the nave which rises clear of the lower roofs of the side aisles is known as the *clerestory* and its walls were pierced with windows for lighting the central part of the basilica's interior. The nave and aisles were the parts occupied by the laity, and movable seats or benches were presumably provided for them here. At its far end the nave opened into the *apse*, which was a semicircular recess, usually covered by a half dome. Between the nave and apse there might be a *transept* or cross aisle. If the latter projected beyond the side aisles it gave the church the form of a cross. The great arch above the half dome of the apse is known as the triumphal arch, and where there was a transept another triumphal arch might separate it from the nave. The part of the church formed by the transept and apse was reserved for the clergy and might be called the *presbyterium*. Low screens sometimes separated it from the rest of the church. They were known in Latin as *cancelli* and later the presbyterium itself was called the *chancel*. There might also be a row of columns standing in front of the presbyterium for adornment. The altar, usually a relatively simple table of wood or stone, stood in the center of the transept or in the apse. If the church was built above the grave of a martyr the altar if possible was placed directly above the holy tomb, and in case this lay at some depth beneath the ground was connected with it by a vertical shaft. To the chamber around the tomb, and the shaft connecting it with the altar, the name *confessio* is applied. The altar might be further dignified by a *ciborium*, or roof erected over it on four columns. The clergy sat behind the altar, on benches running around the wall of the semicircular apse. In the center and raised above the presbyters' seats was the *cathedra*, or official chair in which the bishop sat and from which he preached.[17] An *ambon*

16 Lowrie, *Monuments of the Early Church*, p.179.
17 The famous statue of Hippolytus (d. after A.D. 235), which was probably made

or pulpit in the nave was used for the scripture reading, and sometimes the sermon was preached from it, too, in order for the speaker
to be nearer the people. The baptistery was usually a small, separate
building in the center of which was a round or octagonal pool (*fons*
or *piscina*), entered by a flight of steps, for the act of immersion.[18]
Other structures, too, might be grouped around the church, including chapels, hospices, baths, hospitals, or schools.

In exterior appearance the basilica ordinarily was very plain,
although it was decorated occasionally with mosaic on the façade
or, as in Syria, was developed impressively with single and double
towers. Within, however, the basilica was often richly adorned. A
marble incrustation (*opus sectile*) was frequently applied to the
lower portion of the walls, while on the upper walls of the nave,
on the triumphal arch, and in the half dome of the apse were often
placed the most beautiful representations in mosaic. This was fitting,
since the essential purpose of the basilica was fulfilled in its interior.
There the congregation felt itself a unity, and the thoughts of all
were led forward to the place where the Lord's table stood and
where the gospel was preached.

A mention of such a basilica and a description of the worship
of the Christians within it, is found in the *Apostolic Constitutions*,
written about A.D. 380. It compares the church to a ship and reads
in part as follows:

"Let the building be long, with its head to the east,[19] with its vestries
on both sides at the east end, and so it will be like a ship. In the middle
let the bishop's throne be placed, and on each side of him let the presby-
tery sit down; and let the deacons stand near at hand, with closely girt
garments, for they are like the mariners and managers of the ship. In
accordance with their arrangement, let the laity sit on the other side,
with all quietness and good order. And let the women sit by themselves,
they also keeping silence. In the middle, let the reader stand upon some
high place: let him read the books of Moses . . . and the Epistles of Paul
. . . and the Gospels. . . . In the next place, let the presbyters one by one,
not all together, exhort the people, and the bishop in the last place, as
being the commander. Let the porters stand at the entrances of the men
and give heed to them, while the deaconesses stand at those of the

---

soon after his death and is now in the Lateran Museum, shows this Roman church
leader seated upon such a chair.
    [18] H. Leclercq in DACL II, cols. 382-469; F. W. Deichmann in KRAC I, cols. 1157-
1167.
    [19] This rule calling for the orientation of the apse toward the east, was frequently
but by no means always followed.

women, like shipmen. . . . But if anyone be found sitting out of his place, let him be rebuked by the deacon, as a manager of the foreship, and removed into the place proper for him; for the church is not only like a ship, but also like a sheepfold. For as the shepherds place all the brute creatures distinctly . . . so is it to be in the church. Let the young men sit by themselves, if there be a place for them, but if not let them stand upright. Let those already advanced in years sit in order and let the children stand beside their mothers and fathers. Let the younger women also sit by themselves if there be a place for them but if not let them stand behind the elder women. Let those women who are married and have children be placed by themselves, while the virgins and the widows and the elderwomen stand or sit before all the rest. Let the deacon be the disposer of the places, that every one of those that comes in may go to his proper place and not sit at the entrance. In like manner let the deacon oversee the people that nobody may whisper nor slumber nor laugh nor nod, for all ought in the church to stand wisely and soberly and attentively, having their attention fixed upon the word of the Lord. After this, let all rise up with one consent and looking towards the east, after the catechumens and penitents are gone out, pray to God eastward. . . . As to the deacons, after the prayer is over, let some of them attend upon the oblation of the eucharist, ministering to the Lord's body with fear. Let others of them watch the multitude and keep them silent. But let that deacon who is at the high priest's hand say to the people, Let no one have any quarrel against another; let no one come in hypocrisy. Then let the men give the men, and the women give the women, the Lord's kiss. . . . After this let the deacon pray for the whole church, for the whole world. . . . Let the bishop pray for the people. . . . After this let the sacrifice follow, the people standing and praying silently; and when the oblation has been made, let every rank by itself partake of the Lord's body and precious blood in order, and approach with reverence and holy fear, as to the body of their king. Let the women approach with their heads covered, as is becoming the order of women; but let the door be watched, lest any unbeliever, or one not yet initiated, come in."[20]

4. CHURCHES IN ROME

THE BASILICAS OF CONSTANTINE

THE most famous basilicas of the fourth century were built by Constantine, who after his victory over Licinius and the death of the latter in A.D. 324 and until his own death in A.D. 337 was sole ruler of the Roman Empire. His political and military position was so secure that he could personally devote much time and interest to

[20] II, 57 (ANF VII, pp.421f.); cf. E. H. Short, *A History of Religious Architecture.* 1936, p.65.

religious matters, including the building of great churches. A letter which he directed at this time to all the bishops in the various provinces has been preserved by Eusebius in which the emperor urged "all to be zealous in their attention to the buildings of the churches, and either to repair or enlarge those which at present exist, or, in cases of necessity, to erect new ones."[1] The bishops were authorized to request whatever was needful for the work from the provincial governors, to whom corresponding instructions were sent. "In every province," states Eusebius, "he [Constantine] raised new churches on a far more imposing scale than those which had existed before his time."[2] The personal appearance of this benefactor of early Christianity is seen in Fig. 181, this being the head of a colossal statue which once stood in the Basilica of Constantine in the Roman Forum.

A list of the churches which Constantine erected in Rome is given in the Liber Pontificalis. This list forms a part of the biography of Sylvester who was pope (314-335) at the time of Constantine's reign. Since Sylvester was the thirty-fourth Head of the Roman Church, his biography constitutes Chapter 34 of the Liber Pontificalis. While the text of the Liber Pontificalis dates from the seventh century (p.382 n.20), the notices which are numerous from the time of Sylvester on, concerning churches built or repaired and gifts offered for them, must often have been copied directly from memoranda and records in the papal archives. In particular the list of Constantine's churches and donations gives evidence of genuineness although there is some corruption in the text, as for example where the proper names occasionally become unintelligible.[3]

SAN PIETRO IN VATICANO

The holiest sites upon which churches could be erected at Rome were the graves of Peter and Paul, and the Liber Pontificalis records that Constantine founded basilicas at both of these places. The location of the graves at the Vatican and on the Ostian Way has been discussed already, and also the probable temporary transfer of the remains to Catacumbas in A.D. 258 (pp.382-384, 471-474). When peace came to the church, suitable memorials could be erected in

---

[1] *Life of Constantine.* II, 46.

[2] *ibid.*, III, 47. For the materials in Eusebius relative to the church buildings of Constantine see Ludwig Voelkl in RAC 29 (1953), pp.49-66.

[3] LLP pp.xvii-xviii.

the form of fine basilicas. Concerning the first of these two buildings the Liber Pontificalis records:

"At the same time Constantine Augustus built by the request of Silvester, the bishop, the basilica of blessed Peter, the apostle, in the shrine of Apollo, and laid there the coffin with the body of the holy Peter; the coffin itself he enclosed on all sides with bronze, which is unchangeable: at the head 5 feet, at the feet 5 feet, at the right side 5 feet, at the left side 5 feet, underneath 5 feet and overhead 5 feet: thus he enclosed the body of blessed Peter, the apostle, and laid it away.

"And above he set porphyry columns for adornment and other spiral columns which he brought from Greece.

"He made also a vaulted roof in the basilica, gleaming with polished gold, and over the body of the blessed Peter, above the bronze which enclosed it, he set a cross of purest gold weighing 150 lbs. . . . and upon it were inscribed these words: 'CONSTANTINE AUGUSTUS AND HELENA AUGUSTA THIS HOUSE SHINING WITH LIKE ROYAL SPLENDOR A COURT SURROUNDS,' inscribed in enamelled letters upon the cross."

A list follows of the precious vessels and revenues which Constantine bestowed upon the church.[4]

Constantine's basilica stood until it was destroyed by the popes of the Renaissance to make way for the present Church of St. Peter. In those intervening centuries it was altered somewhat and much added to, but seems basically to have preserved its original structure. Thus, while little now remains of Constantine's original church its essential character can be surmised from sketches and descriptions of the building as it stood in the Middle Ages. A flight of steps led up to a propylaeum which gave access to a large atrium. This court was surrounded by colonnades and had a fountain in the center. The basilica was entered by five doors and divided into nave and two aisles on either side. The columns in the church had been taken from ancient monuments and their bases, shafts, and capitals were varied in size and style. The Constantinian origin of the building was shown plainly when the apse was finally demolished, for the emperor's stamp was on its bricks. The mosaic which at that time still was on the triumphal arch, showing Constantine offering a model of the church to Christ, probably also dated from the original basilica.[5] On the arch, Constantine's inscription addressed to Christ read: "Because, led by thee, the world rises triumphant to the stars, Constantine, victorious, built this hall for thee."[6]

[4] LLP pp.53f.
[5] A. L. Frothingham, *The Monuments of Christian Rome*. 1908, pp.25-27.
[6] E. Diehl, *Inscriptiones latinae christianae veteres.* I (1925), No.1752.

In the course of the fourth and fifth centuries a baptistery was added in the right arm of the transept, the atrium was paved, a mosaic was placed on the façade[7] and the church was connected with Hadrian's mausoleum and bridge by an arcaded boulevard. Many subsidiary buildings grew up around the basilica and eventually an entire suburb surrounded it. In the barbarian invasions Alaric king of the Goths (410) and Genseric king of the Vandals (455) ordered that the Church of St. Peter should be spared, and it also escaped damage in the siege by the Lombards (756). But in the Saracen invasion in 846 it suffered damage and, after that, Pope Leo IV (847-855) built for its protection the so-called Leonine Wall around the basilica and the Vatican hill.

By the time of Pope Nicholas V (1447-1455) Constantine's basilica was leaning badly to one side and generally falling into ruin. It was decided that the old church would have to be torn down and a new one built upon its site. The new structure was designed by Bramante and the first stone laid in 1506. The work was carried forward in following years under the direction of Raphael (1514) and Michelangelo (1546). Dedication was in 1626.

As it stands today the Basilica di San Pietro in Vaticano is the largest church in the world. Its interior is 609 feet in length and its area is about 163,200 square feet. The great dome, which is its crowning glory, is 138 feet in diameter and rises to a height of 405 feet. At an early time the subterranean tomb of Peter was made inaccessible to protect it from marauders and when the old basilica was demolished and the new one built the tomb was not molested. Bramante's plan, indeed, called for moving the tomb in order to give the new church a different orientation, but Pope Julius II (1503-1513) refused to allow this to be done. In 1594, when the present high altar was being built by Pope Clement VIII, it is said that the bottom of the shaft leading to the grave was laid open but that the pope immediately ordered the opening to be filled up again.[8] Through one unblocked place, Hartmann Grisar is said to have caught a glimpse, in 1895, of an ancient marble slab, then broken in half, but presumably still in place over the tomb.[9]

[7] Repair or decoration of the basilica by Leo I (440-461) is mentioned in the Liber Pontificalis (see below p.517) and the mosaic on the façade is known to have borne a dedicatory inscription concerning a restoration by the praetorian prefect Marinianus and his wife Anastasia at Leo's request.

[8] LLP p.53 n.3.

[9] E. Pucci in EB XXIII, p.5.

In front of the church, in the center of the piazza, stands the great obelisk which Caligula brought from Heliopolis to adorn the *spina* of his Circus. The presumed original location of the obelisk in the Circus is still marked by a stone in the small Piazza del Circo Neroniano, just south of St. Peter's. The obelisk was moved to its present site by Xystus V in 1586. The two semicircular colonnades which now beautify the sides of the elliptical piazza were erected by Bernini in 1657-1663 (Fig. 182).

Bernini also designed (1633) the imposing *baldacchino* or bronze canopy which rises to a height of 95 feet over the high altar in St. Peter's. It will be remembered (p.511) that above the tomb of Peter, Constantine set porphyry columns and other spiral columns. Apparently the porphyry columns supported the ciborium above the altar, while the spiral columns formed a colonnade separating the *confessio* from the nave. Several of the spiral columns still exist, some now adorning the upper niches in the four huge piers that support the dome of St. Peter's, and one being preserved in the side chapel known as the Cappella della Pieta. These served Bernini as models for the great gilded spiral columns which support the present ciborium over the high altar (Fig. 183).

In 1940 by the command of Pope Pius XII excavations were undertaken beneath the Church of St. Peter and continued for ten years.[10] Beneath the main part of the church and under its crypts was found a double row of mausoleums, part of the cemetery of a well-to-do class of people. Almost all of the mausoleums were originally vaulted, but most of the vaults were destroyed in the building of Constantine's basilica, the walls of which were set down right in the midst of this cemetery. While the mausoleums were in use mainly from around A.D. 100 to the fourth century, the region was certainly a place of burial even before A.D. 100 as was shown by the ossuaries in which bones from preceding tombs were collected. It is also clear that the cemetery was of pagan origin, although there are a few

---

[10] B. M. Apollonj Ghetti, A. Ferrua, E. Josi, E. Kirschbaum, L. Kaas, and C. Serafini, *Esplorazioni sotto la Confessione di San Pietro in Vaticano, eseguite negli anni 1940-1949.* 2 vols. 1951; Roger T. O'Callaghan in BA 12 (1949), pp.1-23; 16 (1953), pp.70-87; L. E. Hudec in JBR 20 (1952), pp.13-18; Oscar Cullmann, *Petrus, Jünger, Apostel, Märtyrer.* 1952, pp.152-169; Armin von Gerkan in ZNW 44 (1952/53), pp.196-205; J. Gwyn Griffiths in HJ 55 (1956-57), pp.140-149, 285f.; Jocelyn Toynbee in HJ 55 (1956-57), pp.284f.; Jocelyn Toynbee and John Ward Perkins, *The Shrine of St. Peter and the Vatican Excavations.* 1956; Theodor Klauser, *Die römische Petrustradition im Lichte der neuen Ausgrabungen unter der Peterskirche.* 1956; cf. J. M. C. Toynbee in AJA 62 (1958), pp.126-129.

Christian burials toward the latter part of the time of its use. In the case of one mausoleum, although all the sarcophagi it contained probably belonged to one family, the earliest revealed motifs from an Egyptian cult, a later one showed a Dionysian scene, and the latest had Christian motifs. In the area directly beneath the high altar of the church above, was an open area where no mausoleums were ever built. There were burials here, however, one tomb having a tile stamped with a date in the time of Vespasian (A.D. 69-79). Yet these burials left free one particular spot. Across the edge of this spot a red-colored wall was built at about A.D. 160. The date is determined by the bricks of a drainage channel connected with the wall, on several of which are the names of Aurelius Caesar and his wife Faustina Augusta. Since the reference is to Marcus Aurelius before he became emperor (161-180), the date stated above is indicated. In this wall are what the excavators describe as three niches, one above the other. The lowest is very roughly finished, the two above form a sort of shrine which was marked by two marble columns standing on a travertine base and supporting a slab of travertine fixed into the red wall. In loose earth under the lowest niche were some human bones, but since with them were also coins of the second and third centuries it is difficult to assume that these are the remains of Peter. But the date of the niche with its columns seems well established at around A.D. 160, and since this was the exact spot around which Constantine's basilica as well as the present church were built, it would seem probable that this niche is the very "trophy" mentioned by Caius about A.D. 200.[11]

No remains of the Circus of Nero were found in these excavations, making untenable the former supposition that the basilica of Constantine was in part built directly upon the walls of that structure.[12]

---

[11] If the "trophy" was built about A.D. 160 it would probably have been under Anicetus (c.154-c.165), but of this the Liber Pontificalis says nothing (LLP pp.15f.), attributing the building and adorning of "the sepulchral monument of the blessed Peter" to Anacletus instead (LLP p.9), the successor of Clement. It has been suggested that the desire to assign a greater antiquity to events helped produce the probable confusion between the two names in the later tradition (O'Callaghan in BA 16 [1953], pp.80f.).

[12] It is still possible that the circus occupied this location just south of St. Peter's, as the former location of the obelisk (see above p.513) suggests, but in this case the circus must have been a rather simple structure architecturally, perhaps built mostly of wood which perished in the course of time. See Gavin Townend in AJA 62 (1958), pp.216-218. Cullmann (*Petrus*, pp.165f.) thinks that the niches found in the excavations are indeed the "trophy" of Caius, but suggests that the spot thus marked was not that of the grave but of the place of martyrdom of Peter. Since that place, however, was presumably within the Circus of Nero, the suggestion seems unlikely.

But in a mausoleum at the eastern end of the double row of excavated mausoleums, was an extremely important inscription. Here was recorded part of the will and testament of a certain C. Popilius Heraclea, whose estate was bequeathed to his heirs with the understanding that his mausoleum was to be erected *in Vaticano ad Circum juxta monumentum Ulpii Narcisii,* "in the Vatican near the Circus beside the monument of Ulpius Narcissus." This is proof that the famous circus, without doubt that of Caligula and of Nero, was near at hand.

In another of the mausoleums, that of the Valerii, there was recently found the drawing of the head of an old man, represented as bald, furrowed of brow, and with pointed beard. The accompanying inscription has been read as, *Petrus roga Christus Iesus pro sanctis hominibus Chrestianis ad corpus tuum sepultis,* meaning "Peter, pray Christ Jesus for the holy Christian men buried near your body." Since the drawing and inscription had been partly covered by a wall belonging to Constantine's basilica, they must be earlier than the erection of that church and may date from around A.D. 280. It is held by some that this makes unlikely the theory of a temporary removal of the bones of Peter to the cemetery *ad Catacumbas,* but if as we have surmised they were brought back to the Vatican as soon as Valerian's brief persecution was terminated this would not be a difficulty.[13]

The excavations, then, have shown that Nero's Circus was definitely in this region, have revealed a sort of simple shrine which may have been the "trophy" mentioned by Caius, have brought to light an inscription which, if properly read, attests early belief that Peter was buried in the vicinity, and have given much knowledge of the pagan cemetery which Constantine had to invade for the construction of his basilica. All of these facts support the belief that the tomb of the apostle Peter was indeed at this place.[14]

[13] O'Callaghan in BA 16 (1953), pp.82f.; Toynbee and Perkins, *The Shrine of St. Peter and the Vatican Excavations,* p.14.

[14] On the slope of the Janiculum hill in Rome is the Church of San Pietro in Montorio, and in the court of the adjoining convent is the Tempietto, a small circular building erected about 1500 from plans by Bramante, which is also said to mark the place of the martyrdom of Peter. The probable explanation of this variant tradition is as follows. In some of the accounts of the death of Peter it was stated that the place was *inter duas metas.* The *meta* was the turning post at each end of the *spina* in a circus, and this meant that Peter was crucified midway between the two turning posts, that is at the middle of the *spina. Meta* also means pyramid, however, and in Rome two pyramids were conspicuous, that in the Vatican district by the Church of Santa Maria Traspontina, called Meta Romuli, and the pyramid of Cestius by the

SAN PAOLO FUORI LE MURA

The Liber Pontificalis states that the basilica over the grave of Paul, now known as San Paolo fuori le Mura, was also founded by Constantine. One manuscript, however, adds the name of his son, the Emperor Constantius (337-361), who probably carried this church to completion. The statement in the Liber Pontificalis is: "At the same time Constantine Augustus and Lord Constantius Augustus built the basilica of blessed Paul, the apostle, at the bidding of Silvester the bishop, and laid his body away there in bronze and enclosed it, as he did the body of the blessed Peter. . . . Moreover he placed a golden cross over the tomb of blessed Paul, the apostle, weighing 150 lbs." Gifts and revenues devoted to the church also are listed, as in the case of the basilica of St. Peter.[15]

The Constantinian basilica of St. Paul was only a small structure. This seems surprising in comparison with the large church built in honor of Peter, but the explanation is to be found in the character of the available site. The grave of Paul lay between the Via Ostiensis and another small paved street, the Via Valentiniana, which joined it at a sharp angle somewhat to the south. Only the area in the angle between these two streets was available for the basilica, unless the streets were to be destroyed. Also, the site was unfavorable because it stood far distant from the city residences of most of the Christians and because it was in a low-lying area frequently overflowed by the Tiber River. Nevertheless the basilica was erected here. Certainly the location was not invented, but only accepted because it was the actual place of Paul's grave.[16]

In 384 the three emperors, Valentinian II, Theodosius I the Great, and his son Arcadius, issued a decree which moved the inconvenient side street far enough away so that space was gained to accommodate a truly monumental church, and in 386 a letter to Sallust, the prefect of Rome, ordered the construction of the new basilica. The work was completed under the Emperor Honorius (395-423) the

---

Porta San Paolo, known as Meta Remi. So this spot on the Janiculum was chosen because it was midway between the pyramid of Romulus and the pyramid of Remus! These relationships may be seen plainly on the *Forma Urbis Romae Imperatorum Aetate*, delineaverunt Iosephus Lugli et Italus Gismondi (Istituto Geografico de Agostini-Novara). 1949; cf. Rodolfo Lanciani, *Pagan and Christian Rome*. 1892, p.128; Arthur S. Barnes, *St. Peter in Rome and His Tomb on the Vatican Hill*. 1900, p.97.

[15] LLP pp.57f.
[16] Lietzmann, *Petrus und Paulus in Rom*, pp.220f.

younger son of Theodosius, and dedicated by Pope Siricius (384-399), the latter's name and the date 390 still existing on a column of the church.[17] The orientation of the new structure was the reverse of the old, so that the main entrance was from the bank of the Tiber and the apse faced to the east. The church extended across the disused Via Valentiniana and was so much greater than the Constantinian basilica that its transept alone was larger than the entire old church. It was so arranged, however, that the grave of Paul was not changed and the altar and *confessio* remained on their original site.

The basilica of the three emperors stood until destroyed by a great fire in 1823. It was probably damaged by Genseric and the Vandals in 455 and may have been struck by lightning about the same time, since the Liber Pontificalis says that the roof was rebuilt "after the fire from God" by Pope Leo I the Great (440-461): "He replaced all the consecrated silver vessels in all the parish churches after the Vandal devastation. . . . He repaired the basilica of blessed Peter,[18] the apostle, and restored the vaulting of blessed Paul after the fire from God."[19]

Pope Symmachus (498-514) is credited with extensive works of restoration and beautification: "Also in the church of blessed Paul, the apostle, he rebuilt the apse of the basilica, which was falling into ruin, and he embellished it with a picture behind the confession and he made a vaulting and a transept; and over the confession he erected a silver image of the Saviour and the 12 apostles, which weighed 120 lbs.; and before the doors of the basilica he rebuilt steps into the atrium and a fountain; and behind the apse he brought down water and built there a bath from the foundation."[20] Although the Lombards devastated the environs of Rome during the siege of 756, they spared St. Paul's. The Saracens did more damage and may even have rifled the tomb of the apostle Paul. Afterward Pope John VIII (872-882) followed the example of Leo IV at the Vatican (p.512) and surrounded the basilica of St. Paul and the suburb that had grown up around it with a strong battlemented wall. He called the suburb Johannipolis.

Immediately after the terrible fire of 1823, Leo XII began the work of building a new church. The transept of the modern struc-

[17] Frothingham, *Monuments of Christian Rome*, p.48.
[18] Another text reads, "He made the vaulting and decorated the basilica of blessed Peter."
[19] LLP p.100.
[20] LLP p.121.

ture was consecrated in 1840 and the entire church in 1854. The square forecourt, lined with granite columns, was added in 1890-1929. In plan and dimensions the new basilica closely followed its predecessor. The main entrance is by the western façade (Fig. 184), which faces toward the Tiber, and the interior is arranged with nave, double aisles, and transept. Eighty columns of polished gray granite support the ceiling of the nave, which is coffered instead of being open as formerly. The large dimensions of the interior, 394 feet in length and 75 feet in height, and the rich ornamentation combine to produce a very imposing effect (Fig. 185).

The mosaics on the triumphal arch of the basilica of the three emperors were executed in 440-461 by order of the Empress Galla Placidia, sister of the Emperor Honorius, but were damaged badly in the great fire, and the present mosaics are an entirely modern restoration. The mosaic inscription states that the basilica was begun by Theodosius and finished by Honorius and that it was restored and decorated by Placidia under Pope Leo. The mosaics in the apse date from around 1218 and also had to be restored completely after the fire.

When the present church was being constructed there was seen at the bottom of the shaft under the high altar a marble slab with an inscription in letters characteristic of the time of Constantine: PAULO APOSTOLO MARTYRI (Fig. 186). The circular hole seen in the slab was the *billicum* or opening of a little well which led into the tomb, through which it was customary to lower objects to touch the coffin beneath. The two square holes may have been connected with some obscure medieval ceremony.[21]

While all too little from Constantinian and earlier times now remains at the sites of the churches of Paul and Peter, the chain of archeological evidence is such that the last resting places of the two great apostles may confidently be sought beneath the extensive hall of the three emperors and the soaring dome of Bramante and Michelangelo.

SAN GIOVANNI IN LATERANO

In addition to the basilicas of Peter and Paul, five more churches were built in Rome by Constantine. As a matter of fact, in the Liber Pontificalis one of these stands at the head of the list of all the basilicas erected by Constantine, being mentioned even before St. Peter's and St. Paul's. This is "the Constantinian basilica" as the

[21] Barnes, *Martyrdom of St. Peter and St. Paul*, p.148.

Liber Pontificalis calls it,[22] or St. John Lateran (San Giovanni in Laterano) as it is now known. A palace belonging to the senator Plautius Lateranus was confiscated by Nero and thus became imperial property. A portion of it was given by the Emperor Maximian (286-305) to his daughter Fausta, who was married to Constantine in 307. Fausta lived there until she was put to death in 326, and the place became known as the Domus Faustae, or House of Fausta. In 313 a church council under Pope Miltiades met "in the house of Fausta in the Lateran,"[23] and after Fausta's death Constantine gave the palace to Pope Sylvester I as a residence. It continued to be the official residence of the popes for nearly a thousand years. It was burned down in 1308 and the present Palazzo del Laterano was not erected until 1586. In 1843 Gregory XVI made this palace into the Museum Gregorianum Lateranense.

According to tradition, the basilica which Constantine built at the Lateran was dedicated in 324. It was destroyed by an earthquake and reerected by Pope Sergius III (904-911), at that time being dedicated to John the Baptist. After being burned down twice in the fourteenth century it was rebuilt by Urban V (1362-1370) and Gregory XI (1370-1378) and repeatedly altered and modernized at various later times. The interior appears today chiefly in the form given to it by Borromini in the seventeenth century, and the principal façade is the work of Alessandro Galilei in the eighteenth century. Many important church councils have been held here and, as the papal cathedral, the basilica bears the inscription "the mother and head of all the churches of the city and the world." But of the building of Constantine nothing remains.[24]

SANTA CROCE IN GERUSALEMME

"At the same time," continues the Liber Pontificalis after recording the founding of St. Peter's and St. Paul's, "Constantine Augustus constructed a basilica in the Sessorian palace, where he also placed and enclosed in gold and jewels some of the wood of the holy cross of our Lord Jesus Christ, and he dedicated the church under the name by which it is called even to this day, Hierusalem."[25] The Sessorian palace was the residence of Constantine's mother, the Em-

[22] LLP p.47.
[23] LLP p.47 n.1.
[24] The Altar of the Sacrament in the south transept of the present church has four antique columns of gilded bronze which are said to have belonged to the original basilica. Baedeker, *Rome*, p.384.
[25] LLP p.58.

press Helena, and two inscriptions in her honor have been discovered there. While Helena's pilgrimage to the Holy Land is a well known fact, Eusebius says nothing of her discovery of the actual cross of Christ[26] and the accounts of that happening given about the middle of the fifth century by Socrates[27] and Sozomen[28] are certainly legendary in character. The existence of the cross and the sending of pieces of its wood throughout the world were believed in, however, by Cyril of Jerusalem around A.D. 348.[29] It is evident, therefore, that the Sessorian palace hall was transformed into a basilica and named in honor of the discovery of the cross at Jerusalem. The present church, Santa Croce in Gerusalemme, has been rebuilt and restored but still shows traces of once having been a private hall.

SANT'AGNESE FUORI LE MURA

"At the same time," continues the Liber Pontificalis concerning Constantine, "he built the basilica of the holy martyr Agnes at the request of Constantia,[30] his daughter, and a baptistery in the same place, where both his sister, Constantia, and the daughter of Augustus were baptized by Silvester the bishop."[31] St. Agnes was a famous martyr who is mentioned by Jerome[32] and whose place of burial was outside the city on the Via Nomentana, where the catacomb is located which now bears her name. The basilica which Constantine erected in honor of St. Agnes was carried beneath the level of the ground in order to bring its altar immediately over the holy tomb. Rebuilt by Pope Honorius I (625-638) and restored again in the fifteenth and nineteenth centuries, the present Church of St. Agnes outside the Walls (Sant'Agnese fuori le Mura) still lies at a low level, being reached by a descending stairway of forty-five steps, and still retains many characteristics of an early Christian basilica.

SANTA COSTANZA

Nearby is a circular, domed building which is known now as the Church of Santa Costanza. No doubt it represents the baptistery mentioned by the Liber Pontificalis in connection with the basilica

[26] *Life of Constantine.* III, 26, 42.
[27] *Church History.* I, 17 (NPNFSS II, p.21).
[28] *Church History.* II, 1 (NPNFSS II, p.258).
[29] *Catechetical Lectures.* IV, 10; X, 19; XIII, 4 (NPNFSS VII, pp.21,63,83).
[30] Actually the name of Constantine's daughter was Constantina, while his sister was named Constantia.
[31] LLP p.60.
[32] *Letter 130 to Demetrias.* 5 (NPNFSS VI, p.262).

of Agnes, although its original character seems to have been that of a mausoleum. Probably it was used later as a baptistery, the font perhaps having been located in the central space under the dome. The funerary character of the building is shown by the niches in the wall intended to receive sarcophagi, and by the one sarcophagus actually found here and now kept in the Vatican Museum. In the sixteenth century Vincenzo Cartari mentions a ship of Dionysus, executed in mosaic, which was to be seen in the Church of Sant' Agnese "and in what once was a temple of Bacchus," by the latter doubtless meaning Santa Costanza. This suggests that the structure was originally built as a pagan mausoleum, and that the Christian elements are later additions. It has been suggested that it was commissioned by Constantine as an imperial family mausoleum, perhaps as early as A.D. 312 immediately after his victory over Maxentius.[33] In A.D. 354 Constantine's elder daughter, Constantina, died and was buried here. Six years later the younger daughter, Helena, wife of Julian the Apostate, also died and her body was sent to Rome, as the Roman historian Ammianus Marcellinus (c.330-c.395) relates, to be buried on the Via Nomentana where her sister Constantina already lay.[34]

In the low vault of the circular aisle which runs around the interior of Santa Costanza are fine fourth century mosaics in the Roman antique tradition. These include naturalistic representations of flowers, fruit, birds, and sheep, and an interesting vintage scene in which cupids pluck the grapes, carry them to vats, and trample out the juice.[35]

SAN LORENZO FUORI LE MURA

The Liber Pontificalis continues: "At the same time Constantine Augustus built the basilica of blessed Lawrence, the martyr, on the Via Tiburtina in the Ager Veranus over the buried crypt, and he made stairs of ascent and of descent to the body of the holy martyr Lawrence. In that place he erected an apse and adorned it with porphyry and the spot over the tomb he enclosed with silver and beautified it with railings of purest silver, which weighed 1000 lbs."[36] Lawrence was the famous martyr who was put to death over a slow fire in the Valerian persecution of 258. The Constantinian

---

[33] Karl Lehmann in AB 37 (1955), pp.193-196.
[34] XXI, 1, 5. tr. J. C. Rolfe, LCL (1935-39) II, p.93.
[35] E. W. Anthony, *A History of Mosaics.* 1935, p.63; H. H. Powers, *The Art of Mosaic.* 1938, p.79.
[36] LLP pp.61f.

basilica was located so that the altar came over the martyr's crypt to which a stairway gave access. The passage in the Liber Pontificalis is specially interesting since it is one of the earliest descriptions of such a *confessio*.

In 578 Pope Pelagius II rebuilt the church, his work evidently being thorough since the Liber Pontificalis says that "he built from its foundations a basilica over the body of blessed Lawrence."[37] He is also responsible for the mosaic which in restored form is still to be seen on the arch, with Christ in the center, Peter, Lawrence, and Pelagius (with a model of the basilica) on his right side, Paul, Stephen, and Hippolytus on his left, and the cities of Jerusalem and Bethlehem beneath. These are the earliest mosaics in Rome to show Byzantine influence, Christ being seated on the globe of the world as in San Vitale at Ravenna, and Peter being placed in accordance with Byzantine tradition at Christ's right side instead of at the left as was the Roman tradition from the fourth to the thirteenth century.

A complete reorientation and remodeling of this church took place under Honorius III (1216-1227). He turned the nave into a choir with a crypt beneath it, added the present nave at a level ten feet higher on the opposite side of the triumphal arch, thus leaving the mosaics of Pelagius facing the choir, and transferred the entrance to the opposite end of the church. The present San Lorenzo in Agro Verano,[38] or San Lorenzo fuori le Mura, is therefore a basilica far different from that originally built by Constantine.[39]

SANTI PIETRO E MARCELLINO

"At the same time Constantine Augustus built a basilica to the blessed martyrs Marcellinus, the priest, and Peter, the exorcist, at Inter duas Lauros; also a mausoleum where his mother, Helena Augusta, was buried on the Via Lavicana, at the 3rd milestone."[40] The catacomb which still bears the name of these two martyrs has been mentioned (pp.475f.) but the basilica which Constantine built in their honor has disappeared completely. The remains of the octagonal, domed mausoleum of Constantine's mother still stand, however, and the huge porphyry sarcophagus which was found here is

[37] LLP p.168.

[38] The Campo Verano is now the chief cemetery of modern Rome.

[39] For recent excavation at San Lorenzo see W. Frankl, E. Josi, and R. Krautheimer in RAC 26 (1950), pp.9-50; L. E. Hudec in JBR 20 (1952), pp.136-138; R. Krautheimer in *Archaeological Newsletter* (Archaeological Institute of America). 11 (Feb. 28, 1949), pp.85-87.

[40] LLP p.63.

preserved in the Vatican Museum near the sarcophagus from the mausoleum of Constantina. A small church called Santi Pietro e Marcellino has been fitted up in the mausoleum of Helena, which otherwise now is known as the Torre Pignattára. The latter name comes from the *pignatte* or earthenware vessels which were used in the construction of the vaulting for the sake of lightness, as was customary in the late imperial period.

This completes the list of churches erected in Rome by Constantine as given by the Liber Pontificalis. Outside of Rome the same source ascribes to him the building of basilicas at Ostia, Albano, Capua, and Naples,[41] but does not mention the ones he founded in more distant places like Palestine. Before turning to some of the basilicas erected by Constantine in lands outside of Italy a few other Roman churches will be mentioned briefly.

THE "TITLE CHURCHES"

At this time the so-called "title churches" (p.502) formed the majority of the Roman churches and provided the basis of administrative organization, since they were the seats of the presbyters. The priests were divided among the title churches and had responsibility for the corresponding sections of the Roman church members, namely those who lived in that part of the city. The cardinal priests are still assigned to these churches and are titularly in charge of them.[42] By the fifth century the list of title churches numbered twenty-five and included those known today as Santi Giovanni e Paolo, San Clemente, Santi Pietro e Marcellino, San Pietro in Vincoli, San Martino ai Monti, Santa Prassede, Santa Pudenziana, Sant' Eusebio, San Vitale, Santa Susanna, San Marcello, San Lorenzo in Lucina, San Lorenzo in Damaso, San Marco, Sant' Anastasia, Santi Nereo ed Achilleo, Santa Balbina, Santa Sabina, Santa Prisca, Santa Maria in Trastevere, Santa Cecilia, and San Crisogono, as well as the churches of Xysti, of Aemilianae, and of Cyriaci whose identifications are not certain.[43] Of the foregoing, San Clemente and Santi Pietro e Marcellino have already been noted; and of the remainder we shall discuss only Santa Pudenziana and Santa Sabina.

[41] LLP pp.66f.,69f.
[42] J. P. Kirsch, *Die römischen Titelkirchen.* 1918, p.1.
[43] These churches are listed by Frothingham (*Monuments of Christian Rome,* pp.39f.) according to the fourteen *regiones* of ancient Rome.

SANTA PUDENZIANA

The church of Santa Pudenziana is mentioned in an epitaph of A.D. 384 and was rebuilt by Pope Siricius (384-399) who changed it from a hall church into a three-aisled basilica. The date of its original founding is unknown but tradition ascribes it to Pius I (c.142-c.154). To his biography as given by the Liber Pontificalis the following sentences are added in certain eleventh century manuscripts: "He by request of the blessed Praxedis dedicated a church in the baths of Novatus in the Vicus Patricius[44] to the honor of her sister, the holy Pudentiana, where also he offered many gifts and frequently he ministered, offering sacrifice to the Lord. Moreover he erected a font of baptism and with his own hand he blessed and dedicated it and many who gathered to the faith he baptized in the name of the Trinity."[45] Pudentiana and Praxedis[46] were the daughters of Pudens, but whether he is to be identified with the Pudens of II Timothy 4:21 is questionable.

Santa Pudenziana is most famous for the mosaic in its apse which probably dates from the time of Pope Siricius. The mosaic was restored somewhat at the end of the eighth century under Pope Hadrian I (772-795) and was heavily trimmed around the curved margin when the apse was narrowed in 1588. Also a portion of the lower part was removed later by the erection of the *baldacchino* and in 1831 the right side was largely done over. Nevertheless it remains the earliest and most beautiful apse mosaic in existence and is characterized by a solemn and triumphant grandeur (Fig. 187). In the center Christ arrayed in a tunic of gold is seated upon a throne and holds an open book in his hand bearing the inscription "The Lord, Guardian of the Church of Pudentiana." Originally the twelve tunic-clothed apostles were to be seen on either side of Christ, but the outermost figure on each side was lost when the apse was narrowed. Peter stands at the right[47] and Paul[48] at the left. Behind each of the two great apostles stands a woman clothed in gold, holding over his head a laurel crown. These women are believed to represent the Jewish Church (Ecclesia ex Circumcisione) and the Gentile Church (Ecclesia ex Gentibus) respectively. The background is formed by

[44] The Vicus Patricius was near the modern Via Urbana, on which Santa Pudenziana now is located.

[45] LLP p.15 n.3.

[46] To whom the church of Santa Prassede is dedicated.

[47] That is, at the right as seen by the viewer, or at the left hand of Christ. This was the position which was customary in the Roman tradition (p.522).

[48] The opening words of Matthew appear on the open book in Paul's hand but the inscription is a modern restoration.

a portico above which in the center looms the rock of Calvary, surmounted by a great jeweled cross.[49] At the right appears a structure which is probably to be identified with the Church of the Nativity at Bethlehem, while the one at the left probably represents the Church of the Holy Sepulcher in Jerusalem. Above in the clouds are the winged symbols of the four evangelists, now appearing for one of the earliest times in art: the man (angel), lion, ox, and eagle (cf. Ezekiel 10:14; Revelation 4:7) representing respectively Matthew, Mark, Luke, and John.[50]

SANTA SABINA

The church of Santa Sabina was erected by the priest Peter under the pontificate of Celestine I (422-432) as is evident from the dedicatory *titulus* inscription in mosaic which still is in place over the door of the entrance wall. The church was restored in the thirteenth, fifteenth, sixteenth, and twentieth centuries, but with its twenty-four marble columns and open roof the essential structure is still that of an early Christian basilica. Originally, however, it was almost entirely covered within with mosaics, of which all are now lost except the mosaic inscription over the door. On either side of the mosaic inscription is the figure of a woman, the one at the left being shown as a woman of Palestine and labeled Ecclesia ex Circumcisione and the one at the right being represented as a Roman matron and labeled Ecclesia ex Gentibus.[51]

Santa Sabina is most famous for its great cypress doors whose carvings also belong to the time of the origin of the church around 430. Of their original twenty-eight panels only eighteen are left. Eight large panels give scenes from the life of Moses and other Old Testament subjects, while ten small ones are mostly devoted to scenes of the passion of Christ and his appearances after the resurrection. It is thought that the original plan of the door provided a parallelism between the events of the Old Testament and those of the New.[52] The crucifixion appears for perhaps the first time in Christian art.[53]

[49] The style of the cross seems later than that of the rest of the composition and it may be due to Hadrian's restoration.
[50] Anthony, *A History of Mosaics*, pp.66-68; cf. Thomas Albert Stafford, *Christian Symbolism in the Evangelical Churches*. 1942, p.101; Marguerite van Berchem and Étienne Clouzot, *Mosaïques chrétiennes du IVme au Xme siècle*. 1924, pp.11-58.
[51] Anthony, *A History of Mosaics*, p.76.
[52] Morey, *Early Christian Art*, p.138; cf. E. H. Kantorowicz in AB 26 (1944), pp.207-231.
[53] Lowrie, *Monuments of the Early Church*, p.273.

SANTA MARIA MAGGIORE

Our survey of some of the most interesting early Christian churches in Rome may be concluded with mention of Santa Maria Maggiore, which is neither a Constantinian basilica nor a title church but the largest of the eighty churches in the city dedicated to the Virgin, being exceeded in size only by St. Peter's, St. Paul's, and St. John Lateran. It was built by Pope Liberius (352-366), who probably remodeled an already existing palace, and sometimes was known as the Basilica Liberiana. The Liber Pontificalis states in the biography of this pontiff: "He built the basilica of his own name near the Macellum of Libia."[54] The latter is equivalent to "the market of Livia." This basilica was rebuilt by Xystus III (432-440), concerning whom the Liber Pontificalis says, "He built the basilica of the holy Mary, which was called by the ancients the basilica of Liberius, near the Macellum of Lybia."[55]

Santa Maria Maggiore is most famous for its glorious mosaics. Those of the triumphal arch go back to Xystus III, whose inscription still may be read on them: XYSTUS EPISCOPUS PLEBI DEI, "Bishop Xystus to the People of God."[56] The mosaics of the nave, like its ancient marble columns, may go back to Liberius but more probably also belong to the period of Xystus III.[57]

Of the forty-two original panels of nave mosaics, twenty-seven remain. These give a remarkable series of Old Testament pictures of which the Taking of Jericho is shown in Fig. 188. The procession of the ark and trumpeters is shown in the lower panel of the picture, and in the upper the Israelite warriors surround the city whose walls already are falling down. In antique perspective, the man and building which actually are within the city are shown on top of the walls. On the triumphal arch in Santa Maria Maggiore are beautiful scenes relating to the infancy of Christ.

5. CHURCHES IN PALESTINE

THE most sacred sites in all the world on which to erect Christian churches of course were to be found in the Holy Land. Concerning the basilicas which Constantine and his family erected there, we

[54] LLP p.77.   [55] LLP p.94.
[56] A. Schuchert, S. *Maria Maggiore zu Rom.* I, *Die Gründungsgeschichte der Basilika und die ursprüngliche Apsisanlage.* 1939, p.55.
[57] Morey, *Early Christian Art,* p.146; Anthony, *A History of Mosaics,* p.76.

are informed by Eusebius, whose writings are substantially contemporary.[1]

THE CHURCH OF THE HOLY SEPULCHER

For nearly two hundred years a pagan sanctuary (p.330) had stood over the sepulcher of Christ at Jerusalem. But at the command of Constantine this temple and its idols were thrown down and the polluted surface soil carried away. In the course of this work the tomb of Christ came to light again and the emperor forthwith wrote to Macarius, the bishop of Jerusalem, instructing him to erect there at imperial expense a basilica[2] which should surpass in beauty all others everywhere.[3] This church was dedicated in A.D. 335 and is described in considerable detail by Eusebius.[4] Following his description in reverse order, we find that the propylaea or main entrances opened off from the middle of the chief market street of the city, and "afforded to passers-by on the outside a view of the interior which could not fail to inspire astonishment." Beyond and several feet above the level of the street was the first court or atrium which was entered by three doorways, surrounded by porticoes, and left open to the sky. Passing through this one came to the basilica proper, later called the Martyrium, to which access was gained by three doors at the eastern end. Its walls were made of accurately fitted stones, while the roof was covered with lead as a protection against the winter rains. Within, the church was floored with marble slabs of various colors and on each side of the nave were double aisles with galleries above. The ceiling was finished with sculptured panel work like a great sea, "and, being overlaid throughout with the purest gold, caused the entire building to glitter as it were with rays of light." The crowning part of the basilica was what Eusebius calls the Hemisphere. This was at the western end and rose to the very summit of the church, being encircled by twelve columns whose capitals were adorned with large silver bowls presented by the emperor himself.

[1] cf. Paul Mickley, *Die Konstantin-Kirchen im Heiligen Lande, Eusebius-Texte übersetzt und erläutert.* 1923. *The Life of Constantine,* in which much of the relevant material is found, was finished after the death of Constantine (337), since it records that event (IV, 64), but cannot have been written much later, since Eusebius himself died in 340.

[2] Constantine's express designation of the building as a "basilica" is the first appearance of this term in literature in reference to a Christian church (Watzinger, *Denkmäler Palästinas.* II, pp.117f.).

[3] Eusebius, *Life of Constantine.* III, 26-32.

[4] *ibid.,* III, 33-40; cf. J. G. Davies in AJA 61 (1957), pp.171-173.

Beyond the basilica was a second atrium or open court. This was paved with finely polished stone and enclosed with colonnades on three sides. Yet farther to the west was the rock tomb itself. As the place where once the angel had announced the resurrection, this was the chief part of the entire work and was "beautified with rare columns and profusely enriched with the most splendid decorations of every kind." So much is related by Eusebius.

A brief description of the site and church is given also in the itinerary of the famous Bordeaux Pilgrim who visited Jerusalem in A.D. 333. It reads: "On the left hand[5] is the little hill of Golgotha where the Lord was crucified. About a stone's throw from thence is a vault wherein his body was laid, and rose again on the third day. There, at present, by the command of the Emperor Constantine, has been built a basilica, that is to say, a church of wondrous beauty, having at the side reservoirs from which water is raised, and a bath behind in which infants are baptized."[6]

It is evident from these passages that Constantine's architects sought to develop a plan which would be related to two chief points, the rock of Calvary and the tomb itself. The structures which they built were axially on a line which ran from east to west between the market street and the site of the tomb. This left the rock of Calvary just to the south of the main axis. Therefore the second court was colonnaded on three sides, as Eusebius described it, but left open on the south to face directly upon the rock of Calvary. This rock was probably brought to a regular shape by quarrying away superfluous portions of its slopes, and stood in the open air, surrounded by a grille and rising twelve or fifteen feet above the ground. West of the rock of Calvary there was a dip in the ground and then a rise. In the upward slope, "about a stone's throw" from Calvary, was the rock-cut tomb which had been the sepulcher of Christ. Here, too, unimportant portions of the rock round about appear to have been cut away and the sepulcher left standing up prominently from a rock floor. The sacred monument then was enclosed by a round, domed building with a circle of columns on the inside. In the middle stood the tomb itself, probably surrounded by a grille and covered

[5] The description is given from the point of view of one "walking towards the gate of Neapolis." Flavia Neapolis (now corrupted into Nabulus or Nablus) was the name given to the ancient city of Shechem in honor of the Flavian emperor Vespasian, when it was rebuilt after his conquest of the country (p.310). The Gate of Neapolis was therefore in the north wall of Jerusalem.

[6] *The Bordeaux Pilgrim*. tr. Stewart, pp.23f.; cf. R. W. Hamilton in PEQ 1952, pp.83-90.

with a pointed roof. This building became known as the Anastasis because it commemorated the place of the resurrection. Somewhere near at hand must have been the baptistery mentioned by the Bordeaux Pilgrim.[7]

Of these Constantinian structures only a few fragmentary portions remain today. They include a part of the wall of the first court, now embodied in the Russian and Coptic buildings at this place, and a segment of the outer wall of the Anastasis which still forms a part of the wall of the present Rotunda above the sepulcher. Perhaps also the lower courses of masonry in the present chapel of St. John just south of the Rotunda once belonged to the Constantinian baptistery.

Our knowledge of the original Church of the Holy Sepulcher rests primarily, therefore, upon the contemporary accounts of Eusebius and the Bordeaux Pilgrim and upon the fragments of Constantinian masonry which still stand. Confirmation of the general picture which we have drawn is to be found in the writings of Cyril of Jerusalem. Cyril was probably born around A.D. 315 and seems to have grown up in or near the city of which later he was bishop. About A.D. 348 he delivered a famous series of catechetical lectures in the Constantinian basilica itself. In the course of these he referred repeatedly to Golgotha or Calvary, speaking of it sometimes as near the place in which he and his listeners were assembled,[8] and sometimes as standing up above them in their sight.[9] Again he asked his hearers if they saw the spot of Golgotha, and they answered with a shout of praise.[10] A second group of lectures for those newly baptized was held in the "Holy Place of the Resurrection" or the Anastasis itself.[11]

In addition we have one or two very important representations of the Church of the Holy Sepulcher in early Christian art. The fourth century mosaic in the apse of Santa Pudenziana in Rome (Fig. 187; pp.524f.), portrays Christ seated in front of a great rock surmounted by a tall jeweled cross. It is probable that this scene is based upon one of the ceremonies at Jerusalem in which the bishop sat upon a throne in front of the rock of Calvary, surrounded by the deacons. The arcade in the background may then depict the second atrium itself and the buildings at the left be the Anastasis and other structures of Constantine.[12] The other representation of the church is in

[7] E. T. Richmond in W. Harvey, *Church of the Holy Sepulchre, Jerusalem*. 1935, p.vi; Crowfoot, *Early Churches in Palestine*, pp.19f.
[8] *Catechetical Lecture*. XIII, 4 (NPNFSS VII, p.83).
[9] *ibid.*, x, 19.   [10] *ibid.*, XIII, 23.   [11] *ibid.*, XVIII, 33.
[12] Crowfoot, *Early Churches in Palestine*, p.19.

the famous mosaic map at Madeba.[13] Madeba is an ancient site across the Jordan and some fifty miles south of Gerasa. About 1880 it was occupied by Christians from Kerak, who in the course of building operations uncovered a number of churches and floor mosaics. One of the mosaics, dating from the end of the sixth century, gives a map of Palestine. On this map the sea is shown in deep green, plains in light brown, and mountains in dark brown, while place locations are named in Greek letters. Portions of the mosaic are destroyed, but the Jerusalem area is well preserved (Fig. 189) and the city is shown in such detail that even individual buildings can be distinguished. Jerusalem appears as a large oval, with its chief, colonnaded street running from north to south through the heart of the city. On the entire map the directions are recognizable without any doubt, since the street just mentioned parallels the course of the Jordan River and the Dead Sea seen in the distance. The basic outline of the Christian city is still that of Hadrian's colony. At the north end of the main street (left side in our reproduction) is the gate from which the Roman road led to Neapolis and Caesarea. Remains of this gate still exist beneath the present Damascus Gate in Jerusalem. Behind it the mosaic shows an open place and a memorial column on which once stood a statue of Hadrian. The colonnaded street ran through the city to the Roman gate at the south. This was called the middle market street by Eusebius and is identical with the present Khan al-Zeit. A row of columns has been found which probably represents a late Byzantine reconstruction of the western colonnade of this street. The mosaic shows a second colonnaded street running from the plaza at the north gate diagonally to the northwest corner of the temple area and then parallel to the west wall of the temple. The city must have had a main east-west street also but only small, short streets running in this direction are shown on the map. The interior of the city is filled with churchly buildings. Most prominent is the Church of the Holy Sepulcher at a point perpendicular to the middle of the chief market street. The mosaic clearly shows the flights of steps leading up to the first atrium, the three entrance doors, the roof of the basilica, and the dome of the Anastasis.[14]

Not long after the time when the Madeba mosaic map was made, the Constantinian Church of the Holy Sepulcher was destroyed by the Persians. This took place in A.D. 614, and afterward Modestus,

[13] Roger T. O'Callaghan in *Dictionnaire de la Bible*, Supplement, Pt. xxvi, cols. 627-704; Victor R. Gold in BA 21 (1958), pp.50-71.
[14] Watzinger, *Denkmäler Palästinas*. ii, pp.81f.

who was patriarch, carried out a reconstruction in far simpler style but on the same general lines as those of Constantine's work. Thereafter many vicissitudes were in store, including earthquake, fire, pillage, and general neglect. In 935 a mosque was built on the site of the atrium of the church, and in 1009 the church itself was destroyed by the Fatimid Caliph al-Hakim but later rebuilt by the Byzantine emperor Constantine IX Monomachus (1042-1054). The Crusaders, who captured Jerusalem in 1099, found Constantine Monomachus's timber-domed rotunda above the Holy Sepulcher, the tomb itself being surrounded by a circular colonnade of columns and piers. To the east was the court, with the rock of Calvary on its southern side standing to the height "of a lance." Constantine's basilica was in ruins, but its crypt, known by the name of St. Helena, still existed. The Crusaders designed and built a church which covered beneath its roof both the rock of Calvary and the court which formerly adjoined it. This church was connected with the rotunda by a triumphal arch, and with the crypt of St. Helena, now made into a chapel, by a stairway. The basilica of the Crusaders still stands, although eight centuries of neglect have damaged it badly. Constantine Monomachus's dome over the Anastasis was repaired around 1719, then destroyed by fire in 1808. Thereafter the Greeks were authorized by Sultan Mahmud II to repair the church, and they constructed certain walls which obscured the interior arrangement of the rotunda, built a new edicule over the sepulcher, replaced the doors of the main entrance by new ones, and erected a new dome which lasted for about fifty years. The latter was again rebuilt in 1863-1868, but in recent times the general condition of the whole church has become so questionable as to demand a thoroughgoing investigation of its structural weaknesses and a comprehensive plan for works of restoration and preservation.[15]

Thus the handiwork of man over a period of more than nineteen centuries is represented by the existing Church of the Holy Sepulcher. The earliest examples are the traces of the original sepulcher that still survive, as well as another ancient rock tomb still to be seen in the western part of the rotunda, just south of the present Jacobite Chapel. The most recent are the works of repair carried out in the twentieth century. The history and traditions of the centuries are such that we may with confidence seek beneath the roof

[15] William Harvey, *Church of the Holy Sepulchre, Jerusalem, Structural Survey, Final Report.* 1935, pp.vii-xv.

of this structure the true place of Golgotha and the sepulcher of Christ.[16]

A photograph of the main south front of the church is shown in Fig. 190. On the left of the open court are several chapels, including the chapel of St. John, and the bell tower which was built about 1170. The façade of the church is divided into two stories and there are two doors with corresponding windows above. One of the portals is now walled up, as are many of the windows of the church. This is the main entrance and leads directly ahead into the western end of the south aisle of the Crusaders' church which, as will be remembered, was located where the second atrium was in Constantinian times. The chapel of St. Helena, where once Constantine's basilica stood, is descended to by steps leading out from the eastern end of this church. The dome which appears prominently in this picture rises above the western part of the Crusaders' church, while the large dome of the rotunda of the sepulcher is hidden behind the bell tower.

THE CHURCH OF THE NATIVITY

At Bethlehem the Church of the Nativity was built under the leadership of Helena, the mother of Constantine. Not long before her death, which occurred around A.D. 327 at the age of eighty years, this venerable lady visited the Holy Land in person. Eusebius tells how she dedicated a church "at the grotto which had been the scene of the Saviour's birth," and explains, "For he who was 'God with us' had submitted to be born even in a cave of the earth, and the place of his nativity was called Bethlehem by the Hebrews." The sacred cave was beautified with all possible splendor, and the emperor joined his mother in costly offerings.[17]

While the gospel narrative of the birth of Jesus relates only that Mary "laid him in a manger, because there was no place for them in the inn" (Luke 2:7), it is not surprising that this should have been in a cave, since until modern times caves have frequently been employed in Palestine to house both animals and men. The cave is mentioned between A.D. 155 and 160 by Justin Martyr, who says: "when the child was born in Bethlehem, since Joseph could not find a lodging in that village, he took up his quarters in a certain cave near the

[16] Joachim Jeremias in ΑΓΓΕΛΟΣ, *Archiv für neutestamentliche Zeitgeschichte und Kulturkunde.* 1926, p.33; H. T. F. Duckworth, *The Church of the Holy Sepulchre.* 1922, p.11; André Parrot, *Golgotha and the Church of the Holy Sepulchre.* 1957.
[17] Eusebius, *Life of Constantine.* III, 41-43; cf. Socrates, *Ch. Hist.* I, 17; Sozomen, *Ch. Hist.* II, 2.

village."[18] Again in A.D. 246-248, Origen writes: "Corresponding to the narrative in the Gospel regarding his birth, there is shown at Bethlehem the cave where he was born, and the manger in the cave where he was wrapped in swaddling clothes. And this sight is greatly talked of in surrounding places, even among the enemies of the faith, it being said that in this cave was born that Jesus who is worshipped and reverenced by the Christians."[19]

As a matter of fact, this cave was evidently identified as the birthplace of Christ long before the time of Hadrian, for that emperor defiled it with pagan worship just as he did the site of the Holy Sepulcher in Jerusalem. This is related by Jerome, who himself lived at Bethlehem from 386 until his death in 420:[20]

"From the time of Hadrian to the reign of Constantine—a period of about one hundred and eighty years—the spot which had witnessed the resurrection was occupied by a figure of Jupiter; while on the rock where the cross had stood, a marble statue of Venus was set up by the heathen and became an object of worship. The original persecutors, indeed, supposed that by polluting our holy places they would deprive us of our faith in the passion and in the resurrection. Even my own Bethlehem, as it now is, that most venerable spot in the whole world of which the psalmist sings: 'the truth hath sprung out of the earth,'[21] was overshadowed by a grove of Tammuz, that is of Adonis; and in the very cave where the infant Christ had uttered his earliest cry lamentation was made for the paramour of Venus."[22]

The church which was erected over this sacred site by Helena and Constantine is mentioned in A.D. 333 by the Bordeaux Pilgrim. Speaking of Bethlehem, he says, "There a basilica has been built by order of Constantine."[23] Under the Emperor Justinian (527-565), the original Constantinian basilica was demolished and a larger church constructed. This fact is stated in a document written at the beginning of the tenth century by Eutychius, the patriarch of Alexandria. Eutychius says that the Emperor Justinian ordered his legate to pull down the church at Bethlehem, which was a small building, and to

[18] *Dialogue with Trypho.* 78 (ANF I, p.237).
[19] *Against Celsus.* I, 51 (ANF IV, p.418).
[20] *Letter 58 to Paulinus.* 3 (NPNFSS VI, p.120).
[21] Psalm 85:11.
[22] Tammuz was the Mesopotamian god who died and rose annually with the death and rebirth of vegetation. He is here identified with the Greek Adonis, the lover of Venus (Aphrodite). The lamentations of the goddess over his tragic death and descent to the underworld were echoed in the liturgical wailings of his worshipers (cf. Ezekiel 8:14). Frankfort, *Kingship and the Gods*, pp.286-294; T. G. Pinches in HERE XII, pp.187-191.
[23] *The Bordeaux Pilgrim.* tr. Stewart, p.27.

erect another of such size and beauty that not even the temple at Jerusalem might vie with it in beauty. The legate arrived, had the church at Bethlehem destroyed, and built the church as it stands now. When he had finished his work he returned to the emperor, who proceeded to question him as to the way in which he had carried out his commands. But when he described the building the emperor became very angry. "I gave you money," he said, "and you have pocketed it all, but the building you have erected is badly put together, the church is quite dark, and the result is not at all what I intended or according to the plan I told you to follow." And straightway he ordered him to be punished.[24]

Justinian's church, much dilapidated, still stands in Bethlehem. It was spared by the Persians in 614, because they saw on the exterior a mosaic of the adoration of the Magi in which the latter were clothed in Persian dress. The Muslims held the church in veneration and it escaped the general destruction of Palestinian churches ordered in 1009 by the Fatimid Caliph al-Hakim. Baldwin I was crowned king here at Christmas in 1101, and during the period of the Latin kingdom (twelfth century) the church was invested with splendid mosaic decoration. Since that time, however, earthquake, fire, and neglect have reduced it to a sad state of deterioration.[25]

The Church of the Nativity is on the promontory upon which the southeastern part of the town of Bethlehem is now built. The western front and principal entrance of the church are shown in Fig. 191. The large open area paved with stone is where the atrium of the Constantinian basilica must have been. A modern graveyard now encroaches from the north and the buildings of the Armenian Convent project prominently at the right. The narthex was formerly entered through three doors, but these have now been blocked save for a small low rectangular opening in the central door, which remains as the chief public entrance. Within (Fig. 192)[26] the nave is still flanked by Justinian's columns, which form double aisles on either side. Beneath the central area where the transept crosses the main axis of the church, and descended to by steps on either side of the chancel, is the grotto of the Nativity.

The church as described hitherto is essentially that of Justinian. Is anything known of the Constantinian basilica? In 1934 Mr. Wil-

[24] *Annales.* MPG 111 (1863), col. 1070, 159f.
[25] E. T. Richmond in William Harvey, *Structural Survey of the Church of the Nativity, Bethlehem.* 1935, pp.v-xv.
[26] The cross wall shown at the head of the nave in this photograph has now been removed.

liam Harvey discovered the remains of the church of Helena and Constantine beneath the floor of the present church. Only limited excavations were possible, but the essential nature of the original church was determined.[27] The general plan was similar to that of the Church of the Holy Sepulcher. As at Jerusalem the structures were set out axially, but in this case ran from west to east. First there was the atrium. Then three doors gave access to the basilica at its western end. The north and south walls of the basilica stood on the same lines as the existing side walls of the present church, and the interior was divided practically as now into nave and four aisles. At its eastern end the basilica connected directly with an octagonal building which stood above the subterranean cave of the Nativity. Steps arranged on an octagonal plan surrounded the circular mouth of a shaft about twelve feet across, through which it was possible to look down into the grotto itself. The roof of the cave was broken through to make this view possible from the Octagon above.

The floors of the aisles, the nave, and the passage around the shrine in the Octagon, were paved with patterned mosaics. Considerable fragments of these remain, and being probably of Constantinian time are the earliest floor mosaics which have been found in a Palestinian church. Since they were to be trodden underfoot no religious scenes were represented, but geometrical designs, swastikas, acanthus leaves, flowers, fruits, and birds constituted the decorations. A small panel on the north side of the Octagon where no one ordinarily would walk, had the Greek word "Fish" (IXΘYC) in the center (Fig. 193).

An almost contemporary picture of this church is probably to be seen in the apse mosaic of Santa Pudenziana, Rome (Fig. 187). Whereas Jerusalem appears at our left in the mosaic, Bethlehem is seen at our right. In the extreme corner is a high entranceway, to the left of which a long low building represents the atrium of the Church of the Nativity. Adjoining this is a somewhat taller building which is the basilica and immediately to the left of it is the yet loftier Octagon.

THE CHURCH ON THE MOUNT OF OLIVES

Yet another Palestinian church was founded by Helena and likewise enriched by Constantine. The statement of Eusebius concerning

[27] W. Harvey, *Structural Survey of the Church of the Nativity, Bethlehem*, pp.20-30; and in PEFQS 1936, pp.28-32; E. T. Richmond in QDAP 6 (1938), pp.63-66; Crowfoot, *Early Churches in Palestine*, pp.22-30, 119-121.

it is: "And further, the mother of the emperor raised a stately structure on the Mount of Olives also, in memory of his ascent to heaven who is the Saviour of mankind, erecting a sacred church and temple on the very summit of the mount. And indeed authentic history informs us that in this very cave the Saviour imparted his secret revelations to his disciples. And here also the emperor testified his reverence for the King of kings, by diverse and costly offerings."[28] The Bordeaux Pilgrim writes: "From thence you ascend to the Mount of Olives, where before the Passion, the Lord taught his disciples. There by the orders of Constantine a basilica of wondrous beauty has been built."[29]

Evidently the basilica was built near the place on the Mount of Olives where fourth century tradition believed the ascension had taken place (cf. Acts 1:9, 12) and directly over a cave in which it was said Jesus had taught his disciples. The Bordeaux Pilgrim says that these teachings were delivered before the Passion, and perhaps the discourse on the last things was in mind which was described in the gospels as given on the Mount of Olives (Mark 13:3 = Matthew 24:3). Eusebius, however, speaks of the teachings as "secret revelations" which makes one think of the apocryphal teachings which Christ was supposed to have given on the Mount of Olives in the period between the resurrection and the ascension.[30]

However confused some of these traditions may have been, it is certain that a Constantinian basilica did stand over a cave on the Mount of Olives directly across from the Holy City and just south of the summit of the ridge of the Mount. Since the name of the Mount of Olives was Eleona ('Ελαιών, Luke 21:37), the basilica was known as "the church of Eleona," or simply Eleona for short. Although hardly more than a few stones of its walls and small patches of its mosaic floor have survived, the Dominicans have been able to trace the ground plan from the foundation trenches cut in the solid rock, and to establish a very probable reconstruction of its original character.[31]

[28] *Life of Constantine*. iii, 43.
[29] Tr. Stewart, pp.24f.
[30] See e.g. *The Gospel of Bartholomew*. 4:1 (JANT p.173); and above p. 414.
[31] Hugues Vincent and F. M. Abel, *Jérusalem, recherches de topographie, d'archéologie et d'histoire*. ii (1914), pp.337-360,383f. A different reconstruction and a later date have been proposed by E. Weigand (in ZDPV 46 [1923], pp.212-220) and Watzinger (*Denkmäler Palästinas*. ii, p.127), but probably are not to be accepted (see Crowfoot, *Early Churches in Palestine*, pp.30-34; Vincent in RB 21 [1924], pp.310f.; 45 [1936], p.419; 64 [1957], pp.48-71).

According to these investigations, it appears that one approached the basilica through a fine portico with six columns, which gave access to a colonnaded atrium under which was a large cistern. At the farther end of the atrium several steps led up to the level of the basilica itself. The length of the basilica proper was about one hundred feet, this being a little longer than the one at Bethlehem and probably a little shorter than the one in front of the Anastasis. It was divided by two rows of columns into a nave and two side aisles, and the nave terminated in a semicircular apse, on the north side of which was an additional small chamber. The famous cave itself, which was transformed into a crypt, lay beneath the eastern end of the nave and the apse.

The church was destroyed by the Persians in 614, somewhat restored by Modestus, and finally quite ruined. During the Middle Ages two chapels were built on the site, one called the Pater to mark the place where Jesus was supposed to have taught the Pater Noster or Lord's Prayer, and the other named the Credo to commemorate the place where the Apostles were said to have written the Creed. These were destroyed also, and the present Church of the Creed and Church of the Lord's Prayer date only from 1868 when the site was purchased by the Princesse de la Tour d'Auvergne. The east end of the Constantinian basilica and the cave crypt lie directly under the second of these present-day structures.

THE CHURCH AT MAMRE

Not only Constantine's mother, Helena, but also his mother-in-law, Eutropia, joined him in interest in the erection of churches in the Holy Land. Eutropia visited the famous oaks of Mamre (Genesis 18:1) and found the place defiled by heathen idols and sacrifices. When she informed Constantine of the situation the emperor straightway wrote a letter, preserved in full by Eusebius, to Macarius of Jerusalem and the other bishops in Palestine, informing them of his desire that the pagan altar should be demolished and replaced by a church.[32] At this place, which is nearly two miles north of Hebron on the east side of the road to Jerusalem,[33] there is a large enclosure now known as the Haram Ramet el-Khalil. Part of the walls seem to date from the time of Herod and part from the time of Hadrian. Within the enclosure at the east side are the ruins of a church which

---

[32] *Life of Constantine.* III, 51-53.
[33] Sozomen, *Ch. Hist.* II, 4.

has been excavated by Father Mader. It was a small basilica with a long narthex and the apse "inscribed," or built within the rectangle of the church. While the church was restored, perhaps by Modestus, the present ruins doubtless represent the site and plan of the Constantinian basilica.[34]

THE CHURCH OF THE LOAVES AND FISHES
AT ET-TABGHA

Many other churches were built in Palestine during the following centuries, but to them only the briefest allusion here is possible. Most of them were basilical in plan, long buildings with a nave and two aisles. The finest floor mosaics are in the Church of the Loaves and Fishes at et-Tabgha (p.304), the place where fourth century tradition located the feeding of the five thousand (Mark 6:30-44). This church was built above an earlier small chapel on the same site and must be at least as late as the end of the fourth or beginning of the fifth century. The best preserved mosaic is that in the left or north transept (Fig. 194), with its wonderful pictures of birds and plants. Amidst lotus, papyrus, and other plants, ducks are nestling, cormorants flapping their wings, and a flamingo is fighting with a snake.[35]

THE CHURCHES OF GERASA

The Palestinian city of Roman times whose ruins are best preserved today is Gerasa (p.308) in Transjordan. This city was rebuilt in the second century A.D., shattered by earthquakes in the eighth, and left deserted for most of the next thousand years. A number of early Christian churches have been investigated there. The first is known as the cathedral and is a three-aisled basilica with an inscribed apse. It faced upon a paved court in the middle of which was a fountain reported to run with wine annually on the anniversary of the miracle at Cana in Galilee. The church and the miracle are referred to in A.D. 375 by Epiphanius, bishop of Constantia (Salamis) in Cyprus, and the excavators date the church around A.D. 365.[36] In 494 a second basilica, dedicated to the martyr Theodore, was founded on the other side of the fountain court, and with the addition of a baptistery block,

[34] A. E. Mader in RAC 6 (1929), pp.249-312; and in RB 39 (1930), pp.84-117; and *Mambre, Die Ergebnisse der Ausgrabungen im heiligen Bezirk Haram Râmet el-Halîl in Südpalästina 1926-1932.* 2 vols., 1957.

[35] A. M. Schneider, *Die Brotvermehrungskirche von et-ṭâbġa am Genesarethsee und ihre Mosaiken.* 1934.

[36] Kraeling, ed., *Gerasa, City of the Decapolis*, pp.212-219.

baths, and other structures the Christian precinct became a very impressive complex. The baptistery comprised three rooms, in the middle one of which was the baptismal pool. The candidate went down into the pool by four steps and left by steps on the other side.[37] Yet other churches at Gerasa include: the one dedicated to the Prophets, Apostles, and Martyrs, which was built (464-465) in the form of a Latin cross and contains interesting floor mosaics (Fig. 195); the basilica built by a certain Procopius (526-527); the round church of St. John the Baptist with the basilicas of St. George and SS. Cosmas and Damianus on either side of it (529-533); the Synagogue which was rebuilt as a church (530-531); the basilica of SS. Peter and Paul (c.540); the Propylaea church (565); and the basilica containing the name of Bishop Genesius (611).

6. CHURCHES IN SYRIA

THE work of Constantine in the erection of churches was also extended to Syria, according to Eusebius. At Heliopolis (Baalbek), a city whose hitherto exclusively pagan character is emphasized by Eusebius and attested by its world famous ruins of temples and altars, the emperor built "a church of great size and magnificence," and at the same time made arrangements concerning its clergy and provision for the necessities of the poor.[1] At Antioch likewise he erected another church which was "of unparalleled size and beauty." "The entire building," Eusebius continues, "was encompassed by an enclosure of great extent, within which the church itself rose to a vast elevation, being of an octagonal form, and surrounded on all sides by many chambers, courts, and upper and lower apartments; the whole richly adorned with a profusion of gold, brass, and other materials of the most costly kind."[2]

THE CHURCH OF ST. BABYLAS AT KAOUSSIE

While we are dependent upon Eusebius for our knowledge of the Constantinian church at Antioch, excavations in the vicinity of that important site have disclosed two other important early Christian churches. The first of these was found to the north of the city, on the

---

[37] J. Barbee Robertson in *The College of the Bible Quarterly.* 33 (1956), pp.12-20.
[1] *Life of Constantine.* III, 58. For Baalbek see Theodor Wiegand, *Baalbek, Ergebnisse der Ausgrabungen und Untersuchungen in den Jahren 1898 bis 1905.* 4 vols. 1921-25.
[2] *Life of Constantine.* III, 50.

way to the village of Kaoussie, on the right bank of the Orontes River.[3] As may be seen in the air view in Fig. 196, the plan of the church is essentially that of a cross with four equal arms oriented to the four points of the compass. While the walls have been destroyed their foundations remain, together with extensive portions of the mosaics with which the floors were adorned, and thus a good idea of the original structure can be obtained.

The four radiating arms or naves of the church are almost equal in their dimensions, each being about thirty-six feet wide and eighty-two feet long. Of the mosaics with which their floors were covered, those in the north, west, and south naves display a similar pattern of continuous geometric designs. Each of these three floor mosaics is accompanied by an inscription containing substantially the same statement. The one in the north nave reads, "In the time of our most holy bishop Flavian,[4] and in the time of the most pious Eusebius the steward and presbyter, Dorys the presbyter in fulfillment of a vow completed the mosaic of this hall too. In the month of March of the year 435 [A.D. 387]." The mosaics in the east nave are of a different character, being divided into large areas each with its own style of decoration including triangles, circles, and other figures. Any inscription which was here unfortunately is lost.

From all four of the naves attention clearly was directed toward the center of the church. Here the four halls opened into a central room which was about fifty-five feet square. Above, the roofs of the naves abutted upon the presumably yet higher roof of this room. In the center of the room was a raised platform, and beneath the floor were two tombs. One was a tomb of bricks, the other was like a monolithic sarcophagus with a horizontal division in the middle so that it could accommodate two bodies.

The *simple et grandiose* plan of this church, as its excavators call it, was not seriously altered by later additions. Among the smaller structures which were annexed to the main halls the most important was a baptistery. This was entered from the north nave through a hall designated by a mosaic inscription as a Pistikon (ΠΕΙCΤΙΚΟΥ), perhaps the place where the catechumen recited the confession of faith before being baptized. The inscription is dated under Theodotus who was bishop of Antioch in A.D. 420-429. In the baptistery the baptismal basin was large enough to receive the candidate into

[3] Jean Lassus in *Antioch on-the-Orontes. II: The Excavations 1933-1936*, pp.5-44.
[4] Flavian was bishop of Antioch in A.D. 381-404 (NSH IV, p.327).

the water but not large enough to provide for his immersion, so the ceremony must have been carried out by affusion.

As the inscription of Dorys shows, the mosaics which he placed in the main church were completed in A.D. 387. An interesting bit of history enables us with considerable probability to date the original construction of the church a few years earlier and to identify its name.[5] Babylas, bishop of Antioch, suffered martyrdom in A.D. 250 under Decius. His remains presumably were interred first at Antioch, afterward were transferred to Daphne, and finally were brought back to Antioch. In a discourse concerning Babylas, Chrysostom[6] refers to the return of the body to Antioch, and says, "You indeed gave him back to the band of fellow enthusiasts; but the grace of God did not suffer him to remain there forever, but again removed him beyond the river, so that much of the countryside was filled with the sweet odor of the martyr." In connection with this burial of the saint beyond the river, Chrysostom continues, "And he was not destined when he went there to remain alone, but he soon received a neighbor and fellow lodger (γείτονα καὶ ὁμόσκηνον), one of similar life; and he had shared the same office with him."

This second person, Chrysostom says, had been responsible for the construction of the church in which the martyr and he himself were buried. While the church was being built, he had visited it every day and even participated in the actual labor of its erection. This must have been Meletius, the bishop of Antioch, who died in Constantinople in A.D. 381 during the meeting of the ecumenical council over which he presided, and whose remains, according to Sozomen, "were . . . conveyed to Antioch, and deposited near the tomb of Babylas the martyr."[7] Meletius therefore seems to have been buried at Antioch about A.D. 381 in a church in the construction of which he had been instrumental and in a tomb which was in immediate proximity to the interred martyr Babylas. Since Meletius had a stormy career and was most secure in his position as bishop of Antioch in about A.D. 379 and following, it is probable that he began the construction of the church only within the year or so preceding his death.

The identification of the church at Kaoussie with the one which figures in the foregoing account is most probable. Since its main

---

[5] Glanville Downey in *Antioch on-the-Orontes. II: The Excavations 1933-1936*, pp.45-48.

[6] *De Sancto Hieromartyre Babyla*. 3 (MPG 50 [1859], col. 533).

[7] Sozomen, *Ch. Hist.* VII, 10; cf. NSH VII, p.288.

floor mosaics were completed in A.D. 387, the church itself could very well have been built about A.D. 380 by Meletius. In the center of the church, moreover, was a sarcophagus which had once received two bodies. Very possibly this was the place where Babylas received as a "neighbor and fellow lodger" the man who had held the same office that he had, namely Meletius the bishop of Antioch. If these coordinations between the history as known from literary sources and the material findings revealed in the excavations are correct, the church at Kaoussie was constructed and received the remains of the famous martyr Babylas about A.D. 380; Meletius, the builder, was buried there in 381; and the adornment with many of its fine mosaics followed in 387. Its proper name is the Church of St. Babylas.

THE MARTYRION AT SELEUCIA PIERIA

The second church newly discovered in the same vicinity is at Seleucia Pieria, the seaport of Antioch. It seems to have been a memorial church, and commonly is referred to as the Martyrion.[8] According to the style of its mosaics and architecture it is dated tentatively in the last quarter of the fifth century A.D. It is believed to have been destroyed by earthquakes in A.D. 526 and 528 and to have been rebuilt soon after that time.

In its original plan the structure comprised a central quatrefoil, with an ambulatory around it, and a chancel projecting on the east side. The outlines of the quatrefoil and ambulatory appear clearly in Fig. 197, which is a view of the ruins looking north.

The floor of the ambulatory was adorned with a rich mosaic pavement which undoubtedly belonged to the first construction of the building. A portion of the mosaic in the north ambulatory is shown in its original place in Fig. 198. The border is of the type known as rinceau, and shows a continuous stalk of grapevine running in regular undulations, together with bunches of grapes, birds, and fowls. The main field represents a veritable paradise of natural wild life, and shows animals, birds, trees, flowers, and bits of landscape. Among the animals identified by the excavators are a lonely giraffe, a zebra startled by a large crane, inquisitive horses, fleet gazelles, a childishly irritable elephant, ferocious lions, sheep, goats, a hyena, and other beasts. The birds in the field and border include an eagle flapping its wings, a gallinule scratching its head, peacocks,

[8] W. A. Campbell in *Antioch on-the-Orontes. III: The Excavations 1937-1939*, pp.35-54.

flamingoes, cranes, ducks, and geese. Pomegranate, pear, fir, and pine trees, date palms, plants, and flowers add to the beauty of the scene.

The Martyrion was also adorned with an important series of sculptured marble revetments. The fragments recovered fall into two groups, one of which is composed of incised drawings believed to date in the fifth century, the other made up of low plastic reliefs thought to belong to the end of the fifth century or first half of the sixth. The bas-reliefs represent Old Testament subjects exclusively, including Daniel, Moses before the Burning Bush, Samson Fighting with a Lion, and others. The incised reliefs show not only Old Testament scenes such as Joseph in Prison, and Saul Fighting the Amalekites, but also New Testament pictures including the Adoration of the Magi, the Rich Man and Lazarus, the Feeding of the Multitude, and various scenes of healing, and furthermore include figures like Constantine and St. Simeon Stylites. Thus these reliefs include a very comprehensive selection of themes and afford a glimpse of the richness of Christian iconography at this time.[9]

THE CHURCH OF ST. SIMEON STYLITES

In the interior of Syria there were many early Christian churches which were lost to knowledge until, in the second half of the nineteenth century, a number of them were rediscovered and described by the Marquis de Vogüé.[10] More intensive studies have been made since by American and German scholars.[11] The churches date in the time from the fourth to the seventh centuries. On the whole it may be said that it was characteristic of the architecture revealed here to retain the basic form of the basilica but to place a new emphasis upon the development and decoration of the exterior. Single and double towers were employed to achieve an impressive façade, which was often adorned further with an open loggia above a broadly arched entrance.

Of all the Syrian churches the greatest was that of Qalat Siman, the

[9] Kurt Weitzmann in *Antioch on-the-Orontes. III: The Excavations 1937-1939*, pp.135-149; Harold R. Willoughby in JBL 69 (1950), pp.129-136.

[10] C. J. Melchior de Vogüé, *Syrie Centrale*. 2 vols. 1865-77.

[11] *The Publications of an American Archaeological Expedition to Syria in 1899-1900. II: Architecture and Other Arts*, by Howard Crosby Butler. 1903; *Publications of the Princeton Archaeological Expeditions to Syria in 1904-5 and 1909. II: Architecture. A. Southern Syria.* 1919, *B. Northern Syria.* 1920, by H. C. Butler; H. C. Butler, *Early Churches in Syria, Fourth to Seventh Centuries.* ed. E. Baldwin Smith, 1929; Hermann W. Beyer, *Der syrische Kirchenbau.* 1925.

Church of St. Simeon Stylites,[12] which was on a hilly plateau some forty miles northeast of Antioch. Simeon, in whose honor it was built, was born in northern Syria around A.D. 390, and became the first and most famous saint to practice living on top of a pillar. At the age of thirty and after having experimented with numerous other austerities, he built a pillar six feet high and made his home on its summit. He increased the height of the pillar gradually until after ten years it was sixty feet high. Here, protected from falling as we may suppose by a railing and possibly reached by a ladder up which his disciples brought his food, he lived without ever coming down until his death in 459.

The church built in memory of the saint is believed to have been erected shortly after his death, probably between A.D. 460 and 490. The extensive and impressive ruins of this structure which still stand (Fig. 199) provide a good indication of its character. The ground plan was similar to that of the Church of St. Babylas at Kaoussie, in that four rectangular halls were arranged to radiate from a central area, thus forming a cross. In St. Simeon's church the focal point of interest was the column on which the saint had dwelt. This pillar, a piece of which remains today, was left standing in its original position and the memorial edifice was built around it. Each of the four halls which extended out from this center was divided by columns into a nave and two side aisles, and the eastern hall ended in a magnificent triple apse. The central area where the four arms of the cross met was arranged as an octagon and, according to the latest research, was roofed with a soaring wooden cupola or dome.[13]

Hitherto it has been widely believed that the central octagon was left as an unroofed court open to the sky. The chief support for this opinion is a passage in which the church historian Evagrius (b. A.D. c.536) describes the edifice as he saw it upon a visit to the site around A.D. 560. He writes: "The temple is constructed in the form of a cross, adorned with colonnades on the four sides. Opposite the

---

[12] De Vogüé, Syrie Centrale, pp.141-152 and Planches 139-148; Butler in The Publications of an American Archaeological Expedition to Syria in 1899-1900. ii, pp.184-190; in Publications of the Princeton Archaeological Expeditions to Syria in 1904-5 and 1909. II: B., pp.261-284; and in Early Churches in Syria, Fourth to Seventh Centuries, pp.97-110; Beyer, Der syrische Kirchenbau, pp.60-71; Daniel Krencker, Die Wallfahrtskirche des Simeon Stylites in Kal'at Sim'ân I Bericht über Untersuchungen und Grabungen im Frühjahr 1938 ausgeführt im Auftrag des Deutschen Archäologischen Instituts (Abhandlungen der Preussischen Akademie der Wissenschaften. 1938. Phil.-hist. Kl. 4 [1939]).

[13] Krencker, Die Wallfahrtskirche des Simeon Stylites in Kal'at Sim'ân. i, pp.20f.

colonnades are arranged handsome columns of polished stone, sustaining a roof of considerable elevation; while the center is occupied by an unroofed court of the most excellent workmanship, where stands the pillar, of forty cubits, on which the incarnate angel upon earth spent his heavenly life."[14] Since Evagrius explicitly describes the central area as an unroofed or open air court (αὐλὴ ὑπαιθρίος), this must be accepted as the state of the church at the time of his visit. The probability is, however, not that it had been built that way originally, but that by the time Evagrius came the dome had been destroyed by fire or earthquake. When it proved too difficult to rebuild, the central room was left from that time on as an open court.

In the year 979 some further building work was done at Qalat Siman, as is indicated by an inscription which was found written in Greek and in Syrian. The Syrian form of the inscription gives the date in the Seleucid era as 1290, which refers to the year extending from October 7, 978, to October 6, 979. The Greek inscription actually uses the Christian era (κατὰ Χ[ν]), a system of reckoning which in this time occurs but seldom.[15]

Around Qalat Siman were grouped monasteries, and at the foot of the western hill was a town whose ruins show what elaborate accommodations were necessary to care for the large numbers of pilgrims who for centuries came to the place made memorable by the saint whom Evagrius called an "aerial martyr."[16]

7. CHURCHES IN EGYPT

THE CHURCH OF ST. MENAS

For a single example of early Christian churches in Egypt we turn to the remarkable ruined city of St. Menas, Karm Abu Mina, the "vineyard of Menas." According to the legendary lives of this saint, he was an Egyptian born of Christian parents in answer to a prayer of the mother addressed to an ikon of the Virgin. Since a voice seemed to answer this prayer with "Amen," the child was named Amen, or Menas. Growing up, he became a soldier and was on duty at Cotyaea in Phrygia when Diocletian's persecution broke out. Here, around

[14] *Church History.* I, 14 (*Bohn's Ecclesiastical Library.* 1854, pp.275f.).
[15] A slightly earlier example from the year 834 (ἀπὸ δὲ Χριστο[ῦ] ἔτους ω[λ]δ) is found in CIG IV, No.8680.
[16] *Church History.* I, 13.

A.D. 295, Menas bravely confessed his faith in Christ and suffered martyrdom. When his fellow soldiers were sent back from Phrygia to the Mareotis district in Egypt they took his corpse with them. They were threatened en route by terrible sea monsters, but fire went forth from the corpse and drove the creatures back. Arriving safely in Egypt, they buried the body of Menas beside the Lake of Mareotis where he had been born. When the troops were moved again they placed the bones of the saint on a camel to carry with them, but the camel refused to move. When another camel did likewise, it was interpreted as a sign and the bones were interred permanently at the place where the camels had stood. The grave would have been forgotten, save that one day a sick sheep drank from the nearby spring and was miraculously healed. Other wonderful healings, not only of animals but also of men, began to take place, and so many pilgrims were attracted there that a church was built above the martyr's tomb and an entire pilgrim city sprang up. Almost everyone who came carried away in a little flask some of the water from the spring or some oil from the lamp which hung in the church and burned day and night. Wherever the water or oil was carried miraculous healings took place.[1]

As remarkable as are the legends attaching to the name of St. Menas, almost more remarkable still are the actual churches and city which were built at his grave, lost for nearly one thousand years, and rediscovered at the beginning of the twentieth century. The Lake of Mareotis dried up in the Middle Ages and, although during the siege of Alexandria in 1801 the British cut through the dunes at Abusir and let in the sea, the ruins of the city of St. Menas lie now in a barren wilderness. The site, which is thirty miles or more southwest of Alexandria, was rediscovered and excavated by Carl Maria Kaufmann in 1905-1907.[2]

The Burial Church of St. Menas seems to have been consecrated under the Emperor Theodosius I the Great (379-395) although the first building work above the martyr's grave may have been done by Athanasius (c.298-373) with the help and interest of Constantine himself. The Burial Church was a basilica, 125 feet long and 74 feet

---

[1] For a reference to the custom, doubtless based originally upon James 5:14, of taking home oil from the lamps at church to anoint the sick, see Chrysostom, *Homilies on Matthew*. XXXII, 9 (NPNF X, p.217).

[2] C. M. Kaufmann, *Die Ausgrabung der Menasheiligtümer in der Mareotiswüste*. 1906; *Zweiter Bericht über die Ausgrabung der Menasheiligtümer in der Mareotiswüste*. 1907; *Die Menasstadt*. 1910; *Die heilige Stadt der Wüste*. 4th ed. 1924; Leclercq in DACL XI, cols. 324-397.

wide, with nave and aisles each terminating in an apse. It was so arranged that the altar came directly above the martyr's crypt which lay some twenty-six feet below. Not only did this *confessio* enable the holy tomb to be viewed from the room above but also there was provided a great marble stairway at one side which led directly down into the crypt. On the wall opposite the point at which the stairway enters the crypt the place can still be seen where a large marble plate was once affixed, doubtless bearing the famous representation of Menas with two camels bowing down to him. A photograph of the crypt is shown in Fig. 200. The picture is taken from a little chapel on the west of the crypt and looks toward the cryptoporticus which was built later to connect with the basilica of Arcadius. The recess which once held the Menas relief is on the south wall at the immediate right and is approximately three-quarters life size. While this relief no longer exists, it doubtless was the prototype of the picture of Menas between the camels which is stamped on so many of the flasks which were carried away from here by pilgrims. One of these flasks is shown in Fig. 201.

The basilica just described was oriented from west to east. Under the Emperor Arcadius (395-408), in order to accommodate the increasing masses of people a much larger basilica was built on at the eastern end of the first church. A large transept, 164 feet long and 66 feet wide gave the latter structure the form of a cross. At the same time a monumental baptistery church was erected at the western end of the first church. This was a square structure, which was turned into an octagon by the niches in the corners. In the center of its marble pavement was the deep marble tank, entered by steps from each side, in which the immersions were conducted (Fig. 202).

Notably under the eastern Emperor Zeno (474-491) this place developed into a great pilgrim city, and yet other basilicas, baths, and guesthouses were erected. Also there was a flourishing pottery industry which produced lamps, statuettes, plates, vases, and flasks for the pilgrims. Eventually came decline. In the seventh and eighth centuries, the Melchites and Jacobites[3] contended for possession of the sanctuary and in the ninth century a Melchite architect was permitted to carry away the church's marble pillars. Later in the

[3] The Melchites were Egyptian Christians who accepted the decrees of the Council of Chalcedon (A.D. 451) which were directed against the Jacobites and others. The Jacobites took their name from Jacob Baradai, bishop of Edessa (d. 578), the reorganizer of Syrian Monophysitism.

ninth century the place was despoiled by the Muslims and thereafter it became the prey of marauding Bedouins. The Church of St. Menas was seen around A.D. 1000 by an anonymous Arab traveler, but from then until its rediscovery by Kaufmann in 1905 it remained lost beneath the sands of the Mareotic Desert.

8. CHURCHES IN CONSTANTINOPLE

AFTER the defeat and death of Licinius (324), Constantine lived almost continuously in the East and in A.D. 330 officially founded his new capital, Constantinople, which formerly had been the city of Byzantium.[1] New Rome, as Constantinople was also called, was intended to be a wholly Christian city and therefore was adorned not only with a hippodrome, baths, fountains, and porticoes, but also with numerous houses of prayer and memorials of martyrs. A little distance away on the Bosporus was a sanctuary of the Archangel Michael.[2]

THE CHURCH OF ALL THE APOSTLES

At least two churches were founded by Constantine within the city.[3] One of these was dedicated to All the Apostles and intended by Constantine to be his own last resting place.[4] According to Eusebius, the building was carried to a vast height and had a great dome. From foundation to roof it was encased with slabs of various colored marbles while the roof was of brass adorned with gold.[5] This church was reconstructed by Justinian the Great (527-565),[6] but upon the fall of Constantinople to the Turks in 1453 was torn

[1] In Nicomedia of Bithynia, which had served as capital and under Diocletian had been the chief city of the East, Constantine erected a magnificent and stately church as "a memorial of his victory over his own enemies and the adversaries of God" (Eusebius, *Life of Constantine*. III, 50).

[2] Sozomen, *Ch. Hist.* II, 3; Eusebius, *Life of Constantine*. III, 48.

[3] That Constantine later gave encouragement at least toward the building of yet other churches is indicated by his letter to Eusebius (*Life of Constantine*. IV, 36), in which the emperor mentions the need for an increased number of churches in Constantinople to accommodate the growing mass of Christians, and places an order for fifty fine copies of the Bible to be placed in these churches (cf. p.397).

[4] Eusebius, *Life of Constantine*. IV, 70; Socrates, *Ch. Hist.* I, 40.

[5] *Life of Constantine*. IV, 58-60.

[6] Procopius, *Buildings*. I, iv, 9-16. Procopius stated (*ibid.*, I, iv, 19) that the church was built by the Emperor Constantius but the explanation of this difference from Eusebius is doubtless that it was begun by Constantine and completed after his death by his son.

down and replaced by the Mosque of Sultan Mohammed II the Conqueror.[7] The Church of All the Apostles was resembled closely by Justinian's Church of St. John at Ephesus[8] and also is believed to have served as a model for St. Mark's at Venice.

THE CHURCH OF ST. EIRENE

The second church had already been in existence as a Christian sanctuary in the old town of Byzantium, but was considerably enlarged and adorned by Constantine. He dedicated it to holy peace —Eirene—in honor of the peace which he had brought to the world after eighteen years of civil war.[9] In this Constantine followed the example of Augustus who likewise had symbolized the calm and quiet he brought to a torn world by the dedication of an altar at Rome, the Ara Pacis, to the imperial peace. Constantine's church stood for two centuries and then was burned to the ground in the fire of A.D. 532. It was restored by Justinian the Great,[10] but again damaged by fire in 564 and seriously injured by the violent earthquake of 740. The church still stands but has been used by the Turks as an armory and a museum. The present walls of the main body of the building probably date from the new structure erected by Justinian after 532, and the narthex and some other portions represent the same emperor's repairs after 564. The apse and upper part of the church including the dome probably belong to the reconstruction after the earthquake and may have been carried out by the Emperor Leo III the Isaurian (717-740) or by his son and successor Constantine V Copronymus (740-775).[11]

The essential plan of St. Eirene as it now exists is that of the basilica, with atrium, narthex, nave, side aisles, and apse. But a great dome is placed above the nave, even as Eusebius mentioned a dome as a prominent feature of the lost Church of All the Apostles. The combination of a domed superstructure with the earlier ground plan of the basilica became the characteristic theme of Byzantine church buildings. The culminating example of the domed basilica type was to appear in Justinian's church of Hagia Sophia in Constantinople.

[7] A. Van Millingen, *Byzantine Churches in Constantinople.* 1912, pp.3,175; Ernest Mamboury, *Constantinople.* 1925, p.355.

[8] Procopius, *Buildings.* v, i, 6.   [9] Socrates, *Ch. Hist.* i, 16; ii, 16.

[10] Procopius, *Buildings.* i, ii, 13.

[11] Walter S. George, *The Church of Saint Eirene at Constantinople.* 1912; Van Millingen, *Byzantine Churches in Constantinople*, pp.101f.

THE CHURCH OF HAGIA SOPHIA

The first foundations of the famous Church of Hagia Sophia,[12] or "Holy Wisdom," are believed by some to have been laid by Constantine,[13] but the church historian Socrates states only that it was built by Constantine's son and successor, Constantius II (337-361) and consecrated in A.D. 360.[14] It was known as "The Great Church"[15] and was dedicated to the Immortal Wisdom of Christ. The structure of Constantius was of the basilican type, with atrium, narthex, and nave flanked by side aisles marked off with rows of columns. Its roof was of wood, except for the half dome of the apse. This church was burned to the ground in A.D. 404, restored, and again burned down in A.D. 532. Then it was rebuilt in magnificence by Justinian, with Anthemius of Tralles and Isidorus of Miletus as his master builders. Dedication was in A.D. 537. Earthquake damage in 553 and 557 was repaired by Justinian and the dome somewhat raised by Isidorus the younger nephew of the other Isidorus. Since that time the Great Church has survived the vicissitudes of the centuries, little changed. The huge exterior buttresses were added by the Emperor Andronicus II Palaeologus (1282-1328), and the four minarets were erected after the Muslims made the church into "the great mosque of Hagia Sophia" (Fig. 203). In 1931 the Turkish Government issued an order enabling the Byzantine Institute to begin to lay bare and study the ancient mosaics with which the church was adorned.[16] In 1934 the use of the building for a mosque was terminated and it was announced that it would be preserved henceforth as a museum and monument of Byzantine art.

A contemporary description of Hagia Sophia as it appeared in the time of Justinian was given by Procopius of Caesarea, who wrote extensively concerning that emperor's reign and particularly his

[12] Alfons Maria Schneider, *Die Hagia Sophia zu Konstantinopel*; Emerson H. Swift, *Hagia Sophia*. 1940; William Emerson and Robert L. Van Nice in AJA 47 (1943), pp.403-436.

[13] A. Van Millingen, *Byzantine Constantinople*. 1899, p.36.

[14] *Ch. Hist.* II, 16,43.

[15] Procopius, *Buildings*. I, i, 66. This title was sometimes applied to include both Hagia Sophia and St. Eirene, which stood close together and were regarded as forming one sanctuary.

[16] Thomas Whittemore, *The Mosaics of St. Sophia at Istanbul, Preliminary Report on the First Year's Work, 1931-1932, The Mosaics of the Narthex*. 1933; *Second Preliminary Report, Work Done in 1933 and 1934, The Mosaics of the Southern Vestibule*. 1936; *Third Preliminary Report, Work Done in 1935-1938, The Imperial Portraits of the South Gallery*. 1942; and in AJA 42 (1938), pp.219-226; 46 (1942), pp.169-171 and Plates I-X; cf. Harold R. Willoughby in Massey H. Shepherd, Jr., and Sherman E. Johnson, eds., *Munera Studiosa*. 1946, pp.124f.

widespread and notable building achievements.[17] "The church," wrote Procopius, "has become a spectacle of marvellous beauty, overwhelming to those who see it, but to those who know it by hearsay altogether incredible. For it soars to a height to match the sky, and as if surging up from amongst the other buildings it stands on high and looks down upon the remainder of the city."[18] Impressive as was the exterior of the Great Church, the interior (Fig. 204) was more wonderful still. It was adorned with many colored marbles and bathed with an abundance of light until the visitor "might imagine that he had come upon a meadow with its flowers in full bloom."[19] The crowning glory was the huge golden dome which seemed not to rest upon solid masonry but to hang suspended from heaven.[20] In its misty vastness the Spirit of God seemed to descend, and whoever entered to pray felt "that He cannot be far away, but must especially love to dwell in this place which He has chosen."[21] Such was the culminating achievement in the Byzantine development of the basilica.

The mysticism of the East was matched by the aspiration of the West. In the West the path of future development led through the modifications of Romanesque style[22] to the Gothic,[23] whose soaring loftiness is the soul's upward reach toward God. But basic to both Gothic and Byzantine adaptations was the essential structural form and meaning of the early Christian basilica which they preserved. This was the place where was preached the gospel of Jesus Christ.

[17] The treatise on the *Buildings* of Justinian was published in 560 or soon thereafter.

[18] *Buildings.* i, i, 27.   [19] *Buildings.* i, i, 59.

[20] *Buildings.* i, i, 46.   [21] *Buildings.* i, i, 61.

[22] Romanesque means Roman-like and describes the architectural style which prevailed in the West from the fall of Rome (A.D. 476) down to the rise of Gothic. Here the basic basilican idea was modified chiefly through the increasing use of the rounded arch.

[23] Gothic architecture, which developed in Western Europe after A.D. 1100, was an outgrowth of Romanesque but particularly characterized by the use of the pointed arch.

Appendix

The Principles of the Calendar and the
Problems of Biblical Chronology

1. THE UNITS OF TIME

THE chief units in the reckoning of time for calendrical purposes are the day, week, month, and year, while the year is also divided into seasons and the day into hours or other parts. Revelation 9:15 mentions the units, hour, day, month, and year; and Galatians 4:10 speaks of days, months, seasons, and years. There are some indications, to be noted in what follows, which suggest that recognition of the day, week, month, and year was based first upon climatic and agricultural factors; later these units of time were associated with the celestial bodies.

THE DAY

In the Sumerian and Akkadian languages the word for "day" also means "wind." Likewise in the Song of Solomon 2:17 and 4:6 it is said that "the day breathes" or literally that it blows. It has been suggested, therefore, that it was first of all the daily land and sea breezes of the Mesopotamian and Palestinian coastlands which called attention to this time unit long before there was systematic observation of the sun.[1]

The rising and setting of the sun and the alternation of light and darkness were also very obvious facts of nature, however, and these too must have been recognized very early as marking out the day. In Hebrew the word for day is יום (yom). This is used to designate the day in the sense of daytime as distinct from nighttime as, for example, in Genesis 1:5 where "God called the light Day." It is also used for day in the sense of the complete cycle which includes both the daytime and the nighttime as, for example, in Genesis 1:5: "And there was evening and there was morning, one day." In Greek the corresponding word ἡμέρα is used for the daytime as, for example, in Matthew 4:2 where Jesus fasted for "forty days and forty nights."

[1] Hildegard and Julius Lewy in HUCA 17 (1942-43), pp.5f.

552

For the complete cycle of light and darkness there is a word, $\nu\nu\chi$-$\theta\acute{\eta}\mu\epsilon\rho\sigma\nu$, which combines "night" ($\nu\acute{\nu}\xi$) and "day" ($\acute{\eta}\mu\acute{\epsilon}\rho\alpha$) in one term. This is used in II Corinthians 11:25 where it is translated "a night and a day." Usually, however, the "day" which includes the nighttime and the daytime is simply designated with the word $\acute{\eta}\mu\acute{\epsilon}\rho\alpha$ and the context makes plain what is meant as, for example, in John 2:12 or Acts 9:19 where the several "days" are certainly several successive periods each comprising daytime and nighttime.

A "day" in the sense of a complete period of light and darkness might be reckoned as beginning with the coming of the light or with the coming of the darkness, as well as of course theoretically at any other point in the daily cycle, midnight now being used as that point. In Egypt the day probably began at dawn,[2] in Mesopotamia it began in the evening.[3] In the Old Testament the earlier practice seems to have been to consider that the day began in the morning. In Genesis 19:34, for example, the "morrow" (ASV) or "next day" (RSV) clearly begins with the morning after the preceding night. The later practice was to count the day as beginning in the evening. In Leviticus 23:27 it is stated that the day of atonement is to be observed on the tenth day of the seventh month; in verse 32 it is said that the observance is to be "on the ninth day of the month beginning at evening, from evening to evening." These last words can hardly be intended to change the actual date of the fast; rather they appear to be an addition which simply defines what the tenth day of the month was at a time when the day had come to be reckoned as beginning in the evening: the tenth day of the month is the day which begins on the evening of the ninth and continues until the following evening. In making the shift from a morning reckoning to an evening reckoning, the "day" was therefore in fact moved back so that it began a half day earlier than had been the case previously.[4]

In the New Testament in the Synoptic Gospels and Acts the day seems usually to be considered as beginning in the morning. Mark 11:11 states that Jesus entered Jerusalem, went into the temple, and when he had looked at everything, since it was "now eventide" (ASV) or "already late" (RSV), went out to Bethany with the twelve; verse 12 continues the narrative and tells that on the "morrow" (ASV) or the "following day" (RSV) they came back to the city. It is evident

[2] PCAE p.10.   [3] PDBC p.26.
[4] Julian Morgenstern in HUCA 10 (1935), pp.15-28; 20 (1947), pp.34-38.

that the new day has begun with the morning following the preceding evening. Likewise Matthew 28:1, Mark 16:1f., and Luke 23:56-24:1 all picture the first day of the week beginning with the dawn following the preceding sabbath. And Acts 4:3, for an example in that book, tells how Peter and John were put in custody "until the morrow, for it was already evening," thus clearly indicating that the new day would begin the next morning. On the other hand, Mark 1:32 = Luke 4:40 seems to picture the sabbath (Mark 1:21 = Luke 4:31) as coming to an end at sunset, at which time the people of Capernaum were free to bring the sick to Jesus. Likewise in the Gospel according to John the day seems to be reckoned as beginning in the evening. In John 20:1 Mary Magdalene comes to the tomb while it is still dark, yet it is already "on the first day of the week," hence the new day must have already begun. It is evident that this reckoning of the day as beginning with the preceding evening corresponds with the late Old Testament usage described in the preceding paragraph, and it may be assumed that this was the standard custom of the Jews in New Testament times as since. It has been suggested that the other usage, namely that of counting the day as beginning with the morning, is a continuation of the earlier Old Testament practice also already described, and that this usage was maintained in parts of Galilee and was followed by Jesus and the early disciples, which would account for its appearing so frequently in the Synoptic Gospels and Acts.[5]

The coming of light and the coming of darkness are of course gradual events, and it is therefore to periods of transition which are not necessarily sharply defined that the terms "morning" and "evening," as also "dawn" (e.g. Judges 19:25f.) and "twilight" (e.g. I Samuel 30:17), refer. For a more precise line of demarcation between one day and the next the time of sunrise or of sunset could be taken, and we have seen probable examples of such usage in Mark 16:2 and Mark 1:32 respectively. Or the determination could be made in terms of the intensity of the light or the completeness of the darkness. For example, it was held by the Jewish rabbis that Deuteronomy 6:4-7 required the recitation of the Shema in the evening and in the morning, and in the Talmud there is found an extended dis-

---

[5] Julian Morgenstern in *Crozer Quarterly*. 26 (1949), pp.232-240. It may be noted that the Greeks reckoned the day from sunset to sunset, and the Romans began the day at midnight. James Gow, *A Companion to School Classics*. 3d ed. 1891, pp.78, 147; and in Leonard Whibley, ed., *A Companion to Greek Studies*. 3d ed. 1916, p.589.

cussion of exactly what times are thereby intended. The recital could begin in the morning, it was declared, as soon as one could distinguish between blue and white (or between blue and green, as another rabbi taught), and it must be finished before sunrise.[6] As for the evening, Nehemiah 4:21 was cited, where work went on "till the stars came out," and from that analogy it was shown that the appearance of the stars was the sign that the day had ended and the recital could begin.[7] Thus in the morning it was either the dawning light or the following sunrise, and in the evening it was either the sunset or the ensuing nightfall when the stars became visible, that provided the line of demarcation.[8]

Parts of the day were described at an early time in terms of the customary occupation then performed as, for example, the "time for the animals to be gathered together" (Genesis 29:7), or "the time when women go out to draw water" (Genesis 24:11). The nighttime was divided into watches. Lamentations 2:19 speaks of "the beginning of the watches," Judges 7:19 mentions "the middle watch," and Exodus 14:24 and I Samuel 11:11 refer to "the morning watch." The rabbis debated whether there were three watches or four;[9] and Mark 13:35 names four: evening, midnight, cockcrow, and morning. The daytime had recognizable periods such as "the heat of the day" (Genesis 18:1) and "the cool of the day" (Genesis 3:8), and was also divided broadly into morning, noon, and evening (Psalm 55:17). A division of the daytime into three parts, and of the nighttime into three parts, is mentioned in Jubilees 49:10, 12.[10]

The word "hour" (שָׁעָה, *sha'ah*) occurs several times in Daniel (3:6, etc.) in Aramaic, and is common in later Hebrew. In Daniel it still denotes simply a short period of time and the phrase "the same hour" (ASV) may properly be translated "immediately" (RSV). In Greek the corresponding word is ὥρα, and it too is used for an inexactly defined period of time, as for example in John 5:35 where πρὸς ὥραν is translated "for a while."

In Mesopotamia the entire day was divided into twelve periods of what we would call two hours each.[11] Herodotus[12] refers to these

---

[6] *Berakoth.* I, 2; DM p.2.   [7] *Berakoth.* 2b; SBT p.3.

[8] As the line between one day and the next, nightfall was later defined even more precisely as the moment when three stars of the second magnitude become visible. Michael Friedländer in JE III, p.501.

[9] *Berakoth.* 3a-b; SBT pp.5-8.

[10] CAP II, p.80.

[11] Contenau, *Everyday Life in Babylon and Assyria*, p.11.

[12] II, 109.

"twelve divisions (μέρεα) of the day," and observes that the Greeks learned of them from the Babylonians. Among the Greeks themselves the day and the night were each divided into twelve hours.[13] These hours naturally varied in length depending upon the time of year and were known as ὧραι καιρικαί. For scientific purposes, an hour of standard length was used, the entire day (νυχθήμερον) being divided into twenty-four periods of equal length. The astronomer Hipparchus (c.150 B.C.) speaks of these "equinoctial hours" (ὧραι ἰσημεριναί),[14] as he calls them, and Ptolemy[15] also distinguishes between ordinary and equinoctial hours.

In order to measure the hours there were available for the time when the sun was shining the sunclock (πόλος) and the sundial (γνώμων), which are mentioned by Herodotus in the passage cited just above with the statement that they came from Babylonia. The same principle of measurement by the shadow of the sun was of course also known in Egypt, where the obelisks were evidently used for astronomical measurements.[16] For the measurement of time during the darkness as well as the light, there was the water clock (κλεψύδρα), which is mentioned by Aristotle[17] and others.

The division of the day into twelve hours appears in John 11:9 where it is asked, "Are there not twelve hours in the day?" Likewise in Matthew 20:1-12 the householder goes to hire laborers early in the morning, and again at the third, sixth, ninth, and eleventh hours, and the last ones have only one hour to work before the end of the day. If an average daytime lasting from six a.m. to six p.m. was taken as the basis, then the third hour was nine o'clock in the morning, and so on.

In the Talmud[18] there is a discussion in connection with the testimony of witnesses of the extent of reasonable error in a man's estimate of what hour it is, and it is noted that "in the sixth hour the sun stands in the meridian."

Among the parts of the day the "evening" was of special importance. We have already seen how the regularly used day in later Jewish times began in the evening rather than in the morning, and

[13] Gow, *A Companion to School Classics*, p.79.
[14] Hipparchus II, iv, 5. ed. C. Manitius, 1894, p.184.
[15] *Tetrabiblos*. 76. tr. F. E. Robbins, LCL (1948), pp.165-167.
[16] Henry N. Russell, Raymond S. Dugan, and John Q. Stewart, *Astronomy, A Revision of Young's Manual of Astronomy*, I, *The Solar System*. rev. ed. 1945, p.78.
[17] *Athenian Constitution*. LXVII, 2. tr. H. Rackham, LCL (1952), p.187. cf. Sontheimer in PWRE Zweite Reihe, IV, ii, cols. 2017-2018.
[18] *Pesaḥim*. 11b-12b; SBT pp.51-56.

how either the sunset or the appearing of the stars was taken as the exact time of its beginning. The evening was also important because of the sacrifices which were made at that time, and in this connection there was discussion of exactly what period of time was meant. According to Numbers 28:4 the daily burnt offering called for the sacrifice of one lamb in the morning and of another "in the evening." According to Exodus 12:6 the passover lambs were to be killed "in the evening" of the fourteenth day of the first month, and Leviticus 23:5 gives the same date for "the Lord's passover." In all three passages the Hebrew is literally "between the two evenings" (ASV margin), although in the first two cases the Septuagint translates simply πρὸς ἑσπέραν, "towards evening," and only in the Leviticus passage renders ἀνὰ μέσον τῶν ἑσπερινῶν, "between the evenings." The Mishnah[19] states that the daily evening burnt offering was slaughtered at eight and a half hours, that is two-thirty o'clock, and offered at nine and a half hours, that is three-thirty o'clock. If it was the eve of passover it was slaughtered at seven and a half hours, one-thirty o'clock, and offered at eight and a half hours, two-thirty o'clock, whether on a weekday or the sabbath; if it was the eve of passover and this fell on the eve of a sabbath, that is on a Friday, it was slaughtered at six and a half hours, twelve-thirty o'clock, and offered at seven and a half hours, one-thirty o'clock; and then the passover offering was slaughtered after that.

Explaining this procedure the accompanying Gemara[20] states that "between the evenings" means "from the time that the sun commences to decline in the west," and that the "two evenings" give "two and a half hours before and two and a half hours after and one hour for preparation" of the sacrifice. This means that "evening" begins as soon as the sun passes its midday zenith, and that the "two evenings" are from twelve to two-thirty o'clock, and from three-thirty until six o'clock respectively. Thus the daily evening burnt offering is ordinarily sacrificed in the hour between these two evenings, but when the passover must also be sacrificed the same afternoon then the daily sacrifice is moved ahead. In another passage the Mishnah[21] deals with the requirement of Exodus 34:25 that the passover sacrifice not be offered with leaven, and states that everything leavened must be burned at the beginning of the sixth hour, that is at twelve o'clock noon. As the accompanying discussion in the Gemara[22] shows,

[19] *Pesahim.* v, 1; DM p.141.   [20] *Pesahim.* 58a; SBT pp.287f.
[21] *Pesahim.* I, 4; DM p.137.   [22] *Pesahim.* 5a; SBT p.17.

this indicates that the sacrificing could begin immediately after noon. According to Josephus[23] the passover sacrifices were conducted from the ninth to the eleventh hour, that is from three to five o'clock in the afternoon, and this was presumably the standard practice in the first century A.D.

According to the foregoing passages, then, the "evening" was substantially equivalent to the entire afternoon. In Deuteronomy 16:6, however, it is said that the passover sacrifice is to be offered "in the evening at the going down of the sun." The Talmudic explanation of this was that the evening meant the afternoon and was the time when the passover was to be slaughtered, and that the sunset was the time when it was to be eaten.[24] The Sadducees and the Samaritans, however, held that the slaughtering of the lamb itself was to take place between sunset and darkness.[25] The Book of Jubilees seems to agree with this when it says about the passover lamb: "It is not permissible to slay it during any period of the light, but during the period bordering on the evening, and let them eat it at the time of the evening until the third part of the night" (49:12).[26] The Targum of Onkelos also rendered "between the two evenings" in Exodus 12:6 as "between the two suns,"[27] and this was then explained as meaning the time between sunset and the coming out of the stars.[28]

In either case, however, whether it meant the afternoon time up until sunset, or the time from sunset until the stars became visible, the "evening" in the sense and in the regard just discussed evidently belonged to the closing part of the day, and it was only with the sunset or the appearing of the stars that the next day began.

THE WEEK

A sequence of seven days forms a week. Since the ancient Babylonians recognized seven winds, as may be seen in the Creation Epic where Marduk "sent forth the winds he had brought forth, the seven of them,"[29] it has been surmised that originally one day was dedicated to each of the winds and thus a week of seven days was

---

[23] *War.* VI, ix, 3.   [24] *Berakoth.* 9a; SBT pp.46f.
[25] Emil G. Hirsch in JE IX, p.553.   [26] CAP II, p.80.
[27] J. W. Etheridge, ed., *The Targums of Onkelos and Jonathan ben Uzziel on the Pentateuch; With the Fragments of the Jerusalem Targum from the Chaldee.* 2 vols. 1862-65, I, p.370.
[28] S. R. Driver, *The Book of Exodus* (The Cambridge Bible for Schools and Colleges). 1911, p.89 n.
[29] ANET p.66.

formed.[30] In the Bible the days are simply numbered and the seventh day is also named the sabbath (שבת, shabbat; σάββατον). In addition to this, the day before the sabbath was called the day of Preparation,[31] and by the Christians the first day of the week was called the Lord's day (Revelation 1:10). The name of the entire week was derived from the sabbath day and the week was called שבע (shebua') in Hebrew (Genesis 29:27, etc.), σάββατον in Greek (Luke 18:12, etc.).

The custom of naming the seven days of the week after the seven planets is attested in the first century B.C. when Tibullus (d. 19 B.C.) mentions the day of Saturn, and in the first century A.D. when Greek and Latin wall inscriptions at Pompeii (A.D. 79) list "the days of the gods," namely of Saturn, the sun, the moon, Mars, Mercury, Jupiter, and Venus.[32] Dio Cassius[33] (d. A.D. c.235) says this custom was instituted by the Egyptians and was in his own time found among all mankind. Dio's remark in this connection, that the Jews dedicate to their God "the day called the day of Saturn," is of course correct as far as Jewish observance of Saturday or the sabbath is concerned, but they would hardly have designated the day by the name which the pagan writer uses. In an apocryphal rabbinic work, however, the *Pirqe de Rabbi Eliezer*, the final edition of which probably dates in the ninth century A.D., the planets which rule the week are named. For each day a pair is given, the first being the ruler of the nighttime and the second the regent of the following daytime: "The planets serve . . . as the regents of the seven days of the week, to wit: On the first day, Mercury and the Sun; on the second, Jupiter and the Moon; on the third, Venus and Mars; on the fourth, Saturn and Mercury; on the fifth, the Sun and Jupiter; on the sixth, the Moon and Venus; on the seventh, Mars and Saturn."[34]

[30] Hildegard and Julius Lewy in HUCA 17 (1942-43), pp.6-25.

[31] παρασκευή, Josephus, *Ant.* XVI, vi, 2; Matthew 27:62; Luke 23:54; John 19:31, 42; προσάββατον, Mark 15:42.

[32] Θεων ημερας

	(dies)	(the day of)	
Κρονου	Saturni	Saturn	Saturday
Ηλιου	Solis	the Sun	Sunday
Σεληνης	Lunae	the Moon	Monday
Αρεως	Martis	Mars	Tuesday (Tiw's day)
E[ρ]μου	(Mercurii)	Mercury	Wednesday (Woden's day)
Διος	Jovis	Jupiter	Thursday (Thor's day)
[Αφρο]δειτης	Veneris	Venus	Friday (Frigg's day)

Emil Schürer in ZNW 6 (1905), pp.25, 27.

[33] *Roman History.* XXXVII, xvii-xix.

[34] VI, 13b. *Pirkê de Rabbi Eliezer (The Chapters of Rabbi Eliezer the Great) according to the Text of the Manuscript belonging to Abraham Epstein of Vienna.* ed.

THE MONTH

If the day and the week were connected first of all with climatic conditions and only later with astronomical objects it could be that something similar was true of the month. In fact, when the Israelite calendar is discussed below, it will be seen that the Gezer Calendar relates the months to the tasks to be performed in the successive phases of agricultural work, and that the old month names in the Old Testament describe their respective periods of time in terms of agricultural and climatic conditions.

Etymologically, however, the word "month" shows the connection between this time unit and the moon. In Hebrew the word ירח (yerah) means both "moon" and "month," as may be seen for example in Deuteronomy 33:14 where the alternative translations are, "the precious things of the growth of the moons" (ASV), and "the rich yield of the months" (RSV). Likewise the term חדש (hodesh), which originally meant "the shining, glittering new moon," was later used as the designation of the festival of the day of the new moon, and also as the name of the entire month which is, as it were, the lifetime of the newly born moon. In Genesis 29:14, for example, this word clearly means "month," in I Samuel 20:5 and other passages it means the "new moon" day.[35] Likewise in Greek the word μήνη means "moon" and μήν means "month." In the Septuagint μήν is the translation of both ירח (Deuteronomy 33:14, etc.) and חדש (Genesis 29:14). In the New Testament μήν regularly means "month" (Luke 1:24, etc.), but in one case (Galatians 4:10) probably refers to the new moon festival.

In so far as the month was related to the moon, the determination of its length depended upon observation of the phases of the moon. In Egypt, where the day probably began at dawn, it is thought that the month probably began with a lunar phenomenon which could be observed at that time of day. As the moon wanes, the old crescent is finally just visible in the eastern sky before sunrise one morning and on the next morning it is invisible. It may have been, therefore, on the morning when the old crescent could no longer be seen that the Egyptian lunar month began.[36] In Mesopotamia, on the other hand,

---

Gerald Friedlander. 1916, p.32; Solomon Gandz in *Proceedings of the American Academy for Jewish Research*. 18 (1948-49), p.230. See also F. H. Colson, *The Week*. 1926.

[35] Solomon Gandz in JQR 39 (1948-49), pp.259f.

[36] PCAE pp.9-23.

the day began in the evening, and the month began when the crescent of the new moon was first visible in the western sky at sunset.[37]

In modern astronomy the time from one new moon to the next, which is known as the synodic or ordinary month, is determined as 29.530588 days, or 29 days, 12 hours, 44 minutes, 2.8 seconds.[38] This means that on the average the new moon will be seen approximately every twenty-nine and one-half days, and that the full moon will come approximately fourteen and three-quarter days after the appearing of the new moon, that is on the fifteenth day of the lunar month, with the day reckoned from evening to evening.[39]

After the accumulation of data by observation, the month could have been calculated in advance. Likewise it could have been established as a standard unit, say of thirty days, rather than left variable as it must be to agree with the observed phases of the moon.

THE YEAR

The ordinary Hebrew word for "year" is שׁנה (shanah). It is etymologically connected with the idea of "change" or "repeated action," and thus describes a "revolution of time." In the Septuagint it is translated both by ἐνιαυτός (Genesis 1:14, etc.), properly a "cycle of time," and more frequently by ἔτος (Genesis 5:3, etc.), and both Greek words are used for "year" in the New Testament (John 11:49, etc.; Luke 3:1, etc.).

Climatic and agricultural factors doubtless first called attention to the cycle of time that is the year. In Egypt the annual inundation of the Nile was an unusually prominent reminder of the return of the cycle, and was regularly followed by the season of sowing. In Palestine the climate was marked by the "early rain" or "autumn rain" which came in October/November, and the "later rain" or "spring rain" which came in March/April (Deuteronomy 11:14; Jeremiah 5:24),[40] as well as by the recurrence of summer and winter (Zechariah 14:8, etc.), and the agricultural seasons likewise returned regularly with the ripening of the olives in the fall (September/October-October/November), for example, and the shooting into ear of the barley in the spring (March/April).[41]

The autumn and spring seasons, to which attention was thus par-

[37] PDBC p.1.
[38] The American Ephemeris and Nautical Almanac for the Year 1958. 1956, p.xvi.
[39] Julian Morgenstern in HUCA 10 (1935), p.25.
[40] E. Hull in HDB IV, p.195.
[41] W. F. Albright in BASOR 92 (Dec. 1943), pp.22f. n.30 and n.37.

ticularly drawn by climatic and agricultural events, were also marked by the equality in length of day and night which occurs everywhere when the sun crosses the equator in each season. These points are now called the equinoxes, and by our reckoning the autumnal equinox falls about September 23, the vernal equinox about March 21. Likewise the summer and winter were marked respectively by the times when the day was at its greatest length and at its shortest length, or the times when the sun seems to stand still in its northward movement and again in its southward movement. These points are called the summer solstice and the winter solstice, and come by our reckoning about June 21 and December 22. When these several points were recognized they provided definite markers in the course of the year, and it was no doubt possible to establish them with precision by observation of the length of day and night and by measurement of the shadow of the sun.[42]

When such a mark as the vernal equinox is established, the length of the year from that point through a "revolution of time" and back to the same point can be measured. In Egypt, as will be noted in discussing the Egyptian calendar below, the length of the year was probably recognized as early as the third millennium B.C. as being 365 days, and with more exact measurements it was later found to be about 365¼ days. Among the Jews, Mar Samuel (A.D. c.165-c.250), who directed a school at Nehardea in Babylonia and was said to be as familiar with the paths of heaven as with the streets of his own city,[43] reckoned the year at 365 days and 6 hours, while his contemporary, Rab Adda, made it 365 days, 5 hours, 55 minutes, 25 and a fraction seconds.[44] In modern astronomy the length of the ordinary, tropical, or solar year, as it is called, is given as 365.24219879 days, or 365 days, 5 hours, 48 minutes, 45.975 seconds.[45]

When the four points of the vernal and autumnal equinoxes and the summer and winter solstices are taken, the year is readily divisible into four parts. Such a division of the solar year is found in the Talmud,[46] where the word תקופה (*tequfah*) is used as the name of each of the four periods. The word means "cycle" or "season," and a related form was found as "circuit" in the Manual of Discipline (see above p.294).

[42] Russell, Dugan, and Stewart, *Astronomy,* I, p.151.
[43] *Berakoth.* 58b; SBT p.365.
[44] JE III, p.500.
[45] *The American Ephemeris and Nautical Almanac for the Year 1958,* p.xvi.
[46] *Sanhedrin.* 11b; GBT VII, pp.36f.

In the course of the year the sun also seems to trace a path eastward against the background of the stars. This path is known as the zodiac. In a month the sun travels approximately one-twelfth of the way around this circle, and perhaps for this reason, the zodiac was divided into twelve sections.[47] Using the sexagesimal system of ancient Mesopotamia, the entire circle of the zodiac comprises 360 degrees, each of the twelve sections, 30 degrees. These divisions of the zodiac are designated according to the constellations of stars which they contain. Already in the Babylonian epic of creation we read of the work of Marduk:

> He constructed stations for the great gods,
> Fixing their astral likenesses as constellations.
> He determined the year by designating the zones:
> He set up three constellations for each of the
>   twelve months.[48]

Later a single constellation was taken as the sign of each of the twelve parts of the zodiac. In the tractate Berakoth[49] of the Talmud, the "Sovereign of the Universe" says: "Twelve constellations have I created in the firmament, and for each constellation I have created thirty hosts, and for each host I have created thirty legions, and for each legion I have created thirty cohorts, and for each cohort I have created thirty maniples,[50] and for each maniple I have created thirty camps, and to each camp I have attached three hundred and sixty-five thousands of myriads of stars, corresponding to the days of the solar year." In the Sefer Yeṣirah, a Jewish work of unknown antiquity, the names of the constellations are given as follows:[51] Taleh, Shor, Te'omin, Sartan, Aryeh, Betulah, Moznayim, 'Aqrab, Qeshet, Gedi, Deli, and Dagim. The Greek names, as found in Hipparchus, were as follows, the Latin forms and the meanings also being given:

1. ὁ Κριός, Aries, the Ram
2. ὁ Ταῦρος, Taurus, the Bull
3. οἱ Δίδυμοι, Gemini, the Twins
4. ὁ Καρκίνος, Cancer, the Crab
5. ὁ Λέων, Leo, the Lion
6. ἡ Παρθένος, Virgo, the Virgin

[47] F. von Oefele in HERE XII, p.51.
[48] ANET p.67.   [49] 32b; SBT p.201.
[50] Like the other terms, a subdivision of the Roman military organization.
[51] JE XII, p.688.

7. αἱ Χηλαί, Libra, the Balance
8. ὁ Σκορπίος, Scorpio, the Scorpion
9. ὁ Τοξότης, Sagittarius, the Archer
10. ὁ Ἀιγόκερως, Capricornus, the Goat
11. ὁ Ὑδροχόος, Aquarius, the Water Carrier
12. οἱ Ἰχθύες, Pisces, the Fishes

Since most of these were animals, from the word ζῴδιον, "a little animal," the entire zone was called ὁ ζῳδιακὸς κύκλος,[52] the zodiacal circle, or zodiac.

2. THE EGYPTIAN CALENDAR

IN ANCIENT Egypt the year was divided into three seasons. The first was called Akhet or "Inundation" and was the time when the Nile rose and overflowed the fields. The second was Peroyet or "Coming-Forth" when the fields emerged again from the flood waters and seeding, tilling, growth, and harvest took place. The third was Shomu or "Deficiency" and was the season of low water which came after the harvest and before the next inundation.[1] The recognition of these seasons, based upon climatic and agricultural factors, was undoubtedly very old.

It was also recognized that each season comprised approximately four lunar months. The year probably started with the lunar month which began after the river began to rise. The rise of the river normally begins at Aswan in late May or early June, and is about ten days later at Memphis. In addition to the observation of the moon there was another astronomical phenomenon which attracted attention in Egypt at an early time. This was the annual heliacal rising or first reappearance at dawn of the star Sirius, known as Sothis in the Greek spelling of its Egyptian name. In the fifth and fourth millenniums B.C. this rising was taking place at about the same time as the inundation and was probably recognized as the harbinger of the flood. As such it provided a precise point for the beginning of the year. Thus an inscription of the First Dynasty probably reads: "Sothis, the opener of the year; the inundation."[2]

Since the year was composed of lunar months this may be called

---

[52] Hipparchus I, vi, 4. ed. Manitius, p.56.
[1] Frankfort, *Kingship and the Gods*, p.367 n.3; PCAE p.32.
[2] PCAE pp.32, 34, 74 n.22.

a lunar calendar; since the beginning of the year was fixed by reference to a star, it may be described more specifically as a lunistellar calendar. A year composed of twelve lunar months, ordinarily alternating between twenty-nine and thirty days in length, makes 354 days, which is approximately eleven days short of the solar year. To keep the calendar year beginning in the spring in general and at the time of the heliacal rising of Sothis in particular, it must have been necessary to insert an additional month every three years or so. It seems that when this occurred, the intercalary month was put at the head of the new lunar year. This, it is believed, was the original lunar calendar of Egypt, and it was probably still in use in the Protodynastic period.[3]

Whether it was by averaging a series of these lunar years or by counting the days between successive heliacal risings of Sothis, it was also established that the true length of the year to the nearest number of days was 365. The disadvantages of a year composed now of twelve and again of thirteen lunar months must have been evident, and with the recognition of the year's length as 365 days the possibility of a new system emerged. After the analogy of the lunar system the year was still divided into three seasons and twelve months, but for the sake of simplicity and regularity each month was made thirty days in length. This left a shortage of only five days and, after the example of the intercalated month at the beginning of the lunar year, five epagomenal days were inserted before the new year. Since the months were no longer kept in relationship to the real moon but were fixed units in the solar year instead, this may be recognized as essentially a solar calendar, and since the units have an artificial regularity it may be called a "schematic" calendar. This system was introduced, there is reason to believe, between c.2937 and c.2821 B.C. and from then on served as the standard civil calendar of Egypt.[4]

The civil calendar of 365 days was still, however, not in exact agreement with the solar year since the latter is actually closer to 365¼ days in length. At the outset, it may be assumed, the first day of the civil year coincided with the heliacal rising of Sothis. After four years it would begin on the day before the rising of Sothis,

[3] PCAE pp.30-50, 53.
[4] PCAE p.53. This Egyptian calendar consisting of twelve months of thirty days each and five additional days at the end of each year has been called by Neugebauer (*The Exact Sciences in Antiquity*, p.81) "the only intelligent calendar which ever existed in human history."

after eight years, two days before, and so on. Only after 1,460 years, therefore, would the beginning of the civil year have moved all the way around the cycle to coincide once again with the rising of Sothis. Since the original lunar calendar was periodically corrected to keep its beginning point in connection with the heliacal rising of Sothis, the civil calendar gradually diverged more and more from the lunar calendar. It is assumed that this divergence would have become apparent by say 2500 B.C., and that around that time a second lunar calendar was introduced which was thereafter maintained in substantial harmony with the civil year. Thus from that time on, Egypt actually had no less than three calendars and three calendar years, and all of these continued in use throughout the remainder of ancient Egyptian history.[5]

3. THE MESOPOTAMIAN CALENDAR

IN MESOPOTAMIA also there was a lunar, or more strictly a lunisolar calendar. The moon-god was very prominent in Mesopotamia,[1] and observation of the moon no doubt began very early. As based upon the sighting of the new moon, the months were usually alternately twenty-nine and thirty days in length, although sometimes months of the same length in days would come in sequence, and occasionally there seems even to have been a month of twenty-eight days, which is explained on the supposition that two months of twenty-nine days had come together but bad visibility had prevented the seeing of the crescent and the first month had been erroneously assigned thirty days. Whether the months were eventually determined by calculation instead of visual observation is not known.[2]

Twelve lunar months constituted the year, and the year began in the spring. The following list gives the months in order together with their approximate equivalents in our calendar:[3]

[5] PCAE pp.54, 56.
[1] The moon-god was known as Nanna to the Sumerians (ANET p.38), and as Sin to the Akkadians (ANET p.88). Sin was the son of the air-god Enlil, the husband of the goddess Ningal, and they were the parents of the sun-god Shamash (ANET p.164 n.10; p.400 n.3). Sin was called "the lamp of heaven and earth" (ANET p.390), and he was worshiped specially at the temple of Egishnugal in Ur (ANET p.164). The crescent which is his symbol is familiar in Mesopotamian art (ANEP Nos.453, 518, etc.), and the god himself may be represented on the cylinder seal of an official of King Ur-Nammu of Ur (Hugo Gressmann, *Altorientalische Bilder zum Alten Testament*, 2d ed. [1927], Fig. 323).
[2] PDBC p.3.   [3] PDBC p.26.

1.	Nisanu	March/April
2.	Aiaru	April/May
3.	Simanu	May/June
4.	Duzu	June/July
5.	Abu	July/August
6.	Ululu	August/September
7.	Tashritu	September/October
8.	Arahsamnu	October/November
9.	Kislimu	November/December
10.	Tebetu	December/January
11.	Shabatu	January/February
12.	Addaru	February/March

Twelve lunar months fell of course approximately eleven days short of the solar year. At first the rectification of this discrepancy may have been made by simply taking the month which began nearest the vernal equinox as the first month of the new year. Later the method of intercalating an additional month as necessary was employed. This system was developed by the Sumerians and Babylonians and was adopted by the Assyrians probably by the time of Tiglath-pileser I (c.1114-c.1076 B.C.).[4]

By the eighth century B.C. there is evidence that it was recognized in Babylonia that the insertion of seven additional lunar months within a nineteen-year period would closely approximate the additional time needed to stabilize the calendar. By the fourth century B.C. fixed points were established for these seven intercalations, and the nineteen-year cycle was fully standardized. The months added were a second Ululu, the sixth month, or a second Addaru, the twelfth month.[5]

Since new-moon dates can be calculated astronomically for ancient Babylonia, and since the system of intercalation has been reconstructed on the basis of intercalary months actually mentioned in cuneiform texts, it is possible to construct tables which represent the Babylonian calendar with a high degree of probable accuracy.[6]

The achievement of the ancient Babylonian astronomers in devising the nineteen year cycle with its seven intercalated months was indeed remarkable. It has been noted above that one solar year equals 365.24219879 days while one lunar month equals 29.530588

---

[4] P. van der Meer, *The Ancient Chronology of Western Asia and Egypt.* 1947, pp.1f.

[5] PDBC pp.1f. [6] PDBC p.25.

days. Nineteen solar years, therefore, equals 6939.601777 days. In 19 12-month years there are 228 months; adding 7 more months makes a total of 235 months. Two hundred thirty-five lunar months equals 6939.688180 days. Thus, the difference between 235 lunar months and 19 solar years is only .086403 day or 2 hours, 4 minutes, 25.22 seconds. This is how close the ancient Babylonian system came to solving the problem of the relationship between the lunar year and the solar year.[7]

How the system worked in actual practice may be seen in the accompanying tabulation (p.569). This shows the first nineteen years of the reign of Nebuchadnezzar II (604-562 B.C.). The years are numbered and their equivalents in terms of B.C. are given; leap years are indicated by italicizing the last figure of the year when first given. The month names are abbreviated; U II and A II mean a second Ululu and a second Addaru respectively where these are intercalated. From the source table,[8] which shows the first day of each month in terms of our Julian calendar, the number of days in each month is counted and it is this figure which is shown for each month. The total number of days for the nineteen years is 6940; this is the nearest full number to the exact figure already noted above of 6939.-601777 days.

In Egypt we saw that the complexity of the original lunar calendar led to the introduction of a simplified civil calendar with twelve months of thirty days each plus five additional days prior to the new year. In Mesopotamia, too, there was a second calendar of exactly this same sort which was used alongside the real lunar calendar. Since its twelve months of thirty days each, running on in regular sequence regardless of the real moon, were really standardized divisions of the solar year, this was a solar calendar or a "schematic calendar." In Babylonian documents many dates have been found which are evidently given in this schematic calendar, and in some cases it is not possible to prove whether it is the schematic calendar or the real lunar calendar which is intended. But whereas the schematic calendar became the generally used civil calendar in Egypt, in Babylonia it seems to have been the lunar calendar which remained in most general usage, and Mesopotamia has properly been called "the classical country of the strictly lunar calendar."[9]

[7] Small as the difference is, it is precisely this discrepancy of 2 hours, 4 minutes, 25.22 seconds which provides the greatest complication in computing a perpetually fixed lunisolar calendar. cf. Siegfried H. Horn in JBL 76 (1957), pp.169f.
[8] PDBC pp.27f.   [9] O. Neugebauer in JNES 1 (1942), pp.398-401.

Nebuchadnezzar II (First Nineteen Years of Reign)

Yr.	B.C.	Nis	Aia	Sim	Duz	Abu	Ulu	U II	Tas	Ara	Kis	B.C.	Teb	B.C.	Sha	Add	A II	Number of Days in A Year
1	604	29	29	30	29	30	30		29	30	30		30	603	29	29		354
2	603	30	29	29	29	30	30	30	29	30	30	602	29		30	29		384
3	602	30	29	29	30	29	30		30	29	30	601	29		30	30		355
4	601	29	30	29	29	30	29		30	30	29		30	600	29	30		354
5	600	29	30	29	30	29	30	28	30	30	30	599	29		29	30		383
6	599	30	30	29	30	30	29		30	29	29		30	598	30	29		355
7	598	29	30	29	30	30	30	29	30	29	29	597	30		29	29		383
8	597	30	29	30	30	30	30		29	29	30	596	29		30	29		355
9	596	29	30	29	30	30	30	30	29	29	30	595	29		30	29		384
10	595	29	30	29	30	30	29		30	30	29	594	30		29	30		355
11	594	29	29	30	29	30	30		29	30	29	593	30		30	29	30	384
12	593	29	29	30	29	30	29		30	29	30	592	30		30	29		354
13	592	30	29	30	29	29	30		29	29	30	591	30		30	29		354
14	591	30	30	29	30	29	29		30	29	29		30	590	30	29	30	384
15	590	30	29	30	29	30	29		30	29	30	589	30		29	29		354
16	589	30	29	30	29	30	30		29	30	29	588	30		29	29		354
17	588	30	29	30	29	30	30		30	29	30		29	587	30	29	29	384
18	587	30	29	30	29	30	30		30	29	30	586	29		30	29		355
19	586	29	30	29	29	30	30		30	30	29	585	30		29	30		355
																	Total	6940

4. THE ISRAELITE CALENDAR

THE GEZER Calendar, which we have already described (p.182) as a small limestone tablet of around 925 B.C., written perhaps as a schoolboy's exercise, contains a list of months and therewith an outline of the year as it was evidently reckoned at that time in Palestine. The word used for "month" is ירח and the months are grouped and designated according to the type of agricultural work done at the time. Since the agricultural seasons in Palestine are well known (cf. above p. 561), including the ripening of the olive crop in September/October-October/November, the shooting into ear of the barley in March/April, and the subsequent barley harvest in April/May,[1] it is possible to tabulate the sequence of months in the Gezer Calendar together with their equivalents as follows:

1.	2 months	olive harvest	September/October
2.			October/November
3.	2 months	planting grain	November/December
4.			December/January
5.	2 months	late planting	January/February
6.			February/March
7.	1 month	hoeing flax	March/April
8.	1 month	harvest of barley	April/May
9.	1 month	harvest and festivity	May/June
10.	2 months	vine tending	June/July
11.			July/August
12.	1 month	summer fruit	August/September

We see, therefore, that at this time in Palestine the year was reckoned as beginning in the fall, and that it contained twelve months which were related to agriculture.

Turning to the Old Testament we find first a group of month names which are connected with agriculture and climate. There are four of these as follows: (1) The month Abib.[2] This word means a "fresh ear" of grain, as in Leviticus 2:14, and is used of barley when it is "in the ear," as in Exodus 9:31; hence used as a month name and with the article, "the Abib," it refers to the period when the barley shoots into ear. (2) The month Ziv.[3] This term signifies

---

[1] The harvest of barley begins in the Jordan Valley about the middle of April and in the highlands up to a month later. J. W. Paterson in HDB I, p.49.

[2] חדש האביב, Exodus 13:4; 23:15; 34:18; Deuteronomy 16:1.

[3] חדש זו, I Kings 6:1; ירח זו, I Kings 6:37.

"splendor" and is used of the "beauty of flowers"; hence the month name refers to the time of flowers. (3) The month Ethanim.[4] Coming from a word which means "permanent," this term is used in the plural and with the article as a month name which refers to "the permanent streams." (4) The month Bul.[5] The word probably refers to a period of "rain." Of these words both Ethanim and Bul have also been found as month names in North Semitic inscriptions,[6] hence these names, and probably others like them for other months, were no doubt common property among various Semitic peoples in this part of the world. We may call them the Canaanite month names.

Since Abib is, by the etymology of the name, the month when the barley shoots into the ear, we know that it must have been approximately equivalent to March/April (cf. above p.561), and it may therefore be equated with the seventh month in the list of the Gezer Calendar. According to Deuteronomy 16:1 Abib is the month of the passover, and according to Exodus 12:2f. the passover is held in the first month. This manner of reference makes Abib the first month rather than the seventh, and must simply represent a time when the year was reckoned as beginning in the spring rather than the fall and when the months were numbered from the spring. Similarly Ziv, the month of flowers, must be a spring month, and in I Kings 6:1 its name is followed by the explanation, "which is the second month." Likewise Bul, the month of rain, must be the month of "early rain" or October/November (cf. above p.561), and it is called the eighth month in I Kings 6:38. Ethanim, too, is named as the seventh month in I Kings 8:2. Showing, then, the months numbered both from the fall and from the spring, the Canaanite month names fit into the calendar as follows:

1	7	Ethanim	September/October
2	8	Bul	October/November
3	9		November/December
4	10		December/January
5	11		January/February
6	12		February/March
7	1	Abib	March/April

[4] ירח האתנים, I Kings 8:2.
[5] ירח בול, I Kings 6:38.
[6] Mark Lidzbarski, *Handbuch der nordsemitischen Epigraphik nebst ausgewählten Inschriften*. I (1898), pp.231, 236, 412.

8	2	Ziv	April/May
9	3		May/June
10	4		June/July
11	5		July/August
12	6		August/September

It is perhaps not without significance that it is precisely the first two months of the fall and the first two of the spring of which the names are preserved in the Old Testament. These are not only times of special importance in Palestinian agriculture but also the times of the two equinoxes. It will also be remembered (p.553) that in the early period the day was probably reckoned from the morning. These facts suggest that the orientation of this calendar was primarily toward the sun: the rising of the sun began the day; the equinoxes were the turning points of the year. If this was the case then, in the lack of other evidence, the guess may be hazarded that the months were not tied closely to the phases of the moon but were units of the solar year, probably thirty days in length, as in the "schematic" calendars of Egypt and Mesopotamia, and that the resultant shortage of about five days was simply made up by the insertion of additional days at the end of the year.[7]

The supposition is, therefore, that the Israelite calendar was originally agricultural and that as it was harmonized more accurately with the movements of the celestial bodies it was primarily the relationship to the sun that was kept in view. In this period both Egyptian and Phoenician influences were strong in Israel, and both would be expected to have contributed to the solar emphasis. As far as Egypt is concerned, this was the great power which cast its shadow over Palestine until the defeat of Pharaoh Necho by Nebuchadnezzar in 605 B.C. (pp.130, 220). In Egypt the sun was very prominent, as evidenced by the numerous sun deities in the pantheon, and a schematic solar calendar was the standard civil calendar (p.565).

As far as Phoenicia is concerned, we know that Solomon, who reigned shortly before the time ascribed to the Gezer Calendar, entered into close relationships with Hiram, King of Tyre, particularly for help in the building of the temple at Jerusalem (I Kings 5, etc.). According to Josephus,[8] Hiram built new temples to Astarte and

---

[7] In his study of intercalation and the Hebrew calendar (in VT 7 [1957], pp.250-307), J. B. Segal adduces evidence to show that intercalation was already practiced in Israel in the early days of the monarchy (*ibid.*, p.259).

[8] *Against Apion.* I, 18; *Ant.* VIII, v, 3.

Herakles, which suggests interest in the celestial bodies particularly including the sun, since Astarte was generally associated with the planet Venus or with the moon, and Herakles was connected with the sun especially in Phoenicia. According to Porphyry (A.D. 233-c.304) who was born in Phoenicia, probably at Tyre, the Phoenicians gave the name of Herakles to the sun and considered the twelve labors of Herakles to represent the passage of the sun through the twelve signs of the zodiac.[9]

At Jerusalem the temple which Hiram helped Solomon to build may have been so constructed that the sun shone directly in through its eastern gate on the two equinoctial days of the year,[10] and we find that later Josiah "removed the horses that the kings of Judah had dedicated to the sun, at the entrance to the house of the Lord" and "burned the chariots of the sun with fire" (II Kings 23:11), and that again in Ezekiel's time men stood at the door of the temple, "with their backs to the temple of the Lord, and their faces toward the east, worshiping the sun toward the east" (Ezekiel 8:16). Therefore it seems entirely likely that at least from the time of Solomon and under the influence of Egypt and Phoenicia the calendar of Israel was a schematic solar calendar.[11]

5. THE BABYLONIAN CALENDAR IN PALESTINE

IT HAS been noted in the preceding section that the month names Abib, Ziv, Ethanim, and Bul appear in the Old Testament, that these are probably the old Canaanite designations, and that in some instances the occurrence of the names is followed by an explanatory statement indicating, for example, that Ziv is the second month, Ethanim the seventh month, and so on. These numerical equivalents look as if they were added to the records at a time when the old names were no longer so commonly employed and when a different system had come into use, namely a designation of the months by number alone. Such a system is actually found elsewhere in Kings (I 12:32, etc.), Jeremiah (1:3, etc.), Ezekiel (1:1, etc.), and many other books of the Old Testament, and all of the months from the

---

[9] Quoted by Eusebius, *Praeparatio Evangelica.* III, xi, 25. ed. Karl Mras in GCS, Eusebius VIII, 1 (1954), pp.139f. cf. Charles Anthon, *A Classical Dictionary.* 1843, p.599.

[10] Julian Morgenstern in HUCA 6 (1929), pp.16-19.

[11] Julian Morgenstern in VT 5 (1955), pp.67-69.

first to the twelfth are so designated. Likewise in the majority of the apocryphal and pseudepigraphical writings the same system of indicating the months by number is followed.[1]

It has also been noted that in the earlier system the months were listed from the fall, but in the new system where the months are designated by number the numbering begins in the spring. In addition to evidence already cited, there is a plain example of the latter usage when Jeremiah 36:9 mentions the ninth month and the following verse 22 indicates that it was in the winter: counting from the fall, the ninth month would be in the summer; counting from the spring, the ninth month would be in the winter.

The beginning of the year in the spring is in accordance with what we have seen was the usage in Mesopotamia, and it is therefore a reasonable surmise that the new calendrical system was derived from that source. The latest contemporary use of the old Canaanite names is probably in Deuteronomy 16:1.[2] The book of Deuteronomy is commonly supposed to have been edited in connection with the reformation of Josiah and found in the temple in 621 B.C. (II Kings 22:8).[3] The earliest citation in terms of the new system is probably that of the ninth month in the fifth year of Jehoiakim (604/603 B.C.) in Jeremiah 36:9. According to this evidence, the new system was introduced in Judah between 621 and 604 B.C. In 605 B.C., as we have already seen (pp.130, 220), Nebuchadnezzar defeated Necho, and Palestine passed from the sway of Egypt to the domination of Babylon. It may be concluded, accordingly, that it was at that time that the Babylonian way of reckoning was officially established in Palestine.[4]

That the new system of months numbered from a point of beginning in the spring was really the Babylonian system is shown by the fact that the Babylonian names for the months are also found later in the Old Testament. In a number of passages in Esther and Zechariah the month is cited first by number and then by name. The months which so appear are: "the first month, which is the month of Nisan" (Esther 3:7); "the third month, which is the month of Sivan" (Esther 8:9); "the ninth month, which is Chislev" (Zechariah 7:1); "the tenth month, which is the month of Tebeth" (Esther 2:16); "the eleventh month, which is the month of Shebat" (Zechariah

[1] Julian Morgenstern in HUCA 1 (1924), p.19.
[2] Morgenstern in HUCA 1 (1924), p.18.
[3] Pfeiffer, *Introduction to the Old Testament*, p.181.
[4] Elias Auerbach in VT 2 (1952), p.336.

574

1:7); and "the twelfth month, which is the month of Adar" (Esther 3:7, etc.). In Ezra and Nehemiah the month is sometimes referred to by number (Ezra 7:8, etc.; Nehemiah 7:73, etc.), but in the following cases is cited by name alone: Nisan (Nehemiah 2:1), Elul (Nehemiah 6:15), Chislev (Nehemiah 1:1); Adar (Ezra 6:15). The sources just cited are generally considered to be among the latest books in the Old Testament, and thus the use of these month names must have begun relatively late, perhaps from the fourth century B.C. on.[5] The first work in which only the Babylonian names are employed is probably Megillat Ta'anit, the "Scroll of Fasting." This is essentially a list, written probably just after the beginning of the first century A.D., of thirty-six Jewish festivals. The book is divided into twelve chapters, corresponding to the twelve months. The first chapter treats the memorial days of the first month, Nisan, and so on to the twelfth chapter which deals with those of the twelfth month, Adar.[6]

The fact that the numbering of the months according to the Babylonian system came into use among the Jews before the actual month names were adopted may indicate a complex evolution,[7] but would seem to be explicable most simply on the grounds that the numbers did not carry the associations of pagan religion which some of the names did. Thus the month Tammuz (Babylonian Duzu) bore the name of the famous dying god of Mesopotamia, the weeping for whom of the women of Jerusalem was such an abomination in the eyes of Ezekiel (8:14) (cf. above p.533 n.22); and the month Elul may have meant "shouting for joy" in the celebration of the restoration to life of the same deity.[8]

As a result of the development just sketched, then, the list of months in use among the Jews at the end of the Old Testament period was as shown in the following table where the number, Babylonian name, Hebrew name, and approximate equivalent in our months are given:[9]

[5] Morgenstern in HUCA 1 (1924), p.20.
[6] Hans Lichtenstein in HUCA 8-9 (1931-32), pp.257-351; J. Z. Lauterbach in JE VIII, pp.427f.
[7] Morgenstern in HUCA 1 (1924), p.21.
[8] I. Abrahams in HDB IV, p.765.
[9] PDBC p.24.

Number	Babylonian Name	Hebrew Name	Approximate Equivalent
1	Nisanu	Nisan	March/April
2	Aiaru	Iyyar	April/May
3	Simanu	Sivan	May/June
4	Duzu	Tammuz	June/July
5	Abu	Ab	July/August
6	Ululu	Elul	August/September
7	Tashritu	Tishri	September/October
8	Arahsamnu	Marheshvan or, Heshvan	October/November
9	Kislimu	Kislev or, Chislev	November/December
10	Tebetu	Tebeth	December/January
11	Shabatu	Shebat	January/February
12	Addaru	Adar	February/March

The Babylonian calendar was, as we have seen, essentially luni-solar. The months began with the first appearing of the crescent of the new moon in the evening sky, and the intercalation of seven months in nineteen years kept the year of lunar months in close approximation to the solar year. The question which now arises is whether along with the Babylonian order and names of the months, the full Babylonian system of strictly lunar months and of the intercalation of months was also adopted? The sources which will next be cited show that in general this is what was done, but that there were some variations in Jewish practice from Babylonian.

In Palestine it was the responsibility of the Sanhedrin in Jerusalem to determine matters connected with the calendar, and in practice this was done by a council of three men.

As in Babylonia, the month began when the new moon was first seen in the evening, but since the new moon was visible at Jerusalem thirty-seven minutes before it was visible at Babylon, it was possible that upon occasion the new month would begin a day earlier than in Babylonia.[10] The determination that the new moon had actually appeared and the declaration that the new month had thereby begun had to be made by the council just referred to, and the rules according to which this was done are presented and discussed in the Tal-

[10] PDBC pp.23f.

mud in the tractate Rosh Hashanah.[11] The testimony of at least two witnesses was required to establish that the new moon had been seen. So important were the observations of these witnesses that for the fixing of the new moons of Nisan and Tishri, the pivotal points of the year in the spring and fall, they might even exceed the travel limit of two thousand cubits on the sabbath day to bring their report to Jerusalem.[12] In Jerusalem there was a special courtyard where the witnesses were examined and entertained. In earlier time if they came on the sabbath they could not leave this place the whole day, because they had doubtless already used up their allowed travel distance, but Rabbi Gamaliel the Elder ruled that they could go two thousand cubits from it.[13] In the examination of the witnesses they were interrogated with such questions as whether the moon had been seen to the north or to the south of the sun. The point of this question lay in the fact that the new moon always appears due west; hence in the summer when the sun sets in the northwest the new moon is south of the sun, in the winter it is north of the sun.[14] Rabbi Gamaliel II even had a diagram of the phases of the moon on a tablet hung on the wall of his upper chamber, and used this in questioning the witnesses.[15]

When it was determined that the new moon had been seen, the beginning of the new month was proclaimed. On the scriptural warrant of Leviticus 23:44 where "Moses declared . . . the appointed feasts of the Lord," this was done by the solemn declaration of the head of the Sanhedrin that the new moon was "sanctified."[16] Also a trumpet was sounded,[17] as it is said in Psalm 81:3, "Blow the trumpet at the new moon." At one time flares were lighted too to signal the new month, but when the Samaritans introduced confusion by lighting misleading flares, messengers were sent out instead.[18]

While it was considered "a religious duty to sanctify [the new moon] on the strength of actual observation,"[19] it was also recognized that conditions might be such that the actual visual sighting could not be made and in this case it was established that one month would

[11] I, 3-III, 1; 18a-25b; SBT pp.73-115; cf. *Sanhedrin*. I, 2; DM p.382.
[12] *Rosh Hashanah*. 19b; SBT p.81 n.4.
[13] *Rosh Hashanah*. II, 5; 23b; SBT p.101.
[14] *Rosh Hashanah*. II, 6; 23b-24a; SBT pp.102f.
[15] *Rosh Hashanah*. II, 8; 24a; SBT p.105.
[16] *Rosh Hashanah*. II, 7; 24a; SBT p.104.
[17] *Rosh Hashanah*. III, 3; 26a; SBT p.115.
[18] *Rosh Hashanah*. II, 2-4; 22b-23b; SBT pp.96-100.
[19] *Rosh Hashanah*. 20a; SBT p.81.

have thirty days and the next twenty-nine. The month with twenty-nine days was considered "deficient" by half a day, the month with thirty days was "full," being half a day over the true lunar period. It was agreed that the year should not have less than five nor more than seven "full" months. At least in post-Talmudic times Nisan, Sivan, Ab, Tishri, Kislev, and Shebat had thirty days, and Iyyar, Tammuz, Elul, Heshvan, Tebeth, and Adar had twenty-nine. The science by which these determinations were made was known as the "fixing of the month" or as the "sanctification of the new moon."[20]

In his work entitled *Sanctification of the New Moon*, Maimonides (A.D. 1135-1204) gives in Chapters I-V a description of the way in which the calendar was anciently regulated by the Sanhedrin, and in his description of the manner of determining the new moon he shows that calculation as well as observation was employed. Maimonides writes:[21]

"Just as the astronomers who discern the positions and motions of the stars engage in calculation, so the Jewish court, too, used to study and investigate and perform mathematical operations, in order to find out whether or not it would be possible for the new crescent to be visible in its 'proper time,' which is the night of the 30th day. If the members of the court found that the new moon might be visible, they were obliged to be in attendance at the court house for the whole 30th day and be on the watch for the arrival of witnesses. If witnesses did arrive, they were duly examined and tested, and if their testimony appeared trustworthy, this day was sanctified as New Moon Day. If the new crescent did not appear and no witnesses arrived, this day was counted as the 30th day of the old month, which thus became an embolismic[22] month."

It was also necessary for the same council of the Sanhedrin to determine when an intercalary month should be added to the year. There is a discussion of "the intercalating of the year" in the tractate Sanhedrin.[23] Here in addition to mention of the council of three it is also stated that "A year cannot be intercalated unless the Nasi sanctions it."[24] The Nasi was the "prince" or chief of the Sanhedrin, and it would appear that he might or might not be a member of the council of three. An example is given where "Rabban Gamaliel

20 JE III, pp.499f. (Cyrus Adler); 502f. (M. Friedländer).
21 *The Code of Maimonides, Book Three, Treatise Eight, Sanctification of the New Moon*, tr. by Solomon Gandz, with introduction by Julian Obermann, and astronomical commentary by Otto Neugebauer (Yale Judaica Series, 11). 1956, pp.4f. (I, 6).
22 That is, a month containing an added day.
23 I, 2; DM p.382; 10b-13b; SBT pp.42-61.
24 11a; SBT p.47.

was away obtaining permission from the Governor of Syria,[25] and, as his return was delayed, the year was intercalated subject to Rabban Gamaliel's later approval."[26]

The rabbis taught, it is stated, that "a year may be intercalated on three grounds: on account of the premature state of the corn crops; or that of the fruit trees; or on account of the lateness of the Tequfah. Any two of these reasons can justify intercalation, but not one alone."[27] The minute calculations involved are referred to, and an example is given where the rabbis did not finish their calculation until the last day of the month preceding the month to be intercalated.[28] In Babylonia, as we saw, either a second Ululu or a second Addaru might be inserted in the year, but here it is stated flatly that "only an Adar can be intercalated."[29] When the intercalation took place the added month was called the Second Adar.[30] The length of the added month was left to the judgment of the council, and it might be either twenty-nine or thirty days in length.[31]

In the same tractate letters are quoted which were sent out by Rabbi Simeon ben Gamaliel and Rabban Gamaliel II. Simeon, son of Gamaliel I and head of the Sanhedrin in the two decades before the destruction of the Temple, wrote as follows: "We beg to inform you that the doves are still tender and the lambs still young, and the grain has not yet ripened. I have considered the matter and thought it advisable to add thirty days to the year." The letter of Gamaliel II differs only in that he, more modestly as the Talmud observes, associates his "colleagues" with himself in the decision of intercalation.[32]

In agreement with the foregoing, Maimonides[33] also gives a lucid account of the process of intercalation as conducted under the Sanhedrin. Noting that the solar year exceeds the lunar year by approximately eleven days, he says that whenever this excess accumulates to about thirty days, or a little more or less, one month is added and the particular year is made to consist of thirteen months. The extra

---

[25] Probably to obtain confirmation of his appointment as Nasi rather than to secure permission for intercalating the year, since it seems unlikely that the latter would have been required.

[26] 11a; SBT p.47.   [27] 11b; SBT p.49.   [28] 12b; SBT p.57.

[29] 12b; SBT p.55.

[30] The book of Esther was specified to be read in the month Adar, and in Megillah I, 4 (DM p.202) it is discussed whether, if the book has already been read in the First Adar and the year is subsequently intercalated, it must be read again in the Second Adar.

[31] 11a; SBT p.48.   [32] 11a-11b; SBT pp.47-49.

[33] *Sanctification of the New Moon*, I, 2; IV, 1-17. ed. Gandz, pp.4, 16-22.

month is never anything other than an added Adar, and hence an intercalated year has a First Adar and a Second Adar. This added month may consist of either twenty-nine or thirty days. The decision is made by the Council of Intercalation, with a minimum membership of three; if the Nasi or chief of the supreme court was not one of them his assent was also necessary. Continuing with his own exposition of the mathematics involved, Maimonides states that each group of nineteen years contains seven intercalated years and twelve ordinary years.[34] Therefore, in spite of the fact that the Jewish system used only added Adars, the result was the same as in the Babylonian system and seven months were intercalated in each nineteen years.

Both the tractate Sanhedrin and Maimonides[35] also show that the solar year was divided likewise into four seasons or *tequfoth* and into twelve signs of the zodiac (cf. above pp. 562-564). On the basis of a year of 365¼ days, one Tequfah was reckoned at 91 days, 7½ hours. The four Tequfoth were: the Tequfah of Nisan which began at the vernal equinox when the sun enters the constellation of Aries; the Tequfah of Tammuz at the summer solstice when the sun enters Cancer; the Tequfah of Tishri at the autumnal equinox when the sun enters Libra; and the Tequfah of Tebeth at the winter solstice when the sun enters Capricorn.[36]

6. THE CALENDAR OF JUBILEES

IN THE discussion of the Dead Sea Scrolls it was established (pp.293-297) that the Qumran community was zealous in its observance of what it held to be correct times and seasons, that these were different from what other Jews adhered to, that in this connection the community cited and possessed the book of Jubilees, and that in

[34] *Sanctification of the New Moon*, VI, 10. ed. Gandz, p.29.

[35] *Sanhedrin*. 11b; SBT p.49 and n.5; Maimonides, *Sanctification of the New Moon*, IX, 2-3. ed. Gandz, pp.36f.

[36] On the evolution of the calendar see also Hildegard and Julius Lewy in HUCA 17 (1942-43), pp.1-152C; Julian Morgenstern in HUCA 1 (1924), pp.13-78; 10 (1935), pp.1-148; 20 (1947), pp.1-136; 21 (1948), pp.365-496; and in *Occident and Orient, Gaster Anniversary Volume*, ed. Bruno Schindler. 1936, pp.439-456; P. J. Heawood in JQR 36 (1945-46), pp.393-401; Solomon Zeitlin in JQR 36 (1945-46), pp.403-414; Solomon Gandz in JQR 39 (1948-49), pp.259-280; 40 (1949-50), pp.157-172, 251-277; 43 (1952-53), pp.177-192, 249-270; and in *Proceedings of the American Academy for Jewish Research*. 17 (1947-48), pp.9-17; 18 (1948-49), pp.213-254. On chronology see also A. Hermann, F. Schmidtke, and L. Koep in KRAC III, cols. 30-60.

fragments of an actual calendar found in Cave 4 at Qumran historical dates are cited in Babylonian month names but liturgical dates are given in a system in which days of the week are fixed points as well as days of the month. The date of passover, for example, is fixed by Old Testament law (Exodus 12:6) as the evening of the fourteenth day of the first month of the year. It is evident that this date can readily be ascertained in terms of the Babylonian calendar, but that in this calendar the date will fall on different days of the week in different years. The Qumran liturgical calendar, however, also identifies the passover date as the evening of Tuesday, hence this was a calendar in which the days of the week remained constant in relation to the days of the month. Since the clue is available that the community referred to the book of Jubilees in the reckoning of time, it is necessary to ascertain if the calendar of Jubilees satisfies the condition just mentioned and to establish the nature of this calendar.

The book of Jubilees was probably written in the original Hebrew between 135 and 105 B.C., and is preserved in Ethiopic manuscripts and Latin and Greek fragments as well as the two Hebrew fragments which have now been found in Cave 1 at Qumran. Essentially a rewriting of the book of Genesis in the form of a communication from "the angel of the presence" to Moses on Mount Sinai, Jubilees places the biblical narrative within a chronological framework of years, weeks of years, and jubilees, and lays much emphasis upon the institution and proper observance of the festivals of the religious year.[1]

The passage in this book which tells most about the calendar is Jubilees 6:23-32:[2]

"And on the new moon of the first month, and on the new moon of the fourth month, and on the new moon of the seventh month, and on the new moon of the tenth month are the days of remembrance, and the days of the seasons in the four divisions of the year. These are written and ordained as a testimony for ever. And Noah ordained them for himself as feasts for the generations for ever, so that they have become thereby a memorial unto him. And on the new moon of the first month he was bidden to make for himself an ark, and on that (day) the earth became dry and he opened (the ark) and saw the earth. And on the new moon of the fourth month the mouths of the depths of the abyss beneath were closed. And on the new moon of the seventh month all the mouths of the abysses of the earth were opened, and the waters began to descend into them. And on the new moon of the tenth month the tops of the mountains were seen, and Noah was glad. And on this account he ordained them for him-

---

[1] CAP II, pp.1-10; A. C. Headlam in HDB II, p.791.
[2] CAP II, pp.22f.

self as feasts for a memorial for ever, and thus are they ordained. And they placed them on the heavenly tablets, each had thirteen weeks; from one to another (passed) their memorial, from the first to the second, and from the second to the third, and from the third to the fourth. And all the days of the commandment will be two and fifty weeks of days, and (these will make) the entire year complete. Thus it is engraven and ordained on the heavenly tablets. And there is no neglecting (this comandment) for a single year or from year to year. And command thou the children of Israel that they observe the years according to this reckoning—three hundred and sixty-four days, and (these) will constitute a complete year, and they will not disturb its time from its days and from its feasts; for everything will fall out in them according to their testimony, and they will not leave out any day nor disturb any feasts."

From this we learn that the year was divided into four periods or seasons. The beginning of each of the four successive periods was marked by the "new moon," which probably means simply the "first day," of the first month, the fourth month, the seventh month, and the tenth month, in other words each period comprised three months. Each period also contained thirteen weeks. Since this equals 91 days, there must have been two months of 30 days each and one month of 31 days in each group of three months. The complete year was composed, therefore, as it is also explicitly stated, of 52 weeks or of 364 days.

The nature of the calendar just outlined will be discussed further in a moment but first it is necessary to indicate that what seems to be the same system of reckoning is found in the book of Enoch. The book of Enoch[3] is a large and composite work preserved in a number of Ethiopic manuscripts and Greek and Latin fragments. Of the 108 chapters into which it is customarily divided, chapters 72-82 are called the "Book of the Heavenly Luminaries" and constitute a treatise on the laws of the celestial bodies. This part, and at least much of the rest of the book, was probably written originally in Hebrew. This section must be referred to in Jubilees 4:17 where it is said that Enoch "wrote down the signs of heaven according to the order of their months in a book, that men might know the seasons of the years according to the order of their separate months." This citation indicates a date earlier than Jubilees for the "Book of the Heavenly Luminaries," say not later than 110 B.C., and also shows that the

[3] Also known as I Enoch or the (Ethiopic) book of Enoch. On the book see CAP II, pp.163-187; R. H. Charles in HDB I, pp.705-708. For a date for all the principal sections of I Enoch in the reign or shortly after the death of Antiochus Epiphanes see H. H. Rowley, *Jewish Apocalyptic and the Dead Sea Scrolls.* 1957, pp.8f.

author of Jubilees held it in high regard, therefore presumably agreed with it as to calendar.

In the "Book of the Heavenly Luminaries" the motion of the sun is described (I Enoch 72) in relation to twelve "portals" which must be the equivalent of the signs of the zodiac. Beginning at what must be the vernal equinox, the sun rises, it is said, in the fourth of the six eastern portals. It comes forth through that portal thirty mornings in succession, during which time the day grows daily longer and the night nightly shorter. Moving into the fifth portal, the sun rises for thirty mornings; moving on into the sixth portal, it rises for thirty-one mornings. The relative lengths of day and night continue to change, and by this time the day reaches its maximum duration and the night its minimum, in other words it is the summer solstice. Then "the sun mounts up to make the day shorter and the night longer" (v. 15), and after thirty, thirty, and thirty-one mornings the day and night are of equal length, in other words the autumnal equinox is reached. The corresponding sequence is followed on through the second half of the year until at last again day and night are of equal length and the cycle has been completed at the vernal equinox. So, it is concluded, "the year is exactly as to its days three hundred and sixty-four" (v. 32).

This certainly appears to be the same calendar as in Jubilees, and is of special importance because it answers a question on which specific information was not provided in Jubilees, namely which month in each series of three months has the added day to make it thirty-one days in length. Here we learn that in each group of three months their respective lengths are thirty days, thirty days, and thirty-one days.

We may, accordingly, outline a series of three months in the calendar of Jubilees and I Enoch as follows:[4]

I.IV.VII.X.					II.V.VIII.XI.					III.VI.IX.XII.					
1	8	15	22	29		6	13	20	27			4	11	18	25	Wednesday
2	9	16	23	30		7	14	21	28			5	12	19	26	Thursday
3	10	17	24		1	8	15	22	29			6	13	20	27	Friday
4	11	18	25		2	9	16	23	30			7	14	21	28	Saturday
5	12	19	26		3	10	17	24		1	8	15	22	29		Sunday
6	13	20	27		4	11	18	25		2	9	16	23	30		Monday
7	14	21	28		5	12	19	26		3	10	17	24	31		Tuesday

[4] A. Jaubert in VT 7 (1957), p.35.

Since thirteen weeks are thus filled out exactly, it is evident that this same tabulation can represent not only the first three-month period of the year but also the second, third, and fourth groups of months as well. In other words, the first month is identical with the fourth, seventh, and tenth months; the second month is identical with the fifth, eighth, and eleventh months; and the third month is identical with the sixth, ninth, and twelfth months. Thus the one tabulation suffices to represent the entire year.

From I Enoch we also learn that the calendar year must have been considered as beginning at the vernal equinox, since the description there starts at the point where the days are first beginning to grow longer than the nights.

It is also necessary to ask on what day of the week the calendar begins. A clue is found in *The Chronology of Ancient Nations* by the Muslim author al-Biruni (A.D. 973-1048). As a source concerning Jewish sects al-Biruni uses the Kitab al-Maqalat, a manual of the history of religions written by Abu 'Isa al-Warraq in the ninth century. In this work this author speaks, says al-Biruni, "of a Jewish sect called the Maghribis, who maintain that the feasts are not legal unless the moon rises in Palestine as a full moon in the night of Wednesday, which follows after the day of Tuesday, at the time of sunset. Such is their New Year's Day. From this point the days and months are counted, and here begins the rotation of the annual festivals. For God created the two great lights on a Wednesday. Likewise they do not allow Passover to fall on any other day except on Wednesday. And the obligations and rites prescribed for Passover they do not hold to be necessary, except for those who dwell in the country of the Israelites. All this stands in opposition to the custom of the majority of the Jews, and to the prescriptions of the Torah."[5]

The Maghribis were a "cave sect," and there is reason to believe that they may have been the Qumran group or others connected with them.[6] Since it is stated that Wednesday is their New Year's Day, the calendar should probably begin with that day, and the days of the week should fall as shown in the tabulation above. The theological reason given for this beginning point is that on a Wednesday God created the two great lights. This is an obvious reference to Genesis 1:14-19 where God made the sun, moon, and stars on the

---

[5] *The Chronology of Ancient Nations*, ed. C. Edward Sachau. 1879, p.278.
[6] R. de Vaux in RB 57 (1950), pp.422f.; Rowley, *The Zadokite Fragments and the Dead Sea Scrolls*, pp.23f.; cf. Ernst Bammel in ZNW 49 (1958), pp.77-88.

"fourth day," and ordained that these "lights in the firmament" should be "for signs and for seasons and for days and years." It is evident that though the year begins with Wednesday, as far as numbering the days of the week is concerned Wednesday is still the fourth day, Saturday or the sabbath is the seventh, and so on. That the beginning of the year is also marked by the rise of the full moon can hardly be taken as anything other than an ideal statement, since even if in a given year Wednesday was full moon day it would not be so regularly.

While in the calendar that is arranged as we have just indicated, the days of the week and the days of the month cannot possibly remain in a fixed relationship to the phases of the moon, it is plain that the days of the week do remain in a fixed relation with the days of the month. Therefore it is possible to identify the position of festivals or other dates in terms of both the day of the month and the day of the week. Thus if the passover sacrifice is slain on the fourteenth day of the first month (Exodus 12:6) and the fifteenth day is the first day of passover,[7] it is Tuesday which is the eve of passover and Wednesday which is the passover day, and this is the case in every year. This agrees with the date of passover as given in the calendar fragments from Qumran Cave 4, and the other festival dates as given there (see above p.297) are also in exact agreement with what may be ascertained in our present tabulation, falling regularly on Wednesday, Friday, and Sunday.

The fixed relationship of the days of the month with the days of the week is of course precisely what is not found in a calendar of lunar months. As we have stated, in the Babylonian lunisolar calendar the fourteenth day of the first month falls upon different days of the week in different years. The point at issue here was evidently of much importance to those who used the calendar of Jubilees. By the observance of this calendar, it was said, as we have seen, "they will not disturb its time from its days and from its feasts . . . and they will not leave out any day nor disturb any feasts." Together with this positive affirmation concerning its own calendar, the book of Jubilees speaks strongly of the harm that is done by the use of a different calendar (6:36f.):

"For there will be those who will assuredly make observations of the moon—how (it) disturbs the seasons and comes in from year to year ten days too soon. For this reason the years will come upon them when they

---

[7] JE III, p.505.

will disturb (the order), and make an abominable (day) the day of testimony, and an unclean day a feast day, and they will confound all the days, the holy with the unclean, and the unclean day with the holy; for they will go wrong as to the months and sabbaths and feasts and jubilees."

That the calendar to which Jubilees objects is a lunar calendar is shown by the statement that it is based upon "observations of the moon," and also that it makes the year come in annually "ten days too soon." According to Jubilees, "three hundred and sixty-four days . . . constitute a complete year"; in the Babylonian calendar, twelve lunar months of alternately twenty-nine and thirty days each make a year of three hundred and fifty-four days.

If Jubilees objects to lunar reckoning, its own system is presumably essentially solar. That this is indeed its basis is made explicit by the mention of "the rule of the sun" in Jubilees 4:21, and the fuller statement in Jubilees 2:9: "And God appointed the sun to be a great sign on the earth for days and for sabbaths and for months and for feasts and for years and for sabbaths of years and for jubilees and for all seasons of the years." As a solar calendar, then, it evidently began the year with the vernal equinox, and it divided the year into four solar periods, twelve solar months, fifty-two weeks, and three hundred and sixty-four days as has already been outlined.

While the calendar is thus based upon the solar year and actually corresponds with it quite closely and subdivides it quite symmetrically, its total of three hundred and sixty-four days is still actually about one and one-quarter days short of the true solar year of about 365¼ days. With the passage of time this annual shortage would have accumulated into an obvious discrepancy with the seasons and would have required rectification. How the rectification was accomplished is not indicated in the sources with which we have just been dealing, but there is a possible clue in the Pirqe de Rabbi Eliezer where it is stated: "The great cycle of the sun is 28 years."[8] In twenty-eight years an annual shortage of one and one-quarter days would amount to thirty-five days. Thus if there were some system for intercalating five weeks in each 28-year cycle, the calendar would be kept in adjustment. Since a nineteen-year cycle of intercalation was derived from the Babylonian calendar, this 28-year cycle must have had some

[8] vi; ed. Friedlander, p.34. This work, already cited above (p.559), treats of the creation and at this point has reached the fourth day (vi-viii), therefore discusses the course of the planets, the sun, and the moon.

other origin and it would at any rate have fitted perfectly with the calendar of Jubilees.[9]

The calendar of Jubilees seems, therefore, to have been the calendar of the Qumran community. The community was willing to use the Babylonian calendar for matters of everyday life, but for dating the all-important festivals of the religious year it adhered to this other calendar which did "not leave out any day nor disturb any feasts." The Babylonian calendar was no doubt in general and official use at this time, but the community of the covenant evidently did not feel that it did justice to the requirements of the religious year. The calendar to which the community adhered was presumably, therefore, an older one which was believed to be connected with the proper arrangement of the festivals from some authoritative antiquity. Since this was a solar calendar, in distinction from the lunisolar Babylonian calendar, and since, as we have seen reason to believe, the ancient Israelite calendar developed in a solar form, it seems likely that the community believed itself to be maintaining the traditions of an immemorial past.

In the poem on times and seasons in the Manual of Discipline, we found (pp. 294f.) the acrostic Aleph, Mem, Nun, forming the word Amen. The numerical values of these letters of the Hebrew alphabet are 1, 40, and 50, making a total of 91,[10] exactly the number of days in each of the four divisions of the calendar. Thus, to the initiated ear, the liturgical response of the community in its prayers was a solemn affirmation of the divine wisdom so marvelously shown forth in the stately movement of the sun through the four 91-day seasons of the solar year, a movement which set the splendid pattern within which the divine Being was rightly to be worshiped.

[9] For the calendar of Jubilees see Julian Morgenstern in vt 5 (1955), pp.34-76; A. Jaubert in vt 3 (1953), pp.250-264; 7 (1957), pp.35-61; Joseph M. Baumgarten in jbl 77 (1958), pp.355-360. For other suggestions as to the method of intercalation in the calendar of Jubilees see E. R. Leach in vt 7 (1957), pp.392-397.

[10] The numerical values of the letters of the Hebrew alphabet are: Aleph א, 1; Beth (ב), 2; Gimel (ג), 3; Daleth (ד), 4; He (ה), 5; Waw (ו), 6; Zayin (ז), 7; Heth (ח), 8; Teth (ט), 9; Yodh (י), 10; Kaph (כ), 20; Lamedh (ל), 30; Mem (מ), 40; Nun (נ), 50; Samekh (ס), 60; Ayin (ע), 70; Pe (פ), 80; Tsadhe (צ), 90; Qoph (ק), 100; Resh (ר), 200; S(h)in (ש), 300; Taw (ת), 400. For this interpretation of the acrostic see D. Barthélemy in rb 59 (1952), p.200.

7. PROBLEMS OF BIBLICAL CHRONOLOGY

THE application of the calendrical principles worked out above to the solution of problems in biblical chronology is not always easy. It is at once evident that one question that arises in the interpretation of biblical dates is when the year was considered as beginning. In the early Israelite calendar, as we have seen, the year began in the autumn, while in the Babylonian calendar it began in the spring. From the tractate Rosh Hashana[1] we learn that a year beginning in the fall and specifically on the first of Tishri, the seventh month, continued in use for a long time, and also a year beginning in the spring and specifically on the first of Nisan, the first month. "On the first of Tishri is New Year for years, for release and jubilee years, for plantation and for vegetables," it is stated; and, "On the first of Nisan is New Year for kings and for festivals."

But in Bible dates it is not always easy to determine which manner of reckoning is used. Thus from I Kings 6:1, 37, 38 Edwin R. Thiele[2] deduces that the regnal year in the time of Solomon was counted from the first of Tishri in the fall, although the year beginning the first of Nisan was used for reckoning ordinary and ecclesiastical dates; but Julian Morgenstern finds that the same passages indicate a regnal year beginning with Nisan.[3] Again, when Nehemiah 1:1 and 2:1 refer to the month Kislev and the following Nisan, both in the twentieth year of Artaxerxes, Morgenstern[4] thinks Nehemiah was using a year beginning in Tishri, but Hayim Tadmor[5] suggests that Nehemiah simply carried over "the twentieth year" by mistake when the month of Nisan was actually the beginning of the twenty-first year or, alternatively, that the text should read "the twenty-fifth year" as in Josephus,[6] although the latter mistakenly changes the ruler to Xerxes. Thiele[7] thinks that the regnal year was counted from Tishri in Judah but from Nisan in Northern Israel; moreover that while the books of Kings and Jeremiah use a regnal year beginning in Tishri for the kings of Judah, in references to Babylonian or Persian kings the writers of Kings, Jeremiah, Haggai, and Zechariah use a year reckoned from Nisan, as Ezekiel also does in giving the years of the captivity of Jehoiachin; but W. F. Albright[8] finds this

---

[1] I, 1; DM p.188; 2a; SBT p.1.   [2] TMN p.31.

[3] *Occident and Orient, Gaster Anniversary Volume*, p.446.

[4] *op.cit.*, p.441.   [5] In JNES 15 (1956), p.227 n.10.   [6] *Ant.*, XI, v, 7.

[7] TMN pp.32f., 157.   [8] In BASOR 100 (Dec. 1945), pp.17f.

system too elaborate. At all events, whether the year was reckoned from fall or spring, in referring to the months by number the Old Testament always counts from Nisan as the first month.[9]

Another question which arises is as to when the regnal year of a king was considered to begin. The system which prevailed in Babylonia, Assyria, and Persia was that the balance of the calendar year in which a king came to the throne was counted as his accession year, and the first full year of his reign was reckoned as beginning with the next New Year's day. Thus, for example (cf. above p.208), Shalmaneser V died in the tenth month, Tebetu, of his fifth year of reign, and on the twelfth day of the same month, about the last of December, 722 B.C., his successor, Sargon II, ascended the throne. This calendar year was accordingly both the last year of Shalmaneser and the accession year of Sargon. Only with the following Nisan 1 did the first full regnal year of the new king begin. An event dated in the first year of Sargon II would fall, therefore, in 721 B.C. Since the year began in the spring rather than on our January 1, this date would be more precisely indicated as Nisan 721 to Nisan 720, or as 721/720 B.C.

In the alternative nonaccession-year system the year in which the king comes to the throne is counted as his first year of reign. If the reign of Sargon II were referred to according to this system, his first year of reign would be 722/721.

Again in the interpretation of biblical dates it is important to determine if possible which system is followed. Thiele[10] thinks that the kings of Judah followed the accession-year system from Rehoboam to Jehoshaphat, the nonaccession-year system from Jehoram to Joash, and the accession-year system again from Amaziah to Zedekiah; and that the kings of Israel followed the nonaccession-year system from Jeroboam I to Jehoahaz, and the accession-year system from Jehoash to Hoshea. If this is correct, then in the later period of the two monarchies both were using the accession-year system, and at the same time the biblical writers would presumably have used the accession-year system in their references to Babylonian or Persian kings.

Now for concrete illustration of the attempt to apply these principles to the establishment of Old Testament dates we may turn to the closing period in the history of the kingdom of Judah, the rele-

[9] TMN p.31.   [10] TMN pp.157, 281f.

vant archeological materials for which have already been presented in the chapter on Egypt (pp.129ff.) and the section on New Babylonia (pp.220ff.). There it was established from the Babylonian chronicle that the crucial battle of Carchemish took place approximately in Simanu (May/June), 605 B.C. The contemporary prophet Jeremiah equates the date of the battle of Carchemish with the fourth year of King Jehoiakim of Judah (Jeremiah 46:2).[11] We dated the death of Josiah at Megiddo shortly before Duzu (June /July), 609 B.C. The three months of reign of his successor, Jehoahaz (II Kings 23:31), were therefore Tammuz (Babylonian Duzu), Ab (July/August), and Elul (August/September). The accession of the next king, Jehoiakim, was then in Tishri (September/October), 609 B.C. Assuming the accession-year system and a regnal year beginning with Nisan, the first full year of Jehoiakim's reign began on Nisan 1, 608, and his fourth year began on Nisan 1, 605. Since the battle of Carchemish took place in the following summer, this is in agreement with the correlation attested by Jeremiah.[12]

According to II Kings 23:36 and II Chronicles 36:5 Jehoiakim reigned eleven years. If his fourth regnal year was 605/604 B.C., his eleventh year was 598/597.

From the Babylonian chronicle we have learned that it was in his seventh year (598/597 B.C.) and in the month Kislimu that Nebuchadnezzar marched to the Hatti-land and besieged Jerusalem, and that it was on the second day of Addaru, March 16, 597 B.C., that he seized the city.

The reign of Jehoiachin was three months in length (II Kings 24:8) or, more exactly, three months and ten days (II Chronicles 36:9). If it was counted as extending to the day of the fall of the city, Addaru 2, 597 B.C., three months and ten days before that was the twenty-second day of Arahsamnu, December 9, 598 B.C.[13] It will be noted below that Jehoiachin may not actually have been carried away from Jerusalem into exile until a few weeks after the capture of the city, perhaps on the tenth day of the following Nisan, April 22, 597. If his reign was counted as extending to that point, three

---

[11] cf. Josephus, *Ant.* x, vi, 1. In Jeremiah 25:1, according to the usual translation, the fourth year of Jehoiakim is equated with the first year of Nebuchadnezzar, but the Hebrew phrase used here is unique in the Old Testament and may perhaps be held to designate or at least include the accession year.

[12] Hayim Tadmor in JNES 15 (1956), pp.226f.; Edwin R. Thiele in BASOR 143 (Oct. 1956), p.24.

[13] WCCK p.33 equates the twenty-second of Arahsamnu with December 6/7.

months and ten days before would have been the first day of Tebeth, January 16, 597 B.C. It was in the immediately preceding month, Kislimu, that Nebuchadnezzar marched to the Hatti-land and besieged Jerusalem, hence the change in rulers must have come very close to the time of the inauguration of the siege. II Kings 24:8, 10 may even give the impression that Jehoiachin had already come to the throne at the time the siege was started, and Jeremiah 22:18f.; 36:30 may be interpreted as suggesting that Jehoiakim was killed in a court uprising which might have had the purpose of replacing him with the presumably more pro-Babylonian Jehoiachin in a last-minute effort to avert the attack of Nebuchadnezzar;[14] but II Chronicles 36:6 says that Nebuchadnezzar put Jehoiakim in fetters, and Josephus[15] states that it was the Babylonian king who killed him and ordered him cast out unburied before the walls.

Jeremiah 52:28-30 gives the number of people carried away captive by Nebuchadrezzar on three different occasions. The first item is: "in the seventh year, three thousand and twenty-three Jews." Josephus doubtless follows this source when he says[16] that Nebuchadnezzar carried three thousand captives to Babylon. Since Jeremiah here specifies the seventh year of Nebuchadnezzar this seems to be in agreement with the Babylonian chronicle which says that Nebuchadnezzar marched to the Hatti-land and took Jerusalem in his seventh year.

In II Kings 24:12-16, however, it is stated that it was in the eighth year of the king of Babylon that Jehoiachin was taken prisoner and he and "all Jerusalem" carried away to Babylon. Also the total number of those deported is given as ten thousand. The apparent discrepancy may doubtless be explained most simply by supposing that Jeremiah 52:28 is using the Babylonian system in counting the years of Nebuchadnezzar's reign, hence states the date exactly as the Babylonian chronicle does; but that II Kings 24:12 uses the nonaccession-year system, hence calls this Nebuchadnezzar's eighth year; or that II Kings 24:12 uses a year beginning with the preceding Tishri, hence by such reckoning this was already the eighth year. The fact that Jeremiah 52:28-30 is omitted in the LXX might be explained in line with this interpretation as due to the fact that the Babylonian system of dating was not understood in the West.

[14] W. F. Albright in JBL 51 (1932), p.91.
[15] *Ant.* x, vi, 3.
[16] *Ant.* x, vi, 3.

It must be noted on the other hand that the date of the capture of Jerusalem on the second day of Addaru in the seventh year of Nebuchadnezzar means that the city was taken within the very last month of that regnal year of the Babylonian king, and that with the first day of the ensuing month Nisan his eighth year began. If II Kings 24:14 is correct that the total number of persons selected for deportation was ten thousand, and if much booty was taken and prepared for transport, even to the cutting in pieces of the vessels of gold in the temple as II Kings 24:13 states, then it may readily be supposed that the assembling of the captives and goods took several weeks and that the final caravan did not depart until Nebuchadnezzar's eighth year had begun. If some three thousand captives[17] were taken off before the end of Addaru and the balance only after the beginning of Nisan, then both the seventh and the eighth years of Nebuchadnezzar were involved and both Jeremiah and II Kings could be using the accession-year system of reckoning.

That the final deportation took place as a new year was beginning is probably confirmed by II Chronicles 36:10 which gives the time as "in the spring of the year" according to the translation of the Revised Standard Version, but more literally "at the return of the year" (ASV) or "at the turn of the year," which must signify the month Nisan. Likewise Ezekiel 40:1 speaks of what seems to be an exact anniversary ("that very day") of the inauguration of the exile and dates it "at the beginning of the year, on the tenth day of the month." This must mean the tenth day of Nisan, and would date the final deportation on April 22, 597 B.C., a little more than a month after the fall of the city on March 16.

Upon the capture and deportation of Jehoiachin, Zedekiah was put on the throne at Jerusalem (II Kings 24:17; II Chronicles 36:10), and was king there when the city was taken for the second and last time by Nebuchadnezzar. Jeremiah 52:29 states that "in the eighteenth year of Nebuchadrezzar he carried away captive from Jerusalem eight hundred and thirty-two persons." II Kings 25:8 and Jeremiah 52:12 specify the seventh and tenth days of the fifth month in the nineteenth year of King Nebuchadnezzar for the final destruction of Jerusalem.

[17] Since the 3,023 persons are called "Jews" in Jeremiah 52:28 while the deportees mentioned in the next verse are specifically said to have been "from Jerusalem," it has even been suggested (A. Malamat in IEJ 6 [1956], p.253) that the first group were people captured in other towns of Judea and deported forthwith while the siege of Jerusalem was still in progress.

As previously we had given the seventh and the eighth years, so here we have the eighteenth and the nineteenth. Again the simplest explanation is probably that Jeremiah 52:29 uses the Babylonian system, but II Kings 25:8 and Jeremiah 52:12 use either a nonaccession-year system or a year beginning in Tishri, hence designate as the nineteenth year what in the Babylonian system is the eighteenth. The eighteenth year of Nebuchadnezzar was 587/586 B.C., and the seventh and tenth days of the fifth month were August 26 and August 29, 587 B.C.

There is, however, once more another possibility to be considered. The number of 832 persons taken captive from Jerusalem seems very small to represent the final fall of that city, particularly when it is remembered, for example, that Sargon claims 27,290 captives in the capture of Samaria,[18] hence Jeremiah 52:29 may simply record a preliminary deportation of a group of captives apprehended while the siege of Jerusalem was still in progress. II Kings 25:8 and Jeremiah 52:12 might then also use the Babylonian system of reckoning, and in this case the seventh and tenth days of the fifth month in the nineteenth year of Nebuchadnezzar would mean August 15 and 18, 586 B.C.

The fall of Jerusalem is also dated in terms of the reign of Zedekiah. In the ninth year of his reign, in the tenth month, on the tenth day of the month, the siege began (II Kings 25:1).[19] In the tenth year of Zedekiah which was the eighteenth year of Nebuchadrezzar, the siege was in progress and Jeremiah was in custody (Jeremiah 32:1).[20] In the eleventh year of Zedekiah, in the fourth month, on the ninth day, the walls of the city were breached (II Kings 25:2-4; Jeremiah 39:2). In the fifth month, on the seventh or the tenth day, which was in the nineteenth year of Nebuchadnezzar, Nebuzaradan came and destroyed the city (II Kings 25:8; Jeremiah 52:12).

[18] See above p.209 and cf. Thiele in BASOR 143 (Oct. 1956), p.25. The 745 persons carried captive in the twenty-third year of Nebuchadrezzar (582/581), according to Jeremiah 52:30, must have been prisoners taken in some minor uprising subsequent to the fall of Jerusalem, such as the revolt in which Gedaliah was slain (II Kings 25:25). Since this figure is nearly as large as the figure of 832 persons it supports the idea that that number also represented only a minor group and not the total number of prisoners upon the final fall of the capital of Judah.

[19] Jeremiah 39:1 gives the same date lacking the specification of the day.

[20] Since Jeremiah 37:4f. states that the threat of the army of Egypt which caused the Babylonians to lift the siege of Jerusalem temporarily came before Jeremiah was put in prison, that event (cf. above p.131) may have taken place at the end of the ninth or in the early part of the tenth year of Zedekiah.

If the dates in the reign of Zedekiah are stated in terms of the Babylonian system, and his eleventh year coincided with the nineteenth year of Nebuchadnezzar (586/585 B.C.), then his first year would have been the ninth year of Nebuchadnezzar (596/595), and his accession year the eighth year of Nebuchadnezzar (597/596). According to a possible reckoning worked out above, it was in this year on the tenth day of Nisan, April 22, 597 B.C., that Jehoiachin was carried away into exile. Therefore it is quite possible that it was at this time that Zedekiah was installed and that this year, 597/596 B.C., was considered his accession year. On the supposition that 597/596 was the accession year of Zedekiah then his ninth year was 588/587 and the tenth day of the tenth month when the siege began was January 4, 587; his tenth year when Jeremiah was in prison was 587/586; and in his eleventh year (586/585) the ninth day of the fourth month when the walls were breached was July 19, 586, while the seventh and tenth days of the fifth month when the city was finally destroyed were August 15 and 18, 586.

If the second fall of Jerusalem was in the eighteenth year of Nebuchadnezzar rather than the nineteenth, that is in 587 instead of 586, then the accession of Zedekiah could be presumed to have been counted as taking place in 598/597, the seventh year of Nebuchadnezzar, when at almost the end of the year the city and Jehoiachin fell into the hands of the Babylonian king. In this case Zedekiah's ninth year was 589/588 and the siege began on January 15, 588; his tenth year was 588/587; and his eleventh year was 587/586, the walls being breached on July 29, 587, and the destruction coming on August 26 and 29, 587. In this case, however, the tenth and eleventh years of Zedekiah would not correspond with the eighteenth and nineteenth years of Nebuchadnezzar, hence this system seems less likely.

According to II Kings 25:27 Jehoiachin was brought up out of his prison in Babylon in the thirty-seventh year of his exile, the twelfth month, and the twenty-seventh day, which was in the year that Evil-merodach began to reign. Jeremiah 52:31 gives the same date except that the twenty-fifth day of the month is specified, and also says that this was the year that Evil-merodach became king. Evil-merodach is the Babylonian king Amel-Marduk who acceded to the throne in succession to Nebuchadnezzar in 562/561 B.C. If the accession year of Amel-Marduk was the thirty-seventh year of Jehoiachin's exile, the first year of that exile was 598/597, the year in which on the second day of Addaru, March 16, 597 B.C., Jerusalem was captured. It is possible and even probable, however, that the words in II Kings 25:27 and Jeremiah 52:31 concerning Evil-merodach should be translated "in the first year of his reign" (Moffatt Translation).[21] Amel-Marduk's first full year of reign was 561/560, and counting back thirty-seven years from this Jehoiachin's first year of exile would have been 597/596. This would correspond with his going into captivity on the tenth day of Nisan, April 22, 597 B.C., as we have seen reason to believe was the case.

Ezekiel 1:2 refers to the fifth year of the exile of King Jehoiachin, and there follows in the same book a series of dates (8:1; 20:1; 24:1; 26:1; 29:1, 17; 30:21; 31:1; 32:1, 17; 33:21; 40:1) which are evidently stated likewise in terms of the years of Jehoiachin's exile. It must have been a number of months before Jehoiachin actually arrived in Babylon on the long journey from Jerusalem, even as later it took Ezra a full four months to make the reverse trip from Babylon to Jerusalem (Ezra 7:9). Writing from the point of view of Babylon, therefore, it may well be that Ezekiel considered the balance of 597/596 as what we might call the "inception year" of the exile, just as the same year was the accession year of Zedekiah in Jerusalem, and if this was the basis of reckoning then the first full year of Jehoiachin's exile was 596/595, even as it was the first full regnal year of Zedekiah. Such a basis of reckoning seems required by Ezekiel 24:1 where the beginning of the final siege of Jerusalem is dated, presumably with reference to the years of the exile, in the ninth year, tenth month, and tenth day, exactly as in II Kings 25:1 (cf. Jeremiah 39:1) the same event is dated in the ninth year, tenth month, and tenth day of the reign of Zedekiah (January 4, 587 B.C.). If Ezekiel had also given the date of the fall of the city it would then presumably have been the same as that in II Kings 25:8 and Jeremiah 52:12, the seventh-tenth day of the fifth month of the eleventh year, probably August 15-18, 586 B.C. What Ezekiel does give is the date (33:21) when a fugitive from Jerusalem reached Babylon with the first news that the city had fallen. This was on the fifth day of the tenth month in what is given as the twelfth year in the usual text, but as the eleventh year in a number of Hebrew, Greek, and Syriac manu-

---

[21] cf. W. F. Albright in JBL 51 (1932), pp.101f.

scripts.[22] Accepting the latter reading, this date in the eleventh year was January 8, 585, which allows the fugitive slightly less than five months to come from Jerusalem to Babylon, a reasonable length of time compared with the journey of Ezra noted above.

Ezekiel 40:1 speaks of an exact anniversary ("that very day") of the inauguration of the exile on the tenth day of the month at the beginning of the year, that is Nisan 10. This anniversary was in the twenty-fifth year of the exile, that is 572/571. This was also, it is stated, the fourteenth year after the city was conquered. If the city was conquered in the year 586/585, the fourteenth year *after* that was 572/571.

Turning to the New Testament we may note the problem of the date of the Last Supper of Jesus with his disciples. According to the Synoptic Gospels Jesus ate the passover with his disciples before he died (Mark 14:12 = Matthew 26:17 = Luke 22:8f.). According to the Fourth Gospel the crucifixion itself took place on the day of Preparation, that is the day on which the lambs were slain in preparation for the passover meal which followed that night; and this day was itself immediately prior to the sabbath, a sabbath which was a "high day," no doubt meaning that it was at the same time the first day of passover (John 19:31). The representation in the Fourth Gospel is supported by I Corinthians 5:7, "Christ, our paschal lamb, has been sacrificed"; and by the tractate Sanhedrin, "On the eve of Passover Yeshu was hanged."[23]

One suggestion for reconciliation of the difference between the Synoptic and the Johannine accounts is based upon the calendar with which we have become acquainted at Qumran. If by any chance Jesus and the disciples had had reason to follow this calendar they would have eaten their passover already on the preceding Tuesday evening, for by that calendar that was the appointed time for it and Wednesday was the first day of passover in this year as in every year. While the Gospel records are usually held to place the Last Supper on Thursday evening and the crucifixion immediately thereafter on Friday, it may be that all the events of the taking into custody of Jesus and the holding of his trials before Jewish and Roman authorities would fit better within the longer period from Tuesday evening until Fri-

[22] Rudolf Kittel, ed., *Biblia Hebraica*, 1937, p.866 n.21*a*. Herbert G. May in IB 6, p.247; Albright in JBL 51 (1932), p 96; Julius A. Bewer in ZAW 54 (1936), p.114. [23] 43a. GBT VII, p.181; SBT p.281.

day. Interestingly enough, in the early Christian work known as the Didascalia[24] the apostles are quoted as saying that it was on Tuesday evening that they ate the passover with Jesus, and on Wednesday that he was taken captive and held in custody in the house of Caiaphas.[25]

Another suggestion is that Jesus and the disciples, perhaps in conformity with Galilean usage, followed the ancient practice of reckoning the day from morning to morning rather than from evening to evening (cf. above p.553) and that this could account for their eating their passover one day earlier than official Judaism, that is on Thursday evening rather than on Friday evening.[26]

Again it always remains possible that it was simply by deliberate choice and in view of the ominous developments of those days that Jesus moved his observance of the passover ahead one day.[27]

Whether it was on account of calendrical variations or individual choice, it seems likely that the Last Supper was a passover meal held ahead of the official observance and that, as John represents, Jesus died on the day when the passover lambs were slain. According to Jewish law (Exodus 12:6) this date was Nisan 14; according to the sequence of days in the Gospels it was a Friday. According to the Babylonian calendar, in A.D. 30 Nisan 1 fell on March 25 and Nisan 14 came on April 7, a Friday. Again in A.D. 33, supposing only that the Jews did not intercalate a Second Adar at the end of the preceding year (as was probably done in Babylonia), Nisan 1 fell on March 21 and Nisan 14 on April 3, a Friday.[28]

[24] The Didascalia is preserved in Syriac but was probably written originally in Greek, perhaps in the third or second century A.D.; it is now incorporated as the first six books in the *Apostolical Constitutions*, a work of the fourth or fifth century (CAP I, p.613). It is edited by F. X. Funk, *Didascalia et Constitutiones Apostolorum.* 2 vols. 1905.

[25] *Didascalia.* XXI = v, 4-6; ed. Funk. I, p.272. See A. Jaubert in RHR 146 (1954), pp.140-173; and *La date de la cene.* 1957; cf. E. Vogt in *Biblica.* 39 (1958), pp.72-77; BML p.83; James A. Walther in JBL 77 (1958), pp.116-122.

[26] Morgenstern in VT 5 (1955), p.64 n.2. cf. Sherman E. Johnson in IB 7, p.572; and *Jesus in His Homeland*, p.19.

[27] Official practice was to sacrifice the lambs in the temple, according to Deuteronomy 16:2,5-7, which Jesus and the disciples could hardly have done if they diverged from the official dating, and there is in fact no mention of the passover lamb in the Gospel accounts.

[28] PDBC p.46. See A. T. Olmstead in ATR 24 (1942), pp.1-26; *Jesus in the Light of History.* 1942, pp.279-281; T. J. Meek in JNES 2 (1943), pp.124f.; Carl H. Kraeling in ATR 24 (1942), pp.336f.; J. K. Fotheringham in JTS 35 (1934), pp.146-162; Ogg, *The Chronology of the Public Ministry of Jesus*, pp.276f.

In such chronological calculations as we have adduced in regard to both Old Testament and New Testament dates it is evident that the factors involved are complex, and therefore such results as we have indicated must be regarded as provisional. At least the discussion will have shown the sort of materials now available for the study of chronological problems, and it may be hoped that further discoveries will be made in the future which will cast further light upon the framework of days and years in which the biblical events are set.

Index of Scriptural References

General Index

All references are to pages, except where Figures, Maps, or Plans are specifically indicated.

Alexamenos, 373
Alexander I Balas, 245
Alexander I, pope, 458
Alexander II, son of Alexander the Great, 244f.
Alexander II Zabinas, 245
Alexander VII, pope, 383
Alexander Janneus, 253, 300, 308, 312
Alexander, named in inscription in Catacomb of Priscilla, 477
Alexander, son of Herod the Great, 255
Alexander the Great, 37, 42, 133, 150, 244, 310f., 336, 345, 348, 359, 388
Alexandretta, Iskanderun, Gulf of, Map 6; 339, 356
Alexandria, Maps 2, 6; 81, 246, 248, 335, 338, 346, 348, 389, 391, 406, 424, 432f., 435, 438, 446f., 533, 546
Alexandrian Text, 424, 432-441, 447
Alis, 406f., 417
Aliyan, 173
Allenby, E. H., 155, 169, 330
Alorus, 30
Alphabet, 149, 163, 165
Alps, 302
Altaku, Eltekeh, Map 3; 211
Altar of Zeus, Pergamum, 345
Altar to Unknown Gods, Fig. 126; 356f.
Alulim, 30
Amadai, 230
Amalekites, 543
Amanus Mountains, Map 6; 49, 145; Pass, 334
Amasis, 131f., 223
Amaziah, 589
ambon, 507
Ambrose, 443
Amel-Marduk, 227, 594f.
Amelon, 30
Amemit, 101
Amempsinos, 30
Amen, god, 105
Amen, or Menas, 545
Amenemhet I, 90-92
Amenemhet II, 91
Amenemhet III, 171
Amenemhet IV, 91
Amenemopet, 123-125
Amenhotep I, 97
Amenhotep II, Figs. 38, 39; 102f., 119

Amenhotep III, Fig. 41; 103f., 109, 116, 162f., 198f.; colonnade of, at Luxor, Fig. 42
Amenhotep IV, Akhenaton, Fig. 44; 104-112, 115, 149, 198f., 201
Amenmose, 134
Amen-Re, 99, 105f.
American School of Classical Studies at Athens, 354, 360
American Schools of Oriental Research, 18, 183, 308; at Baghdad, 47; at Jerusalem, Plan 1; 160, 163, 189, 268-271, 276, 313, 319
American Tarsus College, 335
Amman, 153, 277, 309
Ammenon, 30
Ammeris, 128
Ammianus Marcellinus, 521
Ammi-zaduga, 73
Ammon, Map 3; 154
Ammonites, 153, 309
Ammonius, Ammonian Sections, 403
Amor, region, 92
Amoretti, 477
Amorites, 53-55, 68, 73, 145f., 153f., 157
Amos, 187
Ampliatus, 464
Amraphel, 73
Amratians, 79-81, 143
Amreh, el-, 80
Amun, god, 90, 99f., 103, 105f., 112, 114, 116, 121f., 126, 134, 390
Amurru, 92, 114, 145f.
Amyntas, 344
Amytis, 220
An, god, 44f.
Anacletus, 514
Ananel, 262
Ananias, 263, 482
Ananos, 262f.
Ananos the son of Annas, 263
Anastasia, wife of Marinianus, 512
Anastasis, in Church of Holy Sepulcher, 529-531, 537
Anastasius I, 252
Anat, goddess, 168, 173
'Anath-bethel, 240
'Anath-Yahu, 240
Anatolia, 266
Ancient Records of Egypt, 76

Ancyra, Angora, Ankara, Maps 4, 6; 198, 344f.
Andrae, Walter, 200
Andronicus II Palaeologus, 550
Angel, earliest known representation of, 51
Anglo-Egyptian Sudan, Map 2
Angora, *see* Ancyra
Ani, 101
Anicetus, 514
Anio River, Plan 3; 366
Ankara, *see* Ancyra
Ankhesenamun, 199
Annals of Tacitus, 378
Annas, high priest, 252, 262f.
Annius Rufus, procurator, 257
Anshan, Map 4; 229, 231f.
Antakya, 337
Anteros, pope, 458f.
Anthemius, 251, 550
Anthius River, 341
Antigonus, 254, 274
Anti-Lebanon, Map 4; 336
Antioch in Pisidia, Map 6; 340-346
Antioch in Syria, Maps 4, 6; 15, 245, 248, 334, 337-340, 346, 389, 446f., 495, 539, 541f., 544
Antiochs, 16 founded by Seleucus I Nicator, 340f.
Antiochus I of Commagene, 200
Antiochus I Soter, 30, 245, 337
Antiochus II Theos, 245
Antiochus III the Great, 245, 248, 345
Antiochus IV Epiphanes, 245f., 253, 282, 335, 338, 354
Antiochus V Eupator, 245
Antiochus VI Epiphanes, 245
Antiochus VII Sidetes, 245
Antiochus VIII Grypus, 245
Antiochus IX Cyzicenus, 245
Antiochus X Eusebes Philopator, 245
Antiochus XI Philadelphus, 245
Antiochus XII Dionysus, 245, 336
Antiochus XIII Asiaticus, 245
Antipater of Sidon, 348

Ashtart, 168, 173; Ashtaroth, House of, 167
Ashi, Robbi, 304
Ashkelon, Map 3; 116
Ashnunnak, *see* Eshnunna
Ashur, god, 63, 202, 205
Ashur, Qalat Shargat, Maps 1, 4; 62f., 200f., 209, 216, 219, 230
Ashurbanipal, 3, 33, 62, 127f., 208, 215-218; on the lion hunt, Fig. 82; victory banquet of, Fig. 81
Ashur-dan III, 200, 206
Ashur-etil-ilani, 218
Ashur-nasir-pal II, Fig. 72; 202-204
Ashur-nirari V, 206
Ashur-sharrat, 216
Ashur-uballit I, 201f.
Ashur-uballit II, 129f., 219
Asia, 6, 22, 108, 130f., 192, 236, 245, 350, 359; Asiatics, 92, 94, 100, 113, 117, 120, 126, 134, 168
Asia, Roman province, Map 6; 346, 374, 380, 382
Asia Minor, Map 4; 146, 198, 226, 236, 247f., 334, 340, 344f., 358, 391, 441, 488
Asiatic columnar style, 488f.
Askar, *see* Sychar
Assyria, Map 1; 3, 5, 57, 68f., 127, 129, 132, 136, 150, 200-219, 309, 589; Assyrians, 128, 220, 309, 567
Assyrian language, 46
Astarte, goddess, 347, 572f.
Astyages, 220, 231f.
Aswan, *see* Elephantine
Asyut, Map 2; 79
Ataroth-addar, 177
Ataroth, Attarus, Map 3; 189
Atbara River, 75
Athanasius the Great, 546
Athanasius the Humble, 438
Athena, goddess, 335, 337, 353; Nike, 353; Parthenos, 357; Promachos, 353, 357
Athenaeus, Greek grammarian, 338
Athenagoras, 385
Athenodorus, Stoic philosopher, 335

Athens, Map 6; 335, 352-358
Aton, god worshiped by Akhenaton, 106-108, 112
Atonement, Day of, 296f.
atrium, 506
Atrium Vestae, 374
Attalus II Philadelphus, 346
Attalus III Philometor, 346
Attarus, *see* Ataroth
Attica, 358
Auaris, 94
Augusta Platea, at Pisidian Antioch, 341
Augusteum, at Ankara, 345
Augustin, 385, 477
Augustus, a man whose daughter was baptized by Silvester, 520
Augustus, Augusti, title, 248, 254
Augustus, Caesar, Fig. 99; 250-252, 254, 256, 258f., 307, 311, 313, 335, 338, 341f., 344f., 350, 352, 354, 360f., 366, 368-375, 490, 549
'Auja-el-Hafir, 429
Aurelian, 251, 366, 383
Aurelians, Region of the, 463
Aurelian Wall, Plans 2, 3; 366, 456
Aurelios Paulos, 428
Aurelius, *see* Marcus Aurelius
Aurora, goddess of dawn, 104
Aushamem, 93
Ausi', 207
Austrian Archaeological Institute, 347
Authorized Version, 449
Auvergne, Princesse de la Tour d', 537
Avaris, Tanis, San el-Hagar, Map 2; 94-96, 114f., 119, 122, 126, 148
Aventine Hill, Plans, 2, 3; 367, 369
Avircius Marcellus, 479
Avitus, 251
Avva, 309
A'waj, el-, River, Map 5; 336
Awan, 36
Awel-Ishtar, 73
Ayasoluk, 346f.
Ayun Musa, 155
Azah, 186f.
Azariah, 206

Azariyeh, el-, *see* Bethany
Azekah, Tell Zakariya, Maps 3, 5; 192f.
Azupiranu, 46
Azzah, 187

Baal, Fig. 61; 172f., 187
Baalbek, *see* Heliopolis
Baal-berith, 184
Baal-meon, 189
Ba' alu, 215
Baal-zebub, 173
Babel, 10; Tower of, 50, 224
Bab esh-Sherqi, Damascus, 337
Bab-ilu, 10, 55
Babin, French archeologist, 21
Babylas, martyr, 541f.
Babylon, Fig. 83; Maps 1, 4; 3, 10, 30, 50, 53, 55, 58, 62f., 65, 68f., 73, 78, 128, 130, 132, 171, 196, 198, 201, 206, 214, 218-227, 228-230, 232-234, 243, 245, 309, 328, 348, 482, 574, 591, 594-596; fall of, 229f.; enameled lion from processional street of, Fig. 84
Babylonia, Map 1; 5, 6, 10, 36, 58, 61, 68-70, 73, 76, 134, 149, 198, 200, 217f., 233, 237, 297, 556, 558, 562, 567, 576, 579, 589, 598
Babylonian Chronicle, 129f., 218-223, 590f.
Babylonian language, 46, 66, 235
Bacchus, 521
Bactria, Bactrians, 237, 242f.
Badari, Map 2; 79f., 143
Badè, William F., 175
Badtibira, 30f.
Bagatti, P. Bellarmino, 333
Baghdad Map 1; 4, 9f., 15f., 29, 38, 54, 211
Baghouz, Map 1; 16
Bagoses, 244
bahr, 6
Bahrein, island, 32
Bahr Yusef, Map 2; 405
Balaam, 154, 288
Balatah, *see* Shechem
baldacchino, 513, 524
Baldwin I, 534
Balikh River, Maps 1, 4; 67f.
Baltimore Museum of Art, 338
Baluchistan, 21f.